The Cambridge Introduction to
French Literature

In this highly accessible introduction, Brian Nelson provides an overview of French literature – its themes and forms, traditions and transformations – from the Middle Ages to the present. Major writers, including francophone authors writing from areas other than France, are discussed chronologically in the context of their times, to provide a sense of the development of the French literary tradition and the strengths of some of the most influential writers within it. Nelson offers close readings of exemplary passages from key works, presented in English translation and with the original French. The exploration of the work of important writers, including Villon, Racine, Molière, Voltaire, Balzac, Flaubert, Zola, Proust, Sartre and Beckett, highlights the richness and diversity of French literature.

Brian Nelson is Professor Emeritus of French Studies and Translation Studies at Monash University, Melbourne, and a Fellow of the Australian Academy of the Humanities. His publications include *Perspectives on Literature and Translation: Creation, Circulation, Reception* (co-edited with Brigid Maher, 2013), *The Cambridge Companion to Émile Zola* (Cambridge, 2007) and translations of the novels of Émile Zola.

The Cambridge Introduction to
French Literature

BRIAN NELSON

CAMBRIDGE
UNIVERSITY PRESS

CAMBRIDGE
UNIVERSITY PRESS

University Printing House, Cambridge CB2 8BS, United Kingdom

Cambridge University Press is part of the University of Cambridge.

It furthers the University's mission by disseminating knowledge in the pursuit of education, learning and research at the highest international levels of excellence.

www.cambridge.org
Information on this title: www.cambridge.org/9780521715096

© Brian Nelson 2015

First published 2015

Printed in the United Kingdom by Clays, St Ives plc

A catalogue record for this publication is available from the British Library

Library of Congress Cataloging in Publication data
Nelson, Brian, 1946–
The Cambridge introduction to French literature / Brian Nelson.
    pages   cm. – (Cambridge introductions to literature)
Includes bibliographical references and index.
ISBN 978-0-521-88708-3 (hardback)
1. French literature – History and criticism.   I. Title.
PQ103.N45   2015
840.9 – dc23   2015012660

ISBN 978-0-521-88708-3 Hardback
ISBN 978-0-521-71509-6 Paperback

This book is dedicated to the memory of my parents,
Frederick and Ida Nelson

Contents

Preface

'INTRODUCTION – Obscene word' writes Gustave Flaubert (1821–80) in his deliciously witty *Dictionary of Received Ideas*. The present volume thus stands condemned in advance; and I should confess that its main form of shamelessness is its commitment to readability. My aim is to provide a critical introduction to French literature that is scholarly yet highly accessible to students and the general reader.

Readability is not simply a matter of nicely turned phrases but also a question of approach and method.[1] First, this book is, precisely, an introduction, not a history. It makes no attempt (how could it?) to provide comprehensive coverage. Rather than adopting a panoramic approach, I focus on a relatively limited number of writers. And to do so I have chosen the form of the essay – inherently more readable than the kinds of writing that normally make up a 'history' or a 'survey'. Each essay-chapter may be read as free-standing, but the sequence of essays may also be read together for the indication they give of the development of French literature as a whole – its themes and forms, its traditions and transformations. Second, my commitment to readability implies a particular view of the function of criticism. I agree with Harold Bloom that literary criticism 'ought to consist of acts of appreciation';[2] the essays in this volume are intended as such. While I wish to inform and illuminate, and explain the ways in which the writers in question are significant, I want to do so in a manner that offers pleasure as well as understanding, that induces in the reader a desire to read (or reread) the texts in question and more generally to pursue his or her own exploration of the riches of French literature. Writers are presented succinctly in the context of their times, but in order to communicate more effectively the pleasures of the texts chosen for analysis, close attention has been paid to exemplary passages. It helps readers to enter the world of the writer, to hear more clearly the writer's voice and to appreciate the shaping forms of his or her imagination. The commitment to readability of this volume is thus a commitment to bringing to life the texts it discusses.

The selection of writers treated is determined partly by personal preference and taste, modified by two criteria: they should all, by common consent or arguably, be major writers (though there is no suggestion that a particular kind of 'canon' is being promoted); and, within a balanced chronological framework, they should all provide compelling insights into their historical and cultural moment. The chapters are generally ordered by the birthdate of the author concerned, but with a few deviations in the interests of literary historical coherence (for example, the pairing of Corneille/Racine, Voltaire/Rousseau, Sartre/Camus). Obvious practical considerations (the limited scale of the volume and the privileging of essays of a certain length) mean that the choice of writers could not be extended beyond those selected.

This book assumes no knowledge of French and little or no prior knowledge of French literature. In the suggestions for further reading, I have borne in mind the needs of the student and a wide general audience: the recommendations are restricted to items in English and pay due attention to works intended for beginners and non-specialists. A separate section lists translations, with suggestions regarding the best available English versions of the main texts discussed. Quotations are given both in translation and in the original, except in the rare cases where the formulation of the original is not significant in itself. It should be noted that the French of some pre-nineteenth-century texts has not been modernized, nor have any peculiar linguistic features been annotated. The titles of texts are given first in their English translation, with the French titles in brackets. Where an item is not available in translation, the French title is given, followed by a literal translation. Footnotes have been kept to a minimum. To this end, I have incorporated into the main text references to items listed in the Further reading section at the end of the book.

So: 'INTRODUCTION – Pleasurable, useful word'? I hope so.

Melbourne
October 2014

Acknowledgements

I am indebted to many people: most of all to my family, but also to numerous friends and colleagues past and present. I would especially like to thank Rosemary Lloyd, Valerie Minogue and Tim Unwin for their valuable support, and I would also like to express my gratitude to Philippe Hamon, Henri Mitterand, Glanville Price and the late Michael Spencer and Philip Thody. I am grateful to the Brown Foundation for a Fellowship that enabled me to spend a richly rewarding month at the Dora Maar House in Ménerbes; to Esther Allen, Jan Owen and Julie Rose for their fellowship in the world of literary translation (and for their fellowship *tout court*); to Ilona Chessid for her judicious editorial comments; to Jade Patterson for her dexterous handling of the index; to Anna Bond, Jo Breeze and Jacqueline French for making the production process so smooth and efficient; and to Linda Bree, my principal editor at Cambridge University Press, for first suggesting that I undertake this volume.

I wish, too, to record my appreciation of the education I received at The Grammar School, Spalding (Lincolnshire, UK). It gave me (son of a railway worker) access to higher education and to the professional life that has flowed from it. To borrow a phrase of John Carey's with regard to his memoir *The Unexpected Professor*, 'this book is, among other things, a tribute of gratitude to a grammar school'. Needless to say, I believe strongly in public policy that treats education as a universally accessible resource, based on merit, rather than as a purchasable commodity.

All translations in this volume are mine except where indicated. My thanks are due to Justin Clemens for permission to use his translation of 'Villon's Epitaph', to Julie Rose for permission to use an extract from her translation of Racine's *Phèdre* and to Jan Owen for permission to use her translations of Baudelaire's 'To a Passer-by' and 'The Swan'. Jan Owen also translated specially for this book extracts from Apollinaire's 'Zone' and Rimbaud's 'The Drunken Boat', and (with Alex Skovron) helped me to translate a sonnet by Mallarmé. I am grateful to the Houghton Mifflin Harcourt Publishing Company for permission to quote from Richard Wilbur's translation of Pierre Corneille's *Le Cid* and to Oxford University Press for permission to quote Christopher Betts's translation of La Fontaine's fable 'The Wolf and the Lamb'.

Chronology

The literary and other works listed below are restricted to those described or mentioned in the essays that compose this book.[1]

486	Roman power in Gaul comes to an end.
771	Charlemagne becomes sole king of the Franks.
800	Pope Leo XIII crowns Charlemagne emperor of the west.
1066	William of Normandy becomes king of England after his victory at Hastings. By linking the English throne to extensive territories in France, this conquest leads to future disputes over sovereignty and lays the ground for four hundred years of conflict.
1337–1453	Hundred Years War.
1348	The Black Death (bubonic plague) spreads across Europe. It kills roughly a third of the French population.
1456	François Villon produces his *Petit Testament*; the *Grand Testament* will follow in 1461.
1469	First printing press in France established at the Sorbonne.
1532	François Rabelais produces *Pantagruel* (followed by *Gargantua* in 1534, *Le Tiers Livre* in 1546 and *Le Quart Livre* in 1552).
1534	The 'Affair of the Placards' (anti-Catholic posters) provokes François I into adopting repressive measures against Protestantism.
1562–98	Wars of Religion. Conflict between Protestants and Catholics was more intense and long-lasting in France than in any other country in Europe.
1572	Saint Bartholomew's Day Massacre: more than 3,000 Protestants are murdered in Paris.
1580	Michel de Montaigne publishes the first two volumes of his *Essais*.

1593	Henri IV converts to Catholicism.
1598	Edict of Nantes ends Wars of Religion, providing for equal rights and, within certain constraints, freedom of worship for Protestants.
1618–48	Thirty Years War against Austria and Spain.
1624	Cardinal Richelieu becomes chief minister to Louis XIII (1610–43).
1635	Richelieu founds the Académie française.
1637	Pierre Corneille's *Le Cid* is performed. Jansenist movement establishes its headquarters at the convent of Port-Royal.
1643	The five-year-old Louis XIV becomes king. Anne of Austria acts as regent and appoints Cardinal Mazarin as chief minister.
1648–53	The 'Fronde': a series of civil wars in which troops loyal to the monarchy confronted (and ultimately defeated) a fluctuating alliance of nobility and *parlementaires* (members of the Paris legislative court).
1659	Molière's *L'École des femmes* is performed (followed by *Tartuffe* in 1664).
1661	On the death of Mazarin, Louis XIV decides to govern France himself. Consolidation of absolute monarchy.
1668	The first collection of Jean de La Fontaine's *Fables* is published.
1677	Jean Racine's *Phèdre* is performed.
1678	Madame de Lafayette publishes her novel *La Princesse de Clèves*.
1680	The Comédie-Française is founded.
1715	Death of Louis XIV.
1726	Voltaire visits England where he will stay for two and a half years. His reflections on what he sees as a liberal Protestant country, in contrast to his own authoritarian Catholic country, becomes the basis of his *Lettres philosophiques* (1734).
1746	Denis Diderot publishes his *Pensées philosophiques*.
1751	The first of the seventeen volumes of the *Encyclopédie* is published, under the editorship of Diderot and Jean le Rond d'Alembert. The work will be completed in 1772.
1755	Jean-Jacques Rousseau publishes his *Discours sur l'origine et les fondements de l'inégalité parmi les hommes*.
1756–63	Seven Years War (France and Austria vs England and Prussia).

1759	Voltaire publishes *Candide*.
1761	Rousseau publishes *Julie ou la Nouvelle Héloïse* (followed in 1762 by *Du contrat social* and *Émile*). In 1764 he begins his autobiographical *Confessions*.
1773	Diderot writes *Jacques le Fataliste*; it will be published in 1796.
1782	Choderlos de Laclos publishes *Les Liaisons dangereuses*.
1787–88	A disastrous financial situation, caused by cumulative war expenditures and profligate court spending, provokes a political crisis. Louis XVI calls a meeting of the Esates General (a consultative body made up of representatives of the nobility, the clergy and the commons) for the first time since 1614.
1789	17 June: The commons (the middle-class Third Estate) proclaims itself the National Assembly, highlighting the fact that it represents the majority of the nation. 9 July: The National Assembly becomes the Constituent National Assembly and establishes a constitutional monarchy. 14 July: The Bastille prison is stormed by an armed crowd. 4 August: The Assembly votes to abolish all feudal privileges. 26 August: *Declaration of the Rights of Man and of the Citizen*: the founding document of the French Revolution.
1791	21 June: Louis XVI and his family are arrested while trying to escape to Austria.
1792	The 'September massacres': more than 1,200 prisoners are executed in Paris. The monarchy is abolished and the First Republic declared.
1793–94	Louis XVI executed (21 January 1793). The Terror begins: a wave of summary executions of perceived enemies of the Revolution. It ends with the arrest and execution of Maximilien Robespierre, leading member of the Jacobin Club and the Committee of Public Safety.
1795	Installation of the Directory, an executive body of five members including the young general Napoleon Bonaparte.
1799	Napoleon seizes power on 18 Brumaire (9 November), marking the beginning of the Consulate (1799–1804).
1804	2 December: Napoleon crowned emperor by Pope Pius VII at Notre-Dame Cathedral.
1814	Napoleon deposed and sent into exile on the island of Elba. Louis XVIII, brother of Louis XVI, becomes king: Bourbon dynasty restored.

1815	The 'Hundred Days': Napoleon escapes from Elba, gathers support and marches to Paris, where he seizes power. Defeated at Waterloo (18 June), he abdicates again and is exiled to the island of St Helena, where he dies in 1821.
1822	Victor Hugo's *Odes et poésies diverses* are published.
1824	Louis XVIII dies and is succeeded by his brother, Charles X, whose reign is marked by reactionary policies.
1827	Hugo's preface to his unperformed play *Cromwell* (*La Préface de Cromwell*) appears.
1830	Hugo's play *Hernani* is performed at the Comédie-Française. Stendhal publishes *Le Rouge et le noir*. The French send an expeditionary force to Algeria and take Algiers. In July, three days of revolution force Charles X to abdicate. Louis-Philippe, duc d'Orléans, becomes the 'Citizen King', beginning the so-called July Monarchy (1830–48).
1831	Hugo's historical novel *Notre-Dame de Paris* is published.
1835	Honoré de Balzac's *Le Père Goriot* is published.
1841	Balzac decides to use the collective title *La Comédie humaine* for his novels.
1846	Charles Baudelaire publishes his influential art and cultural criticism, *Le Salon de 1846*.
1848	24 February: Revolution of 1848. Demonstrations and rioting lead to the fall of Louis-Philippe. 25 February: Second Republic declared. Liberal measures are voted, including universal male suffrage. 22–26 June: 'June Days'. An uprising of workers and students against the bourgeois Republic is violently suppressed (thousands killed, 11,000 imprisoned or deported). 10 December: Louis-Napoleon, nephew of Napoleon Bonaparte, is elected president.
1849	A swing to the right: freedom of the press curtailed, strikes forbidden, right of assembly suspended, universal suffrage abolished.
1851	2 December: Louis-Napoleon seizes power in a *coup d'état*.
1852	Louis-Napoleon proclaims himself Emperor Napoleon III: beginning of Second Empire (1852–70). Foundation of major banking institutions, Crédit Mobilier and Crédit Foncier. Georges-Eugène Haussmann, Prefect of the Seine, starts vast redevelopment of Paris.
1856	Hugo's collection of lyric poetry, *Les Contemplations*, is published.

1857	Gustave Flaubert publishes *Madame Bovary*; Charles Baudelaire publishes *Les Fleurs du mal*.
1859	Colonial expansion: occupation of Saigon; much of Indochina progressively brought under French control.
1862	Hugo's *Les Misérables* is published (though begun in 1840s).
1864	Foundation of the International Workingmen's Association, in which Karl Marx is a leading figure.
1869	Baudelaire's prose poems *Le Spleen de Paris*, sometimes referred to as *Petits poèmes en prose*, are published posthumously; Flaubert's *L'Éducation sentimentale* is published.
1870	19 July: France declares war on Prussia. 2 September: Louis-Napoleon defeated at Sedan. 4 September: Third Republic proclaimed (1870–1940). Prussians besiege Paris.
1871	28 January: Surrender of Paris. Formation, in Paris, of the Commune, a revolutionary government opposed to capitulation. It enacts the first socialist programme in Europe. 22–28 May ('semaine sanglante'): suppression of Commune by French government troops (25,000 killed).
1873	Arthur Rimbaud's first collection of poems, *Une saison en enfer*, is published; his *Illuminations* will follow in 1886.
1874	A painting by Claude Monet, *Impression, soleil levant*, gives the Impressionist movement its name.
1877	Zola's *L'Assommoir*, the seventh of his twenty-volume Rougon-Macquart series (1871–93), is published; *Germinal* will follow in 1885.
1882	Under the prime minister, Jules Ferry, elementary education is secularized and made free and compulsory.
1884	Joris-Karl Huysmans's *À rebours* is published.
1885	Stéphane Mallarmé publishes his hermetic poem 'Prose pour des Esseintes'.
1889	Second International created. Eiffel Tower inaugurated at the Paris World's Fair. Idea of building Paris Métro conceived (first line opened 1900).
1892–93	Panama Canal scandal triggers a campaign by journalist Édouard Drumont against Jewish financing.
1894	Jewish army officer Alfred Dreyfus condemned for espionage and deported to Devil's Island. Discovery of new evidence leads eventually to his acquittal in 1906, but the affair (in which Zola's pro-Dreyfus newspaper article *J'accuse . . . !* is a

key moment) generates heated debate, focusing the ideological divisions within the country: Dreyfusards (anti-clericals, anti-militarists) are set in opposition to anti-Dreyfusards (Catholics, anti-Semites, monarchists).

1899	Foundation of the right-wing Action Française.
1905	Law of Separation of Church and State.
1907	Pablo Picasso's painting *Les Demoiselles d'Avignon* marks the birth of Cubism.
1909	Louis Blériot crosses the English Channel by plane.
1910	Constitution of federation known as French Equatorial Africa.
1913	Guillaume Apollinaire's collection of lyric poetry, *Alcools*, published (followed by *Calligrammes* in 1918). Marcel Proust publishes *Du côté de chez Swann*, first volume of *À la recherche du temps perdu* (completed 1922).
1914–18	First World War (1.3 million French soldiers dead, 1.1 million wounded).
1919	Treaty of Versailles. Alsace and Lorraine reincorporated into France.
1920	French left, formed into a single socialist party in 1905, splits in two. The majority become the new French Communist Party.
1924	André Breton's first Surrealist Manifesto appears; his novel *Nadja* will be published in 1928.
1932	Louis-Ferdinand Céline publishes *Voyage au bout de la nuit*.
1933	Adolf Hitler becomes chancellor of Germany.
1934	6 February: Right-wing demonstrations in the Place de la Concorde. 9 February: Left-wing counter-demonstrations.
1936	The Popular Front, a left-wing coalition led by Léon Blum, wins a majority in the national elections. (Blum's government will fall in 1938 amidst financial chaos.) Creation of the International Brigades, composed of foreign volunteers who join the Republican forces during the Spanish Civil War (1936–40).
1938	Jean-Paul Sartre publishes *La Nausée*.
1939	1 September: Germany invades Poland. Second World War begins.
1940	14 June: Germans enter Paris. 18 June: From London, General Charles de Gaulle broadcasts a call to resistance. 22 June: Marshal Philippe Pétain signs an armistice. France divided into an occupied zone (north and west) and an unoccupied

(southern) zone. Third Republic replaced by the 'French State' (1940–46), with Vichy as the seat of government. The conservative, collaborationist Vichy regime promotes a Catholic France that has no place for Jews or foreigners. People are faced increasingly with a choice between resistance and collaboration.

1942   Albert Camus's first novel, *L'Étranger*, and his philosophical essay *Le Mythe de Sisyphe* are published.

1943   Sartre publishes his major philosophical work *L'Être et le néant*.

1944   6 June (D-Day): The Allies land in Normandy. 25 August: Liberation of Paris. 9 September: De Gaulle forms a government of national unity. Women are given the right to vote. With the liberation of France, the period known as the *épuration* (purification) begins. There are many summary executions and unofficial settling of scores; trials of those thought to have been guilty of collaboration are held throughout the country. The question of justice in relation to Nazi collaborationism becomes (and remains) hotly debated.

1945   8 May: Germany surrenders.

1946   De Gaulle resigns. Fourth Republic (1946–58) established.

1947   Raymond Queneau publishes *Exercises de style*.

1948   Sartre publishes his influential essay on 'committed literature', *Qu'est-ce que la littérature?*

1949   Simone de Beauvoir publishes her seminal text for the development of modern French feminism, *Le Deuxième Sexe*.

1951   Samuel Beckett publishes *Molloy*, his first novel in French; it is followed in 1953 by his play *En attendant Godot*.

1953   Roland Barthes's influential essay *Le Degré zero de l'écriture* is published.

1954   7 May: French army routed by Vietnam Liberation Front at Dien Bien Phu. This marks the end of French military involvement in Indochina. In Algeria, terrorist attacks organized by the National Liberation Front mark the beginning of the Algerian War (which will last until 1962).

1956   France recognizes the independence of Morocco and Tunisia. A series of articles entitled *Pour un nouveau roman* by Alain Robbe-Grillet is published and becomes a form of manifesto; the articles will appear in volume form in 1963. Other

	important works of criticism include Nathalie Sarraute's *L'Ère du soupçon*.
1958	15 May: Deepening crisis in Algeria brings de Gaulle back to power. He establishes Fifth Republic and, in December, is elected president (re-elected 1965).
1960	France proclaims independence of its (sub-Saharan) African colonies. Oulipo is founded.
1962	Algeria's independence recognized.
1964	Sartre's *Les Mots* and Marguerite Duras's *Le Ravissement de Lol V. Stein* are published.
1966	Michel Foucault's essay *Les Mots et les choses* and Jacques Lacan's *Écrits* are published.
1967	Michel Tournier's first novel, *Vendredi ou les limbes du Pacifique*, is published. It is followed by *Le Roi des Aulnes* (which wins the Prix Goncourt) in 1970.
1968	'May Events': Massive anti-government protests by students and workers, leading to a protracted general strike, convulse the Fifth Republic.
1969	De Gaulle resigns and is succeeded as president by Georges Pompidou, who liberalizes some Gaullist social policies.
1971	Sartre publishes his study of Flaubert, *L'Idiot de la famille*.
1973	Barthes publishes *Le Plaisir du texte*.
1977	Luce Irigaray publishes *Ce Sexe qui n'en est pas un*.
1978	Georges Perec publishes *La Vie mode d'emploi*.
1980	Marguerite Yourcenar becomes first woman elected to the Académie française.
1981	François Mitterrand elected president (re-elected 1988).
1984	Duras publishes *L'Amant*, which is awarded the Prix Goncourt.
1987	Opening of the Institute of the Arab World in Paris.
1989	November: Affair of the 'Islamic scarf' highlights racial tensions. The far-right National Front gains in support. Moroccan novelist Tahar Ben Jelloun wins the Prix Goncourt with *La Nuit sacrée*.
1994	Michel Houellebecq publishes *Extension du domaine de la lutte* (followed by *Les Particules élémentaires* in 1998 and *La Carte et le territoire*, which wins the Prix Goncourt, in 2010).
1999	Jean Echenoz wins Prix Goncourt with *Je m'en vais*.

2002	France stunned by success of Jean-Marie Le Pen, leader of National Front, in first round of presidential elections. He forces a run-off with the incumbent Jacques Chirac.
2005	Violent social unrest in the Paris suburbs.
2009	Marie NDiaye wins Prix Goncourt with *Trois femmes puissantes.*
2015	7 January: Attack by Islamist gunmen on the offices of the satirical magazine *Charlie Hebdo*, killing twelve people. 11 January: a crowd of about 1.5 million people (the biggest public rally in France since the end of the Second World War) take part in a 'unity march' through the streets of Paris.

Chapter 1

Villon: a dying man

A dying man can speak his mind.

– Villon, *Testament*, line 728

French literature of the Middle Ages is enormously rich and varied. It comprises, among other genres, heroic epics, courtly romances, verse narratives, religious drama, fables and lyric poetry. In recent years study of medieval French literature has been revitalized by innovative critical approaches that encourage the reading of relevant texts in terms of a literary culture built on sophisticated (and often playful) rewriting of traditional stories. Such approaches imply a fluid notion of literary creation untrammelled by restrictive notions of 'author' and 'text': 'Medieval writers acknowledge that texts do not derive exclusively from or belong to their authors, that they have multiple origins, that they are indeed "a tissue of quotations" and, above all, that they go on developing and evolving as they are read, reread and rewritten in transmission.'[1] The lyric poet François Villon (*c.* 1431 – after 1463) recasts the courtly ideals and conventional pieties of medieval literary tradition, subverting his models by writing in a predominantly ironic mode. Lyric poetry and first-person narratives before Villon are strongly allegorical, and rarely the expression of individualized sentiment; lacking a clear historical dimension, they deal in stock character types (such as the knight-errant, despairing lover, repentant sinner, etc.) and are written in highly stylized poetic language. The greatest impact of Villon's work, as David Georgi argues, is its contribution to the emergence of the intimate first-person voice in European poetry.[2] Villon also created, in his life and work, the figure of the *poète maudit* (the accursed poet, or poet with endless bad luck), who would become a familiar feature of the French poetic tradition.[3] The poetic persona he developed evokes the experience of a marginal man living in a recognizable social reality: he engages imaginatively with the great themes of the literature and art of his age – death, the vagaries of fate, the ravages of time – in conjunction with poverty and the fragility of existence in fifteenth-century Paris.

1

A fictional will

The main elements of what we know about Villon's life are as follows: he attended the University of Paris in the 1450s, obtaining his bachelor's degree in 1449 and a master of arts in 1452; he killed a priest, apparently in self-defence, in 1455, and fled Paris; he petitioned the King for a pardon, which was granted in January 1456; back in Paris at Christmas 1456, he was involved in a burglary of the Collège de Navarre (a rich residential college for students at the Sorbonne) and again fled Paris; his whereabouts during the next few years are unclear, but he seems to have visited the court of Charles (the Duke) of Orléans and was imprisoned for several months at Meung-sur-Loire by the Bishop of Orléans; he was released in a general amnesty in July 1461 when the new king, Louis XI, passed through Meung; he returned to Paris, but in November 1462 was implicated in a serious riot and, given his record, was sentenced to hang; on appeal, in January 1463, the sentence was commuted to ten years' exile from Paris. Nothing further is known of Villon.

Villon's reputation is based on *The Legacy* or *Bequests* (*Le Lais*, 1456), a work of 320 lines; his masterpiece, the *Testament* (1461), consisting of about 2000 lines; and sixteen miscellaneous poems. *The Legacy* is cast in the form of a series of burlesque bequests to friends and acquaintances, in which he gives away a comic collection of items. To the woman who has treated him badly he leaves his heart; to his barber he leaves some hair-clippings; to his cobbler he leaves his worn-out old boots. The *Testament*, similarly, is a mock will, purportedly dictated on his deathbed by a poor, lovelorn scholar named François Villon. It is interspersed with *ballades* and *rondeaux*, of which the most famous are the 'Ballad of Olde-Time Ladies' (*Ballade des dames du temps jadis*), the 'Ballad of Olde-Time Lords' (*Ballade des seigneurs du temps jadis*), and the 'Ballad of Fat Margot' (*Ballade de la Grosse Margot*). Villon takes as his subject matter the familiar *topoi* of his time (the tribulations of love, the brevity of youth, the fact of ageing, the pervasiveness of death), but there is nothing chivalric or idealized about his treatment of them. The tone of the *Testament* is often irreverent and decidedly unromantic. When he speaks directly of poverty, his vision is frankly materialist:

> I have had my loves, it's true enough,
> and I would love to have some more,
> but a sad heart and a stomach
> that's barely ever one-third full
> knock me out of the lovers' race.
> So let another take my place,

One whose keg stands full on his pins;
The feet only dance as the belly allows.

Trans. David Georgi

Bien est verté que j'é aymé
Et aymeroye voulentiers,
Mais triste cueur, ventre affamé,
Qui n'est rassasïé au tiers,
M'oste des amoureux sentiers.
Au fort, quelc'um s'en recompence
Qui est remply sur les chantiers,
Car la dance vient de la pance.

Lines 193–200

Despite Villon's use of a confessional first-person narrator, the *Testament* is not to be read as autobiography. Indeed, it is vital to distinguish between Villon the man and Villon the poet. The poem's appealing directness belies its artful fabrication. Critics such as Tony Hunt and Jane Taylor have persuasively argued that the narrative 'I' is, first and foremost, a literary construct, part of a rhetorical performance which, through its juxtaposition of different voices, disorients the reader and challenges him to question some of the commonplaces (about love and sexuality, morality and the sources of wisdom, etc.) of Villon's time. The narrator-testator, 'Villon', uses a variety of guises and a range of registers – vituperative, sarcastic, melancholic, tender, ribald, derisive – to meditate on life, love and death. The primary characteristic of the *Testament* is its disruptive and subversive nature, especially its subversion of poetic convention. Elevated poetic diction, associated with courtly language, is frequently undercut by everyday speech, including obscenity; parody is used to send up courtly love poems – as in the provocatively vulgar 'Ballad of Fat Margot', in which the narrator, having led the reader to expect that he will be listening to a chivalric speaker celebrating his love, presents himself self-mockingly as the pimp of a fat prostitute, well past her prime; and irony is used to undermine all forms of authority – the authority of conventional wisdom as embodied in classical and biblical tradition (the poem is brimming with learned references), figures of moral authority and, above all, the authority of a consistent authorial voice. This type of authorial inconsistency is strikingly highlighted in the final *ballade* of the *Testament*, in which 'Villon' is depicted as dead, and a new, unidentified narrator steps forward. This narrator describes the protagonist, on his deathbed, expressing not conventional regret for the past, repentance for his sins or a hankering for eternal life, but defiant delight in the pleasures of the moment.

In sober truth it went like this:
he died with nothing but rags to his name,
and even as he died he felt
Love prick him one last cruel time,
sharper than the prong of a buckle
on the strap of a big old baldric;
and with that, he was astonishing
when just about to leave this world.

My Prince, noble as a falcon,
hear what he did as he took his leave:
he downed a gulp of dark red wine
when just about to leave this world.

Trans. David Georgi

Il est ainsi et tellement:
Quant mourut, n'avoit qu'un haillon.
Qui plus, en mourant, mallement
L'espoignoit d'Amours l'esguillon;
Plus agu que le ranguillon
D'un baudrier lui faisoit sentir
– C'est de quoy nous esmerveillon –,
Quant de ce monde voult partir.

Prince, gent comme esmerillon,
Saichiez qu'il fist au departir:
Ung traict but de vin morillon,
Quant de ce monde voult partir.

'The Ballad of the Hanged'

Villon's 'Ballad of the Hanged' (*Ballade des pendus*; also known as 'Villon's Epitaph') is a miscellaneous ballad, not written as part of the *Testament*. It is, along with the 'Ballad of Olde-Time Ladies', his most famous poem and has been described as 'one of the most moving of all lyric poems to have been written in the French language'.[4]

Oh brother humans who live after us,
Do not towards us make your hearts so hard,
For if you can pity us poor men,
Upon you God will lay a winning card;
You see here five or six of us sans lard,

The flesh we nourished when alive quite gone,
Devoured, abandoned, rotted to the bone,
We bones ourselves will soon be ash to fall.
Please no one laugh at what has here been done,
But pray to God that he'll forgive us all.

If we claim you as brothers, you must not
Disdain us, though it's true we were destroyed
By justice; nonetheless, you know the lot
Of men is hardly wisdom to embroid;
Beg pardon for us, for we have annoyed
The Son of Heaven, and it's He we fear,
May He give us his grace, and hold us dear,
Preserve us from the pit's infernal pall –
Now we are dead, no man torments us here,
But pray to God that he'll forgive us all.

The rain has drenched us, and has washed us bare,
The sun has dried us off and blackened us;
Magpies and crows have fed upon our hair,
And pecked our eyes, and drunk our milky pus;
Not for a moment can we stop to cuss,
First here, then there, as the capricious wind
Desires, we're forced eternally to wind;
By birds we've been more pitted than a thimble.
Do not then seek to join our blighted kind,
But pray to God that he'll forgive us all.

Prince Jesus, lord of heaven's golden shower,
Keep us from hell's rapacious abattoir,
That we may never to its abyss fall –
This is no place to mock us, men, nor hour,
But pray to God that he'll forgive us all.

Trans. Justin Clemens
(translation slightly modified)

Frères humains, qui après nous vivez,
N'ayez les cœurs contre nous endurcis,
Car, si pitié de nous pauvres avez,
Dieu en aura plus tôt de vous mercis.
Vous nous voyez ci attachés, cinq, six:
Quant à la chair, que trop avons nourrie,
Elle est piéça dévorée et pourrie,
Et nous, les os, devenons cendre et poudre.
De notre mal personne ne s'en rie;

Mais priez Dieu que tous nous veuille absoudre!
Si frères vous clamons, pas n'en devez
Avoir dédain, quoique fûmes occis
Par justice. Toutefois, vous savez
Que tous hommes n'ont pas bon sens rassis.
Excusez-nous, puisque sommes transis,
Envers le fils de la Vierge Marie,
Que sa grâce ne soit pour nous tarie,
Nous préservant de l'infernale foudre.
Nous sommes morts, âme ne nous harie,
Mais priez Dieu que tous nous veuille absoudre!

La pluie nous a débués et lavés,
Et le soleil desséchés et noircis.
Pies, corbeaux nous ont les yeux cavés,
Et arraché la barbe et les sourcils.
Jamais nul temps nous ne sommes assis
Puis çà, puis là, comme le vent varie,
A son plaisir sans cesser nous charrie,
Plus becquetés d'oiseaux que dés à coudre.
Ne soyez donc de notre confrérie;
Mais priez Dieu que tous nous veuille absoudre!

Prince Jésus, qui sur tous a maistrie,
Garde qu'Enfer n'ait de nous seigneurie:
A lui n'ayons que faire ne que soudre.
Hommes, ici n'a point de moquerie;
Mais priez Dieu que tous nous veuille absoudre!

The poem is redolent of Villon's thematic universe (a haunting preoccupation with mortality, the tension between flesh and spirit, the question of salvation and God's judgement). Its moving quality depends partly on its graphic imagery (especially in the third stanza, which evokes the stripping of the flesh) and partly on the apparent simplicity of the speaking voice; however, this simplicity belies a rhetorical structure marked by characteristic ambiguity. Who is speaking? The first person of the *Testament* has disappeared; instead of an 'I' there is a 'we' who address a plural 'you'. The voice may be singular, speaking for the hanged men on the gibbet, or choral, with the dead speaking as a group. The speaker(s) ask(s) not only that passers-by feel pity for them but that, according to contemporary convention, they (as faithful Christians) intercede with God through their prayers so that the dead men may be absolved of their sins (lines 15–18). The full rhetorical effect of the poem lies, however, in the interplay between speaker(s) and addressees and in the ambiguity inscribed into the 'us' of the refrain ('But pray to God that he'll forgive us all'). And a further ambiguity comes into play: the 'poor' of the third line. 'Poor' is Villon's most-used epithet for himself throughout the *Testament* ('Poor I am, and from my youth, Born of a poor and humble stock', lines 273–74), and he speaks throughout the text of poverty that is both economic and spiritual. A link is made in the poem between criminality (and hence condemnation) and poverty, thus problematizing the concepts of judgement and morality. By the end of the poem the 'us all' ('tous nous') of the refrain embraces the hanged men, the passers-by and all mankind (the English 'us all', absorbing the 'tous', is more emphatic than the French 'nous'). In other words, the initial phrase 'brother humans' is fully realized as part of a rhetorical strategy that culminates in the suggestion that the passers-by are part of the universal brotherhood of man, in which no one may assume the right to judge criminals, for we shall all be viewed as sinners at the Last Judgement.

Chapter 2

Rabelais: the uses of laughter

> ... laughter is of man the very marrow.
>
> – Rabelais, *Gargantua*, 'To the Reader'

The comic fictions of the scholar, physician and one-time monk François Rabelais (?1494–1553), and the senses in which he may be described as 'a Renaissance writer', cannot be fully understood without a knowledge of the historical context in which he wrote. The Renaissance is commonly held to mark the end of the Middle Ages and the beginning of the modern world. The term 'Renaissance', derived from the French word for rebirth, refers to a cultural movement that began in fourteenth-century Italy and lasted in Western Europe into the early seventeenth century. Invigorating both the arts and the sciences, it was marked by a revival of interest in classical Greek and Roman texts, a spirit of intellectual and physical adventure, and a belief in the high potential of human nature and of the individual human being – a belief that fundamentally challenged the theocentric view of the universe embodied in the medieval Church. Above all, the Renaissance gave birth to the idea of learning as the foundation of life. The broad system of values animating the Renaissance has been called 'humanism'. The astonishing intellectual scope, the formal and linguistic inventiveness, and the general ebullience of Rabelais's writings, known collectively as *Gargantua and Pantagruel*, embody Renaissance humanism in all its excitement and thirst for knowledge. As Erich Auerbach writes: 'Rabelais' purpose ... is diametrically opposed to medieval ways of thinking ... [His] entire effort is directed toward playing with things and with the multiplicity of their possible aspects; upon tempting the reader out of his customary and definite way of regarding things, by showing him phenomena in utter confusion; upon tempting him out into the great ocean of the world, in which he can swim freely, though it be at his own peril' (*Mimesis*, pp. 275–76). Laughter, which is central to Rabelais's work, is a sympathetic form of recognition of man's imperfections and an expression of Rabelais's response to the wealth and wonder of the world. However, the Renaissance was not simply a period of cultural and artistic exuberance; it was also a time of turmoil both intellectual and religious. The Lutheran Reformation movement, with its emphasis on individual faith rather than institutional worship, challenged the traditional dogmas and practices of the Catholic Church, leading in the second half of the sixteenth century to the Wars of Religion. The Renaissance was marked also by the sense of disorientation that accompanied man's awareness of a rapidly changing world. It was an age when all phenomena were being reexamined and reinterpreted: the Bible, which led to the Reformation; celestial movements, with Copernicus's planetary revelations; geography, with the voyages of exploration; the human body, with new discoveries in medicine. When Auerbach speaks of the reader's 'peril', he is suggesting that the freedom of vision and thought associated with Rabelais's perpetual 'playing with things' reflects both excitement and apprehension. Rabelais implicitly stresses the burden of individual responsibility that follows from man's discovery of his freedom and capacity for knowledge, and the uncertainty that informs human affairs.

As Milan Kundera has remarked, '*Gargantua-Pantagruel* is a novel from before novels existed. A miraculous moment, never to return, in which an art had not yet come into being as such and therefore was not yet bound by any norms.'[1] Rabelais's narratives are protean in their play with literary forms, episodic in their plots, encyclopedic in their scholarly range. Modelled after the chivalric romances popular at the time, and, more immediately, a recently published chapbook tale of Arthurian giants, *Pantagruel* (1532) and *Gargantua* (1534) chronicle the adventures of the giant Gargantua and his son Pantagruel. Combining vast erudition with vulgar humour, they describe the birth, education and military exploits of their hero-giants. *Gargantua* concludes with a long description of the Abbey of Thélème, a kind of anti-monastery that appears to represent a Renaissance utopia. In stark contrast to the rule-bound life of traditional monasteries, men and women are able to live there in unrestrained freedom. But whether the abbey represents the values of Christian humanism is left in some doubt, for the episode ends with a riddle, which Gargantua reads as a revelation of Divine Truth, whereas Friar Jean, the amiable anti-monk for whom Gargantua has built the abbey, sees in it a coded presentation of the rules for the game of tennis. Throughout Rabelais's work ambiguities are sustained by a shifting tone and an ironic narrative voice. In the prologue to *Gargantua*, he famously presents himself both as a buffoon-like fairground entertainer and as a sage philosopher whose words must be studied intently by the reader if he or she is to discern their hidden meaning – like a dog breaking open a bone in order to suck the marrow. There followed three books: the *Tiers Livre* (Book Three) of 1546 and the *Quart Livre* (Book Four) of 1552, and the so-called *Cinquième Livre* (Book Five) of 1564 (but which is generally thought to be of dubious authenticity). These works place greater emphasis on the quest for truth and meaning in life. They may be read as comedies of interpretation, subverting the idea that life may be contained by any single intellectual system or set of beliefs. In Book Three Pantagruel's companion Panurge sets out to ascertain whether, if he marries, he can be sure that he will never be cuckolded by his future wife. Unable to embrace his own free agency or to accept the inevitable disparity between our wishes and the realities of the world, he consults all manner of 'authorities'. When these authorities fail to provide him with a satisfactory answer, he embarks in Book Four, with Pantagruel and their motley companions, on a mock-epic sea voyage to Cathay to consult the Oracle of the Holy Bottle. By the end of the book, they seem to be in the middle of nowhere, no closer to their goal.

Laughter, satire and language

Laughter is Rabelais's weapon against ignorance, superstition and bigotry. Rabelais was not a 'free-thinker' or a Protestant, or indeed an atheist; but he sympathized deeply with the movement of moderate religious reform that took hold in France in the 1520s. The moderate reformers (known as 'evangelicals' because of their insistence on the supreme importance for Christian faith of Scripture) called into question the Church's attachment to ritualized outer observances such as fasting and pilgrimages, and mercantile practices like the sale of indulgences; they questioned the value of monasticism and the self-serving behaviour of priests; and they attacked the dogmatism of the Faculty of Theology at the University of Paris (the Sorbonne). These evangelical views are reflected in Rabelais's fierce satire of theologians, monks, monasticism and Papal abuses. More broadly, he mocks the pomposity and humourlessness of academics, lawyers, doctors and ideologues of all kinds – in short, all those impermeable to the joys of discovery and closed to the multiple possibilities of life.

Rabelais's satirical laughter is closely linked to questions of language. The Renaissance humanists criticized what they saw as the deliberate obscurity of the Latinate jargon used by the Establishment theologians. It is this obscure language that Rabelais satirizes in his description of Pantagruel's encounter with a student from the Sorbonne whom he induces to speak 'naturally':

> 'So you come from Paris?' said Pantagruel. 'And what do you young gentlemen-students do all day in Paris?'
> The student replied:

'We transportify ourselves across the Seinean river at times auroral and crepuscular; we deambulate via the carfaxes and quadrivia of the urbs; we despumate Latinate verbocination, and, like verisimilar amorabunds, we captivate the benevolence of the omnijudicious, omniform and omnigenous feminine sex . . . '

'Shit!' said Pantagruel. 'What is this idiot saying? . . . '

To which one of his companions replied:

'My Lord, it's obvious that he's trying to imitate the way they talk in Paris; but all he's doing is murdering Latin . . . '

Pantagruel then grabbed him by the throat, saying,

'You're murdering Latin, are you! By Saint John, I'll murder you! I'll flay you alive.'

Whereupon the wretched young man from Limoges began to say:

'Whoa there, Mister! Oh, Saint Marsaut, come an' 'elp me! Hey! For Gawd's sake, lemme go! Git yer 'ands orf me!'

To which Pantagruel said, 'Now you're talking naturally.' And he let go of him, for the poor Limousin was shitting his pants, which were in codtail style, without a full bottom . . .

'Tu viens donc de Paris,' dit Pantagruel. 'Et comment passez-vous le temps, vous autres messires les étudiants, à Paris?'

L'écolier lui répondit:

'Nous transfrétons la Séquane au dilicule et au crepuscule; nous déambulons par les compites et les quadrivies de l'urbe; nous despumons la verbocination latinale, et, comme verisimiles amorabonds, captons la benevolence de l'omnijuge, omniforme, et omnigène sexe feminin . . .

'Eh ben merde, alors,' dit Pantagruel, 'qu'est-ce que veut dire ce fou? . . . '

A ces mots l'un de ces compagnons lui dit:

'Seigneur, sans doute ce galant veut-il contrefaire la langue des Parisiens; mais il ne fait qu'écorcher le latin . . . '

Et Pantagruel le prit à la gorge, en lui disant:

'Tu écorches le latin; par saint-Jean, je te ferai dégorger ce matin, car je t'écorcherai tout vif.'

Et le pauvre Limousin de dire:

'Vée dicou! Gentillâtre. Ho, saint Marsaut, adjouda mi! Hau, hau, laissas à quau, au nom de Dious, et ne me touquas grou.'

A ces mots Pantagruel lui dit:

'Maintenant tu parles naturellement.'

Puis il le laissa, car le pauvre Limousin chiait dans ses chausses, qui étaient fendues en queue de morue, et dont le fond n'était pas cousu . . .

(*Pantagruel,* chapter 6)

Rabelais was a defender of the vernacular, as his mockery of the pretentious young man from Limoges shows; but in matters of language he was also a dazzling innovator. The virtuosity of his vituperations against the scholastic theologians of the Sorbonne is astonishing. Take this passage from the end of his prologue to Book Three:

> Get back, you dirty dogs! Get out of the way! Stop blocking the light, you hooded devils! Did you drag your arses here to sniff my wine and piss all over my barrel? Look! Here's the stick Diogenes ordered in his will to be laid next to him after his death so that he could beat off and drive away all such graveyard ghouls and Cerberean curs. Clear off, you hypocrites! Get back to your sheep! In the devil's name, get out, you filthy humbugs! What? Still here? I'll give up my share of Papimania just to get my hands on you! Grr. Grrr. Grrrrrr. Out! Right out! May you never be able to shit without being whipped, never piss without being flogged, and never get it up except through a good cudgelling!

> Arrière, mâtins! Hors de la carrière, hors de mon soleil, capuchaille du Diable! Venez-vous insinuer ici, culletants, la culpabilité de mon vin et compisser mon tonneau? Voici le bâton que Diogène, par testament, ordonna qu'on dépose près de lui, après sa mort, pour chasser et éreinter ces fantômes de cercueil et ces mâtins cerbériques. Alors, arrière, cagots! Aux moutons, matins! Hors d'ici cafards, de par le Diable, hue! Êtes-vous encore là? Je renonce à ma part de Papimanie si je vous happe. Gzz. Gzzz. Gzzzzzz. Ouste! Ouste! Iront-ils? Puissiez-vous ne jamais fienter que cinglés à coups d'étrivières, ne jamais pisser qu'à l'estrapade, ne jamais être excités qu'à coups de bâton!

As Gérard Defaux has commented: '[Rabelais's] violence, and the sheer pleasure, the raw, intense jubilation he feels at biting, spitting his own venom and inflicting pain, are absolutely unmatched. Nobody...has ever unleashed as fiercely as he the magical energy, the rhythm and power, which are embedded in language.'[2]

Rabelais was writing at a time when the French language was changing at a remarkable pace, when the linguistic resources available to him were unusually large. He delights in language and in man's capacity for language. His work constitutes an exploration of and a reflection on the power and limits of language. He uses multiple styles and mixes registers high and low; he invents extravagant puns and neologisms; he compiles word lists and indulges in rhetorical games. He plays with words in all their possible combinations and permutations. When he speaks of Friar Jean's victims in battle (*Gargantua*, chapter 27) – 'Some died without a word, others spoke without dying; some died as they spoke, others spoke as they died' ('Les uns mouraient sans parler, les autres parlaient sans mourir; les uns mouraient en parlant, les autres parlaient en mourant') – he is not, of course, using language for any representational purpose whatever, but is engaging in pure linguistic play.

The autonomy and delight of language is the theme of the 'frozen words' episode in Book Four. Sailing on the open sea, Pantagruel and his friends start hearing strange words and sounds, which terrify Panurge. The ship's captain explains that they are at the edge of a frozen sea where a great battle had taken place the previous winter, and the air was so cold that all the cries had frozen before they had time to die away; but now, with the coming of spring, they were beginning to thaw and become audible. Some, however, remain frozen.

> 'Here, get hold of these,' said Pantagruel. 'Here are some that haven't yet thawed out.'
>
> Then he threw on the deck before us whole handfuls of frozen words, which looked like sweets of many colours . . . After they had been warmed up a little in our hands, they melted like snow, and we actually heard them, but did not understand them, for they were in some barbarous tongue . . . I saw some very sharp words among them, bloody words too, which, the Captain said, sometimes went back to the place where they'd been spoken, only to find the throat that uttered them had been cut; I saw some horrible words among them, and others unpleasant to behold. When they had all melted together, we heard: *hing, hing, hing, hing, hiss, whizz, tick, tock, gibber, jabber, frr, frrr, frrr, bou, bou, bou, bou, bou, bou, bou, bou. traccc, trac, trr, trr, trrr, trrrrr, ong, ong, ong, ong, ouououong, Gog, Magog,* and God knows what other barbarous words . . .

> 'Tenez, tenez,' dit Pantagruel, 'voyez-en ici qui ne sont pas encore dégelées.'
>
> Alors, il nous jeta sur le tillac de pleines poignées de paroles gelées ressemblant à des dragées perlées de diverses couleurs . . . Après avoir été échauffés entre nos mains, ils fondaient comme neige, et nous les entendions matériellement, mais nous ne les comprenions pas car c'était un langage barbare . . . J'y vis des paroles fort piquantes, des paroles sanglantes, dont le pilote nous disait qu'elles revenaient quelquefois du lieu d'où elles avaient été proférées, mais c'était se couper la gorge: j'y vis aussi des paroles horribles et fort désagréables à voir. Celles-ci ayant fondu toutes ensemble, nous entendîmes hin, hin, hin, hin, his, tic,

torche, lorgne, brededin, brededac, frr, frrr, frrr, bou, bou, bou, bou, bou, bou, bou, bou, bou, traccc, trac, trr, trr, trrr, trrrrr, on, on, on, on, ouououon, goth, magoth, et je ne sais quels autres mots barbares...

(Book Four, chapter 56)

The point implied here is that the words, when pictured as physical objects (like printed signs on the pages of a book),[3] have no meaning until they are interpreted by a human consciousness; and the essential significance of this episode lies in its dramatization of the fact that the words we read in a fictional text are, by definition, the product of the writer's creativity – subjective, private and arbitrary – interacting with the reader's own creative imagination.[4]

Laughter, the marketplace and the body

'Most distinguished boozers, and you, most dearly beloved pox-sufferers (it is to you, and no one else, that my writings are dedicated)' ('Buveurs très illustres et vous, vérolés très précieux [c'est à vous, à personne d'autre que sont dédiés mes écrits]'). Thus begins the prologue to *Gargantua*; and this arresting dedication sets the tone for much of what follows. Just as Rabelais violates hierarchies of language by mixing registers high and low, so he violates hierarchies of social decorum by placing a great deal of emphasis, and thereby generating a great deal of scatological humour, on the visceral energies of the body. Gargantua, Pantagruel and their companions engage in a continual round of eating, drinking, defecating, urinating and copulating. The proximity of humanity to the body is continually stressed, often in spectacular fashion, from the moment of Gargantua's 'very strange' birth. His mother, Gargamelle, has been carrying him in her belly for eleven months, when, after the slaughter of 367,014 fat oxen for a Mardi Gras feast, she indulges her prodigious appetite by eating vast amounts of tripe. After dinner, they dance merrily and drink freely, whereupon Gargamelle believes she can feel the first labour pains.

> Not long after, she began to moan and wail and shout. Immediately, midwives came running from all directions; and feeling her underneath, they found some rather ill-smelling matter, which they thought was the child. But it was her bum-gut coming out, because of the loosening of her right intestine (which you call the back passage) owing to her having eaten too much tripe...

> Peu de temps après, elle commença à soupirer, à se lamenter et à crier. Aussitôt, une foule de sage-femmes surgirent de tous côtés; en la tâtant par en dessous elles trouvèrent quelques membranes de goût assez

désagréable et pensèrent que c'était l'enfant. Mais c'était le fondement qui lui échappait, à cause d'un relâchement du gros intestin (celui que vous appelez le boyau du cul) dû à ce qu'elle avait trop mangé de tripes... (*Gargantua*, chapter 6)

At this juncture, a filthy old hag with the reputation of being a great doctor applies an astringent so horrible that all her sphincter muscles are paralysed – an impediment that loosens the upper cotyledons of the womb, enabling the baby to push his way up through Gargamelle's body via the diaphragm to the shoulders, where he takes a left turn and comes out through her left ear. He does not cry like other babies, but starts shouting 'Drink! Drink! Drink!'

The birth of Pantagruel is described in similar fashion. He is a baby so amazingly big and heavy that he is unable to come into the world without suffocating his mother. The birth is further complicated by the fact that his emergence from his mother's womb is preceded by that of 'sixty-eight muleteers, each leading by the halter a mule laden with salt; after them came nine dromedaries laden with hams and smoked ox-tongues, seven camels with salted eels, then twenty-five cartloads of leeks, garlic, onions and chives: all of which greatly alarmed the midwives' ('soixante-huit muletiers, tirant chacun par le licol un mulet tout chargé de sel; il sortit ensuite neuf dromadaires chargés de jambons et de langues de bœuf fumes, sept chameaux chargés de petites anguilles, puis vingt-cinq charretées de poireaux, d'aulx, d'oignons et de ciboules: ce qui épouvanta bien les sages-femmes') (*Pantagruel*, chapter 3). Gargantua weeps at the death of his wife, but as soon as he thinks of his newborn son, he begins to laugh 'like a calf'.

The 'vulgar' elements in Rabelais have been interpreted by some critics in the light of the influential analyses of the Russian scholar Mikhail Bakhtin (1895–1975), who argues that during the medieval and Early Modern periods two contradictory world-views ran in parallel: 'official' culture, dominated by ecclesiastical authority and the repressive bureaucracy of the Church, and the culture of 'the marketplace', where the irrepressible voice of the people could be heard:

> the unofficial folk culture of the Middle Ages and even the Renaissance had its own territory and its own particular time, the time of fairs and feasts. This territory... was a peculiar second world within the official medieval order and was ruled by a special type of relationship, a free, familiar, marketplace relationship. Officially the palaces, churches, institutions, and private homes were dominated by hierarchy and etiquette, but in the marketplace a special kind of speech was heard, almost a language of its own, quite unlike the language of Church,

> palace, courts, and institutions... In all world literature there is
> probably no other work reflecting so fully and deeply all aspects of the
> life of the marketplace as does Rabelais' novel.
>
> (Bakhtin, *Rabelais and his World*, p. 154)

The language of the marketplace, with its 'curses, profanities and improprieties', is the language of 'natural', uninhibited feeling, expressing a culture at ease with the body and bodily functions, and using its unruliness to laugh at all forms of officialdom and censoriousness. As Stephen Greenblatt writes, 'Rabelais's exuberant laughter turns the world topsy-turvy, challenges the dominant structures of authority, triumphs over fear and constraint, breaks down what had seemed essential boundaries.'[5] Rabelais's scatological laughter clearly reinforces his satirical themes; but it has further, more general significance. Just as language for Rabelais is an expression of our humanity, so a hyperbolic emphasis on the body and the senses reflects humanistic delight in man's earthly existence – a privileging of the human rather than the divine. As a part of nature, man rejoices not only in his intellectual powers and spiritual aspirations but also in 'his breathing life' (Auerbach, *Mimesis*, p. 276).

Rabelais's attempt to portray human nature as a whole formed part of his effort to explore what it meant, in the early sixteenth century, to be a human being in the world. He endeavoured to construct a multi-angled portrait, both serious and playful, of the problems and preoccupations of his age. But what makes his writings so memorable and so influential (notable admirers were Jonathan Swift, Laurence Sterne, Victor Hugo, Gustave Flaubert, Louis-Ferdinand Céline, Raymond Queneau and Milan Kundera) is their extraordinary inventive power. They are among the most innovative works of narrative prose in the French language.

Chapter 3

Montaigne: self-portrait

Every man bears the entire form of the human condition.

– Montaigne, 'On Repenting'

In 1570 Michel de Montaigne (1533–92), suffering increasingly from melancholy, resigned as a magistrate in the high court of Bordeaux to spend more time on his estate in the Périgord, reflecting, reading in his tower library and writing his *Essays*. The death in 1563 of his beloved friend Étienne de La Boétie had deeply affected him. His father and younger brother had died several years later, and his children were also dying (only one lived to grow up). Montaigne felt that he needed to prepare himself for death spiritually, and his morbidity was only increased by his reading in classical philosophy – the Stoics, Epicureans and Sceptics. Moreover, death was everywhere in the world around him in the shape of the Wars of Religion that marked the second half of the sixteenth century. The conflict between Catholics and Protestants, following the Reformation, took a particularly violent form in France. Soon after Montaigne began his *Essays*, there occurred the St Bartholomew's Day Massacre, in 1572 – a coordinated series of assassinations of prominent Huguenot (Protestant) figures, followed by a wave of Roman Catholic mob violence. When Montaigne died, twenty years later, Catholics and Protestants were still killing each other. There were atrocities on both sides, with attendant disorder, famine and outbreaks of plague. The high ideals of the early Renaissance, with its belief in the potential of human nature and of the individual human being, 'dissolved', in Sarah Bakewell's words, 'into violence, cruelty and extremist theology' (*How to Live*, p. 51).[1]

Montaigne took up his pen as a form of therapy, to cure himself of his depression. His desire was to see himself and the world in perspective. To begin with, however, his solitary leisure produced not orderly reflection, but 'chimeras and fantastic monsters'. He became increasingly aware of the unruliness of his own mind, the inconsistency and changeability of his feelings and dispositions. And so he began to see his writing, not as a philosophical search for absolute truth or for his 'real' self, but as an exploration of the way his mind worked, with all its quirks and contradictions. Montaigne's great innovation in Western literature was to make intimate self-revelation a legitimate activity, and to develop a form of writing – a mixture of reflection and self-examination, which he called the 'essay' – that would represent the protean nature of the self. His main contribution to the history of ideas lies in the way he illuminated the importance of what is private or individual in human experience. His originality consists, indeed, in his discovery of what is now called 'individuality' or 'character'. Before him, the generally accepted idea of personality was that it was ruled by one of the body's 'humours'. A person was sanguine, choleric, phlegmatic or melancholic. Montaigne, however, recognized that human character is both complex and fluid.

His influence was enormous. He was the forerunner of the great French 'moralists', in the French sense of the term: that is, writers whose fundamental concern was to use literature to illuminate human behaviour and the human condition. And he was the originator of the tradition of self-study which forms such a strong strand of French literature: Blaise Pascal in the seventeenth century, the Rousseau of the *Confessions* in the eighteenth, Stendhal and Chateaubriand in the nineteenth, and many twentieth-century writers, including Marcel Proust, André Gide, Paul Valéry, Jean-Paul Sartre, Nathalie Sarraute, Marguerite Duras and Roland Barthes.

'... it is my own self that I portray'

Montaigne begins his book thus:

> You have here, Reader, a book written in good faith ... If my intention had been to seek the favour of the world, I would have decked myself out better and presented myself in a studied gait. I want to be seen in these pages, however, in my simple, natural, everyday fashion, without straining or artifice: for it is my own self that I portray.

> C'est ici un livre de bonne foi, lecteur ... Si c'eût été pour rechercher la faveur du monde, je me fusse mieux paré et me présenterais en une marche étudiée. Je veux qu'on m'y voie en ma façon simple, naturelle et ordinaire, sans contention et artifice: car c'est moi que je peins.

Most modern editions of the *Essays* total well over a thousand pages. The topics covered are remarkably diverse, ranging from profound philosophical questions to codpieces and the drinking habits of Germans. A random selection of the titles of the essays might include: 'On Sadness', 'On Idleness', 'On Educating Children', 'On the Cannibals', 'On the Custom of Wearing Clothing', 'On

Sleep', 'On Smells', 'On Conscience', 'On Cruelty', 'On the Art of Conversation', 'On the Lame', 'On Experience'. The following passage, from the beginning of the essay 'On Repenting' (Book III, chapter 2), expresses notions that are fundamental to Montaigne's vision and mode of writing:[2]

> Others form Man; I give an account of him and sketch a picture of a particular one who is very badly formed and whom I would truly make very different from what he is if I had to fashion him afresh. But it is done now. The brush-strokes of my portrait do not go awry even though they change and vary. The world is but a perennial seesaw. Everything in it – the land, the mountains of the Caucasus, the pyramids of Egypt – all oscillate with a common motion and with their own. Constancy itself is nothing but a more languid rocking to and fro. I am unable to stabilize my subject. It staggers confusedly along with a natural drunkenness. I grasp it as it is, at the moment when I give it my attention. I am not portraying being but becoming: not the passage from one age to another (or, as folk put it, from one seven-year period to the next) but from day to day, from minute to minute. I must adapt my account of myself to the passing hour. I shall perhaps change soon, not only accidentally but also intentionally. This is a register of varied and changing occurrences, of ideas that are unresolved and, when needs be, contradictory, either because I myself have become different or because I engage with different attributes or aspects of my subjects. So I may happen to contradict myself now and then, but, as Demades said, I never contradict truth. If my mind could only find a footing, I would not be exploring myself but coming to firm conclusions about myself; but my mind is ever in apprenticeship and being tested. I am expounding a lowly, lacklustre existence; that does not matter. You can attach the whole of moral philosophy to a commonplace private life just as well as to one of richer stuff. Every man bears the entire form of the human condition. Authors communicate themselves to the public by some peculiar mark foreign to themselves; I am the first ever to do so by my universal being, not as a grammarian, poet or jurist, but as Michel de Montaigne. If people complain that I talk too much about myself, I complain that they never even think about their own selves.

> Les autres forment l'homme; je le récite et en représente un particulier bien mal formé, et lequel, si j'avais à façonner de nouveau, je ferais vraiment bien autre qu'il n'est. Meshui, c'est fait. Or les traits de ma peinture ne fourvoient point, quoiqu'ils se changent et diversifient. Le monde n'est qu'une branloire pérenne. Toutes choses y branlent sans cesse: la terre, les rochers du Caucase, les pyramides d'Egypte, et du branle public et du leur. La constance même n'est autre chose qu'un

branle plus languissant. Je ne puis assurer mon objet. Il va trouble et chancelant, d'une ivresse naturelle. Je le prends en ce point, comme il est, en l'instant que je m'amuse à lui. Je ne peins pas l'être. Je peins le passage: non un passage d'âge en autre, ou, comme dit le peuple, de sept ans en sept ans, mais de jour en jour, de minute en minute. Il faut accommoder mon histoire à l'heure. Je pourrai tantôt changer, non de fortune seulement, mais aussi d'intention. C'est un contrerôle de divers et muables accidents et d'imaginations irrésolues, et, quand il y échoit, contraires; soit que je sois autre moi-même, soit que je saisisse les sujets par autres circonstances et considérations. Tant y a que je me contredis bien à l'aventure, mais la vérité, comme disait Démade, je ne la contredis point. Si mon âme pouvait prendre pied, je ne m'essaierais pas, je me résoudrais; elle est toujours en apprentissage et en épreuve. Je propose une vie basse et sans lustre, c'est tout un. On attache aussi bien toute la philosophie morale à une vie populaire et privée qu'à une vie de plus riche étoffe; chaque homme porte la forme entière de l'humaine condition. Les auteurs se communiquent au peuple par quelque marque particulière et étrangère; moi le premier par mon être universel, comme Michel de Montaigne, non comme grammairien, ou poète, ou jurisconsulte. Si le monde se plaint de quoi je parle trop de moi, je me plains de quoi il ne pense seulement pas à soi.

The main themes of this passage – and the hallmarks of Montaigne's writing – are the ideas of flux and changeability, doubt and uncertainty, and self-portraiture as a way of mirroring the human condition. Montaigne stresses the fundamental instability of the mind and, indeed, of the universe. All is flux: 'I am unable to stabilize my subject'; 'I am not portraying being but becoming'. Thus, as he says, he is inconsistent and unpredictable, full of contradictions and shifts of attitude. And so what interests him is not final conclusions, systematically developed arguments and principles, but the mobility of his mind – its 'passage . . . from day to day, from minute to minute'. Moreover, the evocation of the processes of being and thinking corresponds to the form of his writing: the frequent changes of subject and perspective, the digressions and asides, the surprising twists and turns. The apparent disconnectedness of the *Essays* in fact constitutes their essence: the representation of the writer's consciousness as it unfolds. His 'essays' are not essays in the modern sense of a logically organized treatment of a given subject, but tentative forms of experiment or exploration. The ordinary meaning of *essai* is a trial or an attempt; *essayer* means to try or to try out. The essay as Montaigne understood it and used it was a means of testing and weighing up his views on life and himself. He appears to have written whatever came into his head; and later on, when he had a second thought which would qualify or even contradict the first, he would write that down too and include it in subsequent versions of the essay. He would revise (that is, add to) an essay again and again, amending and extending it as his views changed. Harold Bloom calls the *Essays* 'a miracle of mutability', and writes: 'Montaigne changes as he rereads and revises his own book; more perhaps than in any other instance, the book is the man is the book' (*The Western Canon*, p. 147).

Montaigne's stress on the importance of 'ideas which are unresolved' goes to the heart of his project: doubt about the ability of the human mind to know anything with certainty, especially in a world in flux. Only the flux of one's own personal being can be known. Montaigne's intellectual and moral hero was Socrates, who, when asked what he knew, replied that the one thing he did know was that he knew nothing. Montaigne's chosen motto was the question 'Que sais-je?' ('What do I know?'); and one of the maxims he inscribed on his library walls was: 'To any reason an equal reason can be opposed.' This declaration of scepticism, of thought that throws doubt on itself, is fundamental to his vision. He wanted above all to question his own received ideas and first impressions about any subject, to keep exploring different ways of looking at things. His sceptical outlook may be seen as part of the Renaissance current of free thought that would later flow into the Enlightenment. It was but a short step from relativism. Truth, Montaigne concluded, was relative to his own conception of it and might vary from moment to moment. His scepticism troubled the Church. He never explicitly rejected Catholicism, though he refused to believe in miracles or witchcraft; and he celebrated enjoyment of the body, and of living in the here and now of everyday life, rather than the rewards of spirituality. Eventually, in 1676, the *Essays* were placed on the Vatican's Index of Prohibited Books, where they remained until the middle of the nineteenth century.

Towards the end of the passage above, Montaigne makes the striking claim that, through his own self-analysis, he has succeeded in discovering something of universal validity, and that 'the whole of moral philosophy' can be derived from the study of the ordinary individual self. Self-knowledge, he suggests, is the foundation of wisdom. Frank Bowman comments:

> He is proud to be the first to have studied so penetratingly the significant, the *être universel*; he has reached the goal he set for himself. We seem to have a clear case of Renaissance optimism with this sense of being a sort of Columbus discovering the new world of the self-in-flux and thus making a contribution to human consciousness. Montaigne optimistically feels that the self, despite its flux, can be penetrated, known and depicted. He shows none of the anguished Romantic doubts about the validity of self-knowledge, just as he rejects the medieval use of introspection as a means of becoming aware of our sinfulness and

God's glory; for him, self-knowledge is a source of ethical lessons. The whole effort is a novel one, a possible one, and a worthwhile one.

('Montaigne: *Du Repentir*', pp. 45–46)

The idea that by writing about oneself one may create a mirror in which others recognize their own humanity is reflected in various ways throughout the *Essays*. Montaigne implicitly appeals to common experience through the frankness and intimacy of his self-revelations. He tells us that he never sleeps in the daytime and only enjoys sex lying down, that he hates early rising, that his ears often get itchy, that he suffers from kidney stones, that his taste for radishes disappeared but then came back. He confesses to various failures and inadequacies: his memory is terrible; he cannot sing or play musical instruments; the only sport he excels in is horse-riding; he has a rather small penis. He also appeals to more profound sources of empathy: the experience of being brave, indecisive, angry or lustful; or feeling bored by one's responsibilities, or morbidly preoccupied with illness or death. Readers feel drawn into sympathetic identification with Montaigne, who, they feel, is speaking to them as a close friend. Conversational in style and genial in tone, Montaigne, unlike Rousseau, puts himself on a level with his reader, inviting us to accept him as a kind of existential guide, to join him in looking at ourselves and, with him, learning how to live.

'Our most great and glorious achievement is to live our life fittingly'

What kinds of values emerge from the *Essays*? Certain principles are made very explicit (the importance of friendship, hatred of cruelty and violence), but the *Essays* tend to express values by implication rather than by direct statement. Montaigne said that we must all keep 'a little room behind the shop', a part of ourselves that is entirely our own, detached from others and the hurly-burly of the outside world; but he also prized gregariousness, and felt it extremely important to be exposed (and sympathetic) to the experience and ideas of others. Empathy is the key to morality and social behaviour, and friendship in its broadest sense, understood as a common human bond, is a vital component of Montaigne's thinking. The sense of life thus implied is liberal and humane: it values sociability, open-mindedness and tolerance. And so, in his political life, Montaigne sought common ground between some of the extremist positions in the religious wars that wracked France. After his retirement to his estate, he continued to be involved fitfully in public life: he served twice as mayor of Bordeaux, acted several times as mediator between Catholic and Protestant factions, and helped the Catholic king, Henri III (reign: 1574–89), in his negotiations with the heir to the throne, the leader of the Protestants, Henri of Navarre, later Henri IV (reign: 1589–1610).

The final essay, 'On Experience' (Book III, chapter 13), is a kind of summing up of Montaigne's thinking as he reaches the end of his search for knowledge of himself and therefore of all men. The importance of self-knowledge, based on personal experience and the values of honesty and humility, is that it will lead us to reconcile ourselves to our limitations and imperfections; to moderate our judgements and to be ourselves rather than slaves of any orthodoxy or dogma; in sum, to accept that we are fallible human beings. At the beginning of 'On Experience' he writes:

> Is a man not stupid if he remembers having been so often wrong in his judgement yet does not distrust it thereafter? When I find myself convicted of an erroneous opinion by another man's reasoning, it is not so much a case of my learning something new he has told me nor how ignorant I was of some particular matter – there is not much profit in that – but of learning of my weakness in general and of the treacherous ways of my intellect. From that I can reform the whole lump.

> Celui qui se souvient d'avoir été tant de fois trompé par son propre jugement, n'est-il pas un sot s'il ne se méfie pas toujours? Quand je me trouve convaincu de la fausseté d'une opinion par le raisonnement d'un autre, ce que j'apprends n'est pas tant ce qu'il m'a dit de nouveau et cette ignorance particulière (ce serait une maigre acquisition), comme dans toutes les autres circonstances j'apprends ma faiblesse, et la trahison de mon entendement: d'où je tire la reformation de toute la masse.

He ends the essay with a plea for good-humoured acceptance and enjoyment of the world as it is: 'The most beautiful lives, to my mind, are those that conform to the common measure, human and orderly, but without miracles or immoderation' ('Les plus belles vies sont, à mon gré, celles qui se rangent au modèle commun et humain, avec ordre, mais sans miracle et sans extravagance'). Montaigne is implicitly attacking extremism of any kind:

> They want to go beyond themselves and escape from their humanity. That is madness: instead of changing into angels, they change into beasts; instead of raising themselves up, they crash down. Those humours that aspire to transcendency frighten me, like lofty, unapproachable heights . . . It is an absolute accomplishment, virtually divine, to know how to enjoy our being as we ought. We seek other attributes because we do not understand the use of our own; and we look

outside ourselves because we do not know what is within. There is no use in getting up on stilts, for even on stilts we must still walk with our legs! And on the highest throne in the world we are seated, still, on our arse.

Ils veulent se mettre hors d'eux et échapper à l'homme. C'est folie; au lieu de se transformer en anges, ils se transforment en bêtes; au lieu de se hausser, ils s'abattent. Ces humeurs transcendantes m'effraient, comme les lieux hautains et inaccessibles... C'est une absolue perfection, et comme divine, de savoir jouir loyalement de son être. Nous cherchons d'autres conditions, pour n'entendre l'usage des nôtres, et sortons hors de nous, pour ne savoir quel il y fait. Si avons nous beau monter sur des échasses, car sur des échasses encore faut-il marcher de nos jambes. Et au plus élevé trône du monde si ne sommes assis que sur notre cul.

Chapter 4

Corneille: heroes and kings

Do your duty, and leave the rest to the gods

— Corneille, *Horace*

In April 1655 the young Louis XIV made a speech to the *parlement* of Paris in which he was reputed to have used the phrase 'L'État, c'est moi' (I am the State). It was during Louis's long reign (1643–1715) that France moved decisively towards a centralized, 'absolutist' form of government. A key figure in this process was Cardinal Richelieu (1585–1642), chief minister to Louis XIII. Richelieu's central aim was unity under the Crown – a prerequisite, in his view, for prosperity. The turbulent feudal nobility was not finally quelled, however, until the victory of the monarchy in the 'Fronde', the organized resistance to monarchical authority which developed into civil war in the early 1650s. This movement towards the reinforcement of royal authority is the vital background to the plays of Pierre Corneille (1606–84), in which questions of government become increasingly the focus of interest. At the heart of Corneille's theatre is a concern with power relations. His most celebrated plays – *Le Cid* (1637), *Horace* (1640), *Cinna* (1641) and *Polyeucte* (1642) – dramatize the tensions between the individual subject and the institutions of state.

Le Cid

Le Cid is generally regarded as the most significant play in the history of French theatre. Set in medieval Spain at a time of transition between feudal custom and royal power, its dramatic conflict centres on two young lovers, Rodrigo and Chimène. The drama is initiated when the father of Chimène, Don Gomez, insults the father of Rodrigo, Don Diego. The two old nobles, representing a disappearing generation, feel bound to uphold their 'gloire': that is, their reputation and status, in the eyes of their peers, as honourable men. Don Diego commands his son to seek revenge. In Act I, Scene 6, Rodrigo is seen confronting his tragic dilemma.

         Pierced to the very heart
By such an unforeseen and mortal thrust,
The poor avenger of a cause that's just,
Compelled by unjust fate to play that part,
I stand here stunned, and with a head hung low
         Yield to the fatal blow.
How near it was, my heart's desire!
         Oh God, that pain again!
I must take vengeance for a sire
Wronged by the father of Chimène!

         How am I torn apart!
My honor's what desire would free me of,
Yet I must take revenge, despite my love.
One voice commands me, one would sway my heart.
Forced to renounce what is most sweet to me
         Or live in infamy,
I'm pierced by thrust and counterthrust.
         What answer is there, then?
Can I refuse to fight, or must
I slay the father of Chimène?

         Sire, mistress, honor, love,
Delightful tyranny, austere demand,
My glory tarnished or my passion banned.
What one requires, the other would reprove.
O sword, stern gift to a courageous soul
         That's yet in love's control,
Keen enemy of my chief delight,
         What is your mission, then?
To avenge my sire in mortal fight,
And so be sure to lose Chimène?

         Far better, then, to die.
I'm pledged to her as much as to my sire.
By this revenge, I'd earn her hate and ire,
Yet she'd despise me if I passed it by.
One deed would cause the one I love to mourn,
         The other she would scorn.
The more I think, the worse my plight.
         Come, most distraught of men,
Let's die now as her faithful knight,
And do no wrong to my Chimène.

         What! To die unavenged!
To choose a death so fatal to my name!

To let all Spain remember me with shame,
And leave my house's honor sadly changed!
To give my life for a beloved whose
        Love I am sure to lose!
Enough: it's time my folly ceased
        And I grew sane again.
I'll save our honor now, at least,
Since after all I'll lose Chimène.

        Yes, I was wrong indeed.
To serve my sire before my love is right.
Whether I die of grief, or die in fight,
I'll have my forebears' blood with which to bleed.
Now let me haste to vengeance; I upbraid
        Myself that I've delayed,
And that my will has wavered so.
        I shall take action then
For my insulted father, though
His foe's the father of Chimène.

        Trans. Richard Wilbur

        Percé jusqu'au fond du Coeur
D'une atteinte imprévue aussi bien que mortelle,
Misérable vengeur d'une juste querelle,
Et malheureux objet d'une injuste rigueur,
Je demeure immobile, et mon âme abattue
        Cède au coup qui me tue.
Si près de voir mon feu récompensé,
        O Dieu, l'étrange peine!
En cet affront mon père est l'offensé,
Et l'offenseur le père de Chimène!

        Que je sens de rudes combats!
Contre mon propre honneur mon amour s'intéresse:
Il faut venger un père et perdre une maîtresse.
L'un m'anime le Coeur, l'autre retient mon bras.
Réduit au triste choix ou de trahir ma flamme,
        Ou de vivre en infâme,
Des deux côtés mon mal est infini.
        O Dieu, l'étrange peine!
Faut-il laisser un affront impuni?
Faut-il punir le père de Chimène?

        Père, maîtresse, honneur, amour,
Noble et dure contrainte, aimable tyrannie,

Tous mes plaisirs sont morts, ou ma gloire ternie.
L'un me rend malheureux, l'autre indigne du jour.
Cher et cruel espoir d'une âme généreuse,
      Mais ensemble amoureuse,
Digne ennemi de mon plus grand Bonheur,
      Fer qui causes ma peine,
M'es-tu donné pour venger mon honneur?
M'es-tu donné pour perdre ma Chimène?

      Il vaut mieux courir au trépas.
Je dois à ma maîtresse aussi bien qu'à mon père;
J'attire en me vengeant sa haine et sa colère;
J'attire son mépris en ne me vengeant pas.
A mon plus doux espoir l'un me rend infidèle,
      Et l'autre indigne d'elle.
Mon mal augmente à le vouloir guérir;
      Tout redouble ma peine.
Allons, mon âme; puisqu'il faut mourir,
Mourons du moins sans offenser Chimène.

      Mourir sans tirer ma raison!
Rechercher un trépas si mortel à ma gloire!
Endurer que l'Espagne impute à ma mémoire
D'avoir mal soutenu l'honneur de ma maison!
Respecter un amour dont mon âme égarée
      Voit la perte assurée!
N'écoutons plus ce penseur suborneur,
      Qui ne sert qu'à ma peine.
Allons, mon bras, sauvons du moins l'honneur,
Puisqu'après tout il faut perdre Chimène.

      Oui, mon esprit s'était déçu.
Je dois tout à mon père avant qu'à ma maîtresse:
Que je meure au combat, ou meure de tristesse,
Je rendrai mon sang pur comme je l'ai reçu.
Je m'accuse déjà de trop de négligence;
      Courons à la vengeance;
Et tout honteux d'avoir tant balancé,
      Ne soyons plus en peine,
Puisqu'aujourd'hui mon père est l'offensé,
Si l'offenseur est père de Chimène.

The power and lyricism of Corneille's language are remarkable. *Stanza 1:* Rodrigo feels trapped by an agonizing paradox: if he decides to defend his father's honour, he will become the victim of an 'unjust law'. His hopes of love have apparently been destroyed by the actions of his beloved's father. *Stanza 2* dwells on the opposing demands of love and honour. Rodrigo must choose between two kinds of betrayal. The demands of duty and honour, sustained by a feudal, family-centred code of chivalry, are imperious; the claims of courtly love equally so. The series of antitheses and the rhythm of the verses create a sense of paralysis. *Stanza 3:* Rodrigo's mind swims; opposing figures and forces – 'Father, mistress, honor, love' – circle vertiginously round him. The antitheses are obsessively repeated. The apostrophe ('my sword') highlights the symbol of heroism and the obstacle to happiness. *Stanza 4:* Whatever choice Rodrigo makes will alienate him from Chimène, for they share the same code of honour. Suicide beckons. *Stanza 5:* But to die without avenging his father's honour would be to lose everything. Ashamed for hesitating, Rodrigo rejects the idea of suicide and chooses the path of honour. *Stanza 6:* Rodrigo feels exhilaration at having made the heroic choice of vengeance. The language Corneille employs, based on the formal, twelve-syllable alexandrine verse, is taut and sonorous. The balance and concentration of the lines, following the anguished see-sawing of Rodrigo's thoughts, expresses the dialectic of choice: the main formal characteristics of the verse are counterpoint and symmetry. The regularity of the rhythms and the patterned, semi-epigrammatic quality of the language (exceedingly difficult to render in translation) give a sense of a mind striving to overcome conflict and to impose order on the chaos of human feeling.

Rodrigo kills Don Gomez in a duel, thus saving the family honour; Chimène is now honour-bound to seek revenge in turn. But affairs of state suddenly intervene: on the orders of the King, Rodrigo leads an army which defeats Moorish invaders, and becomes a national hero. King Ferdinand, his authority enhanced by the military victory, enjoins Chimène to forgive Rodrigo and to marry him. A degree of tension between the interests of the state (voiced by the King) and the dispositions of its subjects (embodied in Chimène's reluctance to accept the King's will) remains. But the conflict of love and duty has been averted by monarchical fiat; and Rodrigo, the representative of the younger generation, has discovered a new form of 'gloire' – in a code of honour identified with defence of the realm and therefore of royal power and authority.

Le Cid was a huge popular success; but it sparked off a major literary controversy, which became known as 'The Quarrel of *Le Cid*' (1837–40). A war of pamphlets ensued. The context of this war was the formulation during the 1630s of a new set of laws for classical drama, especially tragedy. These laws required that plays observe the 'unities': unity of time (the play's events were to be limited, strictly speaking, to the hours between sunrise and sunset on a single day), place (the entire action was to occur in one location) and action (subplots and the dramatic treatment of more than a single conflict or problem were to be avoided). More generally, the principle of 'propriety' should be observed: no melodramatic actions, no on-stage physical effects, no language that deviated from polite conversation. And the genres of tragedy and comedy were to be kept quite separate. While the function of comedy was to deal with private life and everyday matters, tragedy would take elevated subjects from ancient history to depict the 'human condition'. The implication was that public life – affairs of state – was more important than the life of the individual. The norms that were to determine literary activity thus expressed a vision of the world that was hierarchical and authoritarian; the watchwords were harmony and order. The links between the aesthetics of neoclassicism and the ideology of absolutism have been well stated by the Marxist critic Arnold Hauser: 'The desire is that art should have a uniform character, like the state, should produce the effect of formal perfection, like the movement of a corps, that it should be clear and precise, like a decree, and be governed by absolute rules, like the life of every subject in the state. The artist should be no more left to his own devices than any other citizen; he should rather be guided by the law, by regulations, so as not to go astray in the wilderness of his own imagination.'[1]

The ultimate codification of literary classicism came with the *Art poétique* (1674) of Nicolas Boileau (1636–1711). But already, in 1635, Cardinal Richelieu had established the Académie française, a learned society whose mission was 'to labour with all the care and diligence possible, to give exact rules to our language, to render it capable of treating the arts and sciences': in effect, to exercise state control over cultural activity. Richelieu instructed the Académie to make a judgement on *Le Cid*. Their report acknowledged the play's beauties but criticized its irregularities: it did not strictly observe the laws of the 'unities', and its conclusion – the prediction of the marriage of the hero and heroine – was more in the vein of conventional comedy than tragedy. (Indeed, the original 1637 edition of the play was subtitled 'a tragicomedy'.) Furthermore, the Académie noted the 'immorality' of Chimène's defiance of the King's wishes.

The 'Roman' tragedies

The upshot of 'The Quarrel' was that it led Corneille to pay closer attention to classical dramatic rules. This was evident in the plays produced within five years of *Le Cid*: the so-called Roman tragedies, which made Corneille's reputation as a master of serious drama and created the kind of play known as 'French classical tragedy'. Roman history is used in these plays to dramatize the political conditions that prevailed during the closing years of Louis XIII's reign and the beginning of the autocracy of Louis XIV. *Le Cid* is a kind of prologue to these plays, in terms of both theme (heroism, power, politics) and mode (intense concentration on a moral dilemma). The refusal of Chimène to obey the King and marry Rodrigo signifies a refusal to break with the feudal values of her father and submit to the new, apparently benevolent monarchical order. A self-assertive heroine figures too in *Horace*, which was based on the Roman historian Livy's account of the patriot (Horace) who saves the state and murders his pacifist sister (Camille). One of the enemy champions slain by Horace is betrothed to Camille. When he returns from the battlefield, she denounces his brutality and curses Rome, whereupon he turns his sword on her. Put on trial, his fate lies in the hands of the Emperor, who alone has the authority to pass judgement on him. Although the Emperor describes the murder as monstrous, he spares Horace, declaring that the state needs men like him and that necessity transcends the laws of common humanity. In *Cinna*, the Emperor plays the central role throughout. The play focuses on a conspiracy, led by Cinna, against the first Roman emperor, Augustus. In the final scene, Augustus pardons his enemies, traitors to the state, whose motives are shown to be selfish – in contrast to his own magnanimity, seen as a form of statecraft designed to ensure the state's security. Magnanimity is raised to the level of martyrdom in *Polyeucte*. The eponymous hero, a convert to Christianity, is forced to choose between God, the state and his love for his wife. He chooses martyrdom, his death making immediate converts of his wife and her father. The pagan world of the empire, it is suggested, will be transfigured by Christianity; devotion to the state will be consecrated by devotion to God.

Chapter 5

Racine: in the labyrinth

Where can I hide?
I cannot hide even in Hell

– Phaedra in *Phèdre* (IV, vi)

'Corneille depicts men as they ought to be; Racine depicts them as they are.' This comment by the essayist Jean de La Bruyère (1645–96), in his *Characters* (*Les Caractères*, 1688), neatly states the differences between the two dramatists, whose sensibilities and visions of the world were indeed highly dissimilar. The protagonists of Corneille aspire to a kind of heroic transcendence through the exercise of their will; those of Jean Racine (1639–99) embody a human nature divided against itself, ravaged by conflicting impulses, helpless in the face of its own consuming desires. The suffering and defeat of Racine's protagonists are made all the greater by their agonized awareness of their fate, which they can neither fully comprehend nor do anything to avert. Corneille had sought to arouse in his audiences feelings of admiration; Racine seeks to arouse the Aristotelian responses of pity and fear.

The world of Racinian tragedy

The pessimism that marks Racinian tragedy has been widely attributed to his upbringing. Orphaned in infancy, he was brought up by relatives under the influence of the austere Jansenist strand in contemporary Roman Catholicism. Jansenism was named after its Dutch originator, the theologian Cornelius Jansen (1585–1638), who promoted the doctrine of predestination. The Fall, he taught, had led to the complete ruin of human nature, and since human nature was naturally sinful, all mankind was destined to go to Hell, except for a small minority saved by the direct and mysterious intervention of divine grace. Although Racine came to reject Jansenist belief in his early years, involving himself instead in court affairs and theatre, the emotional and intellectual influence of Jansenism was to haunt him all his life. His education at the

Jansenist schools of Port-Royal gave him not only an intimate knowledge of Jansenist theology but also a remarkable grounding in Greek and Latin literature. The influence on him of Greek tragic drama, especially that of Euripides, was profound. The Greek sense of fatality no doubt converged in his mind with the Jansenist sense of original sin and human worthlessness, contributing to the power of his presentation of man's helplessness in the face of destructive passions and of grace withheld.

The dramatic force of Racine's tragedies, their dense concentration of effect, is generated in aesthetic terms by what has been called their 'simplicity', and which Odette de Mourgues has termed 'the triumph of relevance': in other words, masterly exploitation of the rigour and discipline that were the hallmarks of the neoclassical aesthetic. Every formal element of the plays contributes, in a tightly interwoven, highly economical manner, to their tragic purpose. Strict adherence to the unities (of time, place and action) and a remarkably small vocabulary (fewer than 3,000 words, compared with Shakespeare's 20,000) give Racine's tragedies their sharpness of focus. The plots are very simple. The plays open with the action at crisis point, and, once the first step is taken, tension mounts between a small number of characters, locked together in a claustrophobic world by conflicting desires and ambitions. There is no relief from the inexorable movement towards disaster.

The action is displaced from the physical to the psychological, made manifest through monologues or dialogues; savage emotions are set off, and heightened, by the controlled precision of the alexandrine rhyming couplets in which Racine and Corneille wrote their plays. The entire burden of meaning is placed on language. As George Steiner writes: 'All that happens, happens inside language. That is the special narrowness and grandeur of the French classic manner. With nothing but words – and formal, ceremonious words – at his disposal, Racine fills the stage with the uttermost of action' (Steiner, *The Death of Tragedy*, p. 96). Both Racine and Corneille are seen in France as master poets; tragedies like *Phèdre* were called 'dramatic poems' in the seventeenth century. It is thus not possible to fully appreciate Racine without becoming attuned to the strictly ordered rhetoric, the sublime grandiloquence, of his verse. Successful performances of his plays have something of the quality of music or opera, performed by actors with an appropriate command of diction and rhythm, and able to deliver their lines in a manner halfway between the spoken word and song. Racine's verse is notoriously difficult to render convincingly in English. Rare exceptions are the translations of John Cairncross and, especially, those of *Phèdre* by the English poet Ted Hughes and the Australian translator Julie Rose, who, like Cairncross, composed their versions not in rhyming couplets but in free verse. Hughes and Rose largely succeed in capturing, for a modern theatre audience, some of the tension and power of the original.

Phèdre

Phèdre (1677), based on the *Hippolytus* of Euripides, is generally regarded as Racine's greatest achievement. Phaedra, the wife of Theseus, King of Athens, is in love with her stepson Hippolytus, who in turn loves Aricia, a captive princess. When Theseus is absent, presumed dead, Phaedra allows herself to be persuaded by her old nurse and confidante, Oenone, to declare her passion to Hippolytus, who reacts with horror. Theseus returns unexpectedly. Oenone, to protect Phèdre, accuses Hippolytus of attempting to seduce her mistress. Theseus, enraged, curses his son, calling on the god Neptune to punish him. Hippolytus is killed in a battle with a sea-monster, becoming entangled in the reins of his terrified horses, who drag him to a terrible death. His tutor, Theramenes, returns to tell the story to Theseus. Phaedra, consumed by guilt, confesses all, tells Theseus that his son was innocent and commits suicide by a slow-working poison. Theseus is left alone to mourn his son, having realized his error of judgement and the cruel duplicity of the gods.

A primary feature of Racine's plays is his *tirades*. The French word has no implication of rant, but denotes the great speeches whose function is to fix attention on a character or theme, and whose poetic language, when entrusted to a brilliant actor, can be utterly compelling. The passage below, a *tirade* addressed by Phaedra to Hippolytus, is taken from Act 2, Scene 5, which focuses on Phaedra's terrible declaration of love. In a semi-trance, she sees the pair of them as lovers in the Cretan Labyrinth; the themes of escape and entrapment are held in sustained tension. The passage follows the conventions of classical rhetoric: exordium (lines 1–7); development (lines 8–27); peroration (lines 28–29).

> Yes, Prince, I burn for Theseus.
> I love him, not as he's been in the Underworld,
> A fickle philanderer with a roving eye,
> Bringing disgrace to the God of Hades' bed;
> 5   But loyal, lofty, and a bit fierce,
> Charming, young, trailing hearts wherever he goes,
> The way they depict the Gods, or as I see you before me.
> He had your bearing, your eyes, your way of talking,
> The same noble reticence put colour in his cheeks.
> 10   He sailed through the waves into Crete,

A fine specimen for the daughters of Minos to love.
Where were you then? Why, without Hippolytus,
Did he seem to be the cream of Greece's heroes?
Why – you weren't old enough – but why couldn't you
15   Have been on the ship that sent him to our shores?
You would have slaughtered the Minotaur, our monster half-brother,
Despite all the twists and turns of his endless Labyrinth;
My sister would have armed you with her fatal thread
And led you through the dizzying maze.
20   No – I would have beaten her to it;
Love would have shown me what to do.
I, I alone, Prince, would have come to your rescue, helped you
Negotiate the Labyrinth's entanglements.
How I would have improvised, for that gorgeous face!
25   A miserable thread wouldn't have done *me*.
I'd have stood beside you in the danger you faced,
No – I'd have gone first.
I'd have gone down into the Labyrinth with you
And emerged with you later, or been lost.

Trans. Julie Rose

Oui, prince, je languis, je brûle pour Thésée:
Je l'aime, non point tel que l'ont vu les enfers,
Volage adorateur de mille objets divers,
Qui va du dieu des morts déshonorer la couche;
5   Mais fidèle, mais fier, et même un peu farouche,
Charmant, jeune, traînant tous les cœurs après soi,
Tel qu'on dépeint nos dieux, ou tel que je vous vois.
Il avait votre port, vos yeux, votre langage;
Cette noble pudeur colorait son visage
10   Lorsque de notre Crète il traversa les flots,
Digne sujet des vœux des filles de Minos.
Que faisiez-vous alors? pourquoi, sans Hippolyte,
Des héros de la Grèce assembla-t-il l'élite?
Pourquoi, trop jeune encor, ne pûtes-vous alors
15   Entrer dans le vaisseau qui le mit sur nos bords?
Par vous aurait péri le monstre de la Crète,
Malgré tous les détours de sa vaste retraite:
Pour en développer l'embarras incertain,
Ma sœur du fil fatal eût armé votre main.
20   Mais non: dans ce dessein je l'aurais devancée;
L'amour m'en eût d'abord inspiré la pensée:
C'est moi, prince, c'est moi dont l'utile secours

Vous eût du labyrinthe enseigné les détours.
Que de soins m'eût coûté cette tête charmante!
25   Un fil n'eût point assez rassuré votre amante:
Compagne du péril qu'il vous fallait chercher,
Moi-même devant vous j'aurais voulu marcher;
Et Phèdre au labyrinthe avec vous descendue
Se serait avec vous retrouvée, ou perdue.

The first line, a single sentence, is in a sense deeply ironic, for the remainder of the *tirade* contradicts the opening statement, showing how Theseus has been replaced in Phaedra's feelings by Hippolytus. The exordium climaxes in line 7 with the decisive shift of focus marked by the dramatically monosyllabic, emphatically alliterative 'tel que je *v* ous *v* ois', reinforced by the further alliteration of 'Il a*v* ait *v* otre port, *v* os yeux, *v* otre langage'. The image of Theseus begins to fade as Phaedra compares Hippolytus to her husband as a young man. A series of rhetorical questions (lines 12–15), as Phaedra imagines Hippolytus accompanying his father on the ship that first brought Theseus to Crete, are a prelude to the full displacement of Theseus, as Phaedra then imagines Hippolytus, not Theseus, killing the Minotaur in the Labyrinth at Knossos (lines 16–19). The substitution of Hippolytus for Theseus is followed (lines 20–23) by a further imagined substitution: that of Phaedra for her sister Ariadne, who, with a ball of thread, helped Theseus find his way out of the Labyrinth. The thread is then cast aside, replaced by Phaedra herself: a final substitution, as Phaedra imagines herself walking ahead of Hippolytus in the Labyrinth. Theseus having been eliminated, Phaedra describes herself as Hippolytus's lover. The growing excitement is countered by the sense of fatality that lies in the closing words of the peroration (lines 28–29), 'retrouvée, ou perdue': 'perdue' implies moral perdition and total personal disorientation, not simply death.

If we consider the passage in terms of its basic imaginative patterns rather than its purely rhetorical structure, it may be divided into two parts, following the opening line: lines 2–11 depict Phaedra's nostalgia for the younger Theseus; lines 12–29 evoke Phaedra's fevered imagination as she fantasizes about Hippolytus. The dominant tense of the second part of the *tirade* has become the past conditional ('aurait péri', 'eût armé', 'l'aurais devancée', etc.), describing events which might have, but have not in fact taken place. The erotic fantasy corresponds to a radical rewriting of the myth of Theseus and the Minotaur, with the principal roles completely changed and the Labyrinth invested with complex symbolic value. A tale of heroism is replaced in Phaedra's mind by an ambiguous vision of the Labyrinth as a space in which Hippolytus becomes trapped – trapped, it is implied, by Phaedra's desire for him. In the first part of the passage references to Hippolytus's physical attributes ('port', 'yeux', 'langage') suggest Phaedra's sexual attraction to him, a prelude to the lines in which she imagines herself guiding Hippolytus in the darkness. Racine's poetic rhetoric in the second half of the *tirade* implies that Phaedra's initiation of Hippolytus into the twists and turns of the tunnel is initiation into sexuality. The urgent repetition of 'C'est moi, prince, c'est moi' – the positioning of 'prince' between the two first-person pronouns suggesting that Hippolytus is imprisoned, as it were, by Phaedra – reinforces the fantasy of domination and intimacy ('votre amante', 'avec vous ... avec vous') as her erotic reverie intensifies; while the image of descent suggests the feelings of guilt and help-lessness associated with her 'forbidden' passion. Phaedra knows that pursuit of her secret passion spells perdition ('s'y perdre'), that it must be kept hidden from the eyes of the world, in the depths of the Labyrinth. The Labyrinth is the female sexual organ; it is also a place where Phaedra dreams of seeing Hip-polytus as if trapped at her side; it is a place where Phaedra herself is trapped by her own repressed desires.

The Labyrinth, with its entanglements and its association with the monster, is also the unconscious. The peculiar intensity of *Phèdre* derives to a large extent from its compelling expression of the workings of the unconscious – its complexes, conflicts and sense of guilt. Phaedra, writes Charles Mauron, is 'simultaneously the guilty impulse, the self which confesses and gives in to that impulse, and the conscience which condemns and punishes it'.[1] Throughout the play, Phaedra is tortured by consciousness of her desires. Convinced of her unforgivable guilt, she asks (Act 4, Scene 6) how she can endure the gaze of the sacred sun from which she is descended via her mother, Pasiphaë, and how she will endure the sight of her father (Minos, ruler of the underworld); and in the final scene of the play (Act 5, Scene 7) she reveals to Theseus that her moral conscience has led her to take poison as an act of remorse. Her sense of guilt derives from the conviction that she has sinned. And yet, she is punished for mere desire. She strives to resist her passion for her stepson and confesses her love to Hippolytus only after she believes that her husband is dead. She hopes to die, and she dies – of desire, which, as Terry Eagleton comments, is presented as 'a sort of natural catastrophe ... a sickness or affliction to be lamented as deeply as death, and from which death is ... the only exit'.[2] Desire figures, not as a moral problem, but as a metaphysical condition: that of human beings in the world, and for which a hidden God, transposed into the terms of Greek myth, provides no answer.

As Phaedra sinks into death, the last words of the play are spoken by Theseus. Just as Phaedra is persecuted by Venus, Theseus is tricked by Neptune. He is spared, Leo Spitzer argues, in order to confront what has happened and to acknowledge not only the consequences of his own acts but also the perversity of the world order. The protégé of Neptune, he has been made 'the instrument of doom; the denouement of the action elicits his final understanding that, when he thought himself to be protected by a loving god, he was, in reality, his victim' ('The "Récit de Théramène"', p. 216). The unmitigated nature of the tragedy is thus sealed by the realization of the human condition under the inexorable and arbitrary rule of the gods.

Chapter 6

Molière: new forms of comedy

Making the gentry laugh is a strange business.

— Molière, *The School for Wives Criticized*

Molière (1622–73) is universally recognized as France's greatest comic play-wright. He was also, by all accounts, the finest comic actor of his generation. He himself performed the leading roles in his plays, and at the same time was a director and manager: a complete man of the theatre. To focus on his plays as written texts, and to ignore questions of performance and stagecraft, would obscure our appreciation of his dramatic virtuosity, his specifically theatrical achievements and the remarkable variety of his work. Moreover, he was a highly self-conscious artist whose work constitutes a reflection, in the context of his times, on the nature and possibilities of comic drama. His achievement, as writer-actor-manager, was to renew comic drama in France and to give it something of the status of tragedy.

Comedy high and low

Born Jean-Baptiste Poquelin, in Paris, Molière enjoyed a comfortable bourgeois upbringing. His father was a prosperous *tapissier* (upholsterer and tapestry-weaver) attached to the court of Louis XIII. He could have pursued a profitable career in his father's trade or in the law; however, he chose to abandon his studies in 1643 to become an actor, and this at a time when actors were often categorized on official documents with prostitutes and highwaymen and the Church taught that theatres were places of perdition. With Joseph and Madeleine Béjart, among others, Molière founded the *Illustre Théâtre*. But it went bankrupt in under two years, and the troupe was obliged to leave Paris. They toured the provinces for the next thirteen years, providing private performances for wealthy noblemen in their chateaux and public performances in the towns of southern France. It was during this period that Molière received the theatrical training that provided him with the basis for his later success in Paris. Above all, the provincial years were responsible for consolidating his interest in farce. It was through the performance of a farce that his troupe obtained the permission of the young king, Louis XIV, to try its luck in Paris. Its inaugural performance in the capital was in October 1658 at the Louvre in front of Louis and his court, where they performed Corneille's tragedy *Nicomède* and, as an afterpiece, Molière's own farce, *The Amorous Doctor* (*Le Docteur amoureux*). The King preferred the farce. Molière was granted use of the Petit Bourbon theatre under the patronage of the King's brother, the Duc d'Orleans, who was formally known as 'Monsieur'. The *Troupe de Monsieur* opened its doors in November 1658.

Molière and his troupe shared the Petit Bourbon with a group of Italian actors who specialized in the Italian farce tradition, *commedia dell'arte*. This association with the Italians, who included the legendary Scaramouche, strongly influenced Molière, developing his awareness of the techniques of farce, especially the use of improvisation, gesture and mime. Farce remained an important element of Molière's theatre, even in the major comedies, in terms of theme (conjugal quarrels, cuckoldry, fathers opposing love matches), character type (clever, cheeky servants or slow, stupid ones) and comic business (the scene in *Tartuffe* ([1664/1669]) when Orgon hides under a table while his wife is being seduced on top, or the famous monologue in *The Miser* (*L'Avare*, 1668) during which Harpagon grabs his own arm and thinks he has caught the robber who has stolen his money). The mere fact that Moliere revitalized, and brought back to the Paris stage, a discredited art form made him something of an innovator. However, his real originality revealed itself in the very first play he wrote for Paris audiences: *Precious Provincials* (*Les Précieuses ridicules*, 1659). *Precious Provincials* is an energetic one-act farce, with characters played wearing masks and floured faces; however, it is farce of a particular kind, since a large part of its humour lies in its contemporary satire. It is a savage skit on the manners of the time, in particular the pretentiousness of the female members of bourgeois *salons*. There was an attempt to stop the play's production, but the play was riotously successful and helped to set Molière on the course he was to follow: to fuse popular farce and the comedy of manners and character. Within the next few years, Molière worked towards the formula for which his theatre is most celebrated: the great five-act verse comedies, with their portrayal of the foibles of contemporary man.

The first in this series of so-called 'high' comedies was *The School for Wives* (*L'École des femmes*, 1662). The psychological plausibility of the characters, and the themes touched upon, had never before been seen on the comic stage. The protagonist, Arnolphe, is a middle-aged man with an obsessive fear of being cuckolded. He has chosen as his prospective wife an innocent young girl,

Agnès, whom he has brought up in seclusion, so that she will be too naïve to deceive him. While he is away from home, she meets and falls in love with a young man, Horace; naturally, she rebels against Arnolphe's tyranny. Reduced to a state of bewilderment, he discovers that he is in fact devoted to Agnès. The first really complex character in the history of French comedy, Arnolphe is in some ways a sympathetic figure, but one made ridiculous by his obsession. The play is a rich combination of high comedy, pathos and interludes of farce which serve to highlight the comic tensions in Arnolphe's character.

The formula introduced by this play, and the other famous plays that followed it in a series (*Don Juan* (*Dom Juan*, 1665); *The Misanthrope* (*Le Misanthrope*, 1666); *The Miser*, *Tartuffe*; *The Learned Ladies* (*Les Femmes savantes*, 1672)), represent Molière's great contribution to the history of French comedy. These comedies are built round a conventional romantic intrigue, with a pair of young lovers whose marriage will resolve the plot. But this intrigue is not the point of these plays: grafted onto the traditional plot, and forming the central interest, is a totally new satiric dimension: the portrait of a social problem. *The School for Wives* is not about Horace and Agnès, but about Arnolphe and his attitude to marriage. *The Misanthrope* is not about Alceste and Célimène as lovers, but about Alceste's obsession with sincerity and its absence in the upper-class society in which he and Célimène move. It is thus not surprising that, in spite of its strong elements of farce and fantasy, what struck Molière's contemporaries about his theatre was its 'realism': that is to say, his focus on social observation, his creation of characters who are immediately recognizable in the context of contemporary society yet with caricaturally exaggerated traits that produce laughter.

The School for Wives was a huge success and earned for Molière an annual pension from the King. However, he had not created a new kind of comedy without making some powerful enemies. *The School for Wives* was condemned by a number of churchmen and created much jealousy among Molière's theatrical rivals. The latter, led by Corneille and the rival troupe of actors at the Hôtel de Bourgogne, publicly criticized the play for its mixture of styles (the low comedy of farce and comedy of an elevated, more conventional kind). Molière responded with two little one-act plays in prose, both produced in 1663: *The School for Wives Criticized* (*La Critique de l'École des femmes*) and *The Versailles Impromptu* (*L'Impromptu de Versailles*), in which he answered all the criticisms and outlined his views on theatre in general. In a famous passage of *The School for Wives Criticized*, he states that the business of the comic writer is to paint a true portrait of the men and women of his own age. Molière's imaginary world is the real world of contemporary France, as Corneille's world and Racine's world are not. Comedy, he wrote, is a 'public mirror' in which the spectators must inevitably recognize aspects of themselves. Molière's major plays, as Jacques Guicharnaud has commented, 'show that everyone's life is a romance, a farce, a disgrace'.[1]

Comedy of character: *Tartuffe*

The attacks on *The School for Wives* were mild in comparison with those directed at Molière's most famous play, *Tartuffe*, which was premièred before the King and court in 1664. Although Louis XIV apparently liked the play, its treatment of the theme of religious hypocrisy was found highly provocative by leading churchmen, who campaigned successfully to have the play banned from public performance. The ban was not lifted until 1669, when the play, originally in three acts, was presented in a modified five-act form; this is the play as we know it today.

Tartuffe is ingeniously constructed. The first two acts are entirely taken up with the Orgon family's reactions to Tartuffe's effect on their lives, while Tartuffe himself does not appear until Act 3. Orgon, a well-to-do Parisian, has become obsessed with Tartuffe, who has succeeded in convincing Orgon and his mother that he is a deeply devout man, of exemplary character, who has been misjudged by others. Orgon has not only taken Tartuffe into his household as his spiritual adviser, but also proposes to marry him to his unwilling daughter, Mariane, who is in love with Valère. When Tartuffe finally appears, in Act 3, he attempts to seduce Orgon's wife, Elmire; Orgon's son, Damis, witnesses this and attempts to warn his father, but the latter refuses to believe him and banishes him from the house. Orgon himself eventually witnesses another attempt at seduction, but at this juncture it is revealed that the house now belongs by Orgon's deed of gift to Tartuffe, who has arranged not only to have his benefactor and his family evicted but also to have him jailed for protecting a dissident friend. Orgon is about to be arrested when a deus ex machina in the form of the King's legal representative arrests Tartuffe instead; the all-seeing King, guarantor of ultimate justice, has discovered the truth about the villainous hypocrite and intervenes to restore order.

At the centre of *Tartuffe* is the power struggle within the household. That Tartuffe is a rogue is strongly suggested in the first two Acts and made manifest in Act 3 by his overtures to Elmire. The question is whether he can be prevented from taking over. The spring of the play is the contest over truth and falsehood. Tartuffe brings to the struggle considerable skill as a player of his role (indeed, as an actor in a comedy he himself stages) and brilliant powers of rhetoric (represented in comically exaggerated form, of course). He manipulates Orgon through the language of piety and mystical devotion; and his attempts to persuade Elmire that the religious and the sexual are really reflections of each other ('I can't look at you, you perfect creature, without admiring the Almighty in you') are a masterpiece of casuistry. The play turns, however, not on Tartuffe's villainy, but on Orgon's mania. It is Orgon (played by Molière himself in the original production) who represents the play's most interesting psychological case study and is the real butt of the comedy. He is blinded by his self-regard as a man of charity and by the charms of a piety which, in the words of Erich Auerbach, 'makes it possible for him to satisfy his instinctive urge to tyrannize over and torment his family' (Auerbach, *Mimesis*, p. 361). The central scene of the play is the famous scene in which Orgon is at last forced to recognize the reality of Tartuffe's hypocrisy and lust through a trick played on him by Elmire, who pretends to reconsider his offer of seduction. Orgon hides under a table to witness the encounter. There is dramatic brilliance in the synchronized desires of the lecherous Tartuffe and the credulous Orgon; both want Elmire to provide concrete proof of what they expect (or, in the case of Orgon, do not expect). Tartuffe unmasks himself immediately, but the comic effect of the scene lies in Orgon's refusal to come out from under the table. Elmire keeps coughing desperately to warn him that he should wait no longer, but for a while it seems that only her complete surrender will persuade Orgon of Tartuffe's intentions. 'What, coming out already?' she says sarcastically when Orgon finally emerges. 'There must be some mistake. Get back under the table, you're too early; wait until he's finished, to be absolutely sure . . . ' The tone of the second half of the play is remarkable, as it swings between the registers of farce and tragedy. Paradoxically, Tartuffe's sinister qualities are heightened by his clownishness. The play both amuses and disturbs us, our discomfort deriving from Tartuffe's power of fanaticism over the *paterfamilias*, Orgon.

'Normative' comedy

Molière fought hard to overturn the ban on *Tartuffe*, and in the process engaged with a number of debates regarding the theatre in general and comic theatre in particular. It was in the first of his three 'petitions to the King' that he first alluded to the supposed didactic purpose of comedy, suggesting that its function was 'to correct men while entertaining them'. The argument of moral utility was a highly conventional one, used by Molière to appease his opponents. However, in his 1667 *Letter Concerning the Play 'The Impostor'*, he indicated, more authentically, his vision of comedy and how it works.

The comic is the outward and visible form that nature's bounty has attached to everything unreasonable, so that we should see, and avoid, it. To know the comic we must know the rational, of which it denotes the absence and we must see wherein the rational consists...

Le ridicule est la forme extérieure et sensible que la providence de la nature a attaché à tout ce qui est déraisonnable, pour nous en faire apercevoir et nous obliger à la fuir. Pour connaître ce ridicule il faut connaître la raison dont il signifie le défaut et voir en quoi elle consiste...

The animating principle of Molière's theatre is his exploitation of incongruity: a constant double vision, which depicts the unreasonable alongside the suggestion of its opposite. The 'high' comedies provide grounds for the statement that Molière builds his theatre round monomaniacs: characters who are obsessed with something, whether marital chastity or money or health or learning or social status, which so dominates their thinking that their family threatens to disintegrate around them: 'my mother, brother, wife and children could die,' says Orgon, 'and I wouldn't lose a moment's sleep.'

This focus on extremists and eccentrics who have become disconnected from their social world is better understood if seen in historical context. A variety of factors (the rapid growth of Paris and of fashionable Parisian society, as well as a concern with social stability after the upheaval of the Fronde: see above, p. 25) led in the mid-seventeenth century to a widespread interest in 'manners' – in socially acceptable ways of presenting oneself and interacting politely with others. Being a reasonable person, knowing one's place in society and how to 'fit in', was extolled as a social ideal. This ideal was embodied in the figure of the *honnête homme. Honnêteté* did not connote 'honesty', but the gentlemanly attributes of urbanity, wit, taste, civility and moderation.[2] This is precisely the ethos against which Molière's comic characters offend. However, his plays are not to be understood as embodying a precise form of philosophical or moral commitment; it is rather, as Terence Cave has commented, that we should see his theatre as 'the product of a fertile imagination capable of seizing on the most sensitive questions of his day and embodying them in a dramatic form which preserves their problematic character'.[3] Molière's comedies ask questions, in brilliantly entertaining ways, about what it means to live in society. The *concept* of society is at the heart of *The Misanthrope*, a complex and challenging work considered by many to be Molière's masterpiece. This play dramatizes the conflict between a man's attempt to sustain his individual integrity and the inevitable compromises involved in accommodation to society's complexities and contradictions. To the horror of his friends, the misanthrope, Alceste, rejects the notion of *politesse* and the social conventions of the seventeenth-century *salon*. His form of fanaticism is his unwillingness to compromise, and despite his theoretical attachment to 'truth', his desire to 'correct the world' is ironized – as is the pragmatism of those who ridicule him.

Comedy and/as fantasy

Molière's plays were produced for two quite different audiences: in addition to his predominantly bourgeois Parisian public, he entertained Louis XIV and his court. The court enjoyed satire of the bourgeoisie, as represented in *The School for Wives*, *The Miser* and *Tartuffe*; at the same time, the King became increasingly infatuated with opera. The recently founded Paris Opera was proving a significant rival to Molière's own troupe. This trend is reflected in the plays of Molière's final period. They embody a theatre of spectacle, in which the dramatic action is framed by singing, dancing and music. This new, mixed type of entertainment was known as 'comedy-ballet'. Molière's usual collaborator in these spectacles was the King's Italian master of music, Jean-Baptiste Lulli (1632–87). Molière offered to the King, in his chateaux at Chambord and Saint-Germain, such dazzling creations as *Monsieur de Pourceaugnac* (1669), *The Would-be Gentleman* (*Le Bourgeois gentilhomme*, 1670) and *The Imaginary Invalid* (*Le Malade imaginaire*, 1673). *The Would-be Gentleman* is the pinnacle of this genre. It is a playful satire on the social pretensions of a newly rich middle-class man. With its setting of dancing, music and spectacle, a strong element of fantasy is added to the plot. In this sense, it extends and heightens the elements of fantasy integral to all of Molière's plays: the fantasy implicit in the gestures of farce on stage; the fantastic choreography of comic routines; the fantasy of language, with its patterned dialogue and brilliant word play; the fantastic denouements of many of the plays; the madness of monomaniacs, who live in their own fantasy worlds. The descent (or the happy ascent?) into madness of Monsieur Jourdain, duped towards the end of *The Would-be Gentleman* into believing that he has become a 'mamamouchi' – an invented term to denote a Turkish nobleman – is reminiscent, for example, of the frenzied madness of the miser, Harpagon, when he discovers that his beloved *cassette* (strongbox) has been stolen. The miser's lunatic ravings make up one of the most famous scenes in French dramatic literature.

> Stop thief! Stop thief! Get the murderer! Get the killer! . . . My money's gone. Who was it? Where've you gone? . . . Give me my money, you devil! . . . (*Grabs his own arm.*) Oh god, it's me. I'm going mad. Where

am I? Who am I? What am I doing? My lovely money, my lovely darling money. They've taken you from me. Without you I have nothing to live for. You're my joy, my light, my consolation. I'm finished. Done for. I'm dying. I'm dead. I'm buried. Will no one give me back my life by giving me back my money or telling me who took it. Eh? What are you saying?... (*Peering at the audience.*) What a lot of people, all around! You're all in it, every one of you. I can see it on your faces. You there, what are you saying? Something about the thief?... Please, for pity's sake, tell me anything you know. Are you hiding him? He's there, isn't he? They're all looking at me and laughing.

(*The Miser*, Act 4, Scene 7)

Au voleur! au voleur! à l'assassin! au meurtrier!... on m'a dérobé mon argent. Qui peut-ce être? Qu'est-il devenu?... Rends-moi mon argent, coquin... (*Il se prend lui-même le bras.*) Ah! c'est moi. Mon esprit est trouble, et j'ignore où je suis, qui je suis, et ce que je fais. Hélas! mon pauvre argent, mon pauvre argent, mon cher ami! on m'a privé de toi; et puisque tu m'es enlevé, j'ai perdu mon support, ma consolation, ma joie; tout est fini pour moi, et je n'ai plus que faire au monde: sans toi, il m'est impossible de vivre. C'en est fait, je n'en puis plus; je me meurs, je suis mort, je suis enterré. N'y a-t-il personne qui veuille me resusciter, en me rendant mon cher argent, ou en m'apprenant qui l'a pris? Euh? que dites-vous?... Que de gens assemblés! Je ne jette mes regards sur personne qui ne me donne des soupçons, et tout me semble mon voleur. Eh! de quoi est-ce qu'on parle là? De celui qui m'a dérobé?... De grâce, si l'on sait des nouvelles de mon voleur, je supplie qu'on me le dise. N'est-il point cache là parmi vous? Ils me regardent tous, et se mettent à rire.

Seeing that the audience reacts with nothing but laughter, Harpagon declares, in a paroxysm of irrationality, that he wants everyone in the world to be hanged; and if he still doesn't find his money, he will hang himself. We in the audience continue to laugh – at Harpagon's absurdity and at human folly in general, as it exists in ourselves as well as in others.

Chapter 7

La Fontaine: the power of fables/fables of power

Animals enact my universal theme.

　　　– La Fontaine, 'To His Royal Highness the Dauphin', *Fables*

The Grasshopper and the Ant, The Crow and the Fox, The Town Rat and the Country Rat, The Fox and the Stork, The Lion and the Gnat, The Hare and the Tortoise, The Wolf and the Lamb . . . Jean de La Fontaine (1621–95), a lyric poet and a writer of sporadically bawdy tales in verse,[1] is best known for the 230 *Fables* he published between 1668 and 1694, of which the animal fables are by far the most celebrated. Learnt by heart by generations of French children, they have made La Fontaine one of the most often quoted and one of the best-loved French writers.

The *Fables*: art and ideology

If the fable exists at all in French literature as a poetic form, it is thanks to La Fontaine. By the seventeenth century, the fable was no longer taken seriously. Because he was working in a minor genre, he was free of the rules laid down for other literary forms. The fruit of that freedom can be seen in the variety of tones and styles he adopted. A master of prosody, irregular verse and aural patterning, he was a master, too, of a wide range of registers – satire, comedy, personal lyric, aphoristic wit, heroic rhetoric and down-to-earth speech – which sometimes merge into each other in quick succession. The *Fables* represent a pinnacle of poetic charm and sophistication.

From its origins in classical literature (Aesop most notably), the fable was explicitly designed to offer moral lessons, and was a more obviously didactic form – at least on the surface – than practically any other branch of literature. Like so many of his contemporaries, La Fontaine accepted this view. His originality, however, lay in his rewriting of the old classical tales in a distinctive poetic style, in which the moral is often ambiguous or even omitted altogether. He broadened and recast the old stories in order to depict aspects of the human

condition and to offer a critical view of his society that may be compared with
that of Molière. The function of the animals in the *Fables* is, generally speaking,
to act as conventional embodiments or models of human characteristics; they
are not so much characters as masks, like the figures in the stylized world of
Molière's comedies. One of the effects of transposing human behaviour to the
animal world is that human pretensions are satirized by the ridicule implicit
in their transfer to an inappropriate setting. Part of the pleasure of the *Fables*
lies in our awareness of this double vision.

What emerges from a consideration of the *Fables* as a whole is a vision of
the world that is thoroughly disabused, though not bitter. Like other writers in
the satirical tradition, La Fontaine offers standard diatribes about human corruption. There are several fables in which humans are compared unfavourably
with animals, and in which it is made clear that humans are the beasts. Man
is 'wicked', as he says in 'The Man and the Snake' (X: 1).[2] A large proportion
of the fables are built on the contrast between the wicked and the innocent,
the cunning and the foolish. In the world of the *Fables*, the wicked have power
and the weak can be pitilessly oppressed even when they are totally innocent.
As La Fontaine says in 'The Spider and the Swallow' (X: 6), the powerful sit
down to the rich table of life, while the weak make do with scraps on the other
table – though he also says that this is the result of Jupiter's work, as if social
injustice were divinely ordained. Much of the time, the powerful are explicitly
trying to do evil and ignoring the most sacred of duties in their drive towards
their own advantage. The blackness of the picture is tempered only by certain
considerations that ensure that the powerful do not always escape retribution.
First, the powerful eventually become weak, as the lion discovers, and can be
subjected to indignities that nobody would have dared to visit on them during
their period of strength. Second, the powerful are sometimes stupid and are
particularly open to flattery on the part of the weak – or at least the cunning.
But while this might benefit the fox, it's hardly of much comfort to the weak
and innocent. Third, the powerful also sometimes do their best to harm each
other, as in the case of the fox and the wolf in 'The Lion, the Wolf and the Fox'
(VIII: 3); or, at least, they use each other, as we see with the fox and the wolf
in 'The Fox, the Wolf and the Horse' (XII: 8). La Fontaine's recommendation
is to keep well clear of the powerful and never give them a chance to harm
you.

If there is a positive philosophy in the *Fables*, it pertains to the ideal of freedom, human attachments and Epicurean values. Love of freedom is expressed
in many of the fables, including one where the wolf prefers ostracism, hunger
and freedom to wealth and slavery ('The Wolf and the Dog', I: 5). The theme
of solitude as a value is occasionally expressed. 'The Arbitrator, the Hospital

Visitor and the Visitor' (XII: 29) expresses the value of solitude in a religious context; the same value is expressed in a secular context in 'The Dream of a Dweller in Mogul Lands' (XI: 4). In this life, with death awaiting us all, La Fontaine believes that the sensible attitude to adopt is not the stoic one of mastering – or butchering – the passions ('The Scythian Philosopher', XII: 20), but the Epicurean one of enjoying what life has to offer. The lesson of 'The Wolf and the Hunt' (VIII: 27) can be summed up in the precept: *Enjoy!* We should eat, drink and be merry in the face of death, because we can't know how much time we have to count on ('The Charlatan', VI: 19). When death comes, it comes without being invited, but also without surprising us, because, as he says in 'Death and the Dying' (VIII: 1):

> Death never takes by surprise
> The well prepared, that is, the wise
>
> La Mort ne surprend point le sage;
> Il est toujours prêt à partir

At that moment, we should take our leave courteously of our host at the banquet of life. The wise man is always ready to leave life, though not because life is not worth living. And the greatest gift that life has to offer seems to be love and friendship. In 'The Two Turtle-Doves' (IX: 2), La Fontaine expresses his nostalgia for love and advises lovers to find the world in each other. His recommendation for the wise is, finally, to retreat into the world of private happiness, insulated from the cruelty of life and safe from the attentions of the powerful.

The Poet and the King

The theme of power is at the centre of a fascinating book by the distinguished French critic Marc Fumaroli: *The Poet and the King*. This book offers a highly political reading of La Fontaine's work, focused on the situation of the artist under an absolutist regime.

In September 1661 the 22-year-old Louis XIV (the so-called Sun King whose reign was to last for seventy-two years, from 1643 to 1715) had his superintendant of finances, Nicolas Fouquet, arrested. This arbitrary act signalled dramatically the beginning of Louis's personal, autocratic reign. A sham trial (for embezzlement and treason) ensued, and Fouquet was imprisoned for life. It is true that he had gained his enormous wealth by corrupt means, but this was commonplace at the time. Fouquet had provoked Louis's jealousy; and the

King also saw him as a dangerously liberal figure. Fumaroli stresses in particular Fouquet's prestige as a patron of the arts on a truly grand scale, his popularity in Paris and the hope invested in him – as potential chief minister – to establish a more enlightened political order after the hated absolutist policies of Richelieu (1585–1642) and Mazarin (1602–61), the cardinals who pulled the strings of power under Louis XIII's (reign: 1610–43). The fall of Fouquet destroyed the hopes of a generation of creative artists, who had looked forward to a golden age of patronage under a minister who favoured a great variety of literature, including satire and lyric poetry. Instead, they had to live within a state system that managed and manipulated culture to serve its own ends. A cultural policy of grandeur was instituted. Its orchestrator was Jean-Baptiste Colbert, the chief minister from 1665 to 1683. The most well known monuments built as symbols of Louis XIV's grandeur are, of course, the palace at Versailles and the Louvre. Literature was seen as one of the institutions of kingship; its role was to contribute to the 'glory' of the court.

La Fontaine had been protected and generously supported by Fouquet, whose fall came as a severe blow. For the rest of his life, however, he managed to achieve an uneasy balance between his aesthetic and political integrity and the unavoidable need to humour those in authority. He trod carefully, making certain necessary concessions, and even wrote a number of panegyric poems for the King. Eventually he became a member of the Académie française, but he always kept an ironic distance from the court, writing for the urbane, freethinking world of the *salons* rather than for the state.

Discreet opposition to the ideology of absolutism is expressed beneath the surface of the *Fables*, through lyricism and irony. Against the brutal cult of power, La Fontaine sets, in lyric mode, the values of beauty, love and friendship. His ideal, as noted above, is the private world of the Epicurean garden; and in fables like 'The Two Turtle-Doves' he sings of blissful retreat from the cruelties of public life. Moreover, many of the *Fables* explore ironically the nature, exercise and maintenance of power – the whole phenomenon of autocratic kingship and its workings. The lion and the wolf of the *Fables* are seen as transparent representations of the King. The theme of power and its ironic treatment are illustrated very well by the fable 'The Wolf and the Lamb' (I: 10).

> The reasons given by the strong are best,
>   as this example will attest.
> A lamb stood in a river, pure and clear,
>   quenching his thirst; a wolf came past;
>   his hunger brought him prowling there,
>   looking for food to break his fast.

'How dare you brazenly pollute
my drinking place!' exclaimed this raging brute;
　'such insolence must be chastised.'
'Do not be angry, Sire,' replied the lamb;
'Your Majesty, no doubt, has realized
　that standing where I am
I'm more than twenty paces down the stream
　from where you are; it does not seem
　that I disturb, in any way,
　the water you might drink.' 'I say
　you do disturb it, even so,'
the cruel beast responded; 'and I know
　you spoke much ill of me last year.'
'How could I, when I wasn't born? My mother
has not yet weaned me from her milk, I swear.'
'Then if it wasn't you, it was your brother.'
'I haven't got one.' – 'Then it must have been
some other of your family that I mean.
　You persecute me – not just you,
　but all your dogs and shepherds too.
For that's what I've been told; it proves my case;
　I'll have revenge.' He took his prey,
And ate him deep in woodland far away;
No trial of any kind took place.

　　　　　　Trans. Christopher Betts

La raison du plus fort est toujours la meilleure:
　　Nous l'allons montrer tout à l'heure.
　　Un Agneau se désaltérait
　　Dans le courant d'une onde pure.
Un Loup survient à jeun qui cherchait aventure,
　　Et que la faim en ces lieux attirait.
Qui te rend si hardi de troubler mon breuvage?
　　Dit cet animal plein de rage:
　　Tu seras châtié de ta témérité.
– Sire, répond l'Agneau, que votre Majesté
　　Ne se mette pas en colère;
　　Mais plutôt qu'elle considère
　　Que je me vas désaltérant
　　　　Dans le courant,
　　Plus de vingt pas au-dessous d'Elle,
Et que par conséquent, en aucune façon,
　　Je ne puis troubler sa boisson.

> – Tu la troubles, reprit cette bête cruelle,
> Et je sais que de moi tu médis l'an passé.
> – Comment l'aurais-je fait si je n'étais pas né?
>   Reprit l'Agneau, je tette encor ma mère.
>   – Si ce n'est toi, c'est donc ton frère.
> – Je n'en ai point. – C'est donc quelqu'un des tiens:
>   Car vous ne m'épargnez guère,
>   Vous, vos bergers, et vos chiens.
> On me l'a dit: il faut que je me venge.
>   Là-dessus, au fond des forêts
>   Le Loup l'emporte, et puis le mange,
>   Sans autre forme de procès.

The moral of the fable appears to be enunciated in its first line. But there is ambiguity here. Does 'raison' mean reasoning or motivation? More importantly, does 'meilleure' mean legitimate ('right') or irresistible (through brute force)? The ambiguity is charged with irony; and tongue-in-cheek irony may be read into the narrative voice (apparently aligned with 'the strong'/'[le] plus fort'), given the blatant cynicism of the Wolf's pretence at reasoning. The wolf pretends to demonstrate, by reasoning, why the lamb must be eaten, but his assertions are shown to be wrong at every turn; his pretended demonstration merely indicates his motivation: hunger.[3] The wolf distorts truth in his own interests: that is, in the interests of power. It is the wolf who, in that sense, muddies the clear water of the stream. The statements contained in the first two lines cannot, in other words, be taken at face value. And the placement of the stated moral at the beginning rather than, as usually, at the end, signals the ironic nature of a demonstration ('it proves my case') that does no more than show the wolf's imperviousness to the lamb's ingenuous attempt to argue with him. The cynicism of the wolf and the arbitrariness of his behaviour, encapsulated in the curt coda ('No trial of any kind took place'), could not be clearer. The real moral of the fable, as Ross Chambers has suggested, is: in order to survive, don't argue with the wolfish, out-wolf them:

> [La Fontaine's] *Fables* appear in the first instance as a manual for those who would wield power, not oppose it . . . But it happens that to know the strategies of power serves also the needs of opposition, whose tactics are entirely and exclusively determined by the nature of power and its practices . . . ; so that La Fontaine's revelation of the workings of power turns out simultaneously, if less obviously, to have ironic relevance as an education in oppositional behavior.   (*Room for Maneuver*, pp. 57–58)

This 'education' is embodied in the fable's own narrative performance, which, by imitating the duplicity of the wolf's discourse (mere pseudo-reasoning, hiding true motivation), discreetly but systematically ironizes its own 'demonstration'. As Fumaroli says, and as any student of the ironic uses of art in totalitarian societies knows, poetry does not need to be openly oppositional to be political.

Chapter 8

Madame de Lafayette: the birth of the modern novel

> ... so great was her perplexity that she resolved to avoid
> the very thing she perhaps most desired in all the world.
>
> – Madame de Lafayette, *La Princesse de Clèves*

La Princesse de Clèves (1678), by Marie-Madeleine de Lafayette (1634–93), is generally regarded by literary historians as the first modern novel in French. This may seem surprising given the novel's historical setting: the aristocratic milieu of King Henri II (reign: 1547–59) and his court. The novel's modernity consists in its unprecedented emphasis, in prose narrative, on psychological analysis, and its authentic representation of life at the royal court. Combining elements of the romance and the novella – prose genres that were previously dominant – *La Princesse de Clèves* created a new model for fiction: the type of psychological novel (*roman d'analyse*), foregrounding the inner lives of its characters and the relationships between them, that would become such an important strand of the French literary tradition. It looks forward to the fiction of Laclos and Stendhal.

The beautiful young heroine, the sixteen-year-old Mlle de Chartres, attracts much attention when she is presented at court by her mother. Her mother soon marries her to the Prince de Clèves, a man her daughter respects but does not love. No sooner is she married than she meets the Duke de Nemours, the most brilliant and attractive nobleman in the King's entourage and notorious for his affairs with women. Nemours falls violently in love with her. The princess avoids him as much as she can, but finds herself becoming irresistibly attracted to him. Forced to recognize that she is powerless in the face of her passion, and wishing to preserve her virtue by withdrawing from the court, she turns to her husband for help and confesses to him that she is in love with another man, whom she refuses to name.

The following passage evokes the princess's feelings immediately after this famous scene:

> When the prince had left, when Mme de Clèves found herself alone and considered what she had just done, she was so appalled that she could

hardly imagine it was true. It seemed to her that she had sacrificed the love and respect of her husband and that she had dug for herself a deep pit from which she would never escape. She asked herself why she had done something so perilous, and concluded that she had embarked on it almost without intending to do so. The singular nature of such a confession, for which she could find no parallel, brought home to her all the risks it entailed.

But when she went on to consider that this remedy, drastic though it might be, was the only one that could protect her against M. de Nemours, she decided that she ought to have no regrets and that she had not taken too great a risk. She spent the whole night tormented by uncertainty, confusion and fear, but in the end her mind recovered its tranquillity. She even felt a certain contentment at having given such a token of fidelity to a husband who deserved it so much, who regarded her with such affection and respect, and who had just given her further proof of these feelings by the way in which he had reacted to her confession.

Lorsque ce prince fut parti, que madame de Clèves demeura seule, qu'elle regarda ce qu'elle venait de faire, elle en fut si épouvantée qu'à peine put-elle s'imaginer que ce fût une vérité. Elle trouva qu'elle s'était ôté elle-même le cœur et l'estime de son mari, et qu'elle s'était creusé un abîme dont elle ne sortirait jamais. Elle se demandait pourquoi elle avait fait une chose si hasardeuse, et elle trouvait qu'elle s'y était engagée sans en avoir presque eu le dessein. La singularité d'un pareil aveu, dont elle ne trouvait point d'exemple, lui en faisait voir tout le péril.

Mais quand elle venait à penser que ce remède, quelque violent qu'il fût, était le seul qui la pouvait défendre contre monsieur de Nemours, elle trouvait qu'elle ne devait point se repentir et qu'elle n'avait point trop hasardé. Elle passa toute la nuit pleine d'incertitude, de trouble et de crainte, mais enfin le calme revint dans son esprit. Elle trouva même de la douceur à avoir donné ce témoignage de fidélité à un mari qui le méritait si bien, qui avait tant d'estime et tant d'amitié pour elle, et qui venait de lui en donner encore des marques par la manière dont il avait reçu ce qu'elle lui avait avoué.

The focus here is overwhelmingly on the princess's thoughts and feelings. She is shown struggling to understand, and thus to control, her inner turmoil. As Terence Cave observes: 'There are, of course, external events in *The Princesse de Clèves*, but the story is plotted not through them but through their impact on the princess's changing awareness of her situation and of her own feelings' (Introduction to *The Princesse de Clèves*, p. xvii). Introspection corresponds to the beginnings of self-consciousness and to an almost shocked recognition of complexity. The verb *trouver* (to find, to realize) occurs five times. This is typical of the entire novel, which is replete with words like 'seem', 'observe', 'notice', 'discover' – words denoting the character's perceptions and mental processes.

The princess's perplexity cannot be fully understood without a knowledge of the novel's social and cultural context. The institution of marriage, the practice of arranged marriages and the difficulty for women of realizing their individuality in a world governed by the demands of social expediency were highly topical questions in France in the seventeenth century. Although the novel is set during the reign of Henri II, over a century before the time of writing, the evocation of Henri's court was clearly intended to refer equally to that of Louis XIV (of which Mme de Lafayette herself was a prominent member). The heroine's sheltered upbringing, her early marriage to a man she hardly knows and her training in 'virtue' at the hands of her mother were typical of the times. Mme de Chartres's ethic is a worldly one, based on a concern with social standing and security rather than on moral or religious principles.

> Madame de Chartres ... often gave her daughter descriptions of love, impressing upon her how delightful it can be so that it would be easier to convince her of its dangers. She told her about men's insincerity, their deceit, and their infidelity, and about the disastrous effect of love affairs on married life; on the other hand, she evoked for her the peace of mind which a woman of good reputation may enjoy and the brilliance and social distinction virtue bestows on a woman who is already beautiful and well-born. But she also taught her how difficult it is to preserve this virtue except by an extreme mistrust of oneself and by holding fast to the only thing that can ensure a woman's happiness: to love one's husband and to be loved by him.

> Madame de Chartres ... faisait souvent à sa fille des peintures de l'amour; elle lui montrait ce qu'il a d'agréable pour la persuader plus aisément sur ce qu'elle lui en apprenait de dangereux; elle lui contait le peu de sincérité des hommes, leurs tromperies et leur infidélité, les malheurs domestiques où plongent les engagements; et elle lui faisait voir, d'un autre côté, quelle tranquillité suivait la vie d'une honnête femme, et combien la vertu donnait d'éclat et d'élévation à une personne qui avait de la beauté et de la naissance. Mais elle lui faisait voir aussi combien il était difficile de conserver cette vertu, que par une extrême défiance de soi-même et par un grand soin de s'attacher à ce qui seul peut faire le Bonheur d'une femme, qui est d'aimer son mari et d'en être aimée.

Mme de Chartres dies soon after her daughter's marriage, but not before she has noticed the princess's 'inclination' for Nemours. On her deathbed she warns her daughter of the peril she is in:

> You are on the edge of a precipice. You will have to make a supreme effort and cause yourself great pain in order to hold yourself back. Think of your duty to your husband; think of your duty to yourself, and consider that you are on the point of losing the reputation you have earned for yourself and I so much desired for you.

> Vous êtes sur le bord du précipice: il faut de grands efforts et de grandes violences pour vous retenir. Songez ce que vous devez à votre mari; songez ce que vous vous devez à vous-même, et pensez que vous allez perdre cette réputation que vous vous êtes acquise et que je vous ai tant souhaitée.

The death of the princess's mother deprives her of any source of support except her husband, who now replaces her mother as a friend.

The confession scene aroused heated debate among contemporary readers. Indeed, the princess herself reflects in astonishment and horror at the highly unusual nature of such a confession. Soon after the novel was published, the editor of the *Mercure galant*, Donneau de Visé, invited his readers to express their views on whether the princess's confession to her husband was plausible and whether she should have confided in him at all. The vast majority of respondents found the confession both implausible and reprehensible; however, as W. D. Howarth has noted, the volume of correspondence produced by the survey bore witness to the fascination the novel had for the cultured *salon* public. *La Princesse de Clèves* – and particularly the confession scene – represented, observes Howarth, the translation into sustained literary form of their preoccupation with the psychology of love and the moral problems arising from it. The controversy the novel provoked also indicates the extent to which it disturbed contemporary habits of reading and, by the same token, brought into question the social values of its readers, who expected women to remain silently in their place.

La Princesse de Clèves is typical of much seventeenth-century French literature in its exploration of important questions about the norms of human conduct. Its originality (and achievement) lie in the subtlety and acuity with which Madame de Lafayette depicts the princess's states of mind and feeling, in particular the collision between her education (that is to say, her training at the hands of her mother) and her experience, between her ingrained sense of duty and her own emotions. The princess's uncertainty about how she should behave informs her feelings throughout much of the novel and is exacerbated by her encounters with the social world of the court. As the narrative progresses, she hears various stories of unhappy and difficult love affairs marked by secrecy and duplicity – stories of invented characters as well as of real historical figures like Mary Stuart, Diane de Poitiers and Ann Boleyn. She must somehow assimilate these stories, comparing them with her own experience and with the lessons provided by her mother, if she is to negotiate the promiscuous world around her. It is a world beneath whose polished surface swirl constant undercurrents of amorous and political intrigue; the princess must learn not to judge from appearances, for things are seldom what they seem. She strives to interpret this world but remains in a state of confusion and unease. Critics have commented that this emphasis on human fallibility bears the stamp of the Jansenist world-view (see above, p. 32), which, as Terence Cave has remarked,

> proved to be extraordinarily fertile as an imaginative resource for writers. It provided them with a cogent and complex account of human behaviour in which conscious intention was seen to be constantly belied and undermined by dark, unfathomable motivations: what makes things happen is something we can't quite see, or don't see in time; we live in a world of signs and clues which we must interpret but which are never reliable enough to provide certainty.
>
> ('Introduction', *The Princesse de Clèves*, p. xviii)

The striking thing about the description of the princess's state of mind in the passage quoted above is her ambivalence. Her initial feelings of horror and disbelief give way, despite her uncertainty, to a shaky sense that she might have done the right thing. However, the effects of her confession (like Phaedra's confession of her love for Hippolytus in Racine's *Phèdre*) are, in any case, disastrous. Nemours happens to be eavesdropping outside the window, and the confession thus becomes an indirect confession of love to him. And soon afterwards the Prince de Clèves discovers that the man his wife loves is Nemours, mistakenly supposes that she has yielded to him, is consumed by jealousy, falls ill and dies.

Although the princess and Nemours are now free to marry, she refuses to accept his proposal, partly, she says, out of a sense of duty towards her husband's memory and partly through fear that Nemours's love for her might eventually die and that, in accordance with the norms of masculine behaviour described by her mother, he would become unfaithful.

> 'What I believe I owe to the memory of M. de Clèves would have little power over me were it not sustained by self-interest, by my desire for peace of mind; likewise, the claims of my peace of mind need the

support of those of duty. But, though I distrust myself, I believe that I shall never be able to overcome my scruples, nor can I hope to overcome my attraction to you. It will make me unhappy, and I intend to remove myself from your sight, however painful this will be.'

'Ce que je crois devoir à la mémoire de Monsieur de Clèves serait faible s'il n'était soutenu par l'intérêt de mon repos; et les raisons de mon repos ont besoin d'être soutenues de celles de mon devoir. Mais, quoique je me défie de moi-même, je crois que je ne vaincrai jamais mes scrupules, et je n'espère pas aussi de surmonter l'inclination que j'ai pour vous. Elle me rendra malheureuse et je me priverai de votre vue, quelque violence qu'il m'en coûte.'

She retires to a convent – absence and distance enabling her to maintain her resolve never to see Nemours again – and lives out her days in pious seclusion. However, a sense of extreme ambivalence remains. The princess's rejection of Nemours can hardly be seen as a Cornelian triumph of the will and reason over passion, for the 'duty' she invokes does not spring from absolute principles or any clear moral scruples ('I am sacrificing a great deal', she says, 'to a duty that exists only in my imagination'), but from the values of submission and social respectability instilled in her by her mother and the deep distrust of sexual passion this has formed in her. The princess herself indicates the emotional self-interest that underlies her renunciation: a desire for peace of mind, a desire to return to the tranquillity that preceded passion. Ultimately unable to move beyond her 'uncertainty . . . and fear', she withdraws from the world. The novel's closing sentence is tantalizingly ambiguous. It might be read as a tribute to the princess's exemplary moral character, or as a sadly ironic comment on the socially exceptional quality of her behaviour and the vanity of her sacrifice: 'her life, which was quite short, left inimitable examples of virtue' ('sa vie, qui fut assez courte, laissa des exemples de vertu inimitables').

Chapter 9

Voltaire: the case for tolerance

I have never made but one prayer to God, and a very short one:
'O Lord, make my enemies ridiculous.'
And God granted it.

— Voltaire, *Letter to Étienne Noël Damilaville*, 16 May 1767

'Voltaire is the central figure of the Enlightenment, because he accepted its basic principles and used all his incomparable wit and energy and literary skill and brilliant malice to propagate these principles and spread havoc in the enemy's camp. Ridicule kills more surely than savage indignation: and Voltaire probably did more for the triumph of civilized values than any writer who ever lived.' Thus wrote Isaiah Berlin, the distinguished thinker and historian of ideas.[1] François-Marie Arouet, better known under his pseudonym Voltaire (1694– 1778), has a special place in French literature because of his commitment to secular, humanist values and his defence of intellectual freedom in a society dominated by the Church.

Voltaire first made his name as a writer of verse tragedies and epic poems, but his true genius emerged as the master of brief forms: the short story, the essay, the treatise, the pamphlet, the letter, the epigram. The epigrams, some of which have passed into common use, give a good idea of the style and spirit of Voltaire:

If God did not exist, it would be necessary to invent him.
If God made us in his image, we have certainly returned the compliment.
There are two things for which animals are to be envied: they know nothing of future evils, or of what people say about them.
Prejudice is the reason of fools.
It is dangerous to be right in matters on which the established authorities are wrong.

Voltaire's wit and irony were the weapons he used in his unrelenting struggle against the abuses of the Ancien Régime: obscurantism, intolerance, religious fanaticism. He courted controversy, he made enemies all his life, his books were censored and burnt. His rallying cry, launched in his *Philosophical Dictionary* (1764), was *Écrasez l'infâme!* (literally, 'Crush the infamous!', but more idiomatically translated as something like 'Make War on Injustice!' or 'Destroy Bigotry!'). His works are what Jean-Paul Sartre (see below, pp. 200–07) would later call 'committed literature', and they helped to establish a tradition that led directly from Voltaire via Hugo and Zola to Sartre and Camus.

The Enlightenment

The term 'Enlightenment' is used to describe the movement of ideas that developed in Western Europe from the late seventeenth to the late eighteenth century. The classic definition of the concept is to be found in an essay ('What Is Enlightenment?', 1784) by the German philosopher Immanuel Kant (1724–1804). 'Enlightenment', he wrote, 'is man's emergence from his self-imposed immaturity. Immaturity is the inability to use one's understanding without guidance from another. This immaturity is self-imposed when its cause lies not in lack of understanding, but in lack of resolve and courage to use it without guidance from another. *Sapere Aude!* (Dare to know) – "Have courage to use your own understanding!" – that is the motto of enlightenment.' The leading thinkers of the Enlightenment, the so-called *philosophes* (intellectuals and men of letters rather than philosophers), saw themselves as rationalists whose mission was to imbue the world with a consciousness of the capacity of human reason to improve the human condition. In attempting to free the mind of man, Enlightenment thinkers challenged organized religion, superstition, dogma and priestcraft as barriers to human progress.

The views of the *philosophes* were shaped by the work of two Englishmen, John Locke (1632–1704) and Isaac Newton (1643–1727). Locke argued that men are reasonable beings capable of using their knowledge and intelligence for the promotion of their own happiness. Newton, the greatest figure in early modern science, laid the groundwork of modern physics by working out the mechanical laws of motion, especially the laws of gravity. His work had an enormous impact on the thought of the eighteenth century, inspiring educated people to accept scientific law as a basis for unravelling the mysteries of nature and achieving the technical and material progress that would lead to greater human happiness. This instrumental pursuit of happiness corresponded to the notion of utility. For the individual, utility was whatever increased one's well-being, while for society utility translated into the rule that the measure of whether a policy was right was whether it brought the greatest happiness to the greatest number of people. This was what was meant by 'utilitarianism', which combined morality and self-interest into what the utilitarians called *enlightened self-interest*: in other words, doing good was ultimately in a citizen's own interest, and the pursuit of self-interest contributed to the common good. Utilitarianism permeated the thought of the eighteenth century. The organization of society, in terms of its laws, government and education, was to be remade on rational, utilitarian lines. The stress of Enlightenment thinkers on freedom of thought and expression, and the rights of the individual, corresponded closely to the values and interests of the rising bourgeoisie, which seized power in 1789. Enlightenment principles were reflected in the ideals of the French and American revolutions, embodied in the *Declaration of the Rights of Man and of the Citizen* issued in France in 1789.

Voltaire and Enlightenment

For Voltaire the Church was the greatest enemy of progress. He was not, however, an atheist. Like most *philosophes*, he was a 'Deist': he believed that the existence of a Supreme Being could be inferred from the evidence of design embodied in the complexities and wonders of the world; and he also felt that religious belief helped to maintain moral order among the masses. Anticlerical rather than anti-Christian, he was against *organized* religion, which he thought was a tissue of superstition and fanaticism; moreover, the pernicious role of religious institutions in the power structures of public life was an issue about which he felt passionately. It is important to be aware of the context of his thinking: on 22 October 1685, nine years before Voltaire was born, Louis XIV had committed his most foolish act: he had revoked the Edict of Nantes (1598), which for nearly a century had allowed a measure of religious freedom to Protestants in France. Thus, when Voltaire was born, religious tensions and the persecution of heretics, that is to say, non-Catholics, were still rife.

Voltaire's important early work, the *Philosophical Letters*, also known as *Letters Concerning the English Nation* and *Letters on England* (*Lettres philosophiques*, 1734), was inspired by the two and a half years (1726–29) he spent in England, having chosen to exile himself there as a result of a quarrel with a French aristocrat. He deeply admired England as a land of liberty and religious tolerance – as opposed to the repressive feudal society of his birth. An anthology of essays and travel sketches, the *Philosophical Letters* were written in praise of British liberty and eccentricity, and contained much criticism, largely implicit, of French institutions. The Fifth Letter, on the Church of England, began with the statement: 'This is the country of religious sects. An Englishman, as a free man, goes to Heaven by whatever route he likes.' In the Sixth Letter, he wrote: 'Go into the London Stock Exchange – a more respectable place than many a royal court – and you will see representatives from all nations gathered together for the utility of men. Here Jew, Mohammedan and Christian deal with each other as though they were all of the same faith, and apply the word "infidel" only to people who go bankrupt.' When the *Lettres philosophiques* were published in France, a warrant was immediately issued for Voltaire's arrest and an order sent out for the book to be burnt by the public executioner.

Despite Voltaire's outspoken liberal views, Louis XV appointed him as royal historiographer (a position once held by Racine) in 1745. Nearly ten years later, in 1754, Louis XV banished him from the court at Paris and Versailles, probably because he was piqued that Voltaire had spent long periods at a rival court, that of Frederick the Great of Prussia, the 'Enlightened Despot'. Voltaire took up residence in Geneva, Switzerland, and lived in exile for the last twenty-three years of his life. Soon after settling in Geneva, on the morning of Sunday 1 November (All Saints' Day) 1755, the city of Lisbon was struck by an earthquake killing about 30,000 men, women and children. Voltaire's immediate reaction when the bad news reached Geneva about three weeks later was to write a Poem on the Lisbon Disaster. It embodied his response to the widely held doctrine that the world is governed by a fundamentally benign God. 'We must acknowledge evil is on the earth ... / You foolish philosophers who cried: "All is well", / Come and see these dreadful ruins.' What divine justice, the poem asks, is to be seen in these horrors? How can it be said that the dead have been punished for their sins? Why Catholic Lisbon and not London or Paris, cities of vice? Why did an omnipotent God create a world subject to natural disasters? The poem provoked fury among churchmen throughout Europe.

Voltaire at Ferney

In 1759 Voltaire bought an estate at Ferney, close to the Swiss border, which allowed for a quick escape should Louis XV's censorship police come looking for him. He was to live there for the rest of his life. He entertained lavishly, built a theatre for performances of the stilted neoclassical dramas for which he was celebrated and received an endless stream of visitors from all over Europe. However, he also took a paternal interest in the peasants and was shocked by their wretched conditions of life. He became an enlightened lord of the manor, abolishing feudal dues, starting cottage industries and even rebuilding the parish church. His experience as a landlord, Ian Davidson has argued in *Voltaire in Exile*, led to a remarkable process of moral development, for Voltaire now became a dedicated man of conscience, devoting himself, in the years that followed, to campaigning for the victims of a number of appalling miscarriages of justice, most of them the result of anti-Protestant hysteria whipped up by the Catholic Church. They were the result, too, of the barbaric French legal system, which allowed no presumption of innocence; the sole purpose of a trial was to establish the guilt of the suspect, and torture was used as a matter of course to obtain confessions. So, having spent his early years as a rather arrogant literary dandy moving in aristocratic circles, he spent his late middle age as a champion of human rights.

The first case in which Voltaire became involved concerned a Protestant cloth merchant named Jean Calas, from Toulouse. One of Calas's four sons, Louis, had converted to Catholicism and had left Toulouse. One evening in October 1761, one of the other sons, Marc-Antoine, committed suicide. The whole family was charged with murdering him – allegedly to stop him from carrying out a plan to convert. There was no evidence, just hearsay and rumour, which was stirred up further by the Church. Calas refused to confess, and in March 1762 it was ruled that he was guilty and should be 'broken on the wheel' (tied to a wheel and his arms and legs smashed with an iron bar), exposed for two hours, and then strangled and his body burned on a pyre. To the end he maintained his innocence. When news of the case reached Ferney, Voltaire's suspicions were aroused. After extensive investigations and a long interview with Calas's younger son, Donat, Voltaire took up the case. As Ian Davidson notes, this was one of the most dramatic turning points in Voltaire's life and a key moment in the history of penal reform in Europe. Lawyers were engaged to seek out new evidence, and funds were solicited to help the destitute Calas family. Voltaire wrote moving accounts of the case and mounted a campaign to reform the French legal system. After three years of sustained effort, he succeeded in having the verdict overturned and Calas's name cleared. Louis XV himself gave 36,000 pounds in compensation to the Calas family. This was in many ways Voltaire's finest hour. Calas was, moreover, only one of several cases of injustice that Voltaire took up over the next decade. These cases inspired two overlapping works, the *Treatise on Tolerance* (1763) and the *Philosophical Dictionary* (1764), which are among the most eloquent and characteristic texts of the Enlightenment. 'What is tolerance?' Voltaire asks in his *Treatise*. 'It is the consequence of humanity,' he answers. 'We are all formed of frailty and error; let us pardon reciprocally each other's folly – that is the first law of nature.'

The best of all possible worlds

Candide, or Optimism (1759) is the best and best known of the twenty-six 'philosophical tales' Voltaire wrote between 1752 (*Micromégas*) and 1773 (*The White Bull*). Witty, elegant, brilliantly incisive and combining in parodic manner elements of the picaresque, the voyage of discovery, the adventure novel, the medieval quest and the fable, it is a comic (we might even say Absurdist) vision of disaster. The main object of its satire is the doctrine of optimism: that is, the notion that our world must be 'the best of all possible worlds' because an all-powerful God could have created nothing less. Voltaire's Deist confidence had been shaken to its foundations by the Lisbon earthquake and by the horrors of the Seven Years War between France and Great Britain, which had broken out in 1756. *Candide* expresses the struggle between a Deistic desire to believe that the world is built on a providential design and the chaos and disasters that beset human life. The naïve hero, Candide, travels around the world, trying to make sense of his experiences. Having been taught the philosophy of optimism by his tutor, Pangloss, Candide initially believes that 'everything is for the best in this best of all possible worlds'. But he encounters one horror after another: war, murder, rape, the Inquisition, torture, disease, natural disasters. Life is not only cruel but also incomprehensible and absurd. The see-sawing dialogue between optimism and pessimism, innocence and disenchantment, ends only when Candide concludes that, rather than engaging in endless philosophical speculation, 'we must cultivate our garden' ('il faut cultiver notre jardin'). In other words, instead of striving vainly for final answers to the meaning of life, man should focus resolutely on making material life better. *Candide* satirizes not just optimism but all rigidly doctrinaire systems, which, in their extreme forms, are always dangerous; the ending of the satire is, like Voltaire's thought as a whole, pragmatic, relativistic and rooted in common sense.

With *Candide* Voltaire attained a new international readership: the liberal bourgeois intelligentsia. Moreover, he found that at Ferney he was freer to write what he liked; he came to accept exile from Paris as the price of his outspokenness. Free of royal or aristocratic patronage, he had made himself an independent power in the land: first, by amassing a fortune through his daring speculative ventures (by the end of his life he was the richest, as well as perhaps the most famous, private citizen in Europe), and second, by discovering the power of public opinion through his interventions in social affairs. His consummate use of newspaper articles, letters and cheaply produced pamphlets made him, it might be said, the first great crusading journalist. He lacked entirely the originality of thought of a Rousseau or a Diderot, but he was a brilliant communicator. The significance of his role in the development of literary and intellectual culture in France has been well stated by Priscilla Clark:

> Voltaire's career charted the emergence of a new kind of writer along with a new assessment of literature and its possibilities. The eighteenth-century philosophe already exhibited the acute consciousness of superiority characteristic of the nineteenth-century writer, for Voltaire redefined the relationship of the writer to society by equating the writer's prestige with that traditionally accorded literature. Although the ancien régime always acknowledged literature as such, Voltaire's personal ascendancy did much to force the recognition of the man of letters. The writer spoke with new authority.
>
> (Clark, *Literary France*, pp. 132–33)

By the end of his life, Voltaire had become what he had always wanted to be: a celebrity. In 1778, in his eighty-fourth year, he decided to return to Paris to attend a production of his last tragedy, *Irène*, at the Comédie-Française. His visit to the capital, his first since 1750, was a spectacular triumph. Crowds greeted him like royalty; he was fêted everywhere. More than 300 distinguished visitors, including Benjamin Franklin, called on him, where he was staying, at the *hôtel* of the Marquise de Villette's, now 27 quai Voltaire. But after several weeks, utterly exhausted, he was taken ill, and it became clear that he was dying. According to one account of his final hours, he was urged by a Jesuit priest to renounce the Devil. 'This is no time,' he managed to reply, 'for making new enemies.'

Chapter 10

Rousseau: man of feeling

How blind we are in the midst of so much enlightenment.

– Rousseau, *Lettre à d'Alembert*

'I will . . . venture to say,' wrote Jean-Jacques Rousseau (1712–78) at the beginning of his *Confessions*, 'that I am like no one in the whole world. I may be no better, but at least I am different.' Rousseau was indeed different, in sensibility and temperament, from the other leading figures of the French Enlightenment. Whereas they believed that society could be improved by reform, Rousseau believed that it should be entirely rebuilt; and whereas the former believed that truth could be discovered, and progress achieved, by means of civilization and rational thought, Rousseau believed that truth and a better way of life might be attained by looking within the heart of the simple uncorrupt human being, the 'noble savage', or the child. A powerful and highly original thinker, and a writer of great eloquence, Rousseau's influence on his own and later generations was profound. His *Social Contract* became one of the most celebrated political treatises ever written; his *Emile; or, On Education* (1762) was a radical work of educational theory; his staggeringly successful *Julie, or the New Heloise* (1761) established the novel of sensibility; and his *Confessions* inaugurated modern autobiography as a literary genre. Worshipped and reviled during his own lifetime, he later became a hero of the French Revolution and an icon of Romanticism.

Critique of society

Son of a watchmaker, Rousseau was born on 28 June 1712 in the small Calvinist city-state of Geneva. He ran away from home when he was sixteen, beginning a lifetime of wandering. In the autumn of 1741, he arrived in Paris, where he was drawn into the circle of freethinkers or *philosophes* around the Sorbonne. He became a close friend of Diderot. In the late 1740s he began writing plays, and then preparing articles on music and political economy commissioned by d'Alembert and Diderot for the publishing venture that would become the great *Encyclopédie* (1751–72). In the summer of 1749, Rousseau was walking to Vincennes to visit Diderot, who had been incarcerated in the fortress prison there, when he noticed in the *Mercure de France*, the literary review he had taken with him to read, an announcement by the Academy of Dijon of the subject for their annual prize essay. The topic was: 'Has the progress of the sciences and arts contributed to the corruption of morals or to their improvement?' Rousseau entered the competition with his *Discourse on the Sciences and Arts* (*Discours sur les sciences et les arts*, 1750). Not only did he win the prize, but his essay caused a sensation. He argued that culture and civilization, far from improving human existence (the quintessential view of the Enlightenment), actually made people worse off by corrupting their natural state. Man is naturally good and has only been made bad by society. Rousseau's critique of society was developed, and given stronger political overtones, in his 'Second Discourse', the *Discourse on the Origin of Inequality* (*Discours sur l'origine de l'inégalité*, 1755). For Rousseau man in nature (the 'noble savage') lives a free and happy life. Inequality and injustice have been created and institutionalized by the growth of competition, the division of labour, private property and a political order that gives the strong the power to oppress the weak. Whereas the life of primitive man was peaceful and idle (he had almost no relationship with his fellow men and lived almost entirely in the moment), man as social being lives in a sham world whose reality is exploitation, servitude, inauthenticity and alienation. Recorded history is the story of man's fall from innocence.

Nature, then, is the source of truth. Rousseau's call for a return to nature did not mean, however, a new kind of primitivism, but a return to natural law. This question is explored in *The Social Contract* (*Du contrat social*, 1762). The starting point of this seminal text is man's original freedom, memorably expressed in the opening phrase: 'Man is born free, but everywhere he is in chains.' True liberty and equality can be (re-)established, according to Rousseau, only on the basis of a people who have never yet been divided or corrupted by any form of government, through a social pact of all with all, in which each individual agrees to submit to the 'General Will', which alone has sovereignty. To persuade people to accept the laws of this newly contracted society, Rousseau introduces an authoritarian element: a 'lawgiver', who may use his authority, or an appeal to religious feeling, to induce the mutual cooperation of all citizens. Rousseau's emphasis on the protection of individual rights and the collective will were founding principles of Western liberal democracy; however, his assertion that dissenting citizens should be 'forced to be free' has been criticized by many for its dangerously totalitarian tendency.[1] Some of Rousseau's ideas, prominent among them the idea of the General Will, were incorporated verbatim into the first drafts of the *Declaration of the Rights of Man and of the Citizen*, following the fall of the Bastille in July 1789. The National Assembly deliberated beneath a bust of Rousseau and a copy of *The Social Contact*, which were installed in October 1790. Rousseau's influence during the Revolution is generally considered to have been at its strongest from 1792 to the fall of Robespierre in 1794. Robespierre, author of the Terror, found in Rousseau not just a source of ideas, but a moral ideal, a figure with whom he identified completely. This identification gave Robespierre a great sense of his own virtue and legitimacy, allowing him to take on the mantle of a Rousseauist lawgiver presiding over the birth of a new society.

La Nouvelle Héloïse

Rousseau's romantic epistolary novel, *Julie, or the New Heloise* – set against a background of nature by the shores of Lake Geneva, far from the corruptions of city life – is a story of passion redeemed by virtue. It tells of the passionate but sublime love (echoing the tragic twelfth-century story of the love of Heloise and Abelard) between Julie and her young tutor, Saint-Preux; but Saint-Preux, a commoner, is unacceptable to Julie's aristocratic father as a suitor for her hand. The plot twists and turns for several hundred pages before resolving the question: will the lovers unite? The hallmark of the novel of sensibility was that intense feelings were combined with generosity and virtue. All the characters except Julie's father behave with great magnanimity. The English Lord Bomston, himself attracted to Julie, renounces his suit on discovering her love for Saint-Preux and generously offers to install the lovers on an estate in England if they choose to elope. Julie appeals to her cousin Claire for advice, and the latter, who blames herself for the fact that Julie has surrendered her 'honour' to Saint-Preux, vows that if Julie goes to England she will accompany her, thus destroying her own life. Julie eventually yields to the various pressures brought to bear on her; she tells Saint-Preux that they must part, and obeys her father's command that she must marry the middle-aged, benevolent Baron Wolmar. Wolmar, far from being a repressive figure, emerges as a humane rationalist; he invites Saint-Preux to live in his house and helps the former lovers to exist together platonically. The characters live in a rustic paradise on Wolmar's estate. The climax comes when Julie dies in an accident, as the result of saving her child from drowning; before she dies, she confesses to the survival of her love and suggests to Saint-Preux that her death is timely, since they would not have been able to keep their love platonic indefinitely. Several generations of readers, from 1761 until well into the nineteenth century, shed copious tears over the fate of the ill-starred lovers.

The novel's spectacular success was due not so much to the portrayal of passion as to its praise of moral sublimity. The real subject is the success of the two lovers in overcoming their passion, and the reward for their sacrifice: the peace of a good conscience. The novel is, in that sense, a lyrical celebration of man's original goodness, reflected in the sincerity and generosity of the main characters in their relations with each other. And only in the country, in the midst of nature, far from the artificiality and dissipation of Parisian life, could virtue and honesty prevail and redemption begin. There was also, however, a deeper, less obvious reason for the novel's appeal. Tony Tanner, in an original and persuasive reading of the novel, shows that Julie's most intense emotional relationship – her real adultery, in fact 'barely controlled incest' (*Adultery in the Novel*, p. 126) – is not with Saint-Preux at all, but with her father. The most passionate scenes in the novel feature not Saint-Preux (a passive, virtually emasculated figure) but Julie's father, who in one scene, in a fit of anger (an 'orgasmic eruption', p. 124), assaults her physically; he then takes her on his knee and they embrace. Julie's dream, in the latter half of the book, of a happy-family household comprising herself, her husband (a benign version of her father), Saint-Preux and her cousin Claire, 'is an attempt to realize a dream of total harmony in which all the oppositional elements in human relationships – familial, passional – have been eliminated... The father, he-who-separates, produces a daughter who wishes to be she-who-brings-everyone-together-again. The rule of law engenders a dream of indistinguishability... an abandoning of distinctions' (p. 148). As David Lodge has commented, '[t]he deep appeal of Rousseau's novel for its age was, presumably, that it allowed its readers to peep into this abyss under cover of the most high-minded sentiments, affording a thrilling, frightening glimpse of the polymorphous perversity of feeling that might be enjoyed if the power of the father could be overthrown, but pulling back from final abandonment to it.'[2]

Autobiography

Rousseau's later years were devoted largely to personal works. *Les Confessions* (written 1764–70, published posthumously between 1782 and 1789) is now regarded as his masterpiece. The work begins as follows:

I am resolved on an undertaking that has no precedent, and which,
when complete, will have no imitator. I want to show to my fellow-men
a man in all the truth of nature; and that man will be myself.

Myself alone. I know my own heart and understand men. But I am
not made like any that I have seen; I venture to believe that I am not
made like anyone in the whole world. I may be no better, but at least I
am different. Whether Nature did well or ill in breaking the mould in
which I was cast, that is something that can only be judged after the
reading of my book.

Let the trumpet of judgement sound when it will, I shall step forward
with this book in my hand, to present myself before the Supreme Judge.
I will proclaim out loud: 'Here is what I have done, what I have thought,
what I was. I have told the good and the bad with equal frankness. I have
concealed nothing that was ill, added nothing that was good, and if I
have sometimes used some indifferent ornamentation, this has only
been to fill a void created by my lack of memory; I may have taken as
fact what I knew could have been so, never what I knew to be false. I
have shown myself as I was, vile and contemptible when that is how I
was, good, generous and noble when I was so: I have bared my
innermost self as you alone know it to be. Gather about me, Eternal
Being, the numberless host of my fellow men; let them hear my
confessions, let them groan at my unworthiness, let them blush at my
misdeeds. But let each of them, here on the steps of your throne, reveal
his own heart with equal sincerity; and may any man who dares, say: *I
was a better man than he.*

Je forme une entreprise qui n'eut jamais d'exemple, et dont l'exécution
n'aura point d'imitateur. Je veux montrer à mes semblables un homme
dans toute la vérité de la nature; et cet homme, ce sera moi.

Moi seul. Je sens mon cœur et je connais les hommes. Je ne suis fait
comme aucun de ceux que j'ai vus; j'ose croire n'être fait comme aucun
de ceux qui existent. Si je ne vaux pas mieux, au moins je suis autre. Si la
nature a bien ou mal fait de briser le moule dans lequel elle m'a jeté,
c'est ce dont on ne peut juger qu'après m'avoir lu.

Que la trompette du jugement dernier sonne quand elle voudra; je
viendrai ce livre à la main me présenter devant le souverain juge. Je dirai
hautement: voilà ce que j'ai fait, ce que j'ai pensé, ce que je fus. J'ai dit le
bien et le mal avec la même franchise. Je n'ai rien tu de mauvais, rien
ajouté de bon, et s'il m'est arrivé d'employer quelque ornement
indifférent, ce n'a jamais été que pour remplir un vide occasionné par
mon défaut de mémoire; j'ai pu supposer vrai ce que je savais avoir pu
l'être, jamais ce que je savais être faux. Je me suis montré tel que je fus,

méprisable et vil quand je l'ai été, bon, généreux, sublime, quand je l'ai
été: j'ai dévoilé mon intérieur tel que tu l'as vu toi-même. Être éternel,
rassemble autour de moi l'innombrable foule de mes semblables: qu'ils
écoutent mes confessions, qu'ils gémissent de mes indignités, qu'ils
rougissent de mes misères. Que chacun d'eux découvre à son tour son
cœur au pied de ton trône avec la meme sincérité; et puis qu'un seul te
dise, s'il ose: *je fus meilleur que cet homme-là.*

As this passage clearly indicates, one of the motivating forces behind Rousseau's
self-portrait was his desire to pre-empt his enemies by revealing his faults
before they did, and to state his own case for posterity; but, more significantly,
it reveals his profound belief in the importance of personal feelings as the basis
of morality and self-awareness. Human values, he felt, should be authenticated
not by any external authority, but by the individual's own conscience and
emotions. Sincerity and authenticity – being true to one's own feelings –
become supreme values. Nothing should be censored, all should be revealed:
Rousseau's moments of shame – for instance, his acts of dishonesty and his
adolescent exhibitionism – are treated with the same magnificent literary force
as the moments of lyricism, such as the night in the open air when he listened
to the nightingales. Moreover, it becomes clear as the volume unfolds that
the *Confessions* are strikingly modern in their insistence that self-knowledge is
to be achieved by an understanding of the unconscious, a recognition of the
formative importance of childhood and an acceptance of the role of sexuality in
shaping the personality. Through his exploration of his own dreams, fantasies
and obsessions, he invented, we might say, the way we now try to interpret our
lives; it is certainly true that he greatly enlarged our ideas about the self. As Leo
Damrosch comments: 'psychoanalysis, searching for hidden foundations of the
self, carries forward the quest that he launched in the *Confessions*' (*Jean-Jacques
Rousseau*, p. 494). In his insistence on the uniqueness of the individual and on
the inherently interesting nature of the complex individual self, as well as in
his lyrical evocations of nature, he foreshadowed fundamental characteristics
of Romanticism. Moreover, as Dennis Porter has commented,

What, along with a new frankness, [the *Confessions*] powerfully
inaugurates – and not simply for French literary culture – is an
identification between life and writing that is alien to the ethos of French
classicism. It is an identification that in retrospect we can see
contributed in a crucial way to establishing the very image of 'the writer'.
If the *Confessions* is such an influential work, it is in large part because it
affirms the intimate association between the unfolding of a singular life

and the activity of authorship; self-revelation and self-representation come to be integral to a practice of writing assumed as a vocation.

(*Rousseau's Legacy*, p. 27)

Rousseau's last work, *The Reveries of the Solitary Walker* (*Rêveries du promeneur solitaire*, written 1776–78; unfinished, published with Part I of the *Confessions* in 1782), prefigures even more strongly Romantic attitudes and sensibilities. These texts – akin to prose poems – are built around ten walks in the countryside around Paris. They describe Rousseau's meditations on moral and religious questions, and his reflections on his character and past life in an attempt to understand his contradictory impulses. They express his growing awareness that he could achieve moments of temporary tranquillity by turning in on himself and using his imagination to recapture past experiences, especially moments of intense fulfilment in close proximity to nature. Above all, they evoke memories that point to the conditions of true happiness.

Chapter 11

Diderot: the enlightened sceptic

Does anyone really know where they're going?

– Diderot, *Jacques the Fatalist*

Denis Diderot (1713–84) was a supreme man of letters as understood in the eighteenth century: that is to say, a person seriously concerned with every aspect of human activity and critical inquiry. The range of his writings was astonishing. Moreover, he made important and original contributions in almost every field he engaged with: the natural sciences, moral philosophy, art criticism, the nature of theatre and of acting, the art of fiction. Towards the end of his life, he even travelled to St Petersburg to meet Catherine the Great and advise her on the government of Russia. If his work has a unifying theme, it lies in his exploration of the implications – ethical, political and aesthetic – of a materialist world-view. But rather than proposing firm answers, Diderot asks questions; what is most characteristic of him is his philosophical scepticism and its expression in peculiarly dialogic forms.[1] His intellectual interests and his mode of writing make him the most modern of the great figures of the Enlightenment.

The mind of a sceptic

Diderot was best known by his contemporaries as the editor of the famous *Encyclopédie*, a vast work published between 1751 and 1772 and comprising seventeen folio volumes of text and eleven volumes of plates. The aim of the *Encyclopédie* was to collate all the knowledge of the day – scientific, philosophical, historical and practical – and to disseminate that knowledge with a view to reducing theological superstition and improving the human lot. It was a monument to Enlightenment values and its project of demystification. Diderot challenged conventional thinking of any kind and encouraged his readers to beware of preconceived ideas. However, he was interested less in the accumulation of knowledge than in its instability and limits. He had a sense of existence as dynamic and constantly changing. Whereas his contemporaries thought of science primarily in terms of the ordered world of Newtonian physics, he was more interested in biology and how things mutate. He saw nature as in a state of perpetual flux. As a materialist, he argued that we have no innate ideas derived either from God or any other external source, and that our perception of reality is derived from our experience and, in particular, from our senses. Thus a blind man perceives reality differently from a person with sight. The blind have a different moral sense, for instance: they hate theft but are indifferent to nakedness. One of Diderot's central preoccupations was the contrast between the way things are and the way they seem when experienced from different perspectives. His critical writings, especially on art, reflect this preoccupation with perspective – with the importance of the viewer's or reader's response. What fascinated him was the relative nature of things. His fondness for casting his writing in the form of dialogue is not surprising, for it enabled him to juxtapose different viewpoints on a given subject in order to maintain ceaseless, open-ended debate. His delight in dialogue is eloquently described by Jean Starobinski:

> Diderot never closes his ears to his own internal contradictions and unforeseen trains of thought; his reaction is to embody them in an interlocutor. When he hears in himself the presence of a new thought, he immediately transforms it into an imaginary being with whom he can exchange ideas. In him the dialectic of contradiction and the dialectic of discussion are one and the same thing. Thus is born the dialogue, a succession of moments in the present, where the author's thought is distributed among several voices whose very opposition gives rise to a superior harmony. Dialogue is in Diderot the manifestation of superabundant presence which needs to be divided among a number of actors, each of them giving vivid expression to a feeling, a reflection, or a silence at the very moment when it emerges into existence.[2]

Experimental fiction

Diderot used dialogue extensively in his three great 'philosophic' novels: *Rameau's Nephew* (*Le Neveu de Rameau*, written between 1762 and 1773), *D'Alembert's Dream* (*Le Rêve de d'Alembert*, written in 1769) and *Jacques the Fatalist and His Master* (*Jacques le Fataliste et son maître*; henceforth *Jacques*, written and revised between 1765 and Diderot's death in 1784). These novels, all published posthumously in volume form, were hardly known to Diderot's contemporaries, but they are texts with which the modern reader feels great affinity. *Jacques*, the most modern of them, tells the story of the eponymous hero, formerly a peasant and now a valet, as he rides with his master through France to an unknown destination. They are forever talking, telling one another stories and, as they journey from inn to inn, listening to others telling stories along the way. The novel begins thus:

> How had they met? By chance, like everyone else. What were their names? What's it to you? Where were they coming from? From the nearest place. Where were they going? Does anyone really know where they're going? What were they saying? The Master wasn't saying anything, and Jacques was saying that his Captain used to say that everything that happens to us here on earth, for good or ill, is written up there, on high.

> MASTER: That's really saying a lot.
> JACQUES: My Captain also used to say that every bullet shot out of the barrel of a rifle had someone's name on it.
> MASTER: And he was right...

> After a brief pause, Jacques exclaimed: 'The innkeeper and his inn can go to hell!'

> MASTER: Why would you want to see a fellow man sent to Hell? It's not Christian.
> JACQUES: Because while I'm getting drunk on his awful wine, I forget to water the horses. My father notices and gets angry. I shake my head at him. He picks up a stick and hits me across the shoulders pretty hard. A regiment was passing on its way to camp at Fontenoy. I join up out of pique. We get to our destination and the battle begins...
> MASTER: And you stop the bullet that's got your name on it.
> JACQUES: You've guessed. Got it in the knee, and God knows what adventures, happy and unhappy, followed that shot. They all hang together exactly like the links in a chain, no more and no less. For instance, if it hadn't been for that shot, I don't think I'd ever have fallen in love, or walked with a limp.
> MASTER: So you've been in love?
> JACQUES: Have I been in love!
> MASTER: And all because of a shot from a rifle?
> JACQUES: All because of a shot from a rifle.
> MASTER: You've never said a word about it before.
> JACQUES: That's right.
> MASTER: Why is that?
> JACQUES: Because it could not have been said before or after this moment.

MASTER: And that moment has now come and you can speak about being in love?

JACQUES: Who knows?

MASTER: Well, take a chance. Make a start . . .

Jacques began to tell the story of his loves. It was after lunch. The weather was sultry. His Master nodded off. Night came upon them in the middle of nowhere: there they were, lost. The Master flew into a terrible rage and set about his servant with a whip and at every thwack the poor devil cried out: 'That must have been written up there too . . . '

So you see, Reader, I'm into my stride and it's entirely in my power to make you wait a year, two years, three years, to hear the story of Jacques's love affairs, by separating him from his Master and making both of them undergo all the perils I please. What's to prevent me from marrying off the Master and telling you how his wife deceived him? Or making Jacques take ship for the Indies? And sending his Master there? Or bringing both of them back to France on the same vessel? How easy it is to make up stories! But I'll simply let them off with a bad night's sleep, and you with this delay.

The new day dawned. Now they're on their horses again and on their way.

– And where were they going?

That's the second time you've asked that question, and for the second time I answer: What's it to you? If I get launched on the subject of their travels, you can kiss the story of Jacques's love affairs goodbye . . . They rode on in silence for a while. When both of them had got over their pique, the master said to his servant: 'Well, Jacques, where were we up to in the story of your loves?'

Comment s'étaient-ils rencontrés? Par hasard, comme tout le monde. Comment s'appelaient-ils? Que vous importe? D'où venaient-ils? Du lieu le plus prochain. Où allaient-ils? Est-ce que l'on sait où l'on va? Que disaient-ils? Le maître ne disait rien; et Jacques disait que son capitaine disait que tout ce qui nous arrive de bien et de mal ici-bas était écrit là-haut.

LE MAITRE: C'est un grand mot que cela.

JACQUES: Mon capitaine ajoutait que chaque balle qui partait d'un fusil avait son billet.

LE MAITRE: Et il avait raison . . .

Après une courte pause, Jacques s'écria: Que le diable emporte le cabaretier et son cabaret!

LE MAITRE: Pourquoi donner au diable son prochain? Cela n'est pas chrétien.

JACQUES: C'est que, tandis que je m'enivre de son mauvais vin, j'oublie de mener nos chevaux à l'abreuvoir. Mon père s'en aperçoit; il se fâche. [Je] hoche la tête; il prend un bâton et m'en frotte un peu durement les épaules. Un régiment passait pour aller au camp devant Fontenoy; de dépit je m'enrôle. Nous arrivons; la bataille se donne.

LE MAITRE: Et tu reçois la balle à ton adresse.

JACQUES: Vous l'avez deviné; un coup de feu au genou; et Dieu sait les bonnes et mauvaises aventures amenées par le coup de feu. Elles se tiennent ni plus ni moins que les chaînons d'une gourmette. Sans ce coup de feu, par exemple, je crois que je n'aurais été amoureux de ma vie, ni boiteux.

LE MAITRE: Tu as donc été amoureux?

JACQUES: Si je l'ai été!

LE MAITRE: Et cela par un coup de feu?

JACQUES: Par un coup de feu.

LE MAITRE: Tu ne m'en as jamais dit un mot.

JACQUES: Je le crois bien.

LE MAITRE: Et pourquoi cela?

JACQUES: C'est que cela ne pouvait être dit ni plus tôt ni plus tard.

LE MAITRE: Et le moment d'apprendre ces amours est-il venu?

JACQUES: Qui le sait?

LE MAITRE: A tout hasard, commence toujours...

Jacques commença l'histoire de ses amours. C'était l'après-dînée: il faisait un temps lourd; son maître s'endormait. La nuit les surprit au milieu des champs; les voilà fourvoyés. Voilà le maître dans une colère terrible et tombant à grands coups de fouet sur son valet, et le pauvre diable disant à chaque coup: 'Celui-là était apparemment encore écrit là-haut...'

Vous voyez, lecteur, que je suis en beau chemin, et qu'il ne tiendrait qu'à moi de vous faire attendre un an, deux ans, trois ans, le récit des amours de Jacques, en le séparant de son maître et en leur faisant courir à chacun tous les hasards qu'il me plairait. Qu'est-ce qui m'empêcherait de marier le maître et de le faire cocu? d'embarquer Jacques pour les îles? d'y conduire son maître? de les ramener tous les deux en France sur le même vaisseau? Qu'il est facile de faire des contes! Mais ils en seront quittes l'un et l'autre pour une mauvaise nuit, et vous pour ce délai.

L'aube du jour parut. Les voilà remontés sur leurs bêtes et poursuivant leur chemin. – Et où allaient-ils? – Voilà la seconde fois que vous me faites cette question, et la seconde fois que je vous réponds:

Qu'est-ce que cela vous fait? Si j'entame le sujet de leur voyage, adieu les amours de Jacques... Ils allèrent quelque temps en silence. Lorsque chacun fut un peu remis de son chagrin, le maître dit à son valet: – Eh bien, Jacques, où en étions-nous de tes amours?

Five different levels of narrative interweave here. First, there is the traditional narrative in which the narrator addresses the reader, recounting the story of his characters ('The new day dawned. Now they're on their horses again and on their way'). Second, there is Jacques's narrative; the servant is enjoined by his master to relate the story of his loves. Third, there is the unmediated dialogue between Jacques and his master. Fourth, there is the exchange, with which the novel opens, between narrator and narratee:[3] 'How had they met? By chance, like everyone else.' The narrator stonewalls the questions thrown at him, and the narratee disappears until he suddenly reappears in the last paragraph to ask: 'And where were they going?' This time he is virtually reprimanded by the narrator for his persistent questioning. Fifth, there are the comments addressed to the actual reader by Diderot himself ('So you see, Reader...'). The complexity of the narrative, with its plurality of voices, is compounded by the sudden transitions between the various narrative levels. There is thus not the slightest attempt to create the illusion that the world of the book is continuous with life itself. Diderot is teasing his readers, putting them on notice that they cannot expect to engage with *Jacques* as if it were a conventional narrative; he is flaunting the artificiality of his novel, implying that it has no reality beyond that of the words on the page.

The questions posed by the narratee are those which any reader conventionally asks; and the narrator's pointed refusal to give any indication of possible answers underlines the provocative nature of a text that clearly has no intention of following the conventional form of novels. The convention of the omniscient narrator – the classic narrator of the realist novel, who pulls all the narrative strings and explains the significance of everything – is ironically demystified. The master's derisive comment, 'That's really saying a lot', referring to the army captain's stated belief that 'everything that happens to us here on earth... is written up above, on high', is the opposite of conventional narrative, in which the narrator expounds and comments on his characters' feelings and behaviour rather than vice versa. Whereas Diderot's narrator makes no comments on what is happening, the master comments, approvingly, on the belief in fatality expressed by the captain. It is as if the character, not the narrator, possesses the quality of omniscience; the narrator is elbowed sideways, to a position of virtual redundancy in the text, his marginality emphasized further by the passages of unmediated dialogue which give the characters an unusually dominant position in the narrative. On the other hand, Diderot as author stresses his freedom to manipulate his characters and to arrange the entire pattern of his novel as he wishes. He underlines the arbitrariness of his narrative with a series of rhetorical questions. 'It's entirely in my power,' he proclaims, 'to make you wait a year, two years, three years, to hear the story of Jacques's love affairs.' *Jacques* obliges us to admit that we are dealing with an imaginary world, an artificial construct that declares itself as such. It occupies an important position in the history of the novel, for it illuminates the experience of reading and clarifies the scope and nature of the agreement which the reader enters into with the novelist.

Diderot's stress on the arbitrary powers of the writer is closely related to the central themes of the novel: destiny, free will and the responsibility we have for our actions. Jacques professes to believe in fatality: 'My Captain . . . used to say that every bullet shot out of the barrel of a rifle had someone's name written on it.' The adventures and experiences that make up his life all hang together, he declares, like the links in a chain. He is said to know by heart the works of Baruch Spinoza (1632–77), the Dutch philosopher who was widely regarded as the leading modern proponent of fatalism. Spinoza argued that all mind and matter were modes of the one key substance, which he called either God or Nature. Free will, he held, was an illusion that would be dispelled by man's recognition that every event has a material cause. While Jacques repeatedly states his belief in fatalism, he cannot fully accept this belief; he continues to behave, as the narrator notes, as if he were free to make choices – to behave well or badly. He might thus be said to personify (like Diderot himself) the modern dichotomy between acceptance of scientific determinism and the need to assert the autonomy of the individual. The human desire for freedom is reflected in Diderot's affirmation of the sheer creativity of the writer. 'How easy it is to make up stories!' he exclaims. Diderot appears startlingly modern when read in the light of twentieth-century theories of fiction, and especially so in the light of the postmodern emphasis on textuality, that is, the view that the primary function of writing is not the representation of an extra-textual reality but writing itself, which is seen as an exemplary expression of the creative freedom of the individual.

The philosophical implications of Diderot's experiments with fiction concern not only freedom but also 'truth'. The narrator teasingly refers to his obligation to respect the 'truth' of his story, that is, his powerlessness to change the 'facts'. Yet he constantly demonstrates (and celebrates) his freedom to shape the narrative as he wishes; and the form of his narrative, with its shifting perspectives, unpredictable events and endless digressions, expresses the fluidity of a world where nothing is ever clear-cut or under control. The novel offers the reader three alternative endings – in playful but pointed recognition of the impossibility of 'telling the truth' in any objective sense. The alternative endings express Diderot's recognition of human complexity and self-contradiction, the relativity of our perceptions, and the difficulty – since we only have our own experience to go on – of our ever being certain about anything.

Chapter 12

Laclos: dangerous liaisons

If this book burns, it burns as only ice can burn.

– Baudelaire

Dangerous Liaisons (*Les Liaisons dangereuses*), by Pierre Choderlos de Laclos (1741–1803), caused a sensation when it was published in 1782, just seven years before the French Revolution. With *La Nouvelle Héloïse*, it was the most successful novel of the eighteenth century. But while Rousseau's novel offered ideals that enthused its readers, Laclos's work had a much more troubled reputation. Its success was largely a *succès de scandale*, and in the nineteenth century it was condemned in court for immorality and officially banned. Comparing the world of *La Nouvelle Héloïse* with that of *Les Liaisons dangereuses*, and viewing the latter as a response to the former, Peter Gay writes: 'Where Rousseau is conventional, moral, and edifying, Laclos is unconventional, immoral, and destructive. In Rousseau everybody wins through losing: the sacrifice of gratification leads to purer, more exalted happiness. In Laclos, everybody loses through winning: insistence on gratification leads to restlessness, a sense of being cheated, and tragedy.'[1] Although this quotation misleadingly implies that Laclos's representation of immorality is itself immoral, it evokes very well the distinctive tenor of his novel and suggests how it embodies disillusionment with the optimistic Enlightenment faith in the ability of reason alone to create human happiness.

Sexual games

Dangerous Liaisons evokes the brittle world of the French aristocracy in the final years of the Ancien Régime. It is a realm of pretence and duplicity. Written entirely in the form of letters (one of the literary conventions of the time), the novel centres on the erotic power games played by two libertines, the Marquise de Merteuil and the Vicomte de Valmont.[2] Former lovers, they are now partners in crime. For the eighteenth-century reader, Valmont was a familiar fictional

82

(and theatrical) type: the rake, the Don Juan. A female libertine such as Merteuil would have been a far less familiar (but more striking) figure. Following the death of her elderly husband, Merteuil sets her face against a second marriage, determined to devote herself to the life of free enjoyment she cannot openly pursue in a patriarchal world, where she must maintain an unimpeachable reputation for social respectability. Valmont does not have to disguise his own reputation as a rake (on the contrary, among his own circle his renown is enhanced by his exploits), while Mme de Merteuil would be ruined by one breath of scandal. In the celebrated letter 81, she gives a long account of her 'principles' and methods. She describes how, even as a young girl, she observed the way people behaved in society. Craving knowledge and gratification, she studied the writings of novelists, philosophers and 'the most high-minded moralists' in order to 'know exactly what it was possible to do, what it was best to think and the appearances that must be kept up' in society, thus equipping herself for her entrance, following her period of mourning, onto 'the big stage of life'. Realization of her freedom is synonymous with complete control over herself and, when she so wills, everyone else; it is synonymous with mastery of the arts of masquerade and manipulation. Power and its ruthless exercise is all. As she says, 'One must conquer or die.' She explains to Valmont that she always extracts a secret from her lovers with which she could blackmail them, thus forestalling any attempt they might make to unmask her or damage her reputation.

We learn, soon after the novel opens, that Merteuil wishes to pay back a former lover, who has abandoned her, by ensuring that the rich virgin he is going to marry, the fifteen-year-old, convent-trained Cécile de Volanges, be deflowered and thoroughly debauched before her wedding day. For this task she seeks to enlist Valmont. But Valmont thinks the job so easy that it is unworthy of his talents. He eventually agrees, though he has already set his sights on a more challenging target: a devout young married woman, Mme de Tourvel ('the Présidente'). The deal is sealed by the Marquise's offer to spend one night with him if he can prove, by producing a letter from Tourvel, that he has been successful in his pursuit. Cécile is seduced with ease. The seduction of the Présidente proves more challenging and brings with it a particular surprise, for Valmont begins to realize that he has unwittingly fallen in love with this chaste woman and has caused her to fall in love with him. When he describes (in letter 125) his ecstasy with Tourvel, the Marquise recognizes that he has discovered love. The tone of the novel darkens. Merteuil, the virtuoso of detachment, is made mad with jealousy; ironically, she loses control of her own feelings. She tricks Valmont into renouncing Mme de Tourvel, and in so doing destroying her (though it is Valmont who is the real target of her vengeance). The Vicomte is vain enough to be induced into breaking with Tourvel, afraid of becoming a laughing-stock for falling in love with an entirely unsuitable woman and losing his reputation as a heartless libertine. He returns to Merteuil to claim his night in her bed. But she rebuffs him, indicating that she has a rendezvous with the young Chevalier Danceny (who is in love with Cécile but whom Merteuil has taken as a lover). In response Valmont reveals that he has prompted Danceny to reunite with Cécile, thus leaving Merteuil abandoned yet again. She declares war on Valmont (letter 153) and reveals to Danceny that Valmont has seduced Cécile. Danceny and Valmont duel. Valmont is fatally wounded, but before dying he gives Danceny Merteuil's letters. Their circulation in Paris destroys her reputation; the loss of a lawsuit destroys her financially; and she contracts smallpox, which destroys her beauty. Her disfigurement is seen as the outward sign of her malignancy of character.

A polyphonic novel

Dangerous Liaisons is written in the classic French *moraliste* tradition (see above, p. 18). The analysis of human behaviour and questions of social conduct lie at its heart. It contains erotic episodes and allusions, but the important action takes place in the characters' minds. The epistolary form of the work plays a vital part in this inasmuch as letters allow a direct form of self-revelation. The characters are revealed in terms of the clear-sightedness, strength of purpose or sincerity with which they follow the codes of behaviour that govern them, or in terms of their self-deception or lack of awareness. Valmont and Merteuil are in some measure *moralistes* themselves. Their letters make up a form of commentary on the action and on the other characters. Their skill in analysis – their ability to see why people behave as they do, and to predict how they will behave in response to future contingencies – is virtually a professional skill, since their lives are occupied in deceiving and manipulating others. They need to understand their victims if they are to control them, and they need also to preserve their own secrets from the gaze of others.

Dangerous Liaisons is widely regarded as the supreme example of the epistolary novel. It is ingenious, complex and brilliantly crafted. It has been described as 'polyphonic', in the sense that Laclos has created a distinctive voice or style for each character: the hesitant, naïve voices of Cécile and Danceny; the anguished, candid voice of the Présidente; the worldly, rhetorically self-conscious voices of Valmont and Merteuil. Letters become components of the plot: the letter Danceny hides in Cécile's harp, the letter dictated by Merteuil that effectively kills Tourvel, the letters that bring about Merteuil's downfall. Valmont and

Merteuil manipulate their victims by modulating their language appropriately, skilfully adapting their style and discourse to suit their immediate purpose. The orchestration of letters in counterpoint produces multiple effects of irony and ambiguity. Different voices are juxtaposed, offering different points of view on a given situation. Letters 125 and 128, for example, offer two perspectives on the same event: the seduction of Tourvel.

Letter 125 *The Vicomte de Valmont to the Marquise de Merteuil*

So, I have conquered her, that arrogant woman who dared to think she could resist me! Yes, my love, she is mine, all mine! And ever since yesterday there is nothing left for her to give.

I am still too full of happiness to be able to appreciate it, but I am surprised by the strange delight I felt. Can it be true that a woman's virtue increases her value at the very moment she surrenders? No, let us dismiss this childish idea as an old wives' tale. Do we not nearly always meet some resistance, more or less well-feigned, the first time we have any woman? Have I not experienced with other women the delight I mention? And yet this is not love, because, after all, although I have sometimes felt with that astonishing woman moments of weakness which resemble that unmanly passion, I have always managed to overcome them and remain true to my principles. Even if, as I believe, what happened yesterday carried me further than I expected in that direction and for a moment I shared the ecstasy and the turmoil I created in her, that passing illusion would have disappeared today. And yet the feeling of delight is still there. I don't mind admitting that I would take a certain sweet pleasure in indulging it if it did not worry me somewhat. Am I at my age to be mastered, like some schoolboy, by an involuntary and unfamiliar feeling? No. Above all, I must get to the bottom of it, and fight it.

La voilà donc vaincue, cette femme superbe qui avait osé croire qu'elle pourrait me résister! Oui, mon amie, elle est à moi; et depuis hier, elle n'a plus rien à m'accorder.

Je suis encore trop plein de mon Bonheur, pour pouvoir l'apprécier, mais je m'étonne du charme inconnu que j'ai ressenti. Serait-il donc vrai que la vertu augmentât le prix d'une femme, jusque dans le moment même de sa faiblesse? Mais reléguons cette idée puérile avec les contes de bonnes femmes. Ne rencontre-t-on pas presque partout une résistance plus ou moins bien feinte au premier triomphe? et ai-je trouvé nulle part le charme dont je parle? ce n'est pourtant pas non plus celui de l'amour; car enfin, si j'ai eu quelquefois, auprès de cette femme étonnante, des moments de faiblesse qui ressemblaient à cette passion pusillanime, j'ai toujours su les vaincre et revenir à mes principes. Quand même la scène d'hier m'aurait, comme je le crois, emporté un peu plus loin que je ne comptais; quand j'aurais, un moment, partagé le trouble et l'ivresse que je faisais naître, cette illusion passagère serait dissipée à présent; et cependant le même charme subsiste. J'aurais même, je l'avoue, un plaisir assez doux à m'y livrer, s'il ne me causait quelque inquiétude. Serai-je donc, à mon âge, maîtrisé comme un écolier, par un sentiment involontaire et inconnu? Non: il faut, avant tout, le combattre et l'approfondir.

Letter 128 *Madame de Tourvel to Madame de Rosemonde*

I did not receive your delayed reply until yesterday, Madame. If my life were still mine to call my own, it would have killed me on the spot: but my whole existence belongs to someone else and that other person is M. de Valmont. As you see, I am hiding nothing from you. If you are bound to think of me as no longer worthy of your friendship, I'm still less afraid of losing it than of betraying it. All I can tell you is that having been faced by M. de Valmont with a choice between his death and his happiness, I opted for the latter. I take no pride in this, nor am I blaming myself: I am simply stating a fact.

You will thus have no difficulty in understanding the effect your letter must have had on me with the stern truths it contains. But do not imagine it was able to arouse in me any regrets or that it can ever make me change my feelings or my conduct. It is not that I do not suffer greatly at times, but when my heart is at breaking point, when I fear that I can no longer bear my anguish, I tell myself: Valmont is happy. And that thought drives everything else out of my mind or rather it makes everything a pleasure.

So I have dedicated myself to your nephew; I have ruined myself for him. He has become the absolute centre of my thoughts, feelings, and actions. As long as my life is necessary for his happiness, I shall treasure it and consider myself blessed. If one day he should think differently . . . he will never hear a word of protest or reproach from me. I have already considered this possibility, and my mind is made up.

Je n'ai reçu qu'hier, Madame, votre tardive réponse. Elle m'aurait tuée sur-le-champ, si j'avais eu encore mon existence en moi: mais un autre en est possesseur; et cet autre est M. de Valmont. Vous voyez que je ne vous cache rien. Si vous devez ne me plus trouver digne de votre amitié, je crains moins encore de la perdre que de la surprendre. Tout ce que je puis vous dire, c'est que, placé par M. de Valmont entre sa mort ou son bonheur, je me suis décidée pour ce dernier parti. Je ne m'en vante, ni ne m'en accuse: je dis simplement ce qui est.

Vous sentirez aisément, d'après cela, quelle impression a dû me faire votre lettre, et les vérités sévères qu'elle contient. Ne croyez pas cependant qu'elle ait pu faire naître un regret en moi, ni qu'elle puisse jamais me faire changer de sentiment ni de conduite. Ce n'est pas que je n'aie de moments cruels; mais quand mon cœur est le plus déchiré, quand je crains de ne pouvoir plus supporter mes tourments, je me dis: Valmont est heureux; et tout disparaît devant cette idée, ou plutôt elle change tout en plaisirs.

C'est donc à votre neveu que je me suis consacrée; c'est pour lui que je me suis perdue. Il est devenu le centre unique de mes pensées, de mes sentiments, de mes actions. Tant que ma vie sera nécessaire à son bonheur, elle me sera précieuse, et je la trouverai fortune. Si quelque jour, il en juge autrement... il n'entendra de ma part ni plainte ni reproche. J'ai osé fixer les yeux sur ce moment fatal, et mon parti est pris.

Mme de Tourvel refers to the letter Mme de Rosemonde, Valmont's aunt, recently sent to her, in which she painted her nephew in the blackest of terms, telling Tourvel of his reputation as a libertine and warning her to beware of his charms. Tourvel recognizes that she has abandoned her deep religious convictions; it is to Valmont that she is now passionately devoted. Whereas Valmont savours his seduction of Tourvel, the latter simply states, in an unambiguous statement of love, that her whole existence belongs to Valmont. Whereas Valmont speaks only of his own happiness, Tourvel identifies her happiness with that of Valmont. Tourvel stresses to her friend her complete sincerity: 'I am hiding nothing from you... I am simply stating a fact.' Her integrity of feeling is in stark contrast to the libertine's guile. Valmont's letter expresses the seducer's celebration of mastery over his victim, reflected in images borrowed from military combat and strategy. The greater the woman's resistance, the greater the victory. Rather than naming Tourvel, Valmont refers to her simply as 'that... woman'. Sensual pleasure is subsidiary to the intellectual gratification of power and control, including self-control. Thus, any feelings resembling love ('an unmanly passion') are regarded as a weakness. In the past, Valmont says, he always managed to subdue his feelings and adhere to his 'principles' – a choice of word that turns *libertinage* into an ethical system. But Valmont's letter also reveals his recognition that, despite his efforts, Tourvel has had a powerful effect on him. The word 'charme' ('delight') is used three times, reinforced by the reference to shared passion – a kind of 'ecstasy', a state of being he has not previously known. 'That arrogant woman' becomes 'that astonishing woman'. The libertine's victory is thus only apparent; and the recognition of *feeling* in letter 125 changes the course of the novel.

Interpretation

In the novel's morality-tale ending, the wicked characters are duly punished. However, their victims suffer too: Tourvel dies of a broken heart, Cécile takes refuge in a nunnery, Danceny retires to celibacy and the Knights of Malta. The novel's ambiguity is heightened by the fact that Valmont and, especially, the Marquise have far more intelligence and wit than the other characters. The world of the 'good' (especially as embodied in Mme de Volanges, Cécile's prissy mother) is the world of the stupid, the hypocritical and the self-deceiving. Virtue is unrewarded; religious principles are shown as powerless, religious education as empty. The picture is further complicated by the fact that the modern reader will tend to have some sympathy for a woman like Merteuil, who claims equality and self-fulfilment in defiance of social codes we no longer respect.

The mixed message of *Dangerous Liaisons* is teasingly highlighted in the provocatively ironic prefatory material, the 'Publisher's Note' and the 'Editor's Preface' (both by Laclos, of course). The 'Editor' asserts that the novel's significance and value lie in the moral lessons that may be derived from its picture of corruption:

> It seems to me at least that it is doing a service to society by exposing the methods used by the immoral to corrupt the moral, and I believe these letters will make an effective contribution to this end.

> Il me semble au moins que c'est rendre un service aux mœurs, que de dévoiler les moyens qu'emploient ceux qui en ont de mauvaises pour corrompre ceux qui en ont de bonnes, et je crois que ces lettres peuvent concourir efficacement à ce but.

But this assertion is undermined by the 'Publisher', who casts doubt on the authenticity of the text as a collection of real letters and warns the reader not to be deceived, for there are, he says, compelling reasons to believe that the work is 'only a novel'.

> Furthermore, it seems to us that the author, despite his attempts at verisimilitude, has himself clumsily destroyed all semblance of truth by his choice of the period in which the events are set. Indeed, a number of the characters are so immoral that it is impossible to imagine them living in our own age, this age of philosophy, in which, as we all know, universal enlightenment has made all men so honourable and all women so modest and reserved.

> Il nous semble de plus en plus que l'auteur, qui paraît pourtant avoir cherché la vraisemblance, l'a détruite lui-même et bien maladroitement, par l'époque où il a placé les événements qu'il publie. En effet, plusieurs des personnages qu'il met en scène ont de si mauvaises mœurs, qu'il est impossible de supposer qu'ils aient vécu dans notre siècle: dans ce siècle de philosophie, où les lumières, répandues de toutes parts, ont rendu, comme chacun sait, tous les hommes si honnêtes et toutes les femmes si modestes et si réservées.

The author, barely visible behind the 'Publisher' and the 'Editor', disappears altogether as the reader embarks on the 175 letters that constitute the novel. The reader must make sense of the world of Valmont and Merteuil without the cues provided by a narrator, omniscient or otherwise.

Dangerous Liaisons can be read on various levels: as a portrait of the age; as a study of evil; as the exposure of a society rotten to the core, in which the aristocracy, frittering away its time in decadent games of pleasure and power, is inviting revolution. Malevolence is presented as seductive, but also as sick and sterile. The portrayal of evil is at the same time a critique of rationalism divorced from human feeling, of intellect starved of emotion. As Martin Turnell commented long ago: 'Laclos' theme is the tragedy of the Rational Man, the man who was carefully conditioned through the removal of all moral scruples and the sense of guilt, but inevitably condemned to action in a very limited field.'[3] Merteuil remarks aphoristically in letter 81: 'love, so highly commended as the cause of our pleasures, is at best only a pretext for them' ('l'amour, que l'on nous vante comme la cause de nos plaisirs, n'en est plus que le prétexte'). The cynicism of this remark is striking, but the statement also suggests the libertine's fear of natural emotion. The Marquise is not simply jealous of the Présidente but enraged that she makes Valmont forget his libertine 'principles'. Her savage desire for vengeance and her compulsion to resist Valmont's attempt at domination make her, ironically, lose control of the situation. It is she who provokes the chain of events that lead to Valmont's death and the release of the incriminating letters. The authentic emotion that begins to emerge in letter 125 is so subversive that it leads Merteuil and Valmont to destroy themselves and each other. We witness the collapse of their world and of their system. The Revolution is indeed close at hand.

Chapter 13

Stendhal: the pursuit of happiness

> Beauty is nothing other than the promise of happiness.
>
> – Stendhal, *On Love*

A child of the Enlightenment, a sympathizer with the Romantic movement and, with Honoré de Balzac, the progenitor of the realist novel, Stendhal (the pen name of Marie-Henri Beyle, 1783–1842) was one of the most original writers of his time. The themes and style of his major fictional works – *The Red and the Black* (*Le Rouge et le noir*, 1830), *Lucien Leuwen* (written 1834–35, published posthumously) and *The Charterhouse of Parma* (*La Chartreuse de Parme*, 1839) – have an almost self-contradictory quality: ironic and poetic, comic and tragic, satirical and lyrical. This is reflected in the psychological complexity of the central characters and the subtlety of Stendhal's style of narration. A particular blend of Romantic fervour and eighteenth-century rationalism gives his novels their distinctive quality. The characterization, themes and oblique narrative methods of Stendhal's fiction reflect his preoccupation with the nature of post-Napoleonic France and the problems of selfhood confronting the generation that grew up in the aftermath of Napoleon's downfall at the Battle of Waterloo in 1815.

After Waterloo

An ardent admirer of Napoleon, Stendhal thrived in the heady atmosphere of the Napoleonic age. In 1800 he joined Napoleon's army in Italy (but resigned his commission the following year). From 1806 to 1814 he served as an aide-de-camp during the Emperor's campaigns in Germany, Austria and Russia. After the fall of Napoleon, he experienced French society – that of the Bourbon Restoration (1815–30) – as a dull anti-climax, presenting the spectacle of a philistine, money-grubbing bourgeoisie jostling for power with a stagnant, effete aristocracy. As the momentous events and military triumphs of the Napoleonic era receded into history, the world seemed to shrink and grow grey. The qualities Stendhal valued – energy, passion, spontaneity: the qualities he saw embodied in the Emperor – were those he found lacking in the world around him.

The society of Restoration France is the setting of Stendhal's most famous novel, *The Red and the Black*. The story centres on an ambitious carpenter's son, Julien Sorel, a young man from the provinces who leaves his peasant background (the fictional village of Verrières) to make his way in the world. He feels at odds with a society he despises, sensing that he has been born on the wrong side of history. In 1800 he could have found glory on the battlefield, in Napoleon's army (the 'red' of the title); but in 1830 the only road to advancement for an ambitious young man is via the Church (the 'black'). Seeing himself as an unsentimental opportunist, he uses seduction as a means of advancement – first with Madame de Rênal, the wife of the local mayor, whose children he is employed to tutor; then, after a brief period in a seminary at Besançon, with the aristocratic Mathilde de La Mole, the daughter of his second employer, in Paris, the Marquis de La Mole. He is on the verge of achieving his goals (a wealthy marriage, a title, a brilliant future) when he is denounced by a letter from Madame de Rênal. The letter (in fact written by her priest) declares him a hypocrite who uses women to climb the social ladder; it confronts Julien with a picture of himself that is uncomfortably close to the truth yet utterly intolerable. In a state of shock (semi-insanity is how Stendhal describes it), he leaves at once for Verrières and shoots Madame de Rênal as she stands in church. He wounds her, though not seriously, is tried for his crime and condemned to death. He rejects all attempts by his friends to save him and is executed. Mathilde takes his severed head and buries it. Madame de Rênal dies three days later.

The Red and the Black represented literature of a new kind. This is indicated by the novel's subtitle: 'A Chronicle of 1830'. Stendhal, as much as Balzac, changed the French novel by systematically linking the lives of his characters to current social realities and recent historical events. The historical novel invented in Britain by Sir Walter Scott (1771–1832) was transformed in France into the historical novel of contemporary life. *The Red and the Black* is permeated with a sense of historical processes. The first chapters, describing Verrières and its inhabitants, evoke the complexities of small-town politics; while, as Erich Auerbach points out in *Mimesis*, the love affair between Julien and Mathilde de La Mole is presented in sociopolitical as well as psychological terms. Both characters take up the challenge represented by the social status of the other. Mathilde, the romantic young aristocrat, would not be so drawn to Julien the plebeian if she were less bored by her family's *salon* – this boredom itself deriving from the arid intellectual life of the aristocracy; nor would she attach so many glamorous fantasies to him if she had met him before the Revolution of 1789. Julien, too, might not have had the same mixture of hatred for, and fascination with, the aristocracy either before the Revolution or during Napoleon's reign. His equation of sexual conquest with social victory explains his cry of delight when victory is achieved. Class tensions, political calculations, the reactionary world of the Church, the fears of a weakened aristocracy, the rise of the bourgeoisie – all these themes are woven into the story of Julien's journey from his father's sawmill to the guillotine. As Stendhal anticipated, his bitingly satirical chronicle of his age was not appreciated by a reading public drawn largely from the very classes he satirized. In his famous comparison between the genre of fiction and a mirror being carried along a road, the narrator asks whether he should apologize for what the reader might find unpleasant or shocking in the scene depicted; and he answers himself thus:

> Well, sir, a novel is a mirror carried along a highway. One moment it will reflect into your eyes the blue of the sky, the next the mire in the pot-holes along the road. And the man who carries the mirror on his back will be accused by you of immorality! His mirror shows the mire, and you blame the mirror! You should rather blame the road with the pot-holes, or even better, the inspector of highways who allows the water to gather and the pot-hole to form?

> Eh, monsieur, un roman est un miroir qui se promène sur une grande route. Tantôt il reflète à vos yeux l'azur des cieux, tantôt la fange des bourbiers de la route. Et l'homme qui porte le miroir dans sa hotte sera par vous accusé d'être immoral! Son miroir montre la fange, et vous accusez le miroir! Accusez bien plutôt le grand chemin où est le bourbier, et plus encore l'inspecteur des routes qui laisse l'eau croupier et le bourbier se former.   (Book 2, chapter 19)

For the Stendhalian hero, the class war is not a question of ideology, nor does personal ambition become a simple quest for money or social position; the assault on society represents, for Julien, a need to prove his worth to himself, to assert the superiority of 'merit' over 'rank' and thus to achieve a form of heroism in an unheroic age. And Napoleon – symbol of energy, courage, nobility of soul and the possibility of a young man of humble birth being able to rise in society – is the guiding star. Napoleon pervades *The Red and the Black* as a powerful myth. When we first see Julien, sitting on the rafters of his father's sawmill, he is reading Emmanuel de Las Cases's *Memorial of St Helena*, an account of Napoleon's life based on the author's almost daily conversations with the Emperor during his period of captivity on the island of St Helena; and the portrait Madame de Rênal discovers in Julien's mattress, and which she thinks is the portrait of a rival, is in fact a portrait of Napoleon. Julien sees his experiences in terms of the Napoleonic legend – in terms of triumph, defeat and conquest. He conceives it his Napoleonic duty – he the son of a peasant, she the mayor's wife – to seduce the innocent and virtuous Madame de Rênal. It is a duty that impels him to set himself tasks (such as holding Madame de Rênal's hand before the clock strikes ten) as if they were battlefield objectives. Honour demands that he visit Madame de Rênal in her bedroom. Back in his own room, 'like a soldier returning from a parade', he wonders whether he has played his part well and comments: 'Heavens! Is to be happy, to be loved, no more than that?' ('Mon Dieu! être heureux, être aimé, n'est-ce que ça?') (Book 1, chapter 15). Ironically, Julien's preoccupation with playing his role as seducer prevents him from enjoying 'the happiness that lay at his feet' or from fully realizing that Madame de Rênal is falling in love with him, and he with her; and a further irony, to which Julien also remains blind, is that it is his spontaneous behaviour (throwing himself at her feet and melting into tears) that charms Madame de Rênal, not his 'clumsy manoeuvres'. Similar ironies, accentuated by Julien's blindness, inform his conduct throughout the novel until his imprisonment.

A divided self

The world of the Restoration is portrayed in *The Red and the Black* as a world of petty politics in which all the players are intriguers and hypocrites. In his quest to improve his status, Julien turns the weapons of society – hypocrisy, lies, calculation – against itself. If his chief model is Napoleon, his other model is Molière's masterful imposter, Tartuffe. However, hypocrisy does not come naturally to Julien. He is a passionate man, easily given to impulse and emotion, and his spontaneous feelings keep asserting themselves unexpectedly. He fears, indeed, that their unruliness may subvert his ambitions. Julien is in part a comic character because of the gap between his assumed persona and his real nature. His hypocrisy is itself hypocritical; it's a mask, an assumed role. Throughout the novel, until the last section, Julien's engagement with society is presented in terms of the ironic tension between his public mask and his private self, between spontaneity and calculation. And this tension is embodied in a playful, eighteenth-century style of narration; the unreliable narrator, the urbane and witty author-persona, frequently intrudes into the narrative to express his 'poor opinion' of Julien for his 'failure' to suppress his sensibility in the interests of his career. This ironic criticism invites the reader to ponder the opposition between the values of society (calculation, self-interest) and the nature of the individual (spontaneity, natural impulses) and has the effect of reassuring us that Julien's 'weaknesses' are, in fact, manifestations of his underlying good qualities. Eventually Julien's susceptibility asserts itself once and for all, precipitating the 'state of semi-insanity' in which he shoots Madame de Rênal. His impulsive response to Madame de Rênal's letter unmasks him definitively, revealing a man who reacts not with the calculations of self-interest but with a spontaneous explosion of rage. It is at this point in the story that the narrative irony disappears, as Julien, in prison, begins to make a reckoning of his life.

In his speech to the jury at his trial, Julien, describing himself as 'a peasant who has rebelled against his low position in life' ('un paysan qui s'est révolté contre la bassesse de sa fortune'), says that he expects to be condemned because he sees among the jury only 'outraged members of the bourgeoisie' who want to take the opportunity to punish in him and keep down forever 'the class of young men who, born into an inferior class and in a sense burdened with poverty, are fortunate enough to acquire a good education and the audacity to mingle with what the rich, in their arrogance, call society' ('cette classe de jeunes gens qui, nés dans une classe inférieure et en quelque sorte opprimés par la pauvreté, ont le Bonheur de se procurer une bonne education et l'audace de se mêler à ce que l'orgueil des gens riches appelle la société') (Book two, chapter 41). Although Stendhal undoubtedly sympathized, as a man of liberal convictions, with the class of young men who use their education and talents to rise in the world, Julien's declaration that the class situation is the fundamental explanation of his 'crime' is misleading. His shooting of Madame de Rênal is to be seen, rather, as a deeply felt reaction to the accusation that he is a mere schemer motivated by self-interest. In his speech, he condemns not only his judges but also, by implication, that part of himself that he had cultivated artificially: the counterfeit self who had descended into the corrupt world of the Establishment, in which he had wanted to distinguish himself but which he always detested. In rejecting now any question of compromise with society, and demanding the death sentence, he takes command of his trial and defines his identity.

Tranquillity

Paradoxically, it is in prison that Julien finds freedom and happiness. It is only then, when he is freed from all pretence, that he discovers the happiness that his previous absorption in play-acting had prevented him from knowing. His final state of tranquillity corresponds to self-discovery and to an expression of values, which are above all matters for the individual spirit untrammelled by social considerations. Stendhal admired Napoleonic energy and willed self-assertion, but he valued especially highly, following Rousseau, the individual's ability to realize himself through the spontaneous expression of natural feelings. His Romantic cult of the individual corresponds not only to his distaste for bourgeois society but also to his awareness of the rise of mass culture and the tyranny of the majority.

Julien's thoughts in prison are occupied with Madame de Rênal; only his memory of the exquisite hours spent with her survive in him:

> He felt a special kind of happiness when, left entirely alone and without fear of being disturbed, he could abandon himself completely to the memory of the happy days he had spent at Verrières or at Vergy. The smallest incidents from that time, which had flown by too quickly, now had an irresistible freshness and charm for him. He never gave a thought to his successes in Paris; he was bored by them.

> Il trouvait un bonheur singulier quand, laissé absolument seul et sans crainte d'être interrompu, il pouvait se livrer tout entier au souvenir des journées heureuses qu'il avait passées à Verrières ou à Vergy. Les moindres incidents de ces temps trop rapidement envolés avaient pour lui une fraîcheur et un charme irrésistibles. Jamais il ne pensait à ses succès de Paris; il en était ennuyé.   (Book two, chapter 39)

When Madame de Rênal visits him in the condemned cell, he tells her that he has never loved anyone but her and speaks of the insight he has achieved. It is the transfiguring power of love that enables him to see through his own mythology and the falseness of the contemporary social world, and become truly himself. Love reveals the true ends of existence: beauty and happiness. Thus, the Rousseauistic ideals of spontaneity and natural feeling, sacrificed by Julien to survival in a debased world, are salvaged at the last. And it is only when faced with death that he completes his moral and sentimental education by shedding all worldliness, as he comes to understand that the most important thing is 'the art of enjoying life'. The shadow of death suffuses the denouement of the novel with a tragic, Romantic lyricism.

Chapter 14

Balzac: *'All is true'*

I shall have carried an entire society in my head!

– Balzac, Letter of 1844

The importance of Honoré de Balzac (1799–1850) in the history of French literature lies in his exemplary role in the establishment of the fictional model that came to be known as 'realism' – a sociological type of fiction that emphasized the material and historical circumstances of people's lives rather than individual psychology. The realist novel is concerned above all with man in society. It privileges the world of common experience, presenting man in a dynamic relationship with the forces and institutions that shape collective existence: money, power, class, convention. As an aesthetic category, realism is defined above all by its mimetic urge: that is, by its commitment to the idea that the primary role of the novel is the representation of the 'real' world.

The Human Comedy

Born at the very end of the eighteenth century, Balzac grew up during the turbulent years of Napoleon, came of age during the Restoration of the Bourbon monarchy after Waterloo and wrote most of his fiction during the reign of Louis-Philippe (the so-called citizen king, 1830–48). The central social development of Balzac's lifetime was the rise of the bourgeoisie to a commanding position in French economic and political life. The ethos of the age was encapsulated in the celebrated phrase of François Guizot, Louis-Philippe's prime minister (referring to his belief that suffrage should be restricted to propertied men, and that those who wanted the vote should become rich through thrift and hard work): 'Make money' ('Enrichissez-vous'). Balzac himself was a man of reactionary views, a monarchist and a Roman Catholic who lamented the passing of what he saw as the ordered, organic world of the Ancien Régime. His reactionary stance, however, enabled him to see all the more clearly the inevitable demise of the old order. Oscar Wilde's quip that 'the nineteenth century, as we know it, is largely an invention of Balzac's' is highly insightful, for, in the words of Peter Brooks, 'Balzac "invented" the nineteenth century by giving form to its emerging urban agglomerations, its nascent capitalist dynamics, its rampant cult of the individual personality. By conceptualizing, theorizing, and dramatizing the new – all the while deploring it – he initiated his readers into understanding the shape of a century' (*Realist Vision*, p. 22).

The acute consciousness of a changed world after the Revolution of 1789 led to a widespread interest in history and a vogue for the historical novel. This vogue was at its strongest in the 1820s, when Balzac began his literary career. The first novel he published under his own name was *The Chouans* (1829), a love story set against the background of the royalist insurgency in Brittany at the end of the eighteenth century. *The Chouans* is based on Sir Walter Scott's model of the historical novel; but whereas Scott's novels are 'historical' in the sense of taking the reader back into the past, Balzac's aim was to represent the historical dimension of the present: to depict a new France emerging from revolutionary upheaval. Like Stendhal, Balzac was concerned throughout his fiction to show how his characters reflect and respond to changing social realities. In his first major success, *The Wild Ass's Skin (La Peau de chagrin*, 1831), he recast the genre of the fantastic tale made popular by E. T. A. Hoffmann (1776–1822), directing it, as he had with the genre of the historical novel in *The Chouans*, towards the representation of the contemporary world. *The Wild Ass's Skin* is an excellent introduction to Balzac's world, for it foreshadows the themes he was to explore throughout his fiction. The novel tells the story of a young man, Raphaël de Valentin, whose life is changed when he acquires a piece of shagreen (wild ass's skin) in a curiosity shop. The skin has talismanic powers, enabling its owner to gratify his every wish (even those that are not expressed); but it shrinks with every wish granted, and when it has shrunk to nothing, the owner is dead. The talisman gives Raphaël access to the reality of Paris in 1830; however, as he descends into the urban hell, he is consumed by the destructive desires that animate it.

During the 1830s Balzac's conceptualization of his role as a novelist became more systematic. He began to categorize everything he had written and planned to write in terms of an overarching scheme, which he entitled *The Human Comedy*. Henceforth his individual novels would be only episodes in this vast enterprise, the description of French society in terms of its actual practice (in the section entitled 'Studies of Manners'), its causes ('Philosophical Studies') and its underlying principles ('Analytical Studies'). 'Studies of Manners' makes up the great bulk of *The Human Comedy* and is divided into 'Scenes of Private Life', 'Scenes of Parisian Life', 'Scenes of Provincial Life', 'Scenes of Country

Life', 'Scenes of Political Life' and 'Scenes of Military Life'. Already by 1834, as he was writing *Old Goriot* (*Le Père Goriot*, 1834; published 1835), he had hit on a device that would become a significant feature of his work: the recurring character. Eugène de Rastignac, the young protagonist of *Old Goriot*, later becomes a government minister and peer, appearing as an episodic character in *The Wild Ass's Skin* and reappearing in other novels; the arch-criminal (and future chief of police) Vautrin, to whom we are introduced in *Old Goriot*, plays a prominent part in *Lost Illusions* (*Illusions perdues*, 1837–43) and *A Courtesan's Life* (*Splendeurs et misères des courtisanes*, 1837–44). The importance of this device is that it stimulated Balzac's ambition to present society as a totality, in all its complexities and interconnections. The Promethean nature of this ambition was reflected in the sheer scale of his achievement. By the time of his death, he had written ninety-one novels and stories, containing more than 2,000 named characters, of whom about 500 appear in several different novels.

In 1842 Balzac published a Preface to *The Human Comedy* in which he set out his objectives for the whole enterprise. In this Preface ('Avant-propos') he compares his role as a writer with that of the historian, the scientist and the critic. As a historian, he characterizes himself as the secretary of society. 'French society,' he writes, 'will be the real author; I shall only be its secretary. By drawing up an inventory of its vices and virtues, by detailing its major passions, by depicting characters, by focusing upon the major incidents in its social life, by composing types who embody the traits of a number of homogeneous characters, I might perhaps succeed in writing the history overlooked by so many historians: the history of manners.' As a scientist, he takes his cue from contemporary zoologists, saying that what they were doing to explain and categorize animal species in relation to the shaping force of their environment (*milieu*), he was doing for modern man. Balzac was *inventing* an approach to social existence that has become a commonplace in the contemporary world. He thus sets his novels against a social and physical background observed in compendious detail. His fictional world is famous for its materiality; and one of the most celebrated examples of his explanatory use of milieu is the initial description of Madame Vauquer's shabby boarding house in *Old Goriot*. This setting and the objects and sense-impressions associated with it – the furniture, the ornaments, the food smells, the greasy oilcloth on the table, even the wallpaper – speak eloquently of the social status and psychological make-up of Madame Vauquer and her boarders. As a critic, Balzac says that he must study the causes of the 'social effects' he describes, 'disclose the hidden meaning of this vast array of figures, passions and events' and 'identify which societies approximate to, or deviate from, the eternal rules of the true and the good'. His moral criticism, reinforced by his adherence to Catholicism and the monarchy, is that, with the rise of the bourgeoisie, individualism and self-interest have become the dominant forces in French society.

Old Goriot: the beginning

Old Goriot is one of the most characteristic examples of Balzac's major fictions and the most celebrated 'novel of education' (*Bildungsroman*) – one of the classic patterns of nineteenth-century fiction – in the Balzac canon. The novel is set in 1819, during the Restoration. The novel's three protagonists are lodgers at the Pension Vauquer, in the Latin Quarter: Rastignac, an ambitious but impecunious student with distant relations in high society; Vautrin, a dangerous criminal; and an old man named Goriot, a retired trader who has used his considerable fortune to satisfy the shamelessly exploitative demands of his two daughters: Anastasie de Restaud, who has married into the aristocracy, and Delphine de Nucingen, who has married a crooked banker. Vautrin tries to involve Rastignac in a plot to murder the brother of a wealthy young heiress, Victorine de Taillefer, and to gain a fortune by marrying her. 'There are no such things as principles', Vautrin says, 'there are only events.' However, the plot is thwarted by two other lodgers, who turn out to be police spies. The talented and sensitive Rastignac, as he begins to climb the social ladder, gains a progressive understanding of how the world works, with the Mephistophelean Vautrin and his aristocratic cousin, Madame de Beauséant, as his teachers.

Here is the novel's opening paragraph:

> For the last forty years, an old woman by the name of Madame Vauquer, *née* de Conflans, has run a boarding house in Paris, in the rue Neuve-Sainte-Geneviève, between the Latin Quarter and the Faubourg Saint-Marceau. It is a respectable establishment, known as the Maison Vauquer. Although it accepts both men and women, young and old, its operations have never once attracted malicious gossip. But then, no young lady has been seen there for thirty years and any young man who lodges there must have an exceedingly small allowance from his family. However, in 1819, the year in which our drama begins, one poor young woman was to be found there. The word 'drama' has fallen into some disrepute, having been bandied about in such a loose and perverse way, in this age of tear-stained literature, but it does need to be used here. Not that our story is dramatic in the true sense of the term, but by the end of it, perhaps a few tears will have been shed *intra muros et extra*. Will it be

understood outside Paris? One may wonder. The peculiarities of this
scene packed with commentary and local colour can only be appreciated
between the hills of Montmartre and the heights of Montrouge, in that
illustrious valley of endlessly crumbling stucco and black, muddy
gutters; a valley full of genuine suffering and frequently counterfeit joy,
where life is so amazingly turbulent that only the most outrageous event
will make a lasting impression. Nonetheless, here and there, in this
dense web of vice and virtue, you come across sufferings that seem
grand and solemn: the selfish, the self-interested stop and feel pity,
although for them such things are no sooner seen than swallowed, as
swiftly as a tasty piece of fruit. A stouter heart than most may put a
temporary spoke in the wheel of the chariot of civilization, which is like
the idol of Juggernaut, but it will soon be crushed as the chariot
continues on its glorious course. You will react in much the same way,
you who are holding this book in your white hand, you who are sinking
into an easy chair, saying to yourself: 'This book might amuse me.' After
reading about old Goriot's secret woes, you will dine heartily, blaming
your insensitivity on the author, accusing him of exaggeration, pointing
the finger at his wild imagination. Well! Let me tell you that this drama
is neither fiction nor romance. *All is true*, so true that each one of you
will be able to recognize the elements of it in your own life, perhaps even
in your own heart.

Madame Vauquer, née de Conflans, est une vieille femme qui, depuis
quarante ans, tient à Paris une pension bourgeoise établie rue
Neuve-Sainte-Geneviève, entre le quartier latin et le faubourg
Saint-Marceau. Cette pension, connue sous le nom de la Maison
Vauquer, admet également des hommes et des femmes, des jeunes gens
et des vieillards, sans que jamais la médisance ait attaqué les mœurs de
ce respectable établissement. Mais aussi depuis trente ans ne s'y était-il
jamais vu de jeune personne, et pour qu'un jeune homme y demeure, sa
famille doit-elle lui faire une bien maigre pension. Néanmoins, en 1819,
époque à laquelle ce drame commence, il s'y trouvait une pauvre jeune
fille. En quelque discrédit que soit tombé le mot drame par la manière
abusive et tortionnaire dont il a été prodigué dans ces temps de
douloureuse littérature, il est nécessaire de l'employer ici: non que cette
histoire soit dramatique dans le sens vrai du mot; mais, l'œuvre
accomplie, peut-être aura-t-on versé quelques larmes *intra muros et
extra*. Sera-t-elle comprise au-delà de Paris? le doute est permis. Les
particularités de cette scène pleine d'observations et de couleurs locales
ne peuvent être appréciées qu'entre les buttes de Montmartre et les
hauteurs de Montrouge, dans cette illustre vallée de plâtras
incessamment près de tomber et de ruisseaux noirs de boue; vallée
remplie de souffrances réelles, de joies souvent fausses, et si terriblement

agitée qu'il faut je ne sais quoi d'exorbitant pour y produire une
sensation de quelque durée. Cependant il s'y rencontre çà et là des
douleurs que l'agglomération des vices et des vertus rend grandes et
solennelles: à leur aspect, les égoïsmes, les intérêts, s'arrêtent et
s'apitoient; mais l'impression qu'ils en reçoivent est comme un fruit
savoureux promptement dévoré. Le char de la civilisation, semblable à
celui de l'idole de Jaggernat, à peine retardé par un cœur moins facile à
broyer que les autres et qui enraye sa roue, l'a brisé bientôt et continue
sa marche glorieuse. Ainsi ferez-vous, vous qui tenez ce livre d'une main
blanche, vous qui enfoncez dans un moelleux fauteuil en vous disant:
Peut-être ceci va-t-il m'amuser. Après avoir lu les secrètes infortunes du
Père Goriot, vous dînerez avec appétit en mettant votre insensibilité sur
le compte de l'auteur, en le taxant d'exagération, en l'accusant de poésie.
Ah! sachez-le: ce drame n'est ni une fiction, ni un roman. *All is true*, il
est si véritable, que chacun peut en reconnaître les éléments chez soi,
dans son cœur peut-être.

Here we see Balzac alluding to a number of key characters and themes. Old
Goriot is mentioned by name; the 'young man' is Rastignac; the 'poor young
woman' is Victorine de Taillefer. Thematically, the word 'secret' ('Goriot's
secret woes') has enormous resonances, for Rastignac soon realizes that in
order to achieve the social success he desires he must learn society's secret
codes. *Old Goriot* is a kind of detective story, full of mysteries that need to
be unravelled. Everything in Balzac's world is bursting with meaning, waiting to be fathomed. Much of the narrative energy of a Balzac novel lies in the
protagonist's quest to see beyond appearances (in physiognomy, clothes, build-
ings, etc. as well as in modes of behaviour). The vital context of this drama
of interpretation is the city: 'Will [my novel] be understood outside Paris?'
asks the author-narrator. For Balzac, Paris (which doubled in size during the
first thirty years of the nineteenth century) had become a great melting-pot
of greed, envy and social conflict, dangerous and unstable. The city in Balzac
is modern society; *Old Goriot* is a Parisian story, and Rastignac's education
is intimately connected with the juxtaposition of different urban spaces. The
boarding house, with its hierarchy of levels and rooms for the comparatively
rich and the comparatively poor, is a model of the Parisian social world,
anticipating the opposition between the Latin Quarter (where Rastignac lives
as a poor student) and the *beaux quartiers* inhabited by the aristocracy and
upper bourgeoisie (the world of glamour and power to which he longs to gain
admission).

The main interest of this first paragraph, however, lies in the ways in which
Balzac presents and justifies his new, 'realist' type of writing. Throughout most
of the paragraph (beginning with 'The word drama . . . '), the author-narrator

is flamboyantly centre stage, addressing the reader-narratee directly, even apostrophizing ('Well! Let me tell you …'), in order to affirm the nature of his own text. The allusion to Romantic theatre ('tear-stained literature') implies that, in contrast to its exoticism, he will develop a type of literature in which the drama will spring from the real world. This point is reinforced by the construction of a hypothetical reader who, sinking into a soft armchair, will pick up the book in search of simple entertainment. In Balzac's day, novels were popularly associated with fantasy and escapism – a flight from reality. Balzac stresses that his own novel, by contrast, represents a commitment to the truth; and he enjoins the reader to honour that commitment by being prepared to see his own experience reflected in it. By denying the fictive nature of his novel, Balzac is urging his reader to accept his narrative as a transparent, unmediated representation of the 'real' world. But (with the benefit of critical hindsight) we can hardly take him literally, since all novels are inherently artificial, constructed with language, which has its own rules and cannot represent in any objective or transparent manner what exists independently of those rules; and novels cannot be other than projections, in an inevitably selective manner, of an individual subjectivity. The rhetorical climax of the paragraph is the narrator's paradoxical declaration that what the reader has in front of him is neither fiction nor romance, but a text defined by the phrase '*All is true*' – a phrase made all the more striking by the fact that it is in a foreign language and in italics. Various critics have pointed out that the phrase '*All is true*' is itself a literary allusion. Shakespeare's *Henry VIII*, when it was first produced, was subtitled *All Is True*, a fact revealed in the *Revue de Paris* of 10 August 1831 in an article by Philarète Chasles, a prominent literary figure of the day. The article would still be fresh in the minds of some of Balzac's readers. As Victor Brombert has written: 'The extreme signal of realism (*all is true*) thus places the elaborate opening disclaimer of literarity under the sign of literature.'[1] Similarly, the strident authorial voice, designed to reinforce the truth-telling value of the novel and its importance as exemplifying the major new form of writing of the age, in fact underscores (like Balzac's use of an 'omniscient narrator' throughout his fiction) the extent to which the novel is a rhetorical performance – the work of a kind of literary showman engaged in recreating reality in his own image. In this opening paragraph, Balzac affirms his extra-literary aims (which he will later outline in his 1842 Preface) while indicating, partly through rhetorical exaggeration, and despite himself, that the representational model he is about to establish is no more than a new literary convention: the selection and arrangement of the words on the page in order to give the illusion of reality. He is declaring his mimetic intentions while revealing the artificiality of the means involved.

The 'realist illusion' is achieved through the ways in which Balzac anchors the imaginary world of the text in the real world inhabited by his reader: by precise references to place, time and the social status of his characters. The first sentence provides information about place: the boarding house is situated in Paris, and this information is immediately qualified with mention of its specific location in the rue Neuve-Sainte-Geneviève, between the Latin Quarter and the Faubourg Saint-Marceau – real places, familiar to many readers. (The rue Neuve-Sainte-Geneviève is today's rue Tournefort in the 5th *arrondissement*.) The added detail, 'known as the Maison Vauquer', implies an extra-textual world whose existence makes it possible to verify that the boarding house really exists. The third and fourth sentences situate the boarding house in time: Madame Vauquer has maintained her establishment for the last forty years, and the action of the novel begins 'in 1819'. Though the narrative is situated in the recent past, the repeated use of the present indicative implies direct contact with an extra-textual reality that continues to exist. Madame Vauquer, the character to whom we are introduced, is defined immediately in terms of her sex, age, occupation and social status (Conflans has aristocratic connotations, implying that Madame Vauquer has come down in the world).

These opening sentences read like sociological reportage, and they give *Old Goriot* a 'realistic' feel. Generally, Balzac's fiction provides vast amounts of taxonomically conceived information about French society in the first half of the nineteenth century as well as offering insights into its workings. But although his narratives are intensely focused on 'the real', they could hardly be said to reflect reality in any prosaic or mirror-like sense. Rather, they heighten reality through various forms of stylization: Balzac's plots are melodramatic, full of contrivance and coincidence, stereotypes and antitheses ('suffering'/'joy', 'vice'/'virtue'):[2] his characters, though representative of certain social types and trends, are vividly individualized, often driven by obsessive passions and often (like Goriot) monomaniacal; his language is highly metaphoric (witness the symbolic and mythical associations of the 'illustrious valley' that extends from Montmartre to Montrouge). Immediately after the passage in question, the narrator suggests that anyone walking down the rue Neuve-Sainte-Geneviève to the boarding house is like a traveller descending into the darkness of the catacombs of Paris. The social world of the city becomes a place of fantasy and mystery, described in terms that recall the Gothic novel. 'Exaggeration' goes hand in hand with what is 'so true', documentary realism combining with an extraordinary textual exuberance to produce a kind of hyperrealism. It was thus possible for the Marxist Friedrich Engels (1820–95) to comment that he had learned more from *The Human Comedy* than from all the economists and political scientists combined, and for Baudelaire to write of his astonishment that Balzac's main claim to fame rested on his having been taken for an observer, for it had always seemed to him that his chief merit was that of a visionary: 'All his fictions are as richly coloured as dreams.'

Old Goriot: the end

Goriot ('the Christ of Paternity') dies, having sold and pawned his last possessions for his daughters. His deathbed cry, 'Nothing matters any more but money: money will buy you anything' ('L'argent, c'est la vie. Monnaie fait tout'), might be read as a summary of Rastignac's education and of Balzac's critique of society. For Balzac, all aspects of life – family relations, social ambition, sexual desire – have a price. For Balzac as for Marx, the essence of the bourgeois capitalist system was the transformation of all values into objects of exchange. Rastignac, confronted with this predatory world, arrives at a state of disabused realism; and he resolves to use his understanding to achieve success in society's own terms, as he makes clear in the novel's closing paragraphs, which describe his reflections as he stands on the heights of Père-Lachaise cemetery and looks down at the wealthy districts of Paris. Unlike Stendhal's Julien Sorel, who withdraws from the world after concluding that his fulfilment as an individual is irreconcilable with his social environment, Rastignac determines to plunge ever deeper into society, aware that his knowledge has enabled him to do so. He contemplates Goriot's grave, buries in it 'the last tears of his youth', throws down a challenge to the city and descends into it to make his career by whatever means.

> Alone now, Rastignac walked up towards the highest point of the cemetery and saw Paris spread out below him, winding along the banks of the Seine, its lights beginning to sparkle. His eyes came to rest almost greedily on the area between the column on the Place Vendôme and the dome of the Invalides, the home of the *beau monde*, which he had wanted to enter. He gave the buzzing hive a look that seemed already to drain it of its honey, and uttered these grand words: 'Now it's just the two of us! I'm ready!'
>
> And by way of firing an opening shot at Society, Rastignac went to have dinner with Madame de Nucingen.

> Rastignac, resté seul, fit quelques pas vers le haut du cimetière et vit Paris tortueusement couché le long des deux rives de la Seine, où commençaient à briller les lumières. Ses yeux s'attachèrent presque avidement entre la colonne de la place Vendôme et le dôme des Invalides,

là où vivait ce beau monde dans lequel il avait voulu pénétrer. Il lança sur cette ruche bourdonnant un regard qui semblait par avance en pomper le miel, et dit ces mots grandioses: – A nous deux maintenant!

Et pour premier acte du défi qu'il portait à la Société, Rastignac alla dîner chez madame de Nucingen.

The novel's conclusion is open-ended, though the implication is of future success. However, the line between success and failure is a fine one in the sense that Rastignac's apprenticeship has changed him, deadening his sensibility. The novel's final sentence, noting Rastignac's going to dine with his rich mistress, ironically suggests that the grand challenge is in fact an acceptance of compromise – with the cynical operation of a society in which, as *Old Goriot* has shown, pure feelings can have no part.

Chapter 15

Hugo: the divine stenographer

> I gave the old dictionary a red cap.
>
> – Hugo, 'Réponse à un acte d'accusation' (*Les Contemplations*)

When Hugo died, in 1885, he was given a state funeral grander, certainly more festive, than any Paris had given, even for royalty. The funeral procession, complete with brass bands, attracted 2 million people (a number greater than the population of Paris at the time). It was as a popular hero, an icon of Republican values, a symbol of France itself, that Hugo was laid to rest. How did this extraordinary consecration come about? Writers in France have traditionally been invested with great prestige. Literature in France has always been closely related to national identity and national pride. In one way or another, writers in France have been closely involved in the social and political affairs of the nation, going back to the association of writers with the sources of power in Paris through the creation of the Académie française under Louis XIV in the seventeenth century. French literary culture, in other words, has tended to make a public figure of the writer; and it could be argued that that culture is most fully realized in the 'public' writer, who is simultaneously recorder and agent of change. Classic exemplars of the 'public' writer are Voltaire in the eighteenth century, Hugo in the nineteenth, and Sartre in the twentieth. All three attained phenomenal celebrity during their lifetime.[1]

For many of his contemporaries, Victor Hugo (1802–85) was the most important literary figure of the nineteenth century. He was the leading figure of the Romantic movement in France;[2] he was considered the greatest French poet; and he wrote monumental, hugely popular novels. He was also an iconic political figure. Son of one of Napoleon's generals (a man of staunchly Republican views) and a fervently Catholic-Royalist mother, he was in his youth an ardent Royalist, but moved steadily to the left. As a deputy for Paris, he played an active part in the 1848 Revolution on the side of the Republicans; and in December 1851, when Louis-Napoleon Bonaparte (Napoleon's nephew) staged his *coup d'état* against the Republic and restored the Empire, the Poet stood up against the Despot. He tried unsuccessfully to organize resistance to the coup, and then, fearing for his life, he fled Paris, disguised as a worker, and took refuge in Brussels, where he wrote *Napoléon le Petit*, a brilliant political pamphlet attacking Louis-Napoleon for betraying the idea of the Republic. From Brussels he went to the Channel Islands, where he remained, in self-imposed exile, until the fall of the Second Empire in 1870. He returned to France a national hero.

Drama

In 1827 Hugo published a preface to his (unacted and unactable) play *Cromwell*. Though diffuse and repetitious, this text is of major importance in the development of the theory of modern drama and literature. It was the literary manifesto of Hugo's generation. He championed a form of literature (Romanticism) that would express the democratic spirit of the modern, post-Revolutionary period. He called for a rejection of classical aesthetic doctrine, with its highly regulated poetic diction and its insistence on the separation of the genres of tragedy and comedy, in favour of a new, open conception of dramatic form. It was the free mixing of styles and idioms to be found (and supremely embodied) in Shakespeare that modern literature must emulate in order to express the full complexity and diversity of life; a new style must reflect the rise of a democratic, inclusive society and its displacement of an old order that insisted on propriety, hierarchy and exclusion.

Hugo's ambition was to revolutionize literature by revolutionizing language. The number of words considered permissible in French poetry (including verse drama) had been slowly diminishing since the days of Racine. A distinction had grown up between words that were 'noble' and words (as used by ordinary people) that were 'common'; only the former were allowed in poetry. The strength of these conventions may be measured by the fact that the use of the word 'mouchoir' (handkerchief) during a performance of *Othello* a few years before 1830 produced a riot in the theatre. Hugo and his fellow Romantics threw open the doors of poetry to every available word and form of expression. Their triumph was marked by the première, in February 1830 at the Comédie-Française, of Hugo's historical verse drama *Hernani*. All the traditional 'rules' were broken; freedom of diction and metre were gleefully introduced. Riotous scenes accompanied the première, which took place in a circus-like atmosphere. Hugo was exultant. Romanticism, he declared, in his polemical preface to the first edition of *Hernani* (March 1830), was 'liberalism in literature'. His dislodgement of the cultural norms of the Establishment made it seem that the whole social order was, once more, being brought into question; and indeed, the revolution in the theatre preceded by just four months a revolution in politics: in July 1830 the unpopular Charles X, the last of the Bourbon monarchs of France, abdicated and was replaced by the so-called citizen king, Louis-Philippe, the figurehead of bourgeois liberalism.

Poetry

In some ways it was unfortunate that the main battle over Romanticism took place in the theatre. *Hernani* is a piece of bombastic melodrama, an exercise in rhetoric and the picturesque. Hugo's later play *Ruy Blas* (1838) is somewhat better, but the main achievements of Romanticism lay in poetry and the novel. It is commonly agreed that, in one way or another, the whole of French poetry since Hugo owes him tribute. Without his enormous contribution to the revitalization of poetic forms, the modernist experiments of Baudelaire, Rimbaud, Mallarmé and Valéry would not have been possible. His poetic output was not only vast but also extremely varied in theme and tone. His poetry could be intensely personal, and also deal with the largest of themes: God and the destiny of mankind. He could be grandiloquent and simple, highly dramatic and surprisingly playful. *Odes et ballades* (1826 and 1828) showed Hugo's early efforts to unshackle French verse from the tyranny of Racinian alexandrine regularity. His next important collection was *Les Orientales* (1829), which exhibited even more clearly the technical virtuosity for which he would become famous; his innovative power and his mastery of a wide variety of verse forms were astonishing. The lyric collections, *Les Feuilles d'automne* (1831) and *Les Chants du crepuscule* (1835), contain poems celebrating the poet's personal attachments – to his family and to his faithful mistress, the actress Juliette Drouet; the collections published later in the decade, *Les Voix intérieures* (1837) and *Les Rayons et les ombres* (1840), stress the metaphysical nature of poetic consciousness. In the latter volume, in particular, the poet is presented as a prophet and visionary, probing the mysteries of death, destiny, nature and God, and seeking to guide humanity towards the future.

It was during his years of exile that Hugo wrote his greatest poetry: the powerful satirical verse of *Les Châtiments* (1853), aimed at the Emperor and his regime; his finest collection of lyric poetry, *Les Contemplations* (1856), conceived as a kind of spiritual autobiography and an allegory of human destiny; an epic verse collection, *La Légende des siècles* (first series, 1859), in which Hugo's historical and visionary imagination is given full expression through the creation of a cycle of episodic stories ranging from the biblical Creation to the French Revolution and the scientific discoveries of the nineteenth century;

and finally, the small-scale pastoral lyrics of *Les Chansons des rues et des bois* (1865).

The novel

Hugo's major novels are works of historical fiction that reflect, in one way or another, the political realities of nineteenth-century France. However, they are extraordinarily rich in scope and style, to the extent that they defy conventional generic categorization. They are characterized above all by their visionary and poetic force.[3]

Hugo's particular ability to combine narrative, drama and poetry became apparent in *The Hunchback of Notre-Dame*, a tale of desire set in late medieval Paris, where all life is dominated by the great cathedral. The 'grotesque' hunchback Quasimodo, bell-ringer of Notre-Dame, owes his life to the austere priest Frollo, who is bound by a hopeless passion to the gypsy dancer Esmeralda, who in turn has won Quasimodo's undying devotion through a 'sublime' act of kindness. The novel is built on a pattern of antitheses, including the symbolic opposition between the King (the cruel and superstitious Louis XI) and the underworld of beggars and petty criminals whose night-time assault on the cathedral is one of the most spectacular set pieces of Romantic literature. The generous-spirited outcasts of society – Quasimodo and Esmeralda are exemplary Romantic heroes in this respect – are set in opposition to the dark forces of law and order.

The figure of the sublime outlaw finds its quintessential expression in Jean Valjean, the protagonist of *Les Misérables*, a peasant sentenced to five years' hard labour for stealing a loaf of bread to feed his widowed sister's seven children, then nineteen more for trying repeatedly to escape. Turned into a hardened criminal by his experiences, he reforms, establishes a new identity for himself and becomes a wealthy industrialist and the respected mayor of a French town, where he befriends a young working woman named Fantine, who is forced into prostitution to support her illegitimate child, Cosette, whom Valjean takes into his care. Valjean's conscience compels him to reveal his true identity when an innocent vagrant, falsely accused of stealing apples, is mistaken for him. Imprisoned once more, Valjean escapes. His flight from his nemesis, the police inspector Javert, culminates in one of the most famous scenes in literature, the chase through the sewers of Paris.

The book was an instant bestseller, and was widely translated the moment it came out in 1862 (in Brussels and Paris – having been smuggled out of Hugo's place of exile on Guernsey, legend has it, sewn into the hems of admirers' skirts). Already a celebrity in France, Hugo became a world figure. His novel was popular because it was, precisely, popular: it is popular literature in the sense that it addresses and is accessible to all mankind. Not only did Hugo write about *le peuple*, but he spoke *to* and *for* them as well. The writing of *Les Misérables* was a powerful political act in the sense that he gave a voice to the voiceless: the downtrodden and those whom society saw as not having a right to a voice – criminals, ex-convicts, prostitutes, street urchins. The story of Valjean's struggle to reaffirm his humanity in a world brutalized by poverty became the Bible of the masses.

Les Misérables is less a novel than an immense epic poem (it is close to 1,500 pages long) – an epic of modern times, whose power derives in large measure from its sheer narrative dynamism. It is deeply Romantic both in its humanitarian ideology and in its monumental exuberance of form and content. Expansiveness of ideas is matched by energy and variety of expression. As Simon Leys has written: 'With the richest vocabulary since Rabelais, [Hugo's] linguistic keyboard presents the bewildering range of a grand organ – by turns, solemn, familiar, thundering, whispering, screeching, bellowing, murmuring, roaring ... Technical terms from all sorts of trades and crafts stirred his imagination. He explored in depth the slang of the underworld, the jargon of criminals and of jails.'[4] Hugo's range of styles is extraordinary, from baroque to sober, from lyrical to grimly realist, from naturalistic to surreal. And his vision is kaleidoscopic: there are, of course, his evocations of the life of the city and the drama of the streets (including the underworld of the 1820s), but also the narrative is strewn with his thoughts on society and politics and regularly interrupted by encyclopaedic digressions on such disparate topics as the linguistic structure of slang, the mechanisms of the sewage system, Church history and dogma, religious orders and their practices, the history of warfare and weaponry, of prisons and imprisonment. There are also long, sweeping sections on the Revolution of 1789, the Napoleonic Wars and the Battle of Waterloo. *Les Misérables* seems to be a book about everything, and to contain every kind of novel: adventure story, detective novel, sentimental novel, historical novel, realist novel, Romantic novel, melodrama. Mario Vargas Llosa, in his engaging study of the novel, argues that the most important task of the novelist (that is, the novelist in general) is to invent a narrator and that in *Les Misérables* the narrator, identified with the voice and persona of Hugo himself, becomes the main character, remarkable for his 'omniscience, omnipotence, exuberance, visibility, and egomania'; he embodies the Romantic belief in the creative power of the imagination; he is a 'divine stenographer' intent on writing a 'total novel', a work of fiction designed to enable its readers to 'imagine a different and better world'.

The reputation Hugo acquired in the twentieth century as a master of pompous rhetoric and sentimental clichés has tended to obscure the complexity and inventiveness of his writing. Critics have argued increasingly, however, that a rereading of Hugo's novels, especially *Les Misérables*, will reveal how surprisingly contemporary a writer he is. *Les Misérables* is one of the most ambitious narrative creations of the nineteenth century. Not only does Hugo's prose have a surprising freshness and vigour, but the novel's dazzlingly protean forms – its multiplicity of voices, styles, symbols and images – make it one of the great experimental novels of the modern age.

Chapter 16

Baudelaire: the streets of Paris

All around me howled the deafening street.

– Baudelaire, 'To a Passer-by'

Charles Baudelaire (1821–67) occupies a key position in the development of modern writing, not just as the author of the most celebrated collection of verse in the history of modern French poetry, *The Flowers of Evil* (*Les Fleurs du mal*, 1857), but as the proponent, in his critical writings, of a new aesthetic based on the experience of city life. According to the Marxist cultural critic Walter Benjamin (1892–1940), Baudelaire, by being the first poet of the city, was the first poet of modernity; he was the first writer to recognize in the transformation of Paris during the Second Empire (1852–70) a radical transformation of society itself, and to perceive the impact the new social reality would have on the creative artist. He is seen as the very embodiment of a sensibility and consciousness we regard as modern.

Modernity and the city

In December 1848 Louis-Napoleon Bonaparte, the nephew of Napoleon Bonaparte, was elected president of the Second Republic (1848–51), which had been born out of a revolution in February of the same year. On 2 December 1851 he staged a *coup d'état* that gave him dictatorial powers. A year later he proclaimed the Second Empire. He was now Emperor Napoleon III. To establish his authority, and acquire a kind of legitimacy, he pursued a policy of modernization and 'progress'. He determined to make Paris clean and safe, and above all 'modern', and would do this through a vast scheme of urban redevelopment. He entrusted the project to Georges-Eugène Haussmann (1809–91), whom he appointed Prefect of the Seine. The 'Haussmannization' of the city was social planning on a spectacular scale, glorifying Louis-Napoleon's empire as if it were a new Augustan Rome. Haussmann's overriding aim, however, was to advance the bourgeoisie's business interests by creating a more efficient transport network – by creating a city that would allow the rapid circulation not only of troops but also of goods, people and money. The demolition and building work was unremitting. By 1870 over 1,200 kilometres of new streets had been built, nearly double the number that had existed before. Paris was transformed from an insalubrious warren of crooked streets, congested slums and open sewers into a kind of showplace. Paris became a city of display and consumption, of chic cafés, elegant boulevards and glittering surfaces, in which the outstanding commodity to be looked at was the city itself.

The devastation of *vieux Paris* and the various communities within it was highly controversial, but Haussmann pursued his renovations relentlessly. Large sections of the working class were forced into cheaper outlying areas, dividing Paris into a preponderantly middle- and upper-class west and a working-class east. The explosive growth of the city, and the dramatically new patterns of urban life, dislocated and fragmented traditional human relationships. Haussmann's transformation of Paris not only reshaped the city physically but also broke down or blurred boundaries of every kind – cultural, social, perceptual. In a world in which most Parisians had traditionally lived their lives within the confines of a few streets, many people felt that they had lost Paris and were living in someone else's city; that they had been exiled, so to speak. On the one hand, the modern city was a powerful symbol of progress and enlightenment; on the other hand, the semi-obliteration of the old Paris, with its familiar landmarks, symbolized the deracination of modern man and highlighted the need to establish new reference points for the expression of self and identity.

Baudelaire called for a new aesthetic to match the changes and challenges of 'modernity', understood as a sense of vertiginous change. The city, he wrote, had created a new mode of perception and now demanded a new mode of representation, of aesthetic sensibility and practice. The key text in this regard is his influential essay *The Painter of Modern Life* (*Le Peintre de la vie moderne*, written 1859–60, published 1863), which was the nineteenth century's single most important manifesto of aesthetic modernism. The central idea of this essay is that traditional notions of beauty are no longer adequate. Art, Baudelaire argued, could no longer justifiably concern itself with the conventional types of painting – scenes from ancient history, the Bible, etc. – exhibited at the official state Salon every year; if art was to be relevant, it had to concern itself with the modern world. The exemplary 'painter of modern life', he suggested, was Constantin Guys (1805–92), a relatively minor artist whose pen-and-ink sketches of fashionable Parisian life captured the shock of modern experience – the speed and flux that characterize modernity. With a freshness of vision comparable to that of a child, Guys evoked the thrill of the new, the exhilaration of everything that was novel; and with his rapid sketches he was able to extract the eternal from the transient, to fix on paper fleeting impressions gained from the swirling world around him. Baudelaire thus presented a conception of beauty derived from contemporary urban life, diametrically opposed to the Rousseauian-Romantic cult of nature as well as the 'timelessness' of the classical tradition of history painting. Modern beauty, he wrote, lay not in untouched scenes of nature, but in the artificial creations of city life – in the various artefacts and accessories of the metropolis, such as fashion and make-up. Indeed, the city, being a human creation, represented art itself.

The characteristic embodiment of modernity is the *flâneur*, an urban figure Baudelaire made famous. The *flâneur* is a stroller, a pedestrian who walks slowly and at random through the city, abandoning himself to the sights and impressions of the moment. He observes as others are dragged along by the deadening routines of bourgeois existence, with its utilitarian goals and philistine tastes. But there is nothing passive about the *flâneur*: he is a passionate observer, who delights in plunging into the urban crowd, in being at the centre of the world while remaining hidden from it: 'the spectator is a *prince* who everywhere rejoices in his incognito'.

> For the perfect *flâneur*, for the passionate spectator, it is an immense pleasure to choose to set up house in the heart of the crowd, amid the ebb and flow of movement, in the midst of the fleeting and the infinite. To be away from home and yet to feel everywhere at home; to see the world, to be at the centre of the world, and yet to remain hidden from the world – such are a few of the slightest pleasures of those independent, passionate, impartial creatures ... Thus the lover of universal life enters into the crowd as if it were an immense reservoir of electrical energy. We might thus liken him to a mirror as vast as the crowd itself; or to a kaleidoscope gifted with consciousness, responding to each one of its movements and reproducing the multiplicity of life and the flickering grace of all the elements of life.

> Pour le parfait flâneur, pour l'observateur passionné, c'est une immense jouissance que d'élire domicile dans le nombre, dans l'ondoyant, dans le mouvement, dans le fugitif et l'infini. Être hors de chez soi, et pourtant se sentir partout chez soi; voir le monde, être au centre du monde et rester caché au monde, tels sont quelques-uns des moindres plaisirs de ces esprits indépendants, passionnés, impartiaux ... Ainsi l'amoureux de la vie universelle entre dans la foule comme dans un immense réservoir d'électricité. On peut ainsi le comparer, lui, à un miroir aussi

immense que cette foule; à un kaléidoscope doué de conscience, qui, à chacun de ses mouvements, représente la vie multiple et la grâce mouvante de tous les éléments de la vie.

The *flâneur* is thus a curiously ambiguous figure, existing in a state of strangely detached excitement. Baudelaire wrote about the experience of isolation and loss of connection, but this was the condition of a new and vital kind of perception. The pleasure he feels lies in a vicarious sense of adventure, linked with the satisfaction of decoding, 'reading', the signs of the city. Much of *The Painter of Modern Life* is about the excitement of struggling to master a set of appearances and experiences that threatens to remain illegible. The individual act of creating meaning becomes 'heroic'; the imagination, as Baudelaire declared in his Salon of 1859, is 'the queen of faculties'. For him, the highest expression of the human spirit in a post-religious age is art – a form of art that is autonomous and non-productive, gratuitous and controversial, and that will 'shock the bourgeoisie' (*épater le bourgeois*).

Parisian scenes

The section of *The Flowers of Evil* entitled 'Parisian Scenes' ('Tableaux parisiens') evokes the experience of modern man living in the world of the city. The city had become a dominant theme in the novels of Balzac as the new total context of modern social life. Some of the finest poems of 'Parisian Scenes' (and, later, the prose poems of *Paris Spleen*) deal with urban subject matter, with figures from the street: buskers, acrobats, prostitutes, rag-and-bone men, beggars, the homeless. However, Baudelaire never set great store by realistic 'observation'; and in his own treatment of city life, he sought not to imitate the real but to transform it, to resist its surface meanings in pursuit of the transcendence uniquely available to the artist, who works with his *imagination*. The inaugural poem of 'Parisian Scenes', 'Landscape' ('Paysage'), describes the poet looking out over the rooftops of the city, saying that he will close his shutters and conjure a world out of his own mind.

The world Baudelaire conjures is marked by ambivalence. Life in Paris is perceived and represented by the poet both as the potential source of a kind of imaginative intoxication and as an image of human exile and desolation. The city represents for the artist-*flâneur* both fascination and danger: he is fascinated and inspired by the city's multiple stimuli, its continuously changing streetscapes, its startling incongruities; but the city also represents a danger through the forced cohabitation of the artist with the ever-present masses in the streets and the risk of contamination by their bourgeois materialist pre-occupations. How to protect the individuality and unique vision of the artist, under constant assault by the deafening bustle of the city, by the incoherent and fragmented experience of the 'real'? How to be *in* the city but not *engulfed by* it? This was to become a major preoccupation of the modernist art of the early twentieth century.

The poet-*flâneur* in 'Parisian Scenes', immersed in the moving chaos of the modern street, is concerned above all to make sense of his visions and encounters. At the centre of 'Parisian Scenes' is a preoccupation with the interpretative process itself. The modernist vision embodied in Baudelaire's urban poetry is marked by a sense of dissonance and incompleteness. One of the distinctive features of urban perception in Baudelaire is its fragmentary, often halluci-nated nature. The city and its crowds provide the shock of confrontation, the sudden vision that triggers the poet's imagination. The celebrated poem 'To a Passer-by' ('A une passante') captures, in the appropriately abbreviated, sketch-like form of a sonnet, the experience of an instant, and in so doing transposes into literary language the modernist aesthetics elaborated in *The Painter of Modern Life*. The poet stands in the middle of a noisy street contemplating his detachment from the crowd. For a split second he catches the eye of a passing woman whose glance suddenly arouses in him a feeling of erotic excitement. But just as quickly, she's swept away by the crowd and the poet is left alone, frustrated by the non-realization of this potential encounter, excitement and frustration telescoped into a single moment.

To a Passer-by

All around me howled the deafening street.
Tall and slim, with sorrowful majesty,
a woman in full mourning passed me by,
her sumptuous hand swinging her festooned skirt.

She was lovely as a statue, lithe and tall.
I tensed like a raving fool, drinking in
the heaven of those grey eyes where storms begin –
bewitching sweetness, pleasure that could kill.

One lightning flash … then night! – Fleeting beauty,
whose glance lifted me back to life, will I ever
see you again this side of eternity?

Elsewhere, faraway, too late, maybe *never*!
Where was the other going? Neither of us could tell.
Yet I could have loved you. And you knew it well!

Trans. Jan Owen

A une passante

La rue assourdissante autour de moi hurlait.
Longue, mince, en grand deuil, douleur majestueuse,
Une femme passa, d'une main fastueuse
Soulevant, balançant le feston et l'ourlet;

Agile et noble, avec sa jambe de statue.
Moi, je buvais, crispé comme un extravagant,
Dans son œil, ciel livide où germe l'ouragan,
La douceur qui fascine et le plaisir qui tue.

Un éclair ... puis la nuit! – Fugitive beauté
Dont le regard m'a fait soudainement renaître,
Ne te verrai-je plus que dans l'éternité?

Ailleurs, bien loin d'ici! trop tard! *jamais* peut-être!
Car j'ignore où tu fuis, tu ne sais où je vais,
Ô toi que j'eusse aimée, ô toi qui le savais!

The dramatic effect of the poem derives to a large extent from Baudelaire's ironic transformation of the romantic myth of 'love at first sight' into what Walter Benjamin memorably termed 'love at last sight'. The poem is exemplary in its evocation of what Benjamin called the 'shock' experience characteristic of modern urban life: unforeseeable, momentary experience; a lightning flash followed by night.

The street becomes a kind of stage on which the drama of the poet's mind is acted out allegorically. The allegorization of the Parisian cityscape; the city as a metaphor for all perceptions and relationships; the city as an image of human exile; the juxtaposition of old and new; the feeling of a debased present; a melancholic appreciation of evanescence and change; the poet's sense of his own marginalization: these are major themes in Baudelaire and they are all interwoven in a complex, compelling way in the celebrated poem 'The Swan' ('Le Cygne'):

The Swan

To Victor Hugo

I

It's you I'm thinking of, Andromache.
That little river like a mournful mirror
reflecting back your widowed majesty,
your token Simoïs deepened tear by tear,

came flooding into memory again
as I was crossing the new Carrousel. And I thought

how the old Paris is gone, and how a town
can change more quickly than a mortal heart.

Only the mind's eye holds those booths and stalls,
the rough-hewn shafts and capitals, the stones
in green-scummed piles, the weeds and stagnant pools,
the jumbled bric-a-brac glittering at the panes.

A zoo once spread across this open space
and there one morning at the clear, crisp hour
when sweepers start their chores, and piles of refuse
swirl dark hurricanes into the silent air,

I saw a swan who'd managed to escape
scraping its feet over the bumpy ground
and heaving its plumage on. Beak agape,
it tried to bathe in the dry gutter it found,

nervously dipping its wings into the dust,
and crying for the lovely lake of its birth:
'Water, rain down! Thunder, when will you burst?'
I see it still, a strange and fateful myth

like Ovid's man gazing up at the sky,
its neck convulsing, and its frantic head
stretched to that cruel, ironic blue on high,
addressing its reproaches straight to God.

II

Paris changes, but not my melancholy.
Scaffolding, new palaces, masonry blocks,
the old quarters, all seem allegory.
My dearest memories weigh me down like rocks.

Faced by this new Louvre, I'm overcome
by the image of my heavy, half-crazed swan,
like all exiles, ridiculous, sublime,
gnawed by endless desire. And I think again

of you, Andromache, slipped from Hector's arms
and seized like a lowly beast by haughty Pyrrhus,
of you, rapt with grief by an empty tomb,
Hector's widow married off to Helenus!

I think, too, of the gaunt, consumptive Negress
wearily plodding the mud, her haggard eyes
fixed on sunny Africa's coconut trees
beyond the fortress wall of foggy skies;

of those who've lost what they'll never ever regain!
Of all who swallow down their lonely tears
and suckle from the generous wolf bitch Pain;
of the skinny little orphans fading like flowers!

In the forest of the mind, my own exile,
A hunting horn rings out from memory's core:
I think of castaways on a desert isle,
the conquered and enslaved. And many more...

Trans. Jan Owen

Le Cygne

A Victor Hugo

I

Andromaque, je pense à vous! Ce petit fleuve,
Pauvre et triste où jadis resplendit
L'immense majesté de vos douleurs de veuve,
Ce Simoïs menteur qui par vos pleurs grandit,

A fécondé soudain ma mémoire fertile,
Comme je traversais le nouveau Carrousel.
Le vieux Paris n'est plus (la forme d'une ville
Change plus vite, hélas! que le cœur d'un mortel);

Je ne vois qu'en esprit, tout ce camp de baraques,
Ces tas de chapiteaux ébauchés et de fûts,
Les herbes, les gros blocs verdis par l'eau des flaques,
Et, brillant aux carreaux, le bric-à-brac confus.

Là s'étalait jadis une ménagerie;
Là je vis, un matin, à l'heure où sous les cieux
Froids et clairs le Travail s'éveille, où la voirie
Pousse un sombre ouragan dans l'air silencieux,

Un cygne qui s'était évadé de sa cage,
Et, de ses pieds palmés frottant le pavé sec,
Sur le sol raboteux traînait son blanc plumage.
Près d'un ruisseau sans eau la bête ouvrant le bec

Baignait nerveusement ses ailes dans la poudre,
Et disait, le cœur plein de son beau lac natal:
'Eau, quand donc pleuvras-tu? Quand tonneras-tu, foudre?'
Je vois ce malheureux, mythe étrange et fatal,

Vers le ciel quelquefois, comme l'homme d'Ovide,
Vers le ciel ironique et cruellement bleu,

Sur son cou convulsif tendant sa tête avide,
Comme s'il adressait des reproches à Dieu!

II

Paris change! Mais rien dans ma mélancolie
N'a bougé! palais neufs, échafaudages, blocs,
Vieux faubourgs, tout pour moi devient allégorie,
Et mes chers souvenirs sont plus lourds que des rocs.

Aussi devant ce Louvre une image m'opprime:
Je pense à mon grand cygne, avec des gestes fous,
Comme les exilés, ridicule et sublime,
Et rongé d'un désir sans trêve! et puis à vous,

Andromaque, des bras d'un grand époux tombée,
Vil bétail, sous la main du superbe Pyrrhus,
Auprès d'un tombeau vide en extase courbée;
Veuve d'Hector, hélas! Et femme d'Hélénus!

Je pense à la négresse, amaigrie et phtisique,
Piétinant dans la boue, et cherchant, l'oeil hagard,
Les cocotiers absents de sa superbe Afrique
Derrière la muraille immense du brouillard;

A quiconque a perdu ce qui ne se retrouve
Jamais, jamais! à ceux qui s'abreuvent de pleurs
Et tètent la Douleur comme une bonne louve!
Aux maigres orphelins séchant comme des fleurs!

Ainsi dans la forêt où mon esprit s'exile
Un vieux Souvenir sonne à plein souffle du cor!
Je pense aux matelots oubliés dans une île,
Aux captifs, aux vaincus! … à bien d'autres encor!

The poem begins with a thought that crosses the narrator's mind as he wanders through a monumental new square in Paris, the Place du Carrousel – the area between the two wings of the Louvre and the Carrousel Arch, which before 1852 had been a small warren of streets. He remembers the legendary figure of Andromache, the wife of the Trojan warrior Hector, who, when her husband was killed by Achilles and the ancient city of Troy destroyed, was taken prisoner and placed in exile by Achilles' son Pyrrhus. He remembers the square as part of the old Paris, before it was turned into a building site by Haussmann's workmen, seeing it vividly in his mind's eye, evoking it in detail, with its piles of rough-hewn shafts and capitals, its shacks, junk-shops and jumbled bric-a-brac. And he remembers a menagerie from which a swan had escaped.

Trying to find water in dried-up gutters, the swan longed for the lake of its birth. In part II of the poem the narrator returns to the present and to the image of a changed city. The elegiac tone is deepened and the links between the various elements of the first part – including the significant dedication to Victor Hugo, who was exiled in the Channel Islands for his opposition to the political regime of Napoleon III – become clearer. The narrator recalls once more Andromache (who would have been familiar to French readers through Racine's play *Andromaque*) and the swan, and then, through free association, other exiles of one kind or another: the consumptive black woman missing her native Africa, orphans, castaways, captives, political exiles, 'all those who've lost what they'll never ever regain!' The theme of exile is developed to become a meditation on the human condition. The second part of the poem is a single unified structure of thought, linked by the repeated 'I think', building up and widening its evocation of exile to include, in an infinitely expanding movement, every kind of loss and dispossession. In the last stanza he suggests that he too is in exile in 'the forest of [his] mind'.

In contrast to Victor Hugo, a public figure who spoke magisterially as a voice of political opposition from his self-imposed exile, Baudelaire writes from (and about) his position of exile and alienation *within* the modern city. The poet himself is an exile, swept up in the instability of the modern world, an instability that seems to prevent him from ever occupying a stable position within it. However, if the central motif of the poem is exile, its rhetorical and thematic structure is built on the processes of memory. At the centre of the poem stands the speaking subject: the 'I' who thinks, sees and remembers. The sound of the horn in the last stanza connotes melancholy and distress, but also the solemnity and hope of a heroic call. It is memory – the poet's own consciousness – that sounds the horn. What is suggested – and the suggestion is given affirmative emphasis through its placement in the last stanza – is that, in the face of evanescence and the fragmented experience of 'the real' that characterizes the city, it is poetic consciousness, and by implication language and the imagination, that offer a way, however problematic, of confronting the modern world.

Chapter 17

Flaubert: the narrator vanishes

From the point of view of pure Art, you could almost establish it as an axiom that the subject is irrelevant, style itself being an absolute way of seeing things.

— Flaubert, Letter to Louise Colet, 16 Jan. 1852

Gustave Flaubert (1821–80) was as influential in the field of fiction as Baudelaire was in poetry. His role in the evolution of the French novel is a subversive one. By shifting the novelist's emphasis from *representation* to *composition*, he began to undo the realist novel from within. His two great novels of contemporary life, *Madame Bovary* (1857) and *Sentimental Education* (*L'Éducation sentimentale*, 1869) adhere to a realist framework. They focus on mundane, antiheroic characters and contain an abundance of seemingly objective descriptions of settings and social milieus. What distinguishes Flaubert from Balzac and the 'realist' novelists of his own generation are his stylistic innovations and his self-consciousness as a writer. It is these aspects of his work that situate him on the dividing line between realism and the experimental writing of modernism, and account for his reputation as the creator of the 'modern' self-reflexive novel.

'What I would like to write,' Flaubert declared with provocative hyperbole, 'is a book about nothing, a book dependent on nothing external, which would be held together by the inner strength of its style' (letter to Louise Colet, 16 Jan. 1852). This statement indicates his ambition to give narrative prose the autonomy of stylization and the expressive qualities of poetry, and thereby to establish the novel as the dominant literary form of the nineteenth century. His narrative method has been called 'impersonal', by which is meant a kind of self-suppression by the author – an implicit repudiation of the Romantic notions of creative inspiration and intense self-expression. For Flaubert, the presence of the writer in his work should remain elusive. Whereas the narrator of a Balzac novel is overtly (and often ostentatiously) omniscient, Flaubert's stated ideal was a different kind of God-like narrator, one who would be 'present everywhere but visible nowhere' (9 Dec. 1852).

Meaning in Flaubert's fiction is suggested through the artificer's skill – through the precision of language, the rhythm of the sentences, the structures of the narrative (point of view, patterns of symbolic detail, multiple foreshadowings and echoes, ironic counterpoint, and so on). One of the chief aspects of his writing that works towards the creation of impersonality is the technique known as 'free indirect style' – a technique that makes it impossible to attribute a thought or perception either to the narrator or to a character. The character's thoughts and perceptions are presented as if they are part of the narrative. Free indirect style is closely connected, moreover, to the use of 'focalization' (narration from the point of view of a character); the narrative perspective is predominantly that of the protagonists, whose perceptions are accorded no 'objective' status. These uses of point of view lend themselves to an ironic presentation of character by emphasizing the subjective, relative and often self-deluding nature of experience. Emma Bovary, a country health officer's wife disillusioned with her marriage and frustrated by the dreariness of her environment, turns to adultery to fulfil her romantic dreams; like Don Quixote, she sees the world through the distorting prism of literature and bases her life on the fantasies of passion and happiness she has absorbed from her reading of popular romance. Ironically, *Madame Bovary*, considered a key text of realism, is about someone who takes books too seriously, who thinks of them as real. The strong reflexive tendency in Flaubert's writing is clear, inasmuch as one of his main themes is, precisely, the workings of the imagination.

Flaubert's ideal of impersonality reflects his intellectual attachment to the work of the scientists of his day – an attachment that anticipates Émile Zola's concept of the 'experimental novel'. For Flaubert, the domain of art was converging with that of science, and he equated descriptive scientific inquiry with the kind of objective, analytical writing to which he aspired. Baudelaire, in a perceptive review of *Madame Bovary* in *L'Artiste* on 18 October 1857, echoed Flaubert's view that art must be disinterested ('art for art's sake') – that it must rise above the direct expression of personal opinions, whether moralistic or not:

> A number of critics have said: this work, truly beautiful in the detail and liveliness of its descriptions, does not contain a single character who represents morality, who expresses the true thoughts of the author. Where is the proverbial and legendary character charged with explaining the story and guiding the reader's understanding? In other words, where is the indictment [i.e., of adultery]?
>
>   What rubbish! Eternal and incorrigible confusion of functions and genres! A true work of art need not contain an indictment. The logic of

the work satisfies all claims of morality, and it is up to the reader to draw his conclusions from the conclusion.

Flaubert refuses, indeed, to 'draw conclusions' for the reader. Indeterminacy of narrative voice corresponds to indeterminacy of meaning and theme. Irony suffuses Flaubert's writing both formally and thematically. Style *is* vision. Flaubert's central themes concern the gap between reality and dream, failures of perception, false ideals, the futility of action, the mediocrity and 'stupidity' of the modern world, the clichés that contaminate human thought and language. Much of his writing is sadly comic, as he evokes, in ways often reminiscent of Voltaire's *Candide*, what he sees as the absurdity of the human condition and the grotesque in human behaviour. But ironic detachment, in the case of Emma Bovary, is deeply marked by empathy. Much of the fascination and force of *Madame Bovary* lies in the tension it maintains between irony and sympathy. Emma, for all her foolishness and lack of discrimination, is capable of feelings and impulses that raise her above the mediocrity of her surroundings and the emptiness of those around her. Her abortive attempt to impose the imaginary on the real may even be read as an oblique reflection of Flaubert's own aesthetic aspirations – his anguished (and ultimately impossible) pursuit of a work of pure art. Art – or rather, as he wrote, the highest kind of art – remains for him the only value; it sets us dreaming, enabling us in our imagination to rise above the banality of existence (letter to Louise Colet, 26 August 1853).

Madame Bovary: a visit to a ball

Soon after their marriage, Emma and her husband Charles are invited to an annual ball given by a local landowner, the Marquis d'Andervilliers, at his château, La Vaubyessard. This episode (Part I, chapter 8) is a turning point in the novel, for it confirms Emma's feeling that a better world exists and that her marriage to Charles is responsible for her exclusion from it.

> The air in the ballroom was heavy; the lamps were growing dim. People were drifting back into the billiards room. A servant climbed on to a chair and broke two windowpanes; at the sound of breaking glass, Madame Bovary turned her head and noticed in the garden, against the window, the faces of peasants looking in. And the memory of Les Bertaux came back to her. She saw the farm again, the muddy pond, her father in his smock under the apple trees, and she saw herself as she used to be, skimming cream with her finger from the pans in the milk house.

But in the dazzling splendours of the present moment, her past life, so distinct until now, was vanishing altogether, and she almost doubted that she had ever lived it. She was here now; and, beyond the ball, there was nothing but darkness, spread out over all the rest. She was eating a maraschino ice, holding it with her left hand in a silver shell and half closing her eyes, the spoon between her teeth ...

At three o'clock in the morning, the cotillion began. Emma did not know how to waltz ... Nevertheless, one of the waltzers, whom they familiarly called *vicomte* and whose very low-cut waistcoat seemed moulded to his chest, came up to Madame Bovary and for the second time invited her to dance, assuring her that he would guide her and that she would manage perfectly well.

They began slowly, then went faster. They were turning: everything was turning around them, the lamps, the furniture, the panelled walls, the parquet floor, like a disk on a spindle. As they passed close to the doors, the hem of Emma's dress would catch against his trousers; their legs would slip in between one another; he lowered his gaze towards her, she raised hers to him; a numbness came over her, she stopped. They set off again; and, quickening the pace, the vicomte, drawing her along, disappeared with her to the far end of the gallery, where, gasping for breath, she nearly fell and, for a moment, rested her head on his chest. And then, still turning, but more slowly, he took her back to her seat; she leaned against the wall and put her hand over her eyes ...

Emma put a shawl over her shoulders, opened the window, and leaned out ...

The first light of dawn appeared. She gazed at the windows of the château for a long time, trying to guess which were the rooms of all those people she had observed during the evening. She would have liked to know what their lives were like, to enter into them, to become part of them.

But she was shivering with cold. She undressed and curled up between the sheets against Charles, who was asleep.

L'air du bal était lourd; les lampes pâlissaient. On refluait dans la salle de billard. Un domestique monta sur une chaise et cassa deux vitres; au bruit des éclats de verre, madame Bovary tourna la tête et aperçut dans le jardin, contre les carreaux, des faces de paysans qui regardaient. Alors le souvenir des Bertaux lui arriva. Elle revit la ferme, la mare bourbeuse, son père en blouse sous les pommiers, et elle se revit elle-même, comme autrefois, écrémant avec son doigt les terrines de lait dans la laiterie. Mais, aux fulgurations de l'heure présente, sa vie passée, si nette jusqu'alors, s'évanouissait tout entière, et elle doutait presque de l'avoir vécue. Elle était là; puis autour du bal, il n'y avait plus que de l'ombre, étalée sur tout le reste. Elle mangeait alors une glace au marasquin, qu'elle tenait de la main gauche dans une coquille de vermeil, et fermait à demi les yeux, la cuiller entre les dents …

A trois heures du matin, le cotillion commença. Emma ne savait pas valser … Cependant, un des valseurs, qu'on appelait familièrement *vicomte*, et dont le gilet très ouvert semblait moulé sur la poitrine, vint une seconde fois encore inviter madame Bovary, l'assurant qu'il la guiderait et qu'elle s'en tirerait bien.

Ils commencèrent lentement, puis allèrent plus vite. Ils tournaient; tout tournait autour d'eux, les lampes, les meubles, les lambris, et le parquet, comme un disque sur un pivot. En passant auprès des portes, la robe d'Emma, par le bas, s'éraflait au pantalon; leurs jambes entraient l'une dans l'autre; il baissait ses regards vers elle, elle levait les siens vers lui; une torpeur la prenait, elle s'arrêta. Ils repartirent; et, d'un mouvement plus rapide, le vicomte, l'entraînant, disparut avec elle jusqu'au bout de la galerie, où, haletante, elle faillit tomber, et, un instant, s'appuya la tête sur sa poitrine. Et puis, tournant toujours, mais plus doucement, il la reconduisit à sa place; elle se renversa contre la muraille et mit la main devant ses yeux …

Emma mit un châle sur ses épaules, ouvrit la fenêtre et s'accouda …

Le petit jour parut. Elle regarda les fenêtres du château, longuement, tâchant de deviner quelles étaient les chambres de tous ceux qu'elle avait remarqués la veille. Elle aurait voulu savoir leurs existences, y pénétrer, s'y confondre.

Mais elle grelottait de froid. Elle se déshabilla et se blottit entre les draps, contre Charles qui dormait.

The themes of this passage – dream, desire, reality/fantasy – are at the heart of the novel. Emma, who embodies unlimited desire, is confronted by a world that does not and will not conform to what she believes and wishes it to be. The mediocrity of her domestic life provokes her to 'sensual fantasies' (Part II, chapter 5), and her visit to the great house at La Vaubyessard introduces her to an aristocratic world where luxury seems taken for granted, where material desire – and, by extension, all desire – may, she imagines, be gratified with ease. The first paragraph is focused on the contrast in her mind between the real social world she inhabits – her life with her husband, which is a continuation of her past life on the farm, Les Bertaux, with her father – and the social world she can experience only fleetingly, in the sudden 'fulgurations' ('dazzling splendours') of this particular evening. The image of the peasants

in the garden, their faces pressed to the window (an image all the more striking because of the absence of commentary), provokes acute memories of the
farm. The prosaic images of the muddy pond and the cream she skimmed
from the milk in the dairy are contrasted with the delicate, exotic image of the
present moment – the silver shell – as, trance-like, she eats a maraschino ice,
savouring the sensuous feeling of the spoon between her teeth. The intensity
of the moment seems to obliterate her past ('she almost doubted she had lived
it'), casting into shadow everything beyond the magic circle of the ball. 'She
was here now': her fantasy of inclusion in a world from which, like the peasants outside, she is in reality excluded, is briefly satisfied. Her head, however,
is turned. The next two paragraphs, describing the girations of the waltz as
Emma and the vicomte move round the dance floor, at first slowly and then
more quickly, evoke her abandonment to the delight of being held and guided
by the masterful aristocrat – an experience of erotic excitement that makes her
dizzy, so that she nearly falls, and which, in the momentary freedom and exhilaration of its circular movement, is an ironic counterpoint to the imprisoning
circles of her real life: the deadly routines of domesticity and the frustration of
her marriage, which, as Tony Tanner notes, is symbolized by the circle of the
wedding ring. 'The problem, and the impossibility, of combining the thrilling
rotations of the waltz with the tedious repetitions implicit in the wedding
ring is ineradicably implanted in Emma's life with this particular experience
and further experience can only compound her sense of living among incompatible turnings' (Tanner, *Adultery in the Novel*, p. 300). Emma's imagined
glimpse of passion with the vicomte foreshadows her affairs with Rodolphe
and Léon, which will appear in part as degraded enactments of the aristocratic
fantasy.

The ball over, a sense of anti-climax is suggested when, a page later, she puts a
shawl over her shoulders and opens the window of the guest room in one wing
of the château. In a pointed reversal of perspective, she gazes out at the other
windows, her thoughts now tinged with melancholy as the idea of her exclusion
is given the triple emphasis of 'She would have liked to know what their lives
were like, to enter into them, to become part of them.' Her gaze rejoins, as
it were, that of the peasants at the window, as the time to leave the château
and return to her life at Tostes approaches. The sleeping Charles embodies
the world she really inhabits and, ultimately, cannot escape. After her return
home, her thoughts are frequently drawn back to La Vaubyessard. At the end
of the chapter, the day after the ball, we read: 'Her trip to La Vaubyessard had
made a hole in her life' ('Son voyage à la Vaubyessard avait fait un trou dans
sa vie'). In other words, the episode creates in her a sense of lack – desire for a

satisfaction that cannot be offered in reality. Time passes, but the anticipated second invitation to the château does not come.

The circle, the gaze, the window, the mirror. Scenes and details in *Madame Bovary* resonate in multiple ways, through repetition and variation, in the context of the novel as a whole. Just as the image of a circle recurs throughout the novel, so does the image of Emma gazing out from a window, expressing her frustrations and longings and the play of her imagination. In Tostes it is from her window that she watches the rain fall and contemplates the monotonous routines of the life of the village; from her window in Yonville she sees Léon and, for the first time, Rodolphe; from the window overlooking the garden she dreams of a life elsewhere; at the window of the town hall she looks down with Rodolphe on the agricultural fair and engages in a stilted dialogue that will lead to their fateful ride in the woods, which marks the beginning of their affair; at her attic window, having received the letter from Rodolphe that ends their relationship, she gazes down and is seized by the desire to end her life; at the opera in Rouen, seated in the metaphoric window of the box, she imagines that the drama of her own emotional life is being acted out on the stage below in the performance of Donizetti's *Lucia di Lamermoor* and loses herself in the pure theatricality of the romantic passions and gestures of the protagonists. Her ultimately fatal self-absorption is expressed in a remarkable scene when, following her seduction by Rodolphe, she gazes at herself in a mirror and repeats over and over: 'I have a lover! A lover!' The mirror reflects her fantasy of passion and ecstasy, but we already know that this is illusion. The mirror will tell the truth only when she is on her deathbed, having taken arsenic: 'she looked all around her, slowly, like someone waking from a dream; then, in a distinct voice, she asked for her mirror, and she remained bent over it for some time, until large tears ran down from her eyes' ('elle regarda tout autour d'elle, lentement, comme quelqu'un qui se reveille d'un songe, puis, d'une voix distincte, elle demanda son miroir, et elle resta penchée dessus quelque temps; jusqu'au moment où de grosses larmes lui découlèrent des yeux').

There is no trace of direct authorial commentary in the long passage quoted above, and yet, through its patterning and its resonances, Flaubert captures the rhythm and texture of Emma's feelings in a way that allows the reader to enter into her consciousness. The viewpoint is Emma's, yet the perspective conveyed goes beyond her vision of things. The reader, watching Emma watching, partakes of her sensibility but remains able to discern the stereotypes and illusions that inform, often poignantly, her view of the world. As Flaubert wrote to Louise Colet on 9 October 1852: 'Irony in no way detracts from pathos. On the contrary, it intensifies it.'

Sentimental Education: a visit to a brothel

Flaubert's *Sentimental Education* further unravels the Balzacian model of the novel. In Balzac an impulse towards fulfilment through action is central; in *Sentimental Education* the value of action, individual or collective, is radically undermined. Near the beginning of the novel, the protagonist, Frédéric Moreau, is actually enjoined by his friend Deslauriers to emulate Rastignac: 'Remember Rastignac.' But what ensues shows Frederic to be a kind of anti-Rastignac, passive and ineffectual. He studies law but fails to find a job in the legal profession; he dreams of becoming a writer or a painter, but his interest does not last; and his political ambitions come to nothing. Balzac's plots are purposeful, driven forward by the desire of the characters in their search for money and power; the plot of *Sentimental Education*, though full of incident, describes a discontinuous, meandering drift. Émile Zola, in a highly appreciative article on the novel in 1875, wrote: 'Gustave Flaubert rejected the idea of a central narrative line . . . No episodes carefully prepared and melded, but an apparently random collection of facts, an unexceptional sequence of ordinary occurrences, with characters meeting, separating, meeting again, until they fade away: just faces of passers-by jostling each other on a pavement.'

The indecisive, almost characterless Frédéric represents an entire generation and its failure to realize its dreams. Key moments in Frédéric's personal life are juxtaposed with historical events, but while Balzac linked private and public events to show the powerful agency of history and the individual's capacity to participate in it, the sentimental education of Frédéric and the doomed revolution of 1848 simply echo each other in their common failure. Frédéric remains a passive spectator of the tumultuous events taking place around him: street demonstrations; the revolution of February 1848, the sacking of the Tuileries palace by a mob, and the establishment of the French Second Republic; the eruption of political clubs across Paris; the insurrection of disillusioned workers in June 1848 and their violent suppression by the army and National Guard; and the *coup d'état* of Louis-Napoleon Bonaparte in December 1851. Flaubert's caustic, often comic portrayal of politics in *Sentimental Education* echoes the view of Karl Marx, who, comparing the *coup d'état* of Napoleon Bonaparte with that of his nephew, Louis-Napoleon, in *The Eighteenth Brumaire of Louis Bonaparte* (1852), commented that tragedy cannot be re-enacted by the bourgeoisie without being transformed into a farce. The chaos of the 1848 Revolution is summed up by the description of the political meeting at the splendidly named 'Club de l'Intelligence' in Part III. The Club is intended to be a forum for the debate of revolutionary ideas, and Frédéric goes there to seek support for his candidature in the elections; what ensues, however, is not a meaningful discussion but a babble of voices and incompatible opinions, culminating with the incomprehensible speech, in Spanish, of a comrade from Barcelona. He drowns out Frédéric, whose exasperated response leads to his ejection from the meeting.

Thematically, *Sentimental Education* is an ironic subversion of the *Bildungsroman* form exemplified in a novel like Balzac's *Old Goriot*. Whereas the whole conception of Rastignac's journey from the provinces to Paris, and his experience in the city, implies confidence in the perfect intelligibility of the world and is structured round discovery of the 'laws' that govern social life, Frédéric, at the end of his journey, has learnt nothing. His attempts to find meaning in experience dissolve into ironic inconsequentiality, and the novel eventually closes with Frédéric and Deslauriers, now middle-aged, musing vacantly over their past lives. Here are the novel's closing sentences:

> Frédéric presented his flowers, like a lover to his betrothed. But the heat, the fear of the unknown, a sort of remorse, and even the very pleasure of seeing at a single glance so many women at his disposal, disturbed him so much that he turned deathly pale, and stood rooted to the spot, speechless. The girls all burst out laughing, amused at his embarrassment; thinking they were making fun of him, he fled, and since Frédéric had the money, Deslauriers had no choice but to follow him.
>
> They were seen coming out. This caused quite a stir and was still remembered three years later.
>
> They told one another the story at great length, each filling in the gaps in the other's memory; and when they had finished:
>
> 'That was the best time we ever had!' said Frédéric.
>
> 'Yes, perhaps you're right. That was the best time we ever had!' said Deslauriers.

> Frédéric présenta [son bouquet], comme un amoureux à sa fiancée. Mais la chaleur qu'il faisait, l'appréhension de l'inconnu, une espèce de remords, et jusqu'au plaisir de voir, d'un seul coup d'œil, tant de femmes à sa disposition, l'émurent tellement, qu'il devint très pale et restait sans avancer, sans rien dire. Toutes riaient, joyeuses de son embarras; croyant qu'on s'en moquait, il s'enfuit; et, comme Frédéric avait l'argent, Deslauriers fut bien obligé de le suivre.
>
> On les vit sortir. Cela fit une histoire, qui n'était pas oubliée trois ans après.
>
> Ils se la contèrent prolixement, chacun complétant les souvenirs de l'autre; et, quand ils eurent fini:

– 'C'est là ce que nous avons eu de meilleur!' dit Frédéric.
– 'Oui, peut-être bien? C'est là ce que nous avons eu de meilleur!' dit Deslauriers.

The novel's epilogue cancels out the characters' future retrospectively, as it were, for what the two friends remember as the best time they ever had is an episode – their abortive visit as schoolboys to the local brothel – that occurred several years before the novel actually begins, as if everything that takes place during the intervening period signifies nothing.

Chapter 18

Zola: the poetry of the real

> I have an obsession with authentic detail; the springboard of
> precise observation makes possible the leap into the stars.
>
> – Zola, Letter to Henry Céard, 22 March 1885

Unlike Flaubert, the 'hermit of Croisset', who turned away from his age in an attitude of ironic detachment, Émile Zola (1840–1902) embraced his century in a way no French writer had done since Balzac. Zola's ambition was to emulate Balzac by writing a comprehensive history of contemporary society. His main achievement was his twenty-volume novel cycle, *Les Rougon-Macquart*, published between 1871 and 1893. The fortunes of a family, the Rougon-Macquart, are followed over several decades. The various family members spread throughout all levels of society, and through their lives Zola examines methodically the social, sexual and moral landscape of the late nineteenth century. Zola is the quintessential novelist of modernity, understood as a time of tumultuous change. The motor of change was the rapid expansion of capitalism, with all that that entailed in terms of the altered shapes of the city, new forms of social practice and economic organization, and heightened political pressures. Zola was fascinated by change, and specifically by the emergence of a new, mass society.

Zola rejected much of the social and moral content of the bourgeois worldview, but he retained the central epistemological tenet on which it was based: 'scientific' objectivity. Converted from a youthful romantic idealism to realism in art and literature, he began promoting a scientific view of literature inspired by the aims and methods of experimental medicine. He called this new form of realism 'naturalism'. The subtitle of the Rougon-Macquart cycle, 'A Natural and Social History of a Family under the Second Empire', suggests Zola's two interconnected aims: to use fiction to demonstrate a number of 'scientific' notions about the ways in which human behaviour is determined by heredity and environment; and to use the symbolic possibilities of a family whose heredity is tainted to represent a diseased society – the corrupt yet dynamic France of the Second Empire (1852–70). The 'truth' for which Zola aimed could only be attained, he argued, through meticulous documentation and research; the work of the novelist represented a form of practical sociology, complementing the work of the scientist, whose hope was to change the world not by judging it but by understanding its 'laws'.

At the heart of Zola's naturalism is a concern with integrity of represen- tation. For Zola this meant a commitment to the idea that literature has a social function: to represent the sorts of things that preoccupy people in their daily lives. Industrialization, the growth of the cities, the birth of consumer culture, the condition of the working class, crime, prostitution, the misdeeds of government – these were the issues that concerned Zola; and he wrote about them not simply forensically, as a would-be scientist, but ironically and satirically. Naturalist fiction represents a major assault on bourgeois morality and institutions. The last line of Zola's novel *The Belly of Paris* (*Le Ventre de Paris*, 1873) is: 'Respectable people... What bastards!' ('Quels gredins que les honnêtes gens!').

But although Zola was in many ways a subversive writer, he was not a socialist. His work contains many contradictory strains; indeed, part of his abiding significance lies in the ways in which he articulated the contradictions of his time. The critical controversies surrounding his working-class texts reflect ambiguities in the texts themselves. For Zola, the power of mass working-class movements was a radically new element in human history, and it aroused in him an equivocal mixture of sympathy and unease. *L'Assommoir* (1877) and *Germinal* (1885) create a sense of humanitarian warmth and tragic pathos in their portrayal of the downtrodden, but Zola shows no solidarity with those who propound radical social and economic solutions. Similarly, in his treatment of sex and marriage, Zola broke the mould of Victorian moral cant; but on the other hand, he admired the bourgeois family ideal. The *bête noire* of the bourgeoisie was a moralist who believed deeply in the traditional bourgeois virtues of self-discipline, hard work and moderation.

Scientific observation and poetic vision

Zola's 'scientific' representation of society is informed by a vast amount of ded- icated first-hand observation, note-taking and research – in the great markets of Paris, Les Halles (*The Belly of Paris*), the slums (*L'Assommoir*), the depart- ment stores (*The Ladies' Paradise/Au Bonheur des Dames*, 1883), the coal fields (*Germinal*, 1885), the railways (*La Bête humaine*, 1890), etc. Zola combines the approach of a reporter with the vision of a painter in his observation of particular milieus and modes of life. His fiction acquires its power, however, not from its ethnographic richness but from its imaginative qualities. In his narrative practice, he combines brilliantly the particular and the general, the individual and the mass, the everyday and the fantastic. His various narrative worlds, with their specific atmospheres, are always presented through the eyes of individuals and are never separate from human experience. The interaction between people and their environments is evoked in his celebrated physical descriptions. These descriptions are not, however, mechanical products of his aesthetic credo; rather, they express the very meaning, and ideological tendencies, of his narratives. Consider, for example, the lengthy descriptions of the luxurious physical décor of bourgeois existence – houses, interiors, social gatherings – in *The Kill* (*La Curée*, 1872). The main syntactic characteristic of these passages is the eclipse of human subjects by abstract nouns and things, suggesting the absence of any controlling human agency and expressing a vision of a society which, organized under the aegis of the commodity, turns people into objects. Similarly, the descriptions of the sales in *The Ladies' Paradise*, with their cascading images and rising pitch, suggest loss of control, the female shoppers' quasi-sexual abandonment to consumer dreams, at the same time mirroring the perpetual expansion that defines the economic principles of consumerism. The observed reality of the world is the foundation for a poetic vision.

The originality of Zola's fiction lies in its remarkable symbolizing effects. Emblematic features of contemporary life – the market, the machine, the tenement building, the laundry, the mine, the apartment house, the department store, the stock exchange, the city itself – are used as giant symbols of the society of his day. Zola sees allegories of contemporary life everywhere. In *The Ladies' Paradise*, the department store is emblematic of the new dream world of consumer culture and of the changes in sexual attitudes and class relations taking place at the time. Through the play of imagery and metaphor, Zola magnifies the material world, giving it a hyperbolic, hallucinatory quality. We think of Saccard, the protagonist of *The Kill*, swimming in a sea of gold coins, an image that aptly evokes his activities as a speculator; the fantastic visions of food in *The Belly of Paris*; the still in *L'Assommoir*, oozing with poisonous alcohol; Nana's mansion, like a vast vagina, swallowing up men and their fortunes; the devouring pithead in *Germinal*, lit by strange fires, rising spectrally out of the darkness.

Realist representation is imbued with mythic resonance; reality is transfigured into a theatre of archetypal forces. The pithead in *Germinal* is a modern figuration of the Minotaur, a monstrous beast that breathes, devours, digests and regurgitates. Heredity not only serves as a structuring device, analogous to Balzac's use of recurring characters, but also has great dramatic force, allowing Zola to give a mythical dimension to his representation of the human condition. For Balzac, money and ambition were the mainsprings of human conduct; for Zola, human conduct is determined by heredity and environment, and they pursue his characters as relentlessly as the forces of fate in an ancient tragedy. His use of myth is inseparable from his vision of history and is essentially Darwinian. His conception of society is shaped by a biological model informed by the struggle between the life instinct and the death instinct, the forces of creation and destruction. This vision is marked by an ambivalence characteristic of modernity itself. Despite his faith in science, Zola's vision is marked by the anxiety that accompanied industrialization and modernity. The demons of modernity are figured in images of catastrophe: the pithead in *Germinal*, the runaway train in *La Bête humaine*. Zola's naturalist world is an entropic world, in which nature inevitably reverts to a state of chaos, despite human efforts to create order and to dominate its course; but there is also emphasis on regeneration, on collapse being part of a larger cycle of integration and disintegration. Zola's work always turns towards hope, as the title of *Germinal* implies.

Social class

In 1876 Zola published in serial form his first novel of working-class life, *L'Assommoir*, which describes the social and moral degradation of that class in contemporary Paris. The novel focuses on the life and death of a washerwoman, Gervaise Macquart. It was hugely successful, and it was also scandalous: the serialization of the novel was stopped by the government, and several bourgeois critics noisily accused Zola of pornography. These violently hostile reactions to *L'Assommoir*, together with the novel's immense success, indicated that something significantly new had happened to the novel. In 1877, when the novel appeared in book form, Zola added a preface in response to the storm of controversy the novel had provoked. He characterized *L'Assommoir* as 'a work of truth, the first novel about the common people which does not tell lies but has the authentic smell of the people' ('une œuvre de vérité, le premier roman sur le people, qui ne mente pas et qui ait l'odeur du peuple').

To understand the reasons for the scandal that surrounded the publication of *L'Assommoir*, and its success, we need to consider how the novel undermined the expectations of its contemporary readership. The novel in France was essentially a bourgeois genre, having developed in tandem with the bourgeoisie's political and material rise. It depended on a largely bourgeois readership and was shaped by a bourgeois ideology of literary propriety. Conservative critics clearly considered that Zola had transgressed the limits of what could be written about. To focus entirely on urban workers was itself new and disturbing, and to make a working-class washerwoman a tragic heroine even more so. If the workers could take over the novel, perhaps they could also take over the government; the trauma of the Commune of 1871, when the people of Paris had repudiated their national government and set up their own, was still fresh in people's minds. What also greatly disturbed bourgeois critics was Zola's unflinching realism, the sheer force and candour of his representation of slum life. What disoriented contemporary readers most, however, was not the subject matter of *L'Assommoir*, but its style: its use of working-class language and urban slang. The workers are intrusively present – they can be 'smelt' – in the very language of *L'Assommoir*. During the course of the narrative, popular speech is not simply sprinkled throughout the text but becomes the medium of narration. It is as if the characters themselves take on a narrative function, telling their own story. The language of the characters is absorbed by the (traditionally 'bourgeois') narrator without quotation marks, as if the novel were spoken via the collective voice of the Goutte-d'Or district, using the lexicon and syntax of the street.

Zola achieved this effect by use of a special form of the technique known as free indirect style (see above, p. 123). His brilliant ability to capture popular speech patterns, even when writing indirectly, reflects his powers of empathy, a capacity for evoking the workers' own vision of the world; and it also has significant ideological implications. Not only are the expectations associated with conventional bourgeois narrative disrupted, but the reader is also brought into more direct and authentic contact with the characters and their culture, their attitudes and values, than would have been the case had these been relayed exclusively by means of direct speech and conventional dialogue. It was his bold experiment with style that, according to Zola, explained why his bourgeois readers had been so upset. His 'great crime', as he wrote in his preface, was to have shown that the novel is not an intrinsically bourgeois genre tied to bourgeois discourse.

The novel's central chapter (chapter 7) describes Gervaise's celebration of her saint's day with a Rabelaisian feast where food, drink and companionship are the focus. The doors and windows are opened and the whole neighbourhood is invited to join in the merrymaking. The feast is a pivotal episode, marking the high point of Gervaise's professional success, but also a turning point in her fortunes. The sheer extravagance of the feast suggests the lurking dangers of dissipation, and the occasion also marks the fateful return of Lantier, Gervaise's malevolent former lover. Above all, the extravagance of the feast expresses defiance, through recklessness and prodigality, of the constrictions – the prudence and thrift – of a life always on the edge of starvation. The workers' plight is expressed through the very description of their pleasure: 'The whole shop was dying for a binge. They needed an absolute blow-out' ('Toute la boutique avait une sacrée envie de nocer. Il fallait une rigolade à la mort'). The meal becomes an orgy, and the mounting excitement of the characters is matched by that of the narrative voice, which appears to blend joyously with the voices of the assembled company:

> God, yes, they really stuffed themselves! If you're going to do it, you might as well do it properly, eh? And if you only have a real binge once in a blue moon, you'd be bloody mad not to fill yourself up to the eyeballs. You could actually see their bellies getting bigger by the minute! The women looked as if they were pregnant. Every one of 'em fit to burst, the greedy pigs! Their mouths wide-open, grease all over their chins, their faces were just like backsides, and so red you'd swear they were rich people's backsides, with money pouring out of them.
>
> And the wine, my friends! The wine flowed around the table like the water in the Seine.

> Ah! nom de Dieu! oui, on s'en flanqua une bosse! Quand on y est, on y est, n'est-ce pas? et si l'on ne se paie qu'un gueuleton par-ci par là, on serait joliment godiche de ne pas s'en fourrer jusqu'aux oreilles. Vrai, on voyait les bedons se gonfler à mesure. Les dames étaient grosses. Ils pétaient dans leur peau, les sacrés goinfres! La bouche ouverte, le menton barbouillé de graisse, ils avaient des faces pareilles à des derrières, et si rouges, qu'on aurait dit des derrières de gens riches, crevant de prospérité.
>
> Et le vin, donc, mes enfants ! ça coulait autour de la table comme l'eau coule à la Seine.

The past definite tense used in the first sentence ('on s'en flanqua une bosse!') clearly identifies the passage as a part of the narrative, but the register and syntax – direct, simple, robustly colloquial – reflect the language of the characters. The characters' colloquial language is woven into the fabric of the narrative, absorbing the written discourse of the narrator. The use of *on* in the original ('et si l'on . . . ') is ambiguous (they? we?), blurring further the distinction between narrator and characters. A single voice dominates. The jovial apostrophe 'my friends!', its author and addressees uncertain, draws the reader into sharing in the general euphoria. The narrator sits at the table with his characters, participating stylistically in the revelry and implicitly inviting the reader to join in too, thus subverting the moralistic perspectives on the workers' intemperance that so strongly marked contemporary discourse on social issues and contemporary reactions to the novel. Is it because Gervaise is self-indulgent and given to excess that she undergoes the tragedy of working people? Or is it because she undergoes the tragedy of working people that she becomes self-indulgent and given to excess?

The critical debate surrounding *L'Assommoir*, both at the time of the novel's appearance and afterwards, involved what might be called a politics of representation. The fact that the urban proletariat were considered by the bourgeoisie to be beyond the limits of narrative, beneath the level of narrative representation, was held implicitly to justify their exclusion from political representation. The strident attacks on *L'Assommoir* for pornography were motivated as much by reactionary fear as by prudishness; and the attacks Zola sustained thoughout his career for vulgarity, tastelessness, stylistic crudity and a purported obsession with the filthy underside of society were largely political in nature – attempts by the Establishment to discredit him.

Eight years after *L'Assommoir*, Zola published *Germinal*. Through his description of a miners' strike, he evokes the awakening of the workers' political consciousness. He depicts how torpid resignation is slowly transformed into conscious awareness, and how the miners begin to see themselves as active subjects capable of creating their own history. In *L'Assommoir* Zola had used narrative technique to make articulate the inarticulate, to make us see and hear the world through the workers' eyes and voices. In *Germinal*, he does something similar; however, in the later novel he also depicts a moment in history when the workers find a political voice.

The body and sex

Zola's social and sexual themes intersect at many points. In his sexual themes he ironically subverts the notion that bourgeois supremacy over the workers is a natural rather than a cultural phenomenon; he exposes as myth the reactionary bourgeois supposition that they, unlike the workers, are able to control their natural instincts and that their social supremacy is therefore justified. Adultery among the bourgeoisie was thus much more significant than among the working class because, as transgressors of their own law, the bourgeoisie put at risk an order of civilization structured to sustain their own privileged position. The more searchingly Zola investigated the theme of adultery, the more he risked uncovering the arbitrariness and fragility of the whole bourgeois social order.

In *Pot Luck* (*Pot-Bouille*, 1882) Zola lifted the lid on the realities of bourgeois mores, exposing the hypocrisy of the dominant class, who are no more able to control their natural instincts than the workers, but are simply more dissimulating. The bourgeois go to extreme lengths to maintain the segregation between themselves and the lower classes, whom they insistently portray as dirty, immoral, promiscuous, stupid – at best a lesser type of human, at worst some kind of wild beast. But class difference is shown to be merely a matter of money and power, tenuously holding down the raging forces of sexuality and corruption beneath the surface. We are left with a kind of stew, a melting-pot, a world where no clear boundaries remain.

Zola's naturalism, with its emphasis on integrity of representation, entailed a new explicitness in the depiction of sexuality. Zola broke with academic convention to a degree hitherto unseen in literature. *Nana*, for example, represented a drastic advance towards erotic verisimilitude. The novel's opening scene dramatizes this stripping away of cultural shields as Nana (who is the daughter of Gervaise in *L'Assommoir*) appears with progressively less clothing on the stage of a variety theatre. The theatre functions in *Nana* as a symbiosis of the themes of capitalism and sexuality, in its dual role as theatre and figurative brothel. It is the place where different classes meet and where the actress/prostitute Nana can display her wares, her body, in her role as Venus. This house of ill repute, which holds within its walls people from all walks of life and social stations, presents *risqué* parodies of classical myths as well as other bawdy comedies. Nana's first appearance as Venus prefigures her future as a 'man-eater', for after this performance she becomes the object of desire of every man in the audience. The theatre in *Nana* is a centre of capitalist commerce of the flesh, symbolizing the decadence and hypocrisy of Second Empire society. Theatre is the essence of the world Nana embodies. In her mansion, doors open and close, and men enter unexpectedly, having to be hidden by the maid. Nana's power extends to men of all social strata; she devastates the lives of aristocrats, bankers, journalists and government officials. The power of sex reverses class hierarchies, converting the oppressor into the oppressed.

The public writer

Zola opened up the novel to entirely new areas of experience and representation. He broke taboos. It was entirely appropriate that, in 1898, he crowned his literary career with a political act, 'J'accuse . . . !', his famous open letter to the President of the Republic in defence of Alfred Dreyfus, the Jewish army officer falsely accused of spying for Germany. Zola's courageous stand in the affair – squarely in the tradition of Voltaire and Victor Hugo, and anticipating the work of writers like Sartre and Camus in the twentieth century – showed the public writer at his best. By the time of 'J'accuse...!', French public opinion was polarized, not simply on the question of Dreyfus's innocence or guilt but on the future of the Republic itself. Zola's key strategy in his address to the jury at the time of his trial for libel in connection with the publication of 'J'accuse...!' was to present the unjust condemnation of Dreyfus as an aberration from the true Republic of 1789 and its principles of liberty and justice. Condemned to imprisonment for one year, Zola, like Hugo before him, went into exile, in England. The day after his sentence the League of the Rights of Man was founded. The Dreyfus affair was of seminal importance in relation to the unique role French intellectuals were destined to play on the world stage in the twentieth century as a result of the historical legacy of the Revolution.

Zola died in September 1902, poisoned by carbon monoxide fumes from a blocked chimney. There has been a great deal of speculation that he was in fact murdered by an anti-Dreyfusard working on the roof. Foul play? We don't know. But we do know that 50,000 people turned out for his funeral, including a delegation of miners from Anzin, who chanted 'Germinal! Germinal! Germinal!' as they followed his hearse through the streets to the cemetery at Montmartre.

Chapter 19

Huysmans: against nature

Against Nature fell like a meteorite into the literary fairground and there
was astonishment and fury . . .

— Huysmans, Preface (1903) to *Against Nature*

Joris-Karl Huysmans (1848–1907) began his literary career as a disciple of
Zola, writing naturalist fiction: *Marthe* (*Marthe, histoire d'une fille,* 1876); *The
Vatard Sisters* (*Les Sœurs Vatard,* 1879); 'Knapsack' ('Sac au dos' in *Les Soirées
de Médan,* 1880); *Living Together* (*En ménage,* 1881). But the publication of
Against Nature (*À rebours,* 1884) marked a deliberate break with naturalism,
whose positivist assumptions Huysmans had come to find increasingly uncon-
genial.[1] A startlingly original novel, *Against Nature* epitomizes Decadence,
which was the dominant aesthetic of the *fin-de-siècle.* The novel's protagonist,
a rich, neurotic aristocrat, the Duc Jean Floressas des Esseintes, seeks to escape
from the mediocrity of contemporary society, the capitalist and consumerist
society of the bourgeoisie, by withdrawing into a world of his own making,
dedicated to realizing his private fantasies and pleasures. He attempts to create
for himself an artificial paradise by living life 'à rebours' ('back to front' or
'against nature'), thus carrying to the point of psychopathology the vision of
his master, Baudelaire, who initiated the Decadent obsession with the artificial
and the perverse, and argued that the aim of literature and art was not to
imitate nature but to negate it.

The Decadent dandy

The Baudelairean *flâneur,* of which the dandy was the most flamboyant incar-
nation, attempts to avoid the ultimate terror of contemporary existence: *ennui.*
The emergence of dandyism in France was a response to the rise of the bourgeoisie and the triumph of bourgeois culture. In a society that proclaimed the
virtues of utility, work and thrift, the dandy rejected these values as vulgar.
For Baudelaire, in 'The Painter of Modern Life', dandyism was an attempt to

create a new aristocracy, not by reasserting the superiority of the upper classes over the lower classes, but by setting the individual against the common herd. Fundamentally out of step with the rhythms of modern life, the dandy sought to convey the impression of the man of leisure, ambling unhurriedly through the streets of the city. The self-styled aristocrat of the pavement, the dandy asserts his individuality through the cultivation of *style*, seeking theatrically to create novelty and excitement in a metropolitan environment that frustrates him. The *flâneur*-dandy resists both uniformity of dress and uniformity of motion. He flaunts two precious commodities: expensive clothing and time. The greatest desire of the *flâneur*-dandy is to stand out in the crowd, to retain his individuality while all around are losing theirs. Rejecting the values of the marketplace in favour of the higher values embodied in art and literature, the dandy represents pure artifice.

Des Esseintes takes dandyism to an end point of eccentricity. *Against Nature* represents in Des Esseintes an extreme form of psychological alienation. It is now not society that rejects the artist but the artist who rejects society. Des Esseintes's individualism takes the form of the solitary cultivation of personal lifestyle at the expense of public and social interaction. Having sold his residence in Paris, he withdraws to a house in the country, at Fontenay, and surrounds himself with ever more arcane pleasures: a library of rare books; exotic flowers that resemble artificial ones; a tortoise whose shell he gilds to match the décor, then encrusts with precious stones. He decorates his bedroom to resemble a monk's cell with the most luxurious furnishings, has a fake ship's cabin in his dining room, complete with sea water and mechanical fish, and gives a funeral banquet at which black food is served on black dishes by naked black girls. He attempts to create a world in which he will play all the parts: producer and consumer, *poseur* and public, actor and audience. He revels in the pure subjectivity of experiences – reflecting the Decadent obsession with the mind and the exercise of willpower over one's environment. Nature and artifice are transposed, imagination substituted for reality.

With Baudelaire the paradoxes of dandyism became increasingly apparent. For all his defiance of convention, the dandy can only affirm and measure his existence through the expressions on others' faces. The dandy is a fundamentally theatrical being, dependent on the audience he professes to disdain. In order to be a dandy, one must be seen; and visual dependency complements the dandy's dependence on the economic system he also disdains. Baudelaire concluded that, in order to have money for material elegance, the dandy needed infinite credit, since the alternative was to stoop to a bourgeois preoccupation with earning money. In any case, the dandy could not avoid the marketplace, since he was himself a consumer. The idea of dandyism as a spiritual ideal was belied by the materiality and corporeality inherent in the fact that the chief signs of the dandy's superiority were dress, possessions and personal habits. Des Esseintes's mania for collecting out-of-fashion objects reflects his rejection of the fashions of society; the very nature of the Decadent dandy requires him to seek out that which is rare and unusual. However, his attempt to create an authentic style of consumption uncontaminated by the marketplace is doomed. The market is constantly catching up with Des Esseintes by turning rarities into commonplaces through mass production. And nature, pushed beyond its limits, reasserts itself. The gilded tortoise is so over-embellished that it dies; the exotic plants die from neglect; and Des Esseintes himself almost dies, developing ever more extraordinary allergies and ailments as he continues to live his life against the grain of social and natural law. On a symbolic level, the conflict between Des Esseintes's self and the world takes the form of a conflict between mind and body; and the most obvious source of the disintegration of Des Esseintes's dream world is his own mortality, the deterioration of his health, which eventually causes him to return, on his doctor's orders, to the Paris he despises. Having left the world to protect his mental health, he is forced to return to it to ensure his physical survival. Nature has the last laugh, compelling Des Esseintes to abandon unsustainable artifice and return to the real world.

A journey

Before his recognition of ultimate defeat, however, Des Esseintes decides to go on a journey. The more he devotes himself to exploring, in a vacuum, the world of his own psyche, the worse his nervous state becomes. The solitude he had longed for and finally obtained at his retreat in Fontenay now feels like a form of imprisonment. He is now consumed by a longing for human contact, a need to be part of ordinary life. The novels of Dickens, which he has recently read to calm his nerves, have the opposite effect, and arouse in him an overwhelming desire to visit London to check the accuracy of the visions generated by his reading. He imagines the city as a monstrous metropolis, a terrible world of commerce, swarming with activity. Excited at already feeling part of this world, he travels back to Paris with the intention of taking the train to London. On his arrival in Paris, he visits a bookshop and immerses himself in a collection of guide books. He buys a Baedeker and visits a wine bar where the swarms of English people remind him of characters and scenes from Dickens; he imagines that the hootings of the tugs by the bridge behind the Tuileries are coming from boats on the Thames. Coming back to reality and to the foul weather, and beginning to feel hungry, he leaves the bar and settles down in an English-style tavern in the rue d'Amsterdam, near the Gare Saint-Lazare. He studies the Englishmen and women around him and is struck by their voracious appetites. The sight of their gorging brings back his own appetite, which he had lost long ago. Having eaten and drunk copiously, he begins to feel a kind of naturalized Londoner. However, meditating on his plans, his thoughts turn to another trip he once made to Holland and which, because it failed to live up to the expectations created by the paintings of the Dutch Masters he had seen at the Louvre, left him utterly disillusioned. London, too, he now realizes, cannot live up to his imaginings and bring him what he is looking for. Why travel at all, he asks himself, when one can be transported anywhere while sitting in one's armchair? Reality can only disappoint: the only satisfying journey is a journey into the self. He thus decides to go home to Fontenay.

The description of this aborted trip encapsulates the main themes of the novel, not only expressing Des Esseintes's preference for subjective imagining over actual experience but also echoing his first departure from the world and foreshadowing his ultimate defeat. The episode occupies the whole of chapter 11. The following passage is taken from the end of that chapter.

> Once more he consulted his watch: there were only ten minutes now before his train was due to leave . . .
>
> At that moment the door of the tavern opened and some people came in, bringing with them a wet doggy smell mingled with coal fumes which the wind blew back into the kitchen to the banging of the unlatched door; Des Esseintes felt incapable of moving his legs; a pleasant feeling of warmth and lassitude was seeping into every limb, so that he could not even lift his hand to light a cigar. 'Come on, man, on your feet, you've got to hurry,' he kept telling himself; but these orders were no sooner given than countermanded. After all, what was the point of moving, when one could travel so magnificently by sitting in a chair? Wasn't he already in London, whose smells, weather, citizens, food and even kitchen utensils, were all around him? What could he expect to find over there, except fresh disappointments such as he had suffered in Holland?
>
> He had just enough time to run across to the station, but an immense aversion for the journey, an urgent longing to remain where he was, came over him with ever greater force and intensity. Lost in thought, he let the minutes slip by, thus cutting off his retreat. 'If I went now,' he said to himself, 'I would have to dash up to the barrier and deal with all my luggage in a great rush. What a bore! How tiresome that would be!' And once again he told himself: 'Really, I've seen and experienced everything I wanted to see and experience. I've been steeped in English life ever

since I left home, and it would be madness to risk spoiling such unforgettable impressions by a clumsy change of locality. I must have been suffering from some mental aberration to have thought of renouncing my old convictions, to have rejected the visions of my compliant imagination and to have believed, like an absolute simpleton, that it was necessary, interesting and useful to go on a trip.' He looked at his watch. 'Time to go home,' he said; and this time he managed to get to his feet, left the tavern and told the cab driver to drive him back to the station at Sceaux, from where he returned to Fontenay with his trunks, his packages, his portmanteaux, his rugs, his umbrellas and his sticks, feeling as physically exhausted and mentally depleted as a man who had come home after a long and perilous journey.

Il consulta de nouveau sa montre: dix minutes le séparaient encore de l'heure du train...

A ce moment, la porte de la taverne s'ouvrit; des gens entrèrent apportant avec eux une odeur de chien mouillé à laquelle se mêla une fumée de houille, rabattue par le vent dans la cuisine dont la porte sans loquet claqua; des Esseintes était incapable de remuer les jambes; un doux et tiède anéantissement se glissait par tous ses membres, l'empêchait même d'étendre la main pour allumer un cigare. Il se disait: Allons, voyons, debout, il faut filer; et d'immédiates objections contrariaient ses ordres. A quoi bon bouger, quand on peut voyager si magnifiquement sur une chaise? N'était-il pas à Londres dont les senteurs, dont l'atmosphère, dont les habitants, dont les pâtures, dont les ustensiles, l'environnaient? Que pouvait-il donc espérer, sinon de nouvelles désillusions, comme en Hollande?

Il n'avait plus que le temps de courir à la gare, et une immense aversion pour le voyage, un impérieux besoin de rester tranquille s'imposaient avec une volonté de plus en plus accusée, de plus en plus tenace. Pensif, il laissa s'écouler les minutes, se coupant ainsi la retraite, se disant: Maintenant il faudrait se précipiter aux guichets, se bousculer aux bagages; quel ennui! Quelle corvée ça serait! – Puis, se répétant, une fois de plus: En somme, j'ai éprouvé et j'ai vu ce que je voulais éprouver et voir. Je suis saturé de vie anglaise depuis mon départ; il faudrait être fou pour aller perdre, par un maladroit déplacement, d'impérissables sensations. Enfin quelle aberration ai-je donc eue pour avoir tenté de renier des idées anciennes, pour avoir condamné les dociles fantasmagories de ma cervelle, pour avoir, ainsi qu'un véritable béjaune, cru à la nécessité, à la curiosité, à l'intérêt d'une excursion? – Tiens, fit-il, regardant sa montre, mais l'heure est venue de rentrer au logis; cette fois, il se dressa sur ses jambes, sortit, commanda au cocher de le reconduire à la gare de Sceaux, et il revint avec ses malles, ses paquets,

> ses valises, ses couvertures, ses parapluies et ses cannes, à Fontenay,
> ressentant l'éreintement physique et la fatigue morale d'un homme qui
> rejoint son chez soi, après un long et périlleux voyage.

While representing a powerful current of late nineteenth-century thought and sensibility, both expressing Decadent ideology and reflecting on its failure, *Against Nature* embodies a radical move towards a reflexive form of fiction. Its focus on the self points to the novelistic experiments of Proust; its 'black humour' and spirit of negation were greatly admired by the Surrealists (André Breton's novel *Nadja* begins with a homage to Huysmans as a master of the anti-novel); and Des Esseintes is an archetypal prefiguration of the alienated heroes of existentialist fiction.

Chapter 20

Mallarmé: the magic of words

The pure work implies the elocutionary disappearance of the poet, who leaves the initiative to words.

– Mallarmé, 'Crisis in Verse'

The reader of Huysmans's *Against Nature* learns that the favourite writer of the novel's aesthete hero, Des Esseintes, is the famously enigmatic poet Stéphane Mallarmé (1842–98). Mallarmé returned the compliment, so to speak, with his famous hermetic poem 'Prose pour des Esseintes' (1885). Just as Des Esseintes flees modern life by withdrawing into a world of his own making, the poetry (in both verse and prose) of Mallarmé is based on an aesthetic ideal of self-containment. Central to Mallarmé's poetic principles is his vision of a 'pure work of art' (letter to François Coppée, 20 April 1868) independent of the world outside it – either the life of the author or the society in which the author lives. He dreamed, as he wrote to his fellow poet Paul Verlaine (1844–96), of 'a Text [that] would speak of and by itself, without the voice of an author' (letter dated 16 November 1885). 'The pure work,' he states in 'Crisis in Verse' ('Crise de vers', 1897), 'implies the elocutionary disappearance of the poet, who leaves the initiative to words'.[1] He sought to develop a poetics that emphasized the patterns created within the self-enclosed structure of a poem, by the words composing it, rather than the referential function, however symbolic, of those words. According to a well-known anecdote, the painter Edgar Degas once sought Mallarmé out to ask for his advice on how to complete a sonnet he was trying to write. He had spent the whole day on it, he said, but was going nowhere – despite the fact that he had ideas coming out of his ears. 'But, Degas, you don't make a poem out of ideas,' said Mallarmé. 'You make it with words.'

The writer's compelling task, wrote Mallarmé, was to 'purify the language of the tribe'. He was reacting in part against what he saw as the devaluation of the daily currency of language by mass communications – the press, the *feuilleton*, the cheap book – which, as George Steiner has written, were beneficial to prose fiction but accentuated the minority status of the poem. 'With this industrialization of language and of the means of dissemination

147

of language,' writes Steiner, 'came the semi-literacies characteristic of techno-cratic and mass-consumer society . . . Now it was language as a whole that was being cheapened, brutalized, emptied of numinous and exact force, by mass usage. This view . . . becomes programmatic in Mallarmé's resolve to cleanse the vocabulary and syntax of common speech, to carve out and preserve for poetry an arcane realm of uncompromising significance.'[2] Poetic language, he argued, is fundamentally different from the language of everyday communi-cation. Everyday language is like a coin passed from hand to hand. The value of the coin is not inherent in it but is determined by the use to which it is put: for example, to convey information. Poetic language, on the other hand, is valuable in and of itself. It has a transcendent power. Among Mallarmé's favourite analogies for poetic practice were sorcery, witchcraft, the casting of a spell. His goal of resuscitating the magic of the word should be reflected, he felt, in the experience of reading his poetry – through the reader's confronta-tion with its formal complexities, its density and ambiguity. As he said in a newspaper interview in 1891, 'there must always be enigma in poetry': 'To name an object is to suppress three-quarters of the enjoyment of the poem, which derives from the pleasure of step-by-step discovery; to suggest, that is the dream.'[3] The whole point of Mallarmé's project in poetry lies in his use of uncertainty: in other words, his 'difficulty'. Difficulty, as Malcolm Bowie has shown, plays an integral part in Mallarmé's work. The reader, Bowie suggests, should not waste time trying to work out the true single meaning of his texts, but should attend to the question of how a given poem can be read fully and with pleasure.

The pleasure (and the challenge) that awaits the reader of Mallarmé lies in engagement, 'step-by-step', with the poet's language and with the suggestive structure of his poems: the dislocation of familiar verbal forms and codes of grammar, the twisting of syntax, the teasing ambiguity of theme. Take the following well-known, typically complex sonnet, first published in 1885:

> Virginal, vibrant, beautiful Today –
> Will it cleave with a frenzied blow of its wing
> This hard forgotten lake haunted beneath the frost
> By the crystal glacier of flights never flown!
>
> A swan of old remembers it is he,
> Splendid, but struggling, hopeless to break free,
> Not having sung of a land where one might live
> Through the glittering ennui of sterile winter.
>
> Its neck will shake off the white agony
> Space has inflicted on the bird which denies it,
> But not earth's horror where its plumes are caught.

Phantom assigned to this place by its sheer brilliance,
It is stilled, motionless, in the cold dream of contempt
Worn in useless exile by the Swan.

Le vierge, le vivace et le bel aujourd'hui
Va-t-il nous déchirer avec un coup d'aile ivre
Ce lac dur oublié que hante sous le givre
Le transparent glacier des vols qui n'ont pas fui!

Un cygne d'autrefois se souvient que c'est lui
Magnifique mais qui sans espoir se délivre
Pour n'avoir pas chanté la région où vivre
Quand du stérile hiver a resplendi l'ennui.

Tout son col secouera cette blanche agonie
Par l'espace infligée à l'oiseau qui le nie,
Mais non l'horreur du sol où le plumage est pris.

Fantôme qu'à ce lieu son pur éclat assigne,
Il s'immobilise au songe froid de mépris
Que vêt parmi l'exil inutile le Cygne.

On first reading, the poem appears to present itself as a puzzle. Ambiguity informs it from the very first line. It is not immediately clear that 'vierge', 'vivace' and 'bel' are adjectives rather than adjectival nouns; nor is it clear, once we have grasped that they are adjectives, what descriptive connotations they have, separately or together, in relation to their subject, 'Today'. The second line momentarily implies that 'nous' is the direct object of 'déchirer' (literally, 'to rend', 'tear asunder' or 'strip away'), suggesting that it is 'we' who are to be torn or rent; the ambiguity is removed in the following line, which reveals that 'nous' is an indirect object ('*for* us' is implied). We are led in one direction only to be taken back in another. The swan is adumbrated in the first quatrain before being named at the beginning of the second. But the verbal tricks and ambiguities are part of a larger ambiguity of meaning that turns on the image of the swan (the poet, as we know from tradition). This ambiguity is developed and maintained until the last line. As Malcolm Bowie has commented, the attitudes of the swan *persona* to its imprisoned state are presented in two contrary, interwoven strains.

> ... one of these strains would run: the trapped swan is despairing and self-reproachful for having failed, at the onset of winter, in its responsibilities as singer and harbinger; it rises in pain and protest against its sterile oppressor, but in the end succumbs and resignedly acknowledges its own sterility. The other, however, would run: the

trapped swan is magnificent, its prison resplendent; in captivity it has acquired a pure spiritual energy which it willingly contains and subdues; exile is its badge of honour, allowing it to achieve perfect self-mastery and placing it at a far and fortunate remove from the contingent world of practical endeavour.

(Mallarmé and the Art of Being Difficult, p. 11)[4]

The interplay between these two strains corresponds to a dense pattern of oppositions (present/past, song/silence, potentiality/hopelessness, movement/immobility, entrapment/freedom) that culminates in the final tercet. The 'Il s'immobilise' of the penultimate line may imply not simply abandonment of the struggle but a withdrawal born of contempt for normal reality; while the 'inutile' of the last line (which qualifies both 'l'exil' and, adverbially, 'le Cygne') is equally equivocal, repeating the notions of sterility and entrapment but also implying proud rejection of utilitarian values through commitment to art (thus recalling the heroic dandyism of Baudelaire and the cultivated eccentricity of Des Esseintes). The intricate network of contrasts that make up Mallarmé's 'art of suggestion and counter-suggestion' (Bowie, *Mallarmé and the Art of Being Difficult*, p. 12) has been well evoked by James Lawler: 'The violator is a bird (*avec un coup d'aile ivre*) but so is the phantom presence which is its prey; that which is forgotten (*oublié*) remembers (*se souvient*); the swan whose covering is about to be stripped away (*déchirer*) puts on a cloak of scorn (*vêt*). Imprisonment becomes freedom, sterility a fertile image, while drunkenness (*ivre*) yields to sobriety (*pour n'avoir pas chanté, songe froid*), time to eternity, useless exile to victorious affirmation.'[5]

Mallarmé's influence on the development of modern French literature was enormous. He acquired particular prestige in the eyes of avant-garde critics of the 1960s and 1970s, such as Roland Barthes (1915–80), whose 'death of the author' echoed Mallarmé's 'disappearance of the poet'. Mallarmé's critique of the referential claims of literature has been fundamental to contemporary structuralist and deconstructionist theories of literature, which hold that texts cannot be construed merely as a function of their authors' intentions, that language resists and contradicts the uses to which we try to put it, and that readers construct texts that are to a significant degree of their own making. The multiple meanings of a mature Mallarmé poem invite the reader to read inventively and on various levels, in full awareness of the 'mystery' of his words.

Chapter 21

Rimbaud: somebody else

I is somebody else
> – Rimbaud, Letter to Georges Izambard, 13 May 1871

Arthur Rimbaud (1854–91) was one of the most challenging and liberating influences on modern French culture – always on the move in his life and in his writing, always on his way to somewhere else, assuming and casting off identities as he went. There was the child prodigy, at fifteen writing poetry that showed a complete mastery of French classical forms and prosody, combined with a stunningly original style. There was the teenage rebel, the filthy, foul-mouthed peasant boy, repudiating family and religion, turning up in Paris and scandalizing the literary establishment with his iconoclastic views on poetry and his amazingly anti-social behaviour. There was the relationship with Verlaine and the vagabond years spent with the older poet in Paris, London and Brussels. Meanwhile, by the age of twenty, Rimbaud had composed a body of work that is widely considered one of the most innovative and significant of the French nineteenth century.

The poet as seer

Rimbaud's early years were spent on a farm at Roche, near the Belgian border, and then in the small nearby town of Charleville. He was brought up by his mother – his father, an army officer, having left her when Rimbaud was six. Vitalie Rimbaud, with her peasant avarice, grim piety, social ambition and iron discipline, cast a long shadow over her son's life. Ironically, Rimbaud got from his mother the toughness and determination he needed to escape from her and from everything she represented for him. He ran away to Paris when he was fifteen. His first views of the city were through the grill in the back of a police wagon, for he was arrested on arrival at the railway station for travelling without a ticket. After a few days, he was released, and made his way circuitously back home. He returned to Paris a few months later, this time with a ticket. Back in Charleville, he was greatly excited when Paris declared itself an independent people's republic, and in the spring of 1871 he decided to return to the capital to witness the dawn of the new age. He arrived in the city at the delirious height of the revolutionary Commune, but headed home when the government troops at Versailles began to shell their own capital city.

Rimbaud is often said to have returned from the Commune disenchanted and depoliticized. The Commune had inspired him, however, to pursue his own revolution, his own project of a revolutionized consciousness, embodied in his radical Romantic image of the poet as visionary or seer. He began to formulate a theory of art based on notions that would not be accepted until the twentieth century: art as abstraction, the direct appeal to the mind and senses of a language evolved especially for the purpose, and which involved both the dissociation of reality and the self-alienation of the artist. In May 1871 he sent his former teacher, Georges Izambard, a disjointed letter that included the following statement: 'It's wrong to say: I think. Better to say: I am thought ... I is somebody else' ('C'est faux de dire: Je pense: on devrait dire on me pense ... JE est un autre'). This letter amounted to an argument that the Cartesian ego was a fiction, along with the indivisible, morally responsible self on which Christianity and Western philosophy are founded. In the same mood of excitement and demystification that inspired the Communards, Rimbaud was considering the possibility of freeing the imagination from the controlling force of the intellect, or rather from the superego, the 'I' who was continuous with his mother and the controlling social order she embodied. Two days later, he wrote another letter, to the poet Paul Demeny, elaborating on how this was to be done in poetry:

> The Poet makes himself *a seer* through a long, involved and systematic *derangement* of *all the senses*. All forms of love, suffering, madness; he explores himself, exhausting every possible poison and preserving only their essences. Unspeakable tortures that require the greatest faith and superhuman strength, making him the ultimate Invalid among men, the master criminal, the first among the damned – and the Supreme Scientist! For he arrives at the *unknown!*

> Le Poète se fait *voyant* par un long, immense et raisonné *dérèglement* de *tous les sens*. Toutes les formes d'amour, de souffrance, de folie; il cherche lui-même, il épuise en lui tous les poisons, pour n'en garder que les quintessences. Ineffable torture où il a besoin de toute la foi, de toute la force surhumaine, où il devient entre tous le grand malade, le grand criminel, le grand maudit, – et le suprême Savant! – Car il arrive à l'*inconnu!*

The poet's duty, Rimbaud argued, is to extend his consciousness by submitting himself to every kind of experience – the abuse of the body through alcohol, drugs, fasting, perversions of all kinds – and then transmit what he perceives directly, without any conscious control. These two short letters (the second often referred to as the 'Letter of the Seer'/'Lettre du voyant') were to become central documents of the modern mind. Rimbaud's radical notion of a fluid, multiple personality has played a major role in modern literature's deconstruction of the traditional view of the human self as a distinct, intelligible whole.

By the end of the summer of 1871, a month before his seventeenth birthday, Rimbaud was back once more in Paris, ready to put into practice the ideas articulated in his letters. He was now the young lover of the dipsomaniac poet Paul Verlaine (1844–96), the leading avant-garde poet of the day. Rimbaud turned up on the Verlaines' doorstep with the manuscript of 'The Drunken Boat' ('Le Bateau ivre') in his pocket. This poem was the culmination of his personal and poetic experimentation up to this stage, and it marked the end of his 'childhood'. It was to be his passport to the new world of poets; it was, as he knew, something quite unique.

'The Drunken Boat'

'The Drunken Boat' is an expression, in densely symbolic terms, of Rimbaud's doctrine of *voyance*, of his effort to free the unconscious mind from the long bondage of form and rationality. The poem is about a boat that is more than a boat, a sea that is more than a sea, rivers that are more than rivers. The poem is striking in its physicality: Rimbaud is a poet of nature – not the nature of beautiful landscapes or of ordinary physical relationships, but of the relationship of man to his own body and of man's body to the elements. Mind and body are inseparable; the body thinks, the mind feels.

Here are the beginning and end of the poem:

Stanza 1   As I skimmed down impassive rivers, I guessed
         the ropes were free, I was no longer hauled:
         howling Redskins had my barge men nailed
         as naked targets onto each colour post.

   2   I cared no whit for them, I paid no heed
         to the carriers of cloth or Flemish corn.
         The haulers gone, that hurly-burly done,
         the river let me race on where I would.

3   I, last winter, swept by the choppy tide,
    oblivious as an infant's head, sped on
    down to the sea. Peninsulas unmoored
    had never endured a more triumphant din.

4   The tempest blessed each watch and each sunrise.
    Light as a cork I danced the waves, tossed
    by those eternal rollers of the lost,
    ten nights without the shore lights' foolish eyes.

5   As sweet as those tart apples children like,
    the green seawater breached my hull of pine
    cleansing the stains of vomit and blue wine
    and sweeping off the rudder and grappling hook.

6   I've steeped myself in the Poem of the Sea since then,
    milky with stars and foam's galactic trail,
    devouring azure greens where rapt and pale
    a floating pensive corpse at last slides down;

7   where a sudden stain shocks the blue, the long
    rhythmic deliriums of dawning day
    as, stronger than alcohol and vaster than song,
    the bitter reds of love ferment away.
        . . .

22 I've seen star archipelagoes and isles
    whose heavens open delirious, in flower:
    so you sleep here in depthless nights, exiled,
    you million golden birds, impending Power?

23 It's true I wept too much. Dawn stabs the heart!
    Each sun is drowned, each moon's a ghastly wound:
    I'm drunk on acrid love, dull as a brute.
    Let my keel burst! O let me go under soon!

24 The water of Europe for me is cold and grey,
    a darkening puddle towards sweet-smelling dusk,
    where a lonely child squats down to launch his husk
    of a boat as frail as a butterfly in May.

25 Lulled by your languours, waves, I cannot rise
    and follow in the cotton carriers' wake
    nor flank the pennants and proud flags, nor tack
    the shadow of the prison ships' dreadful eyes.

                                    Trans. Jan Owen

1   Comme je descendais des Fleuves impassibles,
    Je ne me sentis plus guidé par les haleurs:
    Des Peaux-Rouges criards les avaient pris pour cibles,
    Les ayant cloués nus aux poteaux de couleurs.

2   J'étais insoucieux de tous les équipages,
    Porteur de blés flamands ou de cotons anglais.
    Quand avec mes haleurs ont fini ces tapages,
    Les Fleuves m'ont laissé descendre où je voulais.

3   Dans les clapotements furieux des marées,
    Moi, l'autre hiver, plus sourd que les cerveaux d'enfants,
    Je courus! Et les Péninsules démarrées
    N'ont pas subi tohu-bohu plus triomphants.

4   La tempête a béni mes éveils maritimes.
    Plus léger qu'un bouchon j'ai dansé sur les flots
    Qu'on appelle rouleurs éternels de victimes,
    Dix nuits, sans regretter l'œil niais des falots!

5   Plus douce qu'aux enfants la chair des pommes sures,
    L'eau verte pénétra ma coque de sapin
    Et des taches de vins bleus et des vomissures
    Me lava, dispersant gouvernail et grappin.

6   Et dès lors, je me suis baigné dans le Poème
    De la Mer, infusé d'astres, et lactescent,
    Dévorant les azurs verts; où, flottaison blême
    Et ravie, un noyé pensif parfois descend;

7   Où, teignant tout à coup les bleuités, délires
    Et rythmes lents sous les rutilements du jour,
    Plus fortes que l'alcool, plus vastes que nos lyres,
    Fermentent les rousseurs amères de l'amour!
        . . .

22 J'ai vu des archipels sidéraux! et des îles
    Dont les cieux délirants sont ouverts au vogueur:
    – Est-ce en ces nuits sans fonds que tu dors et t'exiles,
    Million d'oiseaux d'or, ô future Vigueur? –

23 Mais, vrai, j'ai trop pleuré! Les Aubes sont navrantes.
    Toute lune est atroce et tout soleil amer:
    L'âcre amour m'a gonflé de torpeurs énivrantes.
    O que ma quille éclate! O que j'aille à la mer!

24 Si je désire une eau d'Europe, c'est la flache
    Noire et froide où vers le crépuscule embaumé
    Un enfant accroupi plein de tristesses, lâche
    Un bateau frêle comme un papillon de mai.

25 Je ne puis plus, baigné de vos langueurs, ô lames,
    Enlever leur sillage aux porteurs de cotons,
    Ni traverser l'orgueil des drapeaux et des flammes,
    Ni nager sous les yeux horribles des pontons.

We are introduced in stanzas 1–4 to the boat and to the boat's introduction
to the sea. The subject of 'I' is the boat itself, the symbol of the child's dream
of total freedom. The boat has drifted down rivers – controlled by them, just
as the rivers are themselves controlled, flowing between banks bordered by
towpaths. Suddenly the control is lost. In a remarkable image from the world
of childhood, howling redskins have nailed the boat-towers to a totem pole.
The redskins might be taken to represent the wild imaginative elements in a
child's life, the things that are not part of morality or a classical education;
while the coloured poles to which the elements of control are nailed suggest
the colours that are about to become part of the boat's life. Once the sub-
conscious elements of aggression have got rid of the first controls, the boat
drifts on, 'insoucieux'; and it becomes free, no longer a common, goods-
carrying barge. Though still in the river, and subject to some control, it has
lost the towrope. Freedom is linked to descent – towards the sea, into the
unconscious. The 'clapotements furieux'(stanza 3) signal the meeting of the
river and the sea. The meeting of river and sea is the moment when education and training give way to openness and freedom, and the conscious
mind, controlled and disciplined, must give way to the unconscious. Movement into the unconscious is evoked as an awakening ('éveils') to a new form of
consciousness.

The next three stanzas (5–7) – an introduction to the sea and its meaning –
form a whole. The meeting with the sea is both cleansing, a kind of baptism
into a new life, and an initiation into the union of nature and the mind. The
green water as sweet as the flesh of sour green apples has multiple meanings.
The physical suggestion of taste combines with that of knowledge, especially
the knowledge possessed by children (identified with the unconscious). This
is not the knowledge that comes with the differentiation of good and evil,
but with their reintegration. The green water has knowledge and power, but
is also an agent of cleansing – identified not with differentiation but with
interpenetration. The water penetrates the hull of the boat and cleans it,

washing away the stains of cheap wine and vomit, the stains of the past of humanity, of the land. The boat steeps itself in the sea, in the unconscious, and loses the last remnants of control. The conscious mind becomes one with the unconscious. This is the moment of *voyance*, when the seer becomes one with the vision he sees. The primordial quality of the sea is stressed by the fact that it contains the sky within itself. The sea is the Great Mother which devours the green and the blue. Within this great primordial force, a drowned man is 'rapt'. '[R]avie' (stanza 6) has two meanings: ecstatic and at peace. The drowned man is not truly dead – he is a symbol of human thought sinking blissfully into the great ocean-mother. The unity between conscious and unconscious, man and nature, thought and dream, is paralleled by the implied unity between art and sex: both are seen as manifestations of the great forces of life. The series of oppositions leading up to 'les rousseurs amères de l'amour', the bitter red staining the blue of the sea-sky (stanza 7), contain not only 'délires' (suggesting intoxication) but also 'rythmes lents' – the slow, compelling rhythm of the sea, of the successful poem and of successful love-making. These are linked with 'rutilements' – the light that suggests the dawn, and also sexuality through the connotations of 'rut' (copulation). Sex is the ferment of life.

The last four stanzas (22–25) may be read as providing four alternative endings – each reader able to choose the mood or vision that suits him/her – or as summing up the different tendencies of Rimbaud's poetry. An optimistic ending is sketched in stanza 22, evoking a feeling of ecstasy. The poem we have read embodies the paradox of a journey that is both an ascent into the sea and a descent into the sky. Both ascent and descent use the forces of the unconscious and free the powers of the libido. The whole poem, with its use of archetypal sensual imagery, is about liberation. The future ('Million d'oiseaux d'or') will see a transmutation of human expectations as well as a transmutation of language through the release of its hidden force. In stanza 23 there is a swing back to the opposite mood ('Mais, vrai ...'), with the suggestion that the price of the new dawn may be too great. This point of view is taken up in *A Season in Hell* (see below) and in all of Rimbaud's poems that end on a note of despair and acceptance of death. If we view the whole of 'The Drunken Boat' as a manifestation of archetypal sexual imagery, then one of the endings of the force of Eros is fusion with the sea – the ultimate resolution of death (Thanatos): 'O que ma quille éclate! O que j'aille à la mer!' The idea of the immense suffering that goes with the visionary experience is clearly expressed in the Letter of the Seer ('Unspeakable torment ... '), where Rimbaud invokes the possibility of his own destruction through his leaps into the unknown.

In stanza 24 the image of the child sailing a paper boat on a dark puddle is set against the immense freedom of the drunken boat itself. The suggestion is that retreat into childhood (or, in Freudian terms, into the womb) may provide security, but also produces sadness. The final stanza is a reaffirmation of revolt and repudiation: once one has experienced ecstasy, one can never go back, no matter what suffering one may endure; the drunken boat can never become again a simple cargo boat carrying cotton. Rimbaud rejects, too, ordinary life, work and discipline, and even some of his original revolutionary ideals, symbolized by 'pennants and proud flags'. The reference to prison hulks expresses his refusal, in part, of the sort of social activity that leads to an unsatisfactory outcome (like the Commune?). He will not go back to accepting anyone else's options, either the ones he barely tolerated at school or naïve political doctrines. He will accept only total freedom.

Bohemia, London, Brussels, Africa

As soon as Rimbaud arrived on his doorstep, Verlaine took him off on a round of the absinthe bars; Rimbaud descended, with Verlaine as his companion, into the Bohemian underworld. The stories of his excesses at this time are legendary. One night, at an all-night café on the Place Pigalle called The Dead Rat, he pulled a penknife from his pocket and cut Verlaine's wrists quite deeply. Rimbaud's stabbing games, like his poems, were experiments and statements: human beings were more interesting in extreme conditions. His excesses were part of a paradoxically disciplined effort to free himself from the constraints of Christian bourgeois society. The precarious tranquillity of the Verlaine household was quickly ruined. Verlaine ran away with Rimbaud to Belgium and then to London. Alcohol, drugs, every form of perversity, were part of their daily behaviour. During all this time both were not only passionately involved with each other but also developing as poets; Rimbaud was experimenting with prosody and syntax until he abandoned traditional poetry altogether and moved into prose poetry and free verse forms.

Rimbaud was delighted by London and returned there three times in less than three years. The London he discovered was a vast, chaotic metropolis that made Paris look rather provincial. As Graham Robb has pointed out, Rimbaud found in the infernal and alienating oddness of London at its industrial apogee a real-life means to achieve the radical estrangement he had been seeking in his poetry. The collections of prose poetry, *A Season in Hell* (*Une saison en enfer*, 1873) and, especially, the *Illuminations* (largely written after *Une saison*, but not published in book form until 1886) are redolent of Rimbaud's experience of the city: 'The mad perspectives of the *Illuminations* were foreign to French literature but not to nineteenth-century inhabitants of Paddington, Holborn and Southwark: subways, viaducts, raised canals; steam engines pass-ing over streets, mastheads suddenly appearing behind chimney-pots. London was ... confirmation of Rimbaud's insight that, when the depiction exactly matched the appearance, reality itself was surreal' (Robb, *Rimbaud*, p. 187).

By the end of June 1873, Verlaine was buckling under the strain of his turbulent domestic life with Rimbaud. The last straw came when Rimbaud laughed at him as he arrived home with a fish for supper. Verlaine smacked him in the face with the fish and caught a ferry to Belgium without packing his bags. After a few days Rimbaud joined him in Brussels, where the famous shooting incident took place: Verlaine shot Rimbaud in the wrist, and served two years in jail. Rimbaud recovered and immersed himself in his work. He abandoned the lyric forms he had used earlier and worked now in a spare, dramatic and allusive prose. Both *A Season in Hell* and *Illuminations* exemplify many of the implications of Rimbaud's statement, 'I is somebody else.' These implications and their significance are well stated by Mark Treharne:

> The language of the self is inhabited by a whole diversity of voices stemming from institutionalized sources such as religious and secular systems of education, from adopted orthodoxies and credos, from literature, from popular cliché, and so on almost *ad infinitum*. Those voices can be quite consciously deployed, but they can also be born of unconscious impulse. They can also be directed to literal or figurative ends, to strategies that range from irony to celebration. They can represent harmonious or conflicting systems of meaning and of ethical perspective. In Rimbaud's case the divided, agonistic voice of *A Season in Hell*, pulled in all directions by instabilities of emotion and belief, extends itself in *Illuminations* to embrace the more positive possibilities of a pluralistic notion of the self ... Rimbaud's practice of the prose poem represents a liberation from what was previously and more conservatively regarded as poetic voice, and his view of self as a plurality of voices orientates poetry radically towards modernism.
>
> (Introduction to Arthur Rimbaud: *A Season*
> *in Hell and Illuminations*, p. xxx)

Rimbaud's literary career continued for over a year after the publication of *A Season in Hell*. The rest, after 1875, was silence. His abandonment of poetry in his early twenties was followed by periods as a language teacher in Reading, England, as a mercenary in the Dutch Colonial Army in Java, as a construction overseer in Cyprus and, for the last ten years of his life, as a remarkably successful trader and explorer in the Horn of Africa. At the time of his death from bone cancer, having had one leg amputated at the Hôpital de la Conception in Marseille, Rimbaud was still unknown beyond the avant-garde.

Although Rimbaud's break with literature in 1875 was total, it is possible to see his life in writing and his life of action as two aspects of a single project. The continuities that run through his life and work include the many correspondences between the essentially peripatetic character of much of his verse, especially in the earlier period ('Sensation', 'Les Reparties de Nina', 'Au Cabaret Vert', 'La Maline', 'Ma Bohème'), and his life as a trader. The motif of movement in Rimbaud's earlier poetry is intimately connected with his passionate desire for freedom – freedom from all constraints, in particular those of bourgeois society and religious hypocrisy. He viciously attacked anyone in authority, from God, Napoleon III and Mme Rimbaud to the customs officers on the nearby Belgian border and the local librarians at Charleville. So how could the archetypal figure of revolt, the Communard sympathizer, have become a colonial entrepreneur and a mercenary? There is continuity, it may be argued, in the radicalism of Rimbaud's self-negations – the ways in which he constantly, and so emphatically, cancelled out his former selves. Leo Bersani is right to stress that '[t]here is one persistent theme – or rather gesture – throughout his life: the gesture of repudiation ... Rimbaud doesn't merely reject certain modes of life and of art against which intelligible objections might be formulated; he repudiates whatever he risks *being*.'[1] The essence of *voyance*, after all, is the absence of any durable and coherent subjectivity. The most essential element that provided the continuity between the two 'halves' of Rimbaud's life was the urge to acquire knowledge by venturing into the unknown, even if that knowledge proved incommunicable. From the start, the basis of his project as a poet lay in the questioning of the frontiers of literature, and his attempts to escape 'literature' altogether. The charting of totally unexplored regions in the Horn of Africa was a practical extension of the schoolboy's poetic dream, expressed in the Letter of the Seer: 'He arrives at the unknown, and when, half-demented, he ends up losing his understanding of his visions, he has, at least, seen them!' ('Il arrive à l'inconnu, et quand, affolé, il finirait par perdre l'intelligence de ses visions, il les a vues!').

Chapter 22

Proust: the self, time and art

I myself seemed to have become the subject of my book

— Proust, *The Way by Swann's*

À la recherche du temps perdu (the *Recherche*, or the *Search*, for short), the 3,000-page, multi-volume novel by Marcel Proust (1871–1922), published between 1913 and 1927, is now recognized as the undisputed masterpiece of twentieth-century fiction. Endlessly rich in its themes and idioms, it is a philosophical novel about time, memory, imagination and art; a psychological novel about human behaviour, love and jealousy; a social novel about France, especially high society, as it evolved from the end of the nineteenth century to the aftermath of the 1914–18 war; and a comic novel of manners, character and language. It is also an experimental novel, quite unlike what contemporary readers normally understood to be a work of fiction. Part of Proust's importance historically is that he redefined the boundaries of fiction. Instead of a conventional linear story with a clearly identifiable plot, the *Search* uses a kaleidoscope of memories to create a startlingly new form of narrative. For those who come to the *Search* for the first time, it reads very much like an autobiography. There is an 'I', a narrator, who is telling the story of his childhood experiences, reminiscing about them, adding analytical comments as he goes. But although there are strong autobiographical elements in the novel – the places and characters can be matched with Proust's own experience, and the narrator's name is revealed to be Marcel – these elements have been transformed, and a world created out of them which, though based on real experiences, is an imaginary one, a fictional creation. The narrative 'I' is, moreover, a double 'I', moving fluidly between the present of the narrator and the past of his younger self, building multiple perspectives into a symphonic structure and promoting a dramatic narration as the narrator comes slowly to understand the significance of his past experiences. The novel invites the reader to enter the narrator's mind, to accompany him on his journey of discovery as he explores in minute detail, in sentences of intricate precision, the workings of his own consciousness and sensibility, and seeks to understand not only the meaning of his life but also the nature of the human condition.

'When a man is asleep . . . '

The novel opens with an extended evocation of the shadowy world of sleep and semi-sleep. The following passage is from the novel's first pages; its motifs will be taken up throughout the novel.

> When a man is asleep, he has in a circle round him the sequence of the hours, the order of the years, and the worlds he has known. He checks with them instinctively as he wakes and in a second reads in them the spot he occupies on the earth, the time that has elapsed up to his waking; but their order can become jumbled and broken. If towards morning, after a night of insomnia, sleep overcomes him as he is reading, in a position too different from the one in which he usually sleeps, his raised arm alone is enough to halt the sun and make it retreat, and, for a few moments after he wakes, he will no longer know what time it is, he will think he has only just gone to bed. If he dozes off in a position even more displaced and divergent, for instance sitting in an armchair after dinner, then the chaos of his worlds will be complete, the magic armchair will transport him at top speed through time and space, and on opening his eyes, he will imagine that he went to bed several months earlier, in another country. But it was enough if, in my own bed, I slept soundly and my mind relaxed entirely; then I would lose all sense of the place where I had fallen asleep and, when I woke in the middle of the night, since I did not know where I was, I did not even know for a moment who I was; all I had, in its primal simplicity, was the dim sense of existence as it may quiver in the consciousness of an animal; I was more bereft than a caveman; but then the memory – not yet of the place where I was, but of several other places where I had lived and where I might now be – would come to me like help from on high to pull me out of the void from which I could not have got out on my own; I passed over centuries of civilization in one second, and the image confusedly glimpsed of oil lamps, then of wing-collar shirts, gradually recomposed my self's original features.

> Un homme qui dort, tient en cercle autour de lui le fil des heures, l'ordre des années et des mondes. Il les consulte d'instinct en s'éveillant et y lit en une seconde le point de la terre qu'il occupe, le temps qui s'est écoulé jusqu'à son réveil; mais leurs rangs peuvent se mêler, se rompre. Que vers le matin, après quelque insomnie, le sommeil le prenne en train de

lire, dans une posture trop différente de celle où il dort habituellement, il suffit de son bras soulevé pour arrêter et faire reculer le soleil, et à la première minute de son réveil, il ne saura plus l'heure, il estimera qu'il vient à peine de se coucher. Que s'il s'assoupit dans une position encore plus déplacée et divergente, par exemple après dîner assis dans un fauteuil, alors que le bouleversement sera complet dans les mondes désorbités, le fauteuil magique le fera voyager à toute vitesse dans le temps et dans l'espace, et au moment d'ouvrir les paupières, il se croira couché quelques mois plus tôt dans une autre contrée. Mais il suffisait que, dans mon lit même, mon sommeil fût profond et détendît entièrement mon esprit; alors celui-ci lâchait le plan du lieu où je m'étais endormi et, quand je m'éveillais au milieu de la nuit, comme j'ignorais où je me trouvais, je ne savais même pas au premier instant qui j'étais; j'avais seulement dans sa simplicité première le sentiment de l'existence comme il peut frémir au fond d'un animal; j'étais plus dénué que l'homme des cavernes; mais alors le souvenir – non encore du lieu où j'étais, mais de quelques-uns de ceux que j'avais habités et où j'aurais pu être – venait à moi comme un secours d'en haut pour me tirer du néant d'où je n'aurais pu sortir tout seul; je passais en une seconde par-dessus des siècles de civilisation, et l'image confusément entrevue de lampes à pétrole, puis de chemises à col rabattu, recomposaient peu à peu les traits originaux de mon moi.

The nameless narrator, whose age and identity are unclear but who is both the subject and the object of his narrative, describes the uncertainty of someone remembering the act of waking and trying to find points of reference that will tell him who he is and where he is in time and space. The mature narrator, in the present, recalls various moments in his past and the different rooms in which he has slept; and throughout the novel these shifting perspectives and patterns of recollection continue until the narrator and his younger selves effectively meet up, so to speak, in old age, in the novel's final volume. The borderland between sleep and waking is where it all begins: that is, the world of the novel is situated inside the narrator's mind. There is virtually no physical description in the passage, just a disembodied voice. The focus of Proust's novel is that voice: pure consciousness. The in-between state described in the passage corresponds to a precarious sense of identity, a kind of vertigo. As the narrator says a little later, 'everything revolved around me in the darkness, things, countries, years' ('tout tournait autour de moi dans l'obscurité, les choses, les pays, les années'). The destabilizing effect of sleep corresponds to a tabula rasa of the self and to feelings of both vulnerability ('I was more bereft than a caveman') and potentiality. What appears as a source of salvation, coming 'like help from on high to pull me out of the void from which I could not have got out on my own', is memory, with its ability to recompose or recreate the self. The structuring motifs of the text are, then, uncertainty, instability, memory and the search for the self. 'Where am I?' leads immediately to 'Who am I?' The *Search* is about the ways in which we come to be who we are, the time it takes us to recognize ourselves for what we are and the manner in which we might articulate our experience. This quest, linked to the narrator's sense of his vocation to be a writer, is the most fundamental theme of Proust's work.

A goodnight kiss

A few pages later, the narrator introduces us to Combray, a village where he had stayed on family holidays as a child. One memory is described at length: the drama of an evening when the presence of a dinner guest, Charles Swann, interferes with the enactment of a nightly ritual in which Marcel's mother gives him a goodnight kiss. That evening, Marcel's father sends his son to bed without the kiss and the child, in anguish, devises a stratagem to make his mother come upstairs – a note he tricks the maid Françoise into transmitting to her at the dinner table. His mother, concerned by her son's highly strung sensibility, has adopted with him a policy of firmness, in order to teach him to master his feelings and strengthen his will, and so tells the maid 'there is no answer'. The tormented child lies awake until he hears the sound of the door-bell and knows that Swann has left. As his mother is coming up to bed, he goes out into the hallway and throws himself upon her. At first she is angry, but Marcel's father unexpectedly takes pity on him and tells his wife to go in and comfort the boy, and even to spend the night in his room. Instead of happiness, however, young Marcel is disturbed to feel that such a concession has caused his mother to be disappointed with him. She slowly calms him, lulling him to sleep by reading to him a novel of George Sand's, *François le Champi.*

This bedtime drama introduces motifs that will become major Proustian themes, developed with great subtlety over many hundreds of pages: desire and the experience of love; the discovery of subjectivity and relativity; the sufferings and solace of the imagination. The child's uncontrollable desire succeeds in obtaining its object, but it creates a feeling of guilt – the guilt of causing distress and disappointment in his mother. The *drame du coucher* represents Marcel's painful initiation into the relativity of the world. He learns, through his father's unexpected indulgence, that personalities are not predictable and principles are not absolute; and he is confronted, too, by the gulf between his own self, his own needs, and the realities of the world in the form of his mother's unwillingness to come upstairs to bestow the kiss. For Proust, desire never succeeds in connecting with the reality of the object on which it fixes. Not only do we attribute to the loved one qualities that are projections of our own imaginations, we are also perversely attracted to the beloved by our belief that he or she represents a world we wish to penetrate but from which we are fatally excluded. Love for Proust is a kind of malady that provokes expectations that can never be fulfilled. It is always marked by jealousy and disillusion. The jealous lover – Swann in his affair with Odette, the grown-up Marcel with Albertine, the young Marcel as he lies awake thinking obsessively about his mother – is always tortured by the thought of what his beloved may be doing in his absence: the 'unknown pleasures' Marcel's mother is enjoying downstairs, for example. The urge to know, to possess, is doomed to failure. But jealous imaginings involving the beloved also become a source of creative fictions; and this takes us to the heart of Proust's work: the development (which does not culminate until the novel's closing volume) of the narrator's understanding that the pain and sorrows of existence can be a source of aesthetic fulfilment (just as Marcel's distraught feelings are soothed by his mother's reading of the novel by George Sand). 'If I had to . . . sum up *A la recherche du temps perdu*,' Leo Bersani writes, 'I would say that it shows how the disappointments the narrator suffers as a result of his extraordinarily rich imagination lead him to give up novelizing in life in order to reminisce about the way he used to novelize, in art' (*Marcel Proust*, p. 17).

'. . . a piece of madeleine'

For many years, the only conscious memory the narrator retains of Combray is the drama of the goodnight kiss. Then, one winter's day, on his return home, his mother, seeing that he is cold, suggests that he have a cup of tea, something he does not normally do.

> She sent for one of those squat, plump sponge-cakes called *petites madeleines*, which look as though they have been moulded in the corrugated valve of a scallop-shell. And soon, mechanically, oppressed by the gloomy day and the prospect of a similar day to follow, I raised to my lips a spoonful of the tea in which I had softened a piece of the cake. But at the very moment when the mouthful of tea and cake-crumbs touched my palate, a thrill ran through me and I immediately focused my attention on the extraordinary thing that was happening inside me.

A delicious pleasure had invaded me, isolating me, without my having any inkling as to its cause. It had instantly made the vicissitudes of life unimportant to me, its disasters innocuous, its brevity illusory, acting in the same way that love acts, by filling me with a precious essence: or rather, this essence was not in me, it was me. I no longer felt mediocre, contingent, mortal. Where could it have come from, this powerful feeling of joy? I sensed that it was connected to the taste of the tea and the cake, but that it went far beyond it, could not be of the same nature. Where did it come from? What did it mean? How could I grasp it? I drink a second mouthful, in which I find nothing more than in the first, then a third that tells me rather less than the second. It is time for me to stop, the potion seems to be losing its effect. It is clear that the truth I am seeking is not in the drink but in me... I put down the cup and turn to my mind. It is up to my mind to find the truth. But how? What grave uncertainty, whenever the mind feels overtaken by itself; when it, the seeker, is also the dark region where it must seek and where all its attributes will be of no avail. Seek? Not only that: create. My mind is faced with something that does not yet exist and that only it can bring into being and into the light.

Elle envoya chercher un de ces gâteaux courts et dodus appelés Petites Madeleines qui semblent avoir été moulés dans la valve rainurée d'une coquille de Saint-Jacques. Et bientôt, machinalement, accablé par la morne journée et la perspective d'un triste lendemain, je portai à mes lèvres une cuillerée du thé où j'avais laissé s'amollir un morceau de madeleine. Mais à l'instant même où la gorgée mêlée des miettes du gâteau toucha mon palais, je tressaillis, attentif à ce qui se passait d'extraordinaire en moi. Un plaisir délicieux m'avait envahi, isolé, sans la notion de sa cause. Il m'avait aussitôt rendu les vicissitudes de la vie indifférentes, ses désastres inoffensifs, sa brièveté illusoire, de la même façon qu'opère l'amour, en me remplissant d'une essence précieuse: ou plutôt cette essence n'était pas en moi, elle était moi. J'avais cessé de me sentir médiocre, contingent, mortel. D'où avait pu me venir cette puissante joie? Je sentais qu'elle était liée au goût du thé et du gâteau, mais qu'elle le dépassait infiniment, ne devait pas être de même nature. D'où venait-elle? Que signifiat-elle? Où l'appréhender? Je bois une seconde gorgée où je ne trouve rien de plus que dans la première, une troisième qui m'apporte un peu moins que la seconde. Il est temps que je m'arrête, la vertu du breuvage semble diminuer. Il est clair que la vérité que je cherche n'est pas en lui, mais en moi... Je pose la tasse et me tourne vers mon esprit. C'est à lui de trouver la vérité. Mais comment? Grave incertitude, toutes les fois que l'esprit se sent dépassé par lui-même; quand lui, le chercheur, est tout ensemble le pays obscur où il doit chercher et où tout son bagage ne lui sera de rien. Chercher? pas seulement: créer. Il est en face de quelque chose qui n'est pas encore et que seul il peut réaliser, puis faire entrer dans sa lumière.

The description of self-rediscovery in this passage develops the theme of the awakening subject in the 'sleeping man' passage, where the narrator writes of memory working like a rope lifting him out of the void. It is because it releases within him all his locked-up memories, transporting him back to his childhood, that the taste of the *madeleine* dipped in tea produces such unaccountable joy. The taste, he soon realizes, is the taste of the little piece of *madeleine* which on Sunday mornings at Combray, when he went to say good morning to Aunt Léonie in her bedroom, she would give him after dipping it in her infusion of tea or lime-blossom. Conscious memory – the memories filed away by the intellect – brings back mere fragments of the past. What the narrator experiences with the *madeleine* is a moment of 'involuntary memory': that is, the triggering of unconscious memory by bodily sensation. This form of memory allows the past to be relived in all its richness and entirety. It breaks open the narrator's sense of habit, allowing all of Combray – the sights and sounds, the people and places, the textures, colours and emotions – to come flooding back in his mind. The last few sentences of the passage above show the narrator, struggling to understand his experience, realizing that what he is seeking is not in the *madeleine* but in himself; he begins to sense that it is not simply a question of an inward search, but also of creation: 'Seek? Not only that: create.'

'. . . a sort of drunkenness'

Another kind of revelation is described in a passage towards the end of the 'Combray' section of *The Way by Swann's*. The young Marcel finds himself in a carriage driving in the country – Dr Percepied is giving him and his family a lift home – and sees the spires of the distant churches of Martinville and Vieuxvicq dancing on the horizon. At a bend in the road, a sudden change of perspective creates the optical illusion of the three spires merging into one.

> As I observed, as I noted the shape of their spires, the shifting of their lines, the sunlight on their surfaces, I felt that I was not penetrating to the core of my impression of them, that there was something else behind their mobility and brightness, something they seemed to contain and conceal at the same time.

The steeples appeared so far away, and we seemed to be approaching them so slowly, that I was surprised when, a few moments later, we stopped in front of the Martinville church. I did not know why the sight of them on the horizon had given me so much pleasure, and the obligation I felt to try and discover the reason for it seemed to me quite irksome; I wanted to store in my head those shapes moving in the sun and not think about them any more now. And it is very likely that, had I done so, the two steeples would have gone forever to join the many trees, rooftops, fragrances and sounds that I had distinguished from others because of the obscure pleasure they had given me and which I had never fully explored. I got down to talk with my parents while we waited for the doctor. Then we set off again, I was back in my place on the seat, I turned my head to see the steeples again, and not long afterwards I glimpsed them one last time as we went round a bend. The coachman did not seem inclined to talk, having barely acknowledged anything I said, and so I was obliged, for lack of other company, to fall back on my own and try to recall my steeples. Soon their lines and their sunlit surfaces split apart, as if they were a kind of bark, a little of what was hidden inside them appeared to me, a thought that had not existed a moment before occurred to me, taking shape in words inside my head, and the pleasure I had experienced at the sight of them was so increased by this that, overcome by a sort of drunkenness, I could no longer think of anything else.

En constatant, en notant la forme de leur flèche, le déplacement de leurs lignes, l'ensoleillement de leur surface, je sentais que je n'allais pas au bout de mon impression, que quelque chose était derrière ce mouvement, derrière cette clarté, quelque chose qu'ils semblaient contenir et dérober à la fois.

Les clochers paraissaient si éloignés et nous avions l'air de si peu nous rapprocher d'eux, que je fus étonné quand, quelques instants après, nous nous arrêtâmes devant l'église de Martinville. Je ne savais pas la raison du plaisir que j'avais eu à les apercevoir à l'horizon et l'obligation de chercher à découvrir cette raison me semblait bien pénible; j'avais envie de garder en réserve dans ma tête ces lignes remuantes au soleil et de n'y plus penser maintenant. Et il est probable que si je l'avais fait, les deux clochers seraient allés à jamais rejoindre tant d'arbres, de toits, de parfums, de sons, que j'avais distingués des autres à cause de ce plaisir obscur qu'ils m'avaient procuré et que je n'avais jamais approfondi. Je descendis causer avec mes parents en attendant le docteur. Puis nous repartîmes, je repris ma place sur le siège, je tournai la tête pour voir encore les clochers qu'un peu plus tard, j'aperçus une dernière fois au tournant d'un chemin. Le cocher, qui ne semblait pas disposé à causer,

> ayant à peine répondu à mes propos, force me fut, faute d'autre
> compagnie, de me rabattre sur celle de moi-même et d'essayer de me
> rappeler mes clochers. Bientôt leurs lignes et leurs surfaces ensoleillés,
> comme si elles avaient été une sorte d'écorce, se déchirèrent, un peu de
> ce qui m'était caché en elles m'apparut, j'eus une pensée qui n'existait
> pas pour moi l'instant avant, qui se formula en mots dans ma tête, et le
> plaisir que m'avait fait tout à l'heure éprouver leur vue s'en trouva
> tellement accru que, pris d'une sorte d'ivresse, je ne pus plus penser à
> autre chose.

The focus of this passage is the mystery and excitement of the urge to create, to translate reality into art, by writing. It evokes the key elements and stages of artistic creation for Proust. The point of departure is Marcel's puzzlement: 'I felt that I was not penetrating to the core of my impression. . .' He does not understand his 'obscure pleasure' at the sight of the steeples and feels impelled to discover the reason for it. The steeples' lines and surfaces are like 'a kind of bark' which, like the scallop-shell valve of the *madeleine*, conceals a secret world. Reality as perceived by the senses is a first step towards the discovery of something more important. Perception creates an impression; reality becomes subjective. The disappearance of the steeples as the carriage turns round a bend, and the coachman's silence, force Marcel to retreat into himself and to 'try to recall' the steeples: the act of memory deepens the impression they have made on him, and 'a little of what was hidden inside them' appears. He begins to understand that the 'something else' the steeples seem to hide lies not in them but in himself, in *his own way* of seeing things. And the 'thought' engendered by memory is not the result of a conscious intellectual process, but erupts unconsciously, 'taking shape in words' inside Marcel's head. He asks the doctor for a pencil and some paper and, despite the jolts of the carriage, composes a kind of prose-poem that makes him feel 'so perfectly relieved of those steeples and what they had been hiding behind them' ('si parfaitement débarrassé de ces clochers et de ce qu'ils cachaient') that, like a hen who has laid an egg, he begins to sing at the top of his voice. The significance of the steeples episode lies not so much in its highlighting a literary description of an experience as in its description of the experience of literature.

Although his piece of writing fills him with strange satisfaction, Marcel dismisses it because, as he notes, he does not fully realize that 'what was hidden behind the steeples of Martinville had to be something analogous to a pretty sentence, since it had appeared to me in the form of words that gave me pleasure' ('ce qui était caché derrière les clochers de Martinville devait être quelque chose d'analogue à une jolie phrase, puisque c'était sous la forme de mots qui me faisaient plaisir, que cela m'était apparu'). His failure to grasp the full meaning

of the steeples experience, and of a number of similar experiences, prevents
him from fulfilling his life's ambition to be a writer – until, towards the end of
Finding Time Again, he attends a reception at the Princesse de Guermantes's
after many years' absence. He has been away in a sanatorium, his health is
failing, his past seems distant, and he feels his life has been wasted. But a series
of *madeleine*-like episodes – for example, stumbling on an uneven paving stone
that transports him back to Venice by reminding him of a similar experience
when he had stood on two uneven flagstones in the baptistry of St Mark's –
shows him that his past, which he thought lost, still lives within him. These
episodes give him the same intense pleasure he had felt at the sight of the steeples
or the taste of the *madeleine*. 'I no longer felt mediocre, contingent, mortal,'
writes the narrator in the *madeleine* episode; and the full significance of that
statement can be fully appreciated only by reading the whole novel, of which
major themes are evanescence, impermanence and the radical contingency that
informs human experience. Whereas the nineteenth-century realist novelists
portrayed the self as something that is stable, developing through the various
stages of life, Proust's portrayal of selfhood stresses its discontinuous, shifting
nature. An individual life, according to this vision, is made up of a multiplicity
of different, often contradictory selves; for Marcel the end of a relationship
spells the death of a self and the birth of a new self. And just as individuals are
portrayed as being subject to perpetual flux and mobility, so is society itself, as
the old aristocracy disintegrates, absorbed by the bourgeoisie, and the glittering
world of the Belle Époque is swept away by the First World War. The ravages of
time are written on the now barely recognizable faces of Marcel's old friends
and acquaintances at the Princess's reception, which appears to him like some
kind of grotesque masked ball. The guests seem already to have been claimed by
death. The redemptive significance of involuntary memory is that, through the
unbidden return of the past, the narrator grasps not only that he lives in time
but that time lives within him, awaiting resurrection. This illumination defines
the task of art: to give durable life to departed life. Only art can give significance
to what would otherwise be mere contingency; only the aesthetic will to form
can show us the value of the individual human mind and the real quality of an
individual's contact with the world. Marcel sees that he can possess in art – the
marriage of reality and imagination – the happiness he could not possess in
life. He finally understands what the steeples had been trying to tell him, and
discovers the subject matter of his book: himself and his own past life. The task
of the artist, he writes, is to express subjectivity, to 'translate' our own unique
experience of the world; the value of art generally lies in its ability to reveal
the multiplicity of different ways in which individuals perceive the world; and
the reader of fiction will thereby become a more sophisticated reader of his

or her own self. The novel closes with the narrator's realization that the book it is his vocation to write is the very novel that describes the genesis of his discovery.

The *Search* represents a remarkably original development of the early modernism of Flaubert and Baudelaire. The aesthetic principles articulated by Proust through his narrator are modernist, and emphatically anti-realist/naturalist, in the sense that they extol an art focused not on representing external reality but on expressing the reality within ourselves, and the act of creation, in forms shaped for that purpose. 'Proust's modernity,' writes Malcolm Bradbury, 'comes from the great withdrawal he made into the intelligence, the sensuousness, the synaesthesia, the psychology of art. He is one of the great *creators*, even though it seems as if he did not create at all, but just lay there and remembered.'[1]

Chapter 23

Jarry: the art of provocation

> The work of art is a stuffed crocodile.
>
> – Alfred Jarry

The eccentric figure of Alfred Jarry (1873–1907), best known for his taboo-breaking farce *Ubu roi* (1896), occupies an important place in the history of the avant-garde in France. As much a culture-hero, a symbol of wild nonconformity, as an important author in his own right, he became a point of reference and inspiration for the Dadaists and Surrealists, and his theatre is often seen as a precursor of the twentieth-century theatre of the Absurd. Writers who explicitly acknowledged Jarry's influence include Tristan Tzara, André Breton, Antonin Artaud, Raymond Queneau, Eugène Ionesco, Boris Vian and Georges Perec. 'Jarry's history', writes Jerrold Seigel, 'was one of unremitting challenge to convention and tradition. He was perhaps the first figure to make direct confrontation with his audience a generating principle of his work. All the twentieth-century movements that make action and provocation central to artistic practice were foreshadowed by him' (*Bohemian Paris*, p. 310).

Ubu

Ubu roi had its origins in the subversive fun-making of intelligent schoolboys. At the *lycée* Jarry attended in Rennes, there was a tradition of extravagant skits, performed mainly with puppets, based on a bumbling, pompous physics teacher named Félix Hébert, around whom a whole mythology had grown up. Jarry was an enthusiastic participant in this tradition, and, at the age of fifteen, wrote a series of episodes that he was to develop over the next few years. Among Hébert's nicknames was 'Père Ébé', which got transformed into Père Ubu. Jarry moved from Brittany to Paris in 1891, and in 1896 was employed as secretary to the theatre director Aurélien Lugné-Poe, of the avant-garde Théâtre de l'Œuvre, known for its connections with Symbolism and anarchism. Jarry persuaded Lugné-Poe to include two performances of *Ubu roi* in the company's programme, and he was allowed in effect to become the production's director. The première took place at the Nouveau Théâtre on 9 and 10 December 1896.

These two performances were among the most tumultuous in the history of French theatre. They were nothing less than an orchestrated attempt, based on an elaborate publicity campaign, to create a scandal comparable to that over Victor Hugo's Romantic drama *Hernani* in 1830. Anyone who was anyone in the literary world was there. The shock effect from the beginning was tremendous, starting with Ubu's first utterance. The actor playing Ubu, Firmin Gémier, strode to the front of the stage, looked out at the audience, and shouted, 'Merdre!' – a deformation of 'merde' (shit), translated variously as 'Pschitt!', 'Shittr!' 'Shikt!', 'Shite!', etc. The extra 'r' allows the actor to enunciate the word in a more aggressive manner, accentuating its offensiveness. Parts of the audience erupted in outrage. For fifteen minutes the actors stood gaping, wondering who was putting on the show, them or the audience. When the play continued, its mix of absurd humour and scatology, and its provocative violation of all the prevailing conventions of theatre, created further unrest. Members of the audience booed and hissed, some shouted vulgarities back at the stage, objects were thrown, fights broke out in the auditorium.

Ubu is the ultimate anti-hero. Monstrous, animalistic and foul-mouthed, he is a child-man who spreads devastation throughout the world and indulges in one vile act after another. Egged on by his equally monstrous, lecherous wife, Mère Ubu, he murders, plots and pillages his way to the throne of Poland, inaugurating a reign of terror with the help of a so-called 'disembraining' machine before he is deposed and exiled. A burlesque of heroic theatre from Sophocles to Shakespeare (notably *Macbeth*), the play offers a vision of a man of insatiable appetites. The world of Ubu is a world of endless self-gratification, anarchy and destruction: 'I'll quickly make my fortune, then kill the whole world and bugger off' ('j'aurai vite fait fortune, alors je tuerai tout le monde et je m'en irai').

To get under his audience's skin, Jarry was using for the first time theatrical devices audiences would become accustomed to in the twentieth century: embarrassment, sick humour and – anticipating the Dadaists and Surrealists – shock. Jarry's aim was to provoke his predominantly bourgeois audience not only by challenging their sense of propriety but also by confronting them with a monstrous caricature of their own greed and rapacity. He also suggests the arbitrariness, as he saw it, of all forms of authority. But the play goes far beyond social and political satire. The 'filth' that characterizes Ubu is characteristic of humanity in general. As a personification of unbridled indulgence of appetites, Ubu is an image of the destructive potential of the human personality itself, of the disruptive Freudian *Id* – anticipating Surrealism, which was strongly influenced by Freudian ideas. Violence and its extravagantly stylized expression are central to the theatrical experience in *Ubu roi*. The play has the vicious energy of a Punch and Judy show. It is continuously funny, but also bleak in its representation of how bad the world can be; and sinister in its anticipation of the monstrous history of the twentieth century.

The play was revolutionary in that every aspect of it – action, character, staging, design, language – was anti-naturalistic. The action is characterized by its caricatural extravagance. The main characters are presented as animated puppets. Firmin Gémier was masked, given a huge false belly decorated with a vortex along with an elongated pear-shaped head, and spoke his lines in the strange staccato style which Jarry himself had begun to use several months earlier. The nobles, judges and financiers of Poland were represented by wicker dummies. The entire Polish and Russian armies were played by one actor each. Cardboard horses' heads were used for the Russian cavalry. The set, created by artists including Pierre Bonnard and Henri de Toulouse-Lautrec, combined multiple settings, some of which were quite unrelated to the action of the play. A 'formally dressed' actor would walk across the set with a printed placard (in the manner of the Elizabethan stage) to indicate the precise location of the action. And the stylized, Rabelaisian language, with its bombast, neologisms ('pschittasword', 'phynance-hook') and pompous archaisms ('cornegidouille', 'rastron') maintained the sense of wild unreality. The style established by the opening 'Merdre!' is sustained from beginning to end:

> PÈRE UBU: Pschitt!
>
> MÈRE UBU: Oh! That's a fine way to talk, Père Ubu. You're such a great lout.
>
> PÈRE UBU: Watch out I don't bash yer face in, Mère Ubu.
>
> MÈRE UBU: It's not me you ought to do in, Père Ubu, there's somebody else.
>
> PÈRE UBU: By my green candle, I'm not with you.
>
> MÈRE UBU: So, you mean, Père Ubu, that you're content with your lot?
>
> PÈRE UBU: By my green candle, pschitt, Madame, I bloody well am. More than content! I'm a Captain of Dragoons, aide de camp to King Wenceslas, decorated with the Order of the Red Eagle of Poland, and ex-King of Aragon. You can't do any better than that!
>
> PÈRE UBU: Merdre!
>
> MÈRE UBU: Oh! Voilà du joli, Père Ubu, vous estes un fort grand voyou.
>
> PÈRE UBU: Que ne vous assom'je, Mère Ubu!

MÈRE UBU: Ce n'est pas moi, Père Ubu, c'est un autre qu'il faudrait assassiner.

PÈRE UBU: De par ma chandelle verte, je ne comprends pas.

MÈRE UBU: Comment, Père Ubu, vous estes content de votre sort?

PÈRE UBU: De par ma chandelle verte, merdre, madame, certes oui, je suis content. On le serait à moins: capitaine de dragons, officier de confiance du roi Venceslas, décoré de l'ordre de l'Aigle Rouge de Pologne et ancien roi d'Aragon, que voulez-vous de mieux?

Anarchism, Dadaism, Absurdism

After the scandal of the first performances of *Ubu roi*, Jarry spent the remaining eleven years of his life turning himself into a type of Ubu figure. The intentional eccentricity of his own life, and his generally outrageous behaviour, made him a legend even before his early death at the age of thirty-four from a mixture of tuberculosis and alcoholism. His eccentricities included the adoption of the Ubu persona in everyday life (he affected Ubu's staccato speech and signed his letters 'Père Ubu'), recklessness with firearms (he regularly carried a loaded revolver) and his remarkable low-ceilinged apartment (he was short enough to stand upright, but many visitors had to stoop). Above all, he drank constantly. Roger Shattuck calls his prodigious drinking practices 'suicide by hallucination', while Jerrold Seigel comments that, in this, he was less the heir of Baudelaire than the double of Rimbaud, like him seeking to become a 'seer' through the systematic derangement of all the senses (*Bohemian Paris*, p. 321). The idea he embodied in his ultimately self-destructive lifestyle – an idea that had its origins in the Romantic cult of the 'artificial paradises' of drugs and alcohol, and was to become an important principle for the Surrealists – was that true artists should not simply create art but also live their art in their own lives, preferably at fever pitch.

Jarry's highly individualistic approach to life was no doubt shaped by its cultural and political contexts. It was matched in the political field by the emergence of anarchism. The period of anarchism's greatest activity and influence in Paris was, precisely, the last decade of the nineteenth century, when there was an epidemic of bomb-throwing and the figure of the anarchist cast a frightening shadow over the life of the city. The anarchist – the fanatical extremist bent on destroying the hated bourgeois society – represented individualism taken to excess. Anarchism (whose etymology derives from two words meaning *not* and *power*) is an ideology based on the belief that the individual should not be subject to any external restraints, any governmental mechanism, whatever.

The artistic continuation of anarchism in a collective sense was the movement known as Dada or Dadaism. Just as anarchism believed in the destruction of bourgeois society to allow new, free growth, so the Dadaists believed that institutionalized 'high' art must be destroyed before culture can be reborn on the basis of a new, liberated individualism. The name 'Dada' (the French word for hobby-horse, the wooden children's toy) was chosen for its apparent meaninglessness by a group of young rebels led by the Romanian poet Tristan Tzara (1896–1963), who started the Dada movement in Zurich, Switzerland, in 1916. Their rebellion was a reaction to the meaningless horrors of the First World War. The world had gone so incurably mad, they argued, that nothing – no art, no literature, no doctrine, no programme – had any value; like Jarry, they used the indiscriminate negation of accepted values in order to shock and scandalize. If Dada had any value, it lay precisely in its capacity to provoke a radical questioning of social and aesthetic values; it forced people to reassess art in general. Among its provocations was the organization of what used to be known as *happenings*, and which they called *manifestations*: a race between a typewriter and a sewing machine; a poetry reading in which the English, French, German and Italian versions of a poem were read simultaneously; a work of art built by making a pile with bits of old machine parts, and so on. They attached great importance to spontaneity. And, like Jarry, they realized the iconoclastic value of humour: if we laugh at something, we are well on the way to getting rid of it.

During the last decade of his life Jarry wrote a great deal. There were several more Ubu plays (*Ubu cocu*, 1897; *Ubu enchaîné*, 1900; *Ubu sur la butte*, 1901), a short novel, *The Supermale* (*Le Surmâle*, 1902), a strange, virtually unclassifiable text entitled *Exploits and Opinions of Dr Faustroll, Pataphysician* (*Gestes et opinions du docteur Faustroll, pataphysicien*, completed 1898, published 1911), and various finely nuanced critical texts, especially on theatre, as expressed in, for example, introductory talks written to precede performances of *Ubu roi*. *Dr Faustroll* includes a definition of pataphysics, the spoof science Jarry invented, in which contradictions are embraced and all possible viewpoints have equal validity. Pataphysics is, in Jarry's words, 'the science of imaginary solutions' and 'the law governing exceptions'. Jarry claimed that 'talking about things that are understandable only weighs down the mind and falsifies the memory, but the absurd exercises the mind and makes the memory work'. Like Ubu, pataphysics grew out of the fantasies inspired by Jarry's old physics teacher, Félix Hébert. But it was more than pure mischief-making, for it reflected Jarry's scepticism towards the faith in science and its deterministic laws that so strongly marked the educational system and the general intellectual environment in which he grew up. Written in the spirit of absurdity, it was a kind of inverted parody of scientific determinism – a celebration of originality and spontaneity, an affirmation of the importance of art and imagination.

Jarry died on 1 November 1907. His last utterance, apparently, was to ask for a toothpick.

Chapter 24

Apollinaire: impresario of the new

... fed up with this ancient world

– Apollinaire, 'Zone'

If Alfred Jarry was the agent provocateur of the avant-garde, Guillaume Apollinaire (1880–1918) was, in the words of Roger Shattuck, its impresario. Both in his own work and in his indefatigable activities as critic and propagandist, he championed everything that was new and challenging in the arts in the early twentieth century. His was the most influential new voice in poetry when it was bursting out of old forms and themes to discover what Baudelaire had proclaimed years earlier as the 'heroism of modern life'. His two major collections of poetry are *Alcools* (1913) and *Calligrammes* (1918).

Tradition and modernity

'What has our culture lost... that the *avant-garde* had in 1890?' asks Robert Hughes in the opening chapter of his book *The Shock of the New*. He answers: 'Ebullience, idealism, confidence, the belief that there was plenty of territory to explore, and above all the sense that art, in the most disinterested and noble way, could find the necessary metaphors by which a radically changing culture could be explained to its inhabitants.' The great metaphor of this sense of change – 'its master-image, the one structure that seemed to gather all the meanings of modernity together' – was, Hughes suggests, the Eiffel Tower. The Tower was built to serve as the central icon of the 1889 Exposition Universelle (World's Fair), the theme of which was industrial manufacture and *transformation*. The speed at which culture reinvented itself through technology from around 1880 to the outbreak of the First World War was astonishing. Inventions and discoveries included the automobile, the aeroplane, the telephone, the wireless, the phonograph, the telegraph, the light-bulb, the cinematograph, the gramophone disc, wireless telegraphy, radium and radiography.

[What emerged from] the growth of scientific and technical discovery... was the sense of an accelerated rate of change in all areas of human discourse, including art. From now on the rules would quaver, the fixed canons of knowledge fail, under the pressure of new experience and the demand for new forms to contain it. Without the heroic sense of cultural possibility, Arthur Rimbaud's injunction to be *absolument moderne* would have made no sense. With it, however, one could feel present at the end of one kind of history and the start of another.[1]

The changes in man's view of himself and the world between 1880 and 1914 – an excited sense of dynamism, an affirmation of the present in relation to the past – were reflected in an extraordinary ferment of the arts during this period. Traditional practices were radically questioned. This break in the arts reached its moment of most intense activity in France in the decade that immediately preceded the outbreak of the First World War in 1914. The art movement that captured this spirit in a particularly seminal way was Cubism, led by Pablo Picasso (1881–1973) and Georges Braque (1882–1963). Cubism represented an absolute break with the whole nature of traditional figurative painting. Since the Renaissance, painting had followed the convention of one-point, or single, perspective. Picasso and Braque wanted to represent the fact that our perception of an object is made up of multiple perspectives; Cubist painting aimed to represent the coexistence of several different planes on the same surface. In 1904 Apollinaire met Picasso and other members of the avant-garde. The following year, he published an article on Picasso, effectively the first critical appraisal of that painter ever to appear. He began to write exhibition reviews and catalogue prefaces, and became an energetic champion of Cubism. He became well established as an art critic. His essays on art were published in volume form in 1913 as *The Cubist Painters: Aesthetic Meditations* (*Les Peintres cubistes: Méditations esthétiques*). He was a brilliant propagandist. He seemed to know everyone and to be everywhere. It is hard to think of an important artist living in Paris before the First World War whose later fame did not owe something to Apollinaire's friendship and his writings about art.

Apollinaire's art criticism, though effective, was undistinguished, but it contributed greatly to his development and influence as a poet. His studies of the new painting stimulated him to envisage new techniques for poetry: simultaneity of points of view, juxtaposition of images, stream of consciousness, etc. Above all, he insisted on innovation. While Picasso and Braque were breaking up the conventional forms of art, Apollinaire was breaking up regular metre and grammatical sentences. While the Cubists were experimenting with *collage* (from 'to glue', reflecting the technique of making works of art out of emblems of modernity based on industrial mass production – scraps of newspaper, product packaging, rope, metal and so on, glued together), Apollinaire was putting words and letters together in new patterns, using typography to produce what came to be called 'concrete' poetry: that is, poetry in which the words are arranged in the shape of the object or phenomenon described in the poem (rain, a tie, a heart, etc.). Apollinaire's followers were influenced by his daring experimentation with the conventions of the genre: the 'Cubist' technique of juxtaposition, the combination of visuals and text in the *Calligrammes*, the abolition of all punctuation from *Alcools* onwards, uneven line length, occasional rhyme – all these features of his poetry signified the liberation of poetry from centuries-old formal conventions. In 1913, when *Alcools* was going to press, Apollinaire wrote a new poem, 'Zone', to introduce the book, to give the whole of it a modernist cast and to emphasize the importance he now attached to innovation. 'Zone' has been described as '*the* great poem of early modernism. A decade before the oft-quoted date of 1922, the year of [T. S. Eliot's] *The Wasteland* and [James Joyce's] *Ulysses*, Apollinaire has given us, in this long poem of wandering and dislocation, a sketch map of the modern.'[2]

'Zone'

Here are the first twenty-four lines of this 155-line poem:

> Finally you're fed up with this ancient world
>
> O Eiffel shepherdess tower your bridges this morning are bleating
>
> You've had it with living amongst the shards of Greece and Rome
>
> Even the cars are antiquities here
> Only religion has stayed entirely new
> Religion remains as simple as airport hangars
>
> In Europe you alone Christianity are not antique
> Europe's most modern man is yourself Pope Pius X
> And as for you whom the windows watch shame keeps you
> from venturing into a church for morning confession
> You scan the flyers leaflets and placards proclaiming
> the poetry of the day is here and for prose there are newspapers
> stacks of the latest thrillers twenty-five cents a piece
> the private lives of the famous and umpteen titles besides
>
> This morning I saw a pretty street whose name I forget
> New and sparkling clean it was the clarion of the sun
> The managers workers and chic stenographers

pass there four times a day Monday through Saturday
Three times a morning the siren blares
A bad-tempered bell bays out around noon
The pronouncements on billboards and walls
posters and plaques parrot and screech
I like the style of this industrial street
in Paris between rue Aumont-Thiéville and avenue des Ternes.

– Trans. Jan Owen

A la fin tu es las de ce monde ancien

Bergère ô tour Eiffel le troupeau des ponts bêle ce matin

Tu en as assez de vivre dans l'antiquité grecque et romaine

Ici même les automobiles ont l'air d'être anciennes
La religion seule est restée toute neuve la religion
Est restée simple comme les hangars de Port-Aviation

Seul en Europe tu n'es pas antique ô Christianisme
L'Européen le plus moderne c'est vous Pape Pie X
Et toi que les fenêtres observent la honte te retient
D'entrer dans une église et de t'y confesser ce matin
Tu lis les prospectus les catalogues les affiches qui chantent tout haut
Voilà la poésie ce matin et pour la prose il y a les journaux
Il y a les livraisons à 25 centimes pleines d'aventures policières
Portraits des grands hommes et mille titres divers

J'ai vu ce matin une jolie rue dont j'ai oublié le nom
Neuve et propre du soleil elle était le clairon
Les directeurs les ouvriers et les belles sténo-dactylographes
Du lundi matin au samedi soir quatre fois par jour y passent
Le matin par trois fois la sirène y gémit
Une cloche rageuse y aboie vers midi
Les inscriptions des enseignes et des murailles
Les plaques les avis à la façon des perroquets criaillent
J'aime la grace de cette rue industrielle
Située à Paris entre la rue Aumont-Thiéville et l'avenue des Ternes

The form and language of the poem – which describes a walk through Paris,
beginning one morning and continuing throughout a whole day and night
until the next morning – are new and adventurous: uneven stanza and line
lengths, kaleidoscopic changes in perspective, constant switches in tone, abrupt
juxtaposition, startling imagery (the Eiffel Tower as a shepherdess; the bridges
across the Seine as her flock; Christ, later on, as an aviator who holds the world

altitude record; the setting sun, in the poem's closing line, as a human neck from which a head has been severed). And Apollinaire affirms his wish to be 'modern' ('you're fed up with this ancient world', 'You've had it . . . with Greece and Rome'). As he strolls through the streets – an exercise in Baudelairean *flânerie* – he incorporates into his poem, *collage*-like, the 'art' and 'literature' of the city

> You scan the flyers leaflets and placards proclaiming
> the poetry of the day is here and for prose there are newspapers
> stacks of the latest thrillers twenty-five cents a piece . . .

> The pronouncements on billboards and walls

> posters and plaques parrot and screech

as well as references to the new mechanical age (automobiles, airfield hangars, factory sirens and, later, an aeroplane and omnibuses). The celebratory tone ('a pretty street', 'I like the style . . . ') is partly undercut, however, by discordant notes ('A bad-tempered bell', 'The pronouncements . . . parrot and screech'). The disjointed form of the poem, lacking any regular rhythm and rhyme or, indeed, punctuation, reflects the disorder of urban experience. And we become increasingly aware of the ambivalence of Apollinaire's attitude towards modern experience as embodied in the city, a profound tension in his mind between tradition and modernity. As David Kelley has written: 'The deliberately incongruous associations of the Eiffel Tower with pastoral sheperdesses, of religion with aircraft hangars, of Christ with the first aeroplane, of childhood piety and innocence with the brash brightness of an industrial street in the morning sunlight . . . are part of a subtle play with the private and cultural associations of youth and age, innocence and world-weariness, modern and ancient' ('Defeat and Rebirth', p. 84). The poem veers constantly between past and present, in both personal and cultural terms, as the poet wanders through the streets searching for new reference points for the self and identity. Personal memories obtrude into the present moment, while, on the other hand, the poet's mind is increasingly crowded with images from the mythology of Christianity and the ancient world, suggesting a desire to find, through (or by analogy with) the cohesion of traditional myth, a system of expression that will allow him to reconcile the richness of the past and the fragmentation of the present – the modern world of factories and omnibuses, automobiles and aeroplanes – in the name of a new art of the future.

Chapter 25

Breton & Company: Surrealism

Beauty will be CONVULSIVE or will not be at all.

– André Breton, *Nadja*

The literary precursors of Surrealism include the Marquis de Sade (1740–1814), Victor Hugo (1802–85), Gérard de Nerval (1808–55), Charles Baudelaire (1821–67), the Comte de Lautréamont (1846–70), Arthur Rimbaud (1854–91), Alfred Jarry (1873–1907) and Guillaume Apollinaire (1880–1918). The social origins of the movement lay, first and foremost, in the French experience of the First World War (1914–18). The cataclysm of the 'Great War' made the values and culture of the nineteenth century, with its proud belief in progress and reason, God and patriotism, seem meaningless. The very concept of 'civilization' was thrown into question; civilization was a sham, and this meant that art could no longer be a celebration of it. The disillusion of the younger generation of artists and intellectuals was reflected in the aggressive anti-art antics of the literary movement known as Dada or Dadaism (see above, p. 176). The aim of the Dadaists was to expose the culture of the past for the nonsense the war had proved it to be. The Dadaists' leader, the Romanian poet Tristan Tzara (1896–1963), chopped up newspaper articles, pasted them in random order and called them poems. When he arrived in Paris in 1919, he was warmly welcomed by a group of young poets: André Breton (1896–1966), Louis Aragon (1897–1982), Philippe Soupault (1897–1990), Robert Desnos (1900–45), Paul Éluard (1895–1952) and others. These young men, some of whom had served in the war, rejected outright the civilization that seemed to have betrayed them. Within a few years Dada had burnt itself out, but its spirit of shock and provocation carried over into the more positive concept of avant-garde art which was to become Surrealism (the word was borrowed from Apollinaire, who coined it in his 1917 programme note for the ballet *Parade*). Surrealism was arguably the most influential avant-garde movement of the twentieth century, international in scope and extending to every form of artistic practice from poetry and prose narrative to painting, photography, film and theatre.

Rebellion of the mind

Breton, the self-styled leader of the Surrealists, declared that he wanted to set people free from bourgeois society and every form of repression associated with it. He saw Surrealism less as a new poetics than as a kind of cultural therapy that would refresh and expand people's sense of reality by uniting them with their desires, giving them access to what he called 'the marvellous' in everyday life. His aim was no less than the regeneration of humanity through the transformative power of the imagination – to change the world by changing consciousness. The impetus for this exalted goal was provided by popular notions of Freudian psychoanalysis. Breton had spent nearly three years of the war as a medical student in the army psychiatric services, treating shellshock victims, and this experience had deeply marked him. Helping patients to analyse their dreams 'constituted', as he stated later, 'almost all the groundwork of Surrealism ... interpretation, yes, always, but above all liberation from constraints – logic, morality and the rest – with the aim of recovering their original powers of spirit'. In his 1924 *Surrealist Manifesto*, in which he attempted to codify the aims of Surrealism, he wrote: 'SURREALISM, n.m. Pure psychical automatism, which has the aim of expressing, whether verbally, in writing, or in some other manner, the actual functioning of the mind freed from any control by reason and any aesthetic or moral preoccupation.' Several years earlier, his familiarity with the Freudian techniques of free association had led him to discover automatic writing. In collaboration with Philippe Soupault, he had composed what may be regarded as the first Surrealist text, *The Magnetic Fields* (*Les Champs magnétiques*, 1920), where, as Breton described it, the two poets 'undertook to cover some paper with writing, with a laudable contempt for what might result in terms of literature'. They believed that automatic writing, by seeking to draw on the resources of the unconscious, would retrieve new truths from the hidden depths of the mind. Surrealism, Breton announced, was a means of uniting conscious and unconscious realms of experience so completely that the world of dream and fantasy would be joined to the everyday rational world in a new, higher reality – a surreality.

Freud was merely an excuse for the Surrealist project. While Freud was interested in the *interpretation* of dreams, with a view to curing the patient's neuroses, the Surrealists were interested in the dream as a source of pure imagination;[1] while Freud emphasized the destructive power of the libido, the Surrealists viewed the libido as a springboard for social transformation; and while Freud regarded mental disorders as an illness, a condition to be cured, for the Surrealists the unconscious mind represented a great reservoir of creative energy waiting to be released. For the Surrealists, moreover, madness and irrationality were qualities to be prized. Hadn't the men in authority who had led their fellows to the senseless slaughter of the Great War always claimed that society could only be governed on the basis of reason? The Surrealists saw the irrational as an essential means of attacking the world of purportedly ordered (though in fact disordered) structures; similarly, they saw madness as an anti-value, a source of truth about human existence and a supreme form of revolt against an intolerable society.

To shock the bourgeoisie and the Catholic Church, the Surrealists cultivated scandalous behaviour. To jolt human awareness out of the tired habits of every-day perception, and to subvert the process of rational thought, they delighted, in their literary and artistic work, in incongruity – in imagery that juxta-posed, in often startling ways, things that would not normally be associated. The example Breton gave as a quintessential illustration of the Surrealist ideal of beauty was the phrase of the nineteenth-century poet Lautréamont in his *Songs of Maldoror* (*Les Chants de Maldoror*, 1868): 'As beautiful as the chance encounter on an operating table of a sewing machine and an umbrella'. Tech-niques of shock and surprise, a fascination with automatic writing, self-induced hypnosis, artificially altered states of consciousness, dreams and dream-states, chance encounters and 'mad love', all corresponded to a conception of art as offering a view onto a world transfigured by the imagination, which was seen by Breton as the only index of human possibility.

Paris Peasant and *Nadja*

Visual language is closer to the processes of the unconscious mind than thinking in words, and Surrealism's emphasis on imagistic modes of expression meant that its most natural vehicles were poetry and, especially, the visual arts (we all remember Marcel Duchamp's Mona Lisa with a moustache, Man Ray's iron with spikes, Salvador Dalí's lobster telephone, etc.). However, some of the most celebrated examples of Surrealist writing are to be found in experiments with prose narrative – in, most notably, Aragon's *Paris Peasant* (*Le Paysan de Paris*, 1926) and Breton's *Nadja* (1928). Indeed, both of these texts are admirable introductions to Surrealism.

For the Surrealists, art is *revelation* of reality, something that endeavours to produce and expand reality rather than to reproduce it. Rather than imitate life through writing, they wanted writing to embody the creative mind at work. They therefore felt that the traditional realist novel was an entirely inade-quate form of expression. For them the deterministically conceived characters and concrete descriptions of the realist novel were deeply banal; their own texts, by contrast, would seek to disclose the 'marvellous' that lies hidden just beneath the surface of reality. In *Paris Peasant* and *Nadja*, Paris itself becomes a beguiling dream-space where the extraordinary aspects of the everyday may be encountered. The Surrealists' favourite haunts were the covered arcades of the Right Bank, the *passages* built in the nineteenth century and which were still full of specialist shops, bazaars of the bizarre selling all manner of artefacts. If Baudelaire was the first strolling poet of the metropolis, the Surrealists followed in his footsteps. In his study of Baudelaire, Walter Benjamin (see above, p. 112) recognizes the phantasmagoria of culture provoked by Haussmann's transformation of Paris and embodied in the *passages* – waiting, as it were, for Surrealism. 'The father of Surrealism was Dada', he wrote; 'its mother was an arcade'.[2] The quest for the 'marvellous' corresponds to a fascination with the objects, often obsolete and unfashionable, washed up by modern consumerism – what Aragon calls 'the unconscious of the city'. The phantasmagoric eye selects and transforms these objects, celebrating the sense of the 'marvellous suffusing everyday existence'. *Paris Peasant*, a novel of 'casual strolling', contains a long section entitled 'The Passage de l'Opéra'. This *passage* is a double arcade which, even as Aragon was writing about it, was due for demolition. The narrator describes the arcade in minute detail. The shop window displays cast an unsettling spell, destabilizing rational thought and replacing it with the world of dreams. The shop, for instance, that sells canes and walking-sticks, 'displayed so as to show both stems and handles to their best advantage', their pommels fantastically varied: 'ivory roses, dogs' heads with jewelled eyes, damascened semi-darkness from Toledo, niello inlays of delicate sentimental foliage, cats, women, hooked beaks'. The panoply of the urban environment is transfigured in his imagination, producing a disquieting sense of the instability of the real.

The dominant effect of Aragon's prose, however, is one of enchantment. At one point the narrator describes his imaginings as he contemplates a ladies' hairdresser.

> I should like to know what nostalgias, what crystallizations of poetry, what castles in the air, what edifices of longing and hope are constructed in the head of the apprentice at the moment when, at the outset of his career, he forms the intention of becoming a ladies' hairdresser and begins to look after his hands. What an enviable destiny for the common man, to spend the whole day undoing the rainbow of feminine modesty, gossamer heads of hair, vaporous hair, those charming bedchamber curtains. He will spend his life in this haze of love, his fingers intertwined

with the very emblem of woman at her most unguarded, with this most subtle of erotic accessories, which she wears with such apparent nonchalance. There are surely some hairdressers who, like miners down the pit, have dreamed of specializing in brunettes, and others who will make a career of blondes. Have they never thought of deciphering these networks which, just before, gave a hint of the disorder of sleep? I have often stopped at the threshold of these shops which men may not enter, and I have seen the heads of hair unfurling in their grottoes.

Je voudrais savoir quelles nostalgies, quelles cristallisations poétiques, quels châteaux en Espagne, quelles constructions de langueur et d'espoir s'échafaudent dans la tête de l'apprenti, à l'instant qu'au début de sa carrière il se destine à être coiffeur pour dames, et commence de se soigner les mains. Enviable sort vulgaire, il dénouera désormais tout le long du jour l'arc-en-ciel de la pudeur des femmes, les chevelures légères, les cheveux-vapeur, ces rideaux charmants de l'alcôve. Il vivra dans cette brume de l'amour, les doigts mêlés au plus délié de la femme, au plus subtil appareil à caresses qu'elle porte sur elle avec tout l'air de l'ignorer. N'y a-t-il pas des coiffeurs qui aient songé, comme des mineurs dans la houille, à ne servir jamais que des brunes, ou d'autres à se lancer dans le blond? Ont-ils pensé à déchiffrer ces lacis où restait tout à l'heure un peu du désordre du sommeil? Je me suis souvent arrêté au seuil de ces boutiques interdites aux hommes et j'ai vu se dérouler les cheveux dans leurs grottes.

The ordinary young hairdresser becomes a surrogate poet; the sight of his shop triggers the evocation of a fantasy world; the rhapsodic prose affirms the powers of human desire and imagination.

Like *Paris Peasant*, *Nadja* is autobiographical, a similarly hybrid text combining confession, testimony and manifesto. It also contains photographs, in order to dispense with any need for conventional 'realist' description of place. The narrative begins with a quest for identity: it opens with the question 'Who am I?' In the first section, Breton discusses the ways in which he intends to explore his own life.

I intend to relate, in the margin of the narrative on which I am about to embark, only the most significant episodes of my life *such as I can conceive it apart from its organic design*, that is, to the extent that it is subject to chance events, from the smallest to the greatest, where, reacting against my ordinary idea of existence, my life leads me into a kind of forbidden world, a world of sudden connections, petrifying coincidences, reflexes that head off any other mental activity, chords struck as though on the piano, flashes of light that would make you see, really *see*, if only they were not so much quicker than all the rest.

Je n'ai dessein de relater, en marge du récit que je vais entreprendre, que les épisodes les plus marquants de ma vie *telle que je peux la concevoir hors de son plan organique*, soit dans la mesure même où elle est livrée aux hasards, au plus petit comme au plus grand, où regimbant contre l'idée commune que je m'en fais, elle m'introduit dans un monde comme défendu qui est celui des rapprochements soudains, des pétrifiantes coincidences, des réflexes primant tout autre essor du mental, des accords plaqués comme au piano, des éclairs qui feraient voir, mais alors *voir*, s'ils n'étaient encore plus rapides que les autres.

The essential theme of the early pages of *Nadja* is the importance of apprehending the messages of the unconscious in order to enrich our conscious life with the full creative potential of desire; and the focus of the passage above is what Breton calls 'objective chance' – 'sudden connections', 'petrifying coincidences', 'flashes of light', miraculous occurrences in the external world that seem to have no obvious causality nor to reflect conscious volition. They respond, rather, to our unconscious desire and transfigure our mental world. The Surrealists believed that at certain moments we come upon places, objects or people with an uncanny ability to reveal us to ourselves, or to open new horizons. Such a person is the enigmatic Nadja, a real person with whom Breton had a brief relationship. He meets her, quite by accident, in the street (she 'enjoyed being nowhere but on the streets, the only region of valid experience for her'). She accompanies him on his wanderings around Paris, anticipating and entering into his thoughts and fantasies, acting as a catalyst for the irruption of the marvellous in everyday life as a result of 'signs' she is able to produce and interpret – showing Breton how 'reality' becomes Surreal. She has gone over to 'the other side of the mirror', and Breton longs to be able to join her.

Woman as muse, enabling men to find their own creative voice, was a prominent feature of the male-dominated Surrealist enterprise. Woman is presented as being in closer touch than man with her unconscious and with the prized irrationality of dreams. Not only is Nadja clairvoyant, she is also deranged. Breton as narrator adopts a tone of clinical observation, presenting his account of Nadja as a medical case study. She eventually fades from his life. Some months later, he hears that she has been committed to an asylum, but he does not visit her. Cast as poetic muse, she is a vehicle for Breton's realization of his Surrealist agenda. As 'her' story unfolds, he weaves his own discourse around it, his voice gradually effacing and ultimately eradicating hers. He incorporates her spirit into himself, rendering her dispensable. By the end she seems only to have been the figment of the imagination she has been instrumental in liberating.

Significance and legacy

Surrealism has been described as the last swoon of Romanticism. Just as Romanticism was a form of revolt against Enlightenment rationalism and neoclassical convention after the upheavals of the French Revolution and the Napoleonic Wars, so Surrealism was a form of rebellion against nineteenth-century positivism and the self-righteousness of bourgeois culture after the catastrophe of the First World War. Like the Romantics, the Surrealists worshipped liberty and love, and were fascinated by the creative power of the imagination.

The Surrealists made a tortuous attempt, from the late 1920s onwards, to integrate their revolutionary goals with those of the Communist International. The movement eventually split into political activists (Aragon, Éluard) and those who remained committed to the liberation of the imagination (Breton). The coming of the Second World War sounded the death-knell of Surrealism, just as the First World War had founded it; but it was less the war that killed it than the inevitability of compromise by absolutists in the face of fascism and the horrors of Nazism – the need for *engagement* in the world of the here and now, rather than rejection of it. Aragon and Éluard stayed in France to join the Resistance, while Breton fled to New York. When he returned to Paris in 1946, he found Albert Camus and Jean-Paul Sartre occupying central positions in French intellectual and literary life.

Despite the changed climate of the post-war world and its aftermath, the influence of Surrealism remains strong and pervasive. The lasting legacy of Surrealism in an international context has been admirably characterized by Al Alvarez:

> Surrealism ... changed the way the world is perceived. By creating a universal hieroglyphics for the unconscious, it helped to obscure the dividing line between waking and dreaming. Surrealist literature was never as persuasive as the painting, but the Surrealist perspective – the belief that experience is multi-layered and permeable, and that dreams and the unconscious soak through – became a basic premise of modern art ... In their different ways, Borges, Márquez, Ionesco and Calvino are surreal; so is the humour of the Marx Brothers, S. J. Perelman and Zero Mostel, the films of Buñuel, the soap operas of David Lynch, the stories

and pictures of Maurice Sendak; so too, in retrospect, are *Alice in Wonderland*, Gogol's 'The Nose' and Kafka's meticulously factual narratives. We now take for granted that reality is not what it seems and, at any moment and in any place, a trapdoor may swing open without warning and drop us into our unconscious.[3]

The influence of Surrealism on pop culture and the world of entertainment has been particularly strong (Alvarez might have placed *The Goon Show* and Monty Python alongside the Marx Brothers). Much postmodernist writing owes a debt to Surrealism, whether acknowledged or not. And it is easy to see why Surrealism had a great revival at the time of the students' revolt in the Paris of 1968 and why many of the slogans that appeared on walls in that month of May were phrases taken from the writings of the Surrealists or those who had passed in and out of the Surrealist movement. One of those slogans, which seemed to sum up all the others, was 'Dream is truth'.

Chapter 26

Céline: night journey

> The sadness of the world has different ways of getting to people, but it
> seems to succeed nearly every time.
>
> – Louis-Ferdinand Céline, *Journey to the End of the Night*

Céline's dark, raging vision of the horrors of the twentieth century exploded
on to the French literary scene with *Journey to the End of the Night* (*Voyage
au bout de la nuit*), his first novel, in 1932. Céline (the pen name of Louis-
Ferdinand Destouches, 1894–1961) never stopped raging, in a voice – derisive,
savage, funny, immensely eloquent – that broke with all the canons of French
narrative prose and pointed the novel in radically new directions. Just as Proust
liberated the French novel from the restrictions of linear plot and consistent
characterization, Céline freed it from the confines of formal artistic language
and conventional grammar, creating a powerfully original prose style based on
the expressive resources of popular speech.

Elements of a life

Céline was the product of the petit-bourgeois Paris of the small shopkeeper –
the nation of thrift, hard work, patriotism and anti-Dreyfus inclinations. The
son of an insurance clerk and a lacemaker, he was born in Courbevoie, in the
western suburbs of Paris. His mother ran a shop for many years in the Passage
Choiseul, specializing in old lace. In September 1912, after leaving school and
holding various short-term jobs, he volunteered for military service, serving
in a cavalry regiment. Soon after the outbreak of war in 1914, he was badly
wounded in his right arm, and suffered a concussion as the result of a bursting
German shell; he was mentioned in despatches and awarded the Médaille
Militaire. Deeply affected by his experience of the war, he was invalided out of
the army in 1915. After convalescing in Paris he worked for a while at the French
Consulate in London. In 1916 he set sail for the recently acquired colony of the
Cameroons in West Africa, where he stayed for almost a year as manager of a

cocoa plantation. After the war, he studied privately to obtain his Baccalauréat, undertook medical studies at the University of Rennes and, in 1924, qualified as a doctor. There followed a medical posting to Geneva with the League of Nations and a visit to the United States in 1925. In 1927 he established a medical practice in Clichy, and in 1929 set up home in Montmartre, where he lived for the next fifteen years, continuing to work as a doctor, mostly in working-class areas. He volunteered for military service at the outbreak of war in 1939, but was rejected on medical grounds.

Journey to the End of the Night (henceforward *Journey*) was a huge success, especially with the French left. Céline's portrayal of the trenches, of colonial Africa, of the brutalizing factories of the United States and of a corrupt and impoverished France was taken to be a political critique of the iniquities of world capitalism. However, after a two-month visit to Russia in 1936, Céline published a short pamphlet, *Mea Culpa*, in which he expressed his complete disillusion with Communism. A second novel followed in 1936: *Death on the Installment Plan/Death on Credit* (*Mort à crédit*), in which the narrator Ferdinand relates, often in a deeply comic mode, his childhood and adolescence in turn-of-the-century Paris. Céline then published, in 1937, a virulently anti-Semitic tract, *Bagatelles pour un massacre* (Trifles for a Massacre). This was followed by further anti-Semitic texts, *L'École des cadavres* (The School of Corpses, 1938) and *Les Beaux Draps* (A Fine Mess, 1941). Why Céline wrote these pamphlets – which are intellectually absurd and often repetitious – has greatly exercised commentators. One aspect of Céline's strange character was his apparent urge always to insult accepted opinion to a degree where he was made an outcast; his aim, he said, was to be reviled as 'the biggest bastard alive'. This was certainly the distinction he achieved with his pamphlets, which damned him utterly in the eyes of generations of French readers and critics, and continue to taint his literary reputation. During the Occupation, he obsessively voiced his anti-Semitic views and had contacts with right-wing writers and German authorities, but had nothing to do with the Vichy regime. However, fearing reprisals because of his notoriety, he fled France in June 1944 soon after the Normandy landings, and, with his third wife Lucette, his cat Bébert and his friend, the actor Robert Le Vigan, he spent months wandering across a chaotic, disintegrating Germany, finally arriving in the town of Sigmaringen, where the Vichy government in exile was established. There followed six difficult years in Denmark, including a spell of imprisonment for over a year. When the Danes refused to extradite him, a French court in 1950 tried him *in absentia* and found him guilty of wartime collaboration with the Germans. A year later, a second court granted him amnesty, and he was able to return safely to France. He settled in Meudon just outside Paris, resumed his medical practice and continued to write until his death in 1961. His last three novels, sometimes referred to as the German Trilogy – *Castle to Castle* (*D'un château l'autre*, 1957), *North* (*Nord*, 1960) and *Rigadoon* (*Rigodon*, 1969) – evoke in apocalyptic terms the last days of the Third Reich.

Céline's anti-Semitic tracts were, and are, odious to any civilized person. However, Céline was not a collaborator, he was contemptuous of the Vichy government and he cannot reasonably be described as pro-Nazi. His political vision, such as it was, was anarchistic. He was deeply hostile to the ideologies, of left or right, that proposed political panaceas to save humanity. This was partly because he had little faith in humanity itself. As Ferdinand Bardamu, the narrator of *Journey*, says: 'It's people you've got to be afraid of, and nothing else – always' ('C'est des hommes et d'eux seulement qu'il faut avoir peur, toujours'). Although Céline wrote, with some compassion, about the plight of the ordinary man, the lost and vulnerable individual, and although, throughout his life, he was deeply involved with the predicament of the poor, his vision was anti-humanist. His work, in that sense, is violently at odds with a literary tradition, from Montaigne to Voltaire and beyond, that often wrote in praise of man's possibilities. Part of the French literary tradition to which Céline might be said to belong is that of the outcast writer which runs from Villon (whom Céline admired more than any other French writer) through Rousseau and Rimbaud to Jean Genet. Céline's apocalyptic narratives are driven by a fierce desire to portray life as it is – to tell the truth, as Céline saw it, about the awfulness of men, the brutality of human society and the absurdity of lives always lived in the shadow of death and physical decay. He is a descendant of Zola in that, like Zola in *L'Assommoir*, his aim in *Journey* was to represent faithfully a certain state of affairs; it is an aim in no way incompatible with compassion. The integrity of Céline as an artist is mirrored in the stress Bardamu places on his wish as narrator to be a conscientious witness of the harsh realities of existence:

> The biggest defeat, in every department of life, is to forget, especially what has finally done you in, and to die without ever fully realizing what bastards men are. When the open grave is there in front of us, we mustn't try to be smart, but we mustn't forget either, we've got to tell the whole story without changing a word – tell all about the most vicious things we've seen men do and then throw in the towel and crawl on down. That's a big enough job for a whole lifetime.

> La grande défaite, en tout, c'est d'oublier, et surtout ce qui vous a fait crever, et de crever sans comprendre jamais jusqu'à quel point les hommes sont vaches. Quand on sera au bord du trou faudra pas faire les

malins nous autres, mais faudra pas oublier non plus, faudra raconter tout sans changer un mot, de ce qu'on a vu de plus vicieux chez les hommes et puis poser sa chique et puis descendre. Ça suffit comme boulot pour une vie tout entière.

A nightmare journey

Journey is built on Céline's own experiences, though it would be a mistake to identify its first-person narrator too closely with the author himself. It is the picaresque story of Ferdinand Bardamu, whose fifteen-year journey across the world, from Paris to Africa and the United States and back to Paris, is also a journey into the horrors of the twentieth century: war, nationalism, colonialism, industrial capitalism, economic depression and poverty. The first part of the novel describes Bardamu's experience of the destructive idiocy of the First World War. It then describes his experience in a trading company in Bambola-Bragamance in West Africa. Colonial Africa is portrayed as a torrid, mosquito-ridden world of disease, malevolence, corruption and exploitation. From Africa, Bardamu escapes to the United States. He arrives in New York, the soulless banking capital of the world, and then moves to Detroit, where he works for a while in the mechanized hell of the Ford car plant. Finally, he returns to a Paris menaced by economic depression and works as a doctor among the poor in suburban Rancy. Bardamu's life is an endless series of dislocations and disappointments, leading nowhere. The essence of *Journey* lies in the confrontation between a vile world and a bewildered individual – a twentieth-century *Candide* – whose experiences usually prove overwhelming and incomprehensible. The novel is a manifestation of what has been called the European revolt against culture; that is to say, it gives expression, compellingly, to the disillusionment with the very notion of progress of the immediate post-First World War generation.

The form of expression

The impact of *Journey* is visceral. Céline seeks to transmit emotion, not ideas; and he seeks to do so through style. In a letter to a critic dated 24 May 1936, Céline wrote: 'I don't want to narrate, I want to make people FEEL. It's impossible to do this with standard academic language – style that is correct and elegant . . . This type of language is *out of the question, it's dead*, as unreadable (in an emotive sense) as Latin' ('Je ne veux pas narrer, je veux faire

RESSENTIR. Il est impossible de le faire avec le langage académique, usuel –
le beau style . . . Leur langage est *impossible, elle est morte*, aussi illisible (en ce
sens émotif) que le latin'). The originality and power of Céline's writing lie in
two main aspects of his work: narrative and language.[1]

The narrative content and tone of his novels often take the form of a kind of
fantasy – delirious, hallucinatory visions whose élan sweeps the reader along
at considerable speed. Take this description, in *Journey*, of the killing-fields of
Flanders:

> Could I, I wondered, be the last coward left on earth? The thought was
> terrifying! . . . Lost in the midst of two million heroic madmen, all baying
> for blood and armed to the teeth! With and without helmets, without
> horses, on motorbikes, yelling, in cars, screeching, shooting, plotting,
> flying, kneeling, digging, prancing past, capering along, revving up, shut
> up on earth as if it was a loony bin, bent on destroying everything on it,
> Germany, France, whole continents, everything that breathes, destroy it
> all, madder than mad dogs, loving their madness (which dogs don't), a
> hundred, a thousand times madder than a thousand dogs, and so much
> more vicious! . . . What a sorry lot we were! No doubt about it, I
> thought: this crusade I'd got myself into was an apocalypse.
>
> Serais-je donc le seul lâche sur la terre, pensais-je? Et avec quel
> effroi! . . . Perdu parmi deux millions de fous héroïques et déchaînés et
> armés jusqu'aux cheveux? Avec casques, sans casques, sans chevaux, sur
> motos, hurlants, en autos, sifflants, tirailleurs, comploteurs, volants, à
> genoux, creusant, se défilant, caracolant dans les sentiers, pétaradant,
> enfermés sur la terre comme dans un cabanon, pour y tout détruire,
> Allemagne, France et Continents, tout ce qui respire, détruire, plus
> enragés que les chiens, adorant leur rage (ce que les chiens ne font pas),
> cent, mille fois plus enragés que mille chiens et tellement plus
> vicieux! . . . Nous étions jolis! Décidément, je le concevais, je m'étais
> embarqué dans une croisade apocalyptique.

There are innumerable scenes and episodes like this, characterized by their great
visionary power. The intensity of this type of narrative delirium is reinforced by
a prose style invested with the freshness and immediacy of the spoken tongue.
It is a style whose virtuosity invites comparison with Rabelais's 'carnivalesque'
style in the early Renaissance, before canons of correctness were imposed on the
French language (see above, p. 12). Forged from the vernacular, it involves the
lexicon, grammar and syntax of oral language. What is more, this style, which
gives the effect of uncontrolled spontaneity, was only arrived at after constant
rewriting. Astonishingly, *Journey* is in Céline's terms relatively traditional.
Stylistically, *Death on the Installment Plan* marked a radical development of

the methods deployed in *Journey*: argot, verbal invention and fragmentation of syntax, notably through the use of abrupt, exclamatory phrases, a feverish staccato, punctuated by Céline's trademark 'three dots' – the endless ellipses with which he broke the orthodox French sentence into pieces and stood French syntax on its head, permitting him to divide his text into rhythmical rather than syntactic units. His later novels would go even further.

Céline wanted to shock and provoke; his annexation of spoken French, spiced with slang and so-called 'obscenities', embodied his distaste for respectability, for the bland conventions of received usage in any context – linguistic or social. He also wanted to bewitch and seduce; the rhythms and effects of his 'little music', as he called his style, were intended in part to form a persuasive rhetoric that would seduce the reader, just as Bardamu is seduced into enlisting in the army by the music of the military band he hears by chance at the very beginning of the novel. This rhetoric is apparent in the following passage taken from the section of the novel that describes Bardamu's life as a doctor, after he has returned from the United States, in the Parisian suburbs at Rancy:

> With my medical degree, I could set up shop anywhere, that was true enough . . . Not that, anywhere else, it would be better or worse . . . A bit better to begin with, of course, because it takes a while for people to get to know you, to get into gear and find the trick of sinking their claws in you. Until they've found the chink in your armour, you can have a bit of peace, but once they've found it, it's the same old story no matter where you are. There's no doubt that the best time in a new place is that brief period when you're not yet known. After that, the same shit starts all over again. That's what people are like. The main thing is not to wait too long and let the sods find out exactly where your weak spots are. You've got to squash bedbugs before they can crawl back into their cracks. Don't you reckon?
>
> As for the patients, the clients, I had no illusions at all about them . . . They wouldn't be one bit less scrounging, stupid or spineless in any other part of town than they were here. The same booze, the same old dramas, the same sports gossip, the same happy subjection to their natural urges – food, booze, sex – would produce the same filthy horde, blathering endless bullshit, bragging, scheming, and very aggressive when not in a panic.
>
> But just as sick people turn over in bed, so, in life, we have a perfect right to heave ourselves over on to the other side, it's all we can do, the only defence that's ever been found against Destiny. No use hoping to drop your troubles off somewhere along the way. It's as if your Misery is like some hideous woman you're married to. Maybe it would be better

in the end to give her a little bit of love rather than wear yourself out fighting with her all your life. Because obviously you can't bump her off, can you?

Avec mon diplôme, je pouvais m'établir n'importe où, ça c'était vrai... Mais ce ne serait autre part, ni plus agréable, ni pire... Un peu meilleur l'endroit dans les débuts, forcément, parce qu'il faut toujours un peu de temps pour que les gens arrivent à vous connaître, et pour qu'ils se mettent en train et trouvent le truc pour vous nuire. Tant qu'ils cherchent encore l'endroit par où c'est le plus facile de vous faire du mal, on a un peu de tranquillité, mais dès qu'ils ont trouvé le joint, alors ça redevient du pareil au même partout. En somme, c'est le petit délai où on est inconnu dans chaque endroit nouveau qu'est le plus agréable. Après, c'est la même vacherie qui recommence. C'est leur nature. Le tout c'est de ne pas attendre trop longtemps qu'ils aient bien appris votre faiblesse les copains. Il faut écraser les punaises avant qu'elles aient retrouvé leurs fentes. Pas vrai?

Quant aux malades, aux clients, je n'avais point d'illusion sur leur compte... Ils ne seraient dans un autre quartier ni moins rapaces, ni moins bouchés, ni moins lâches que ceux d'ici. Le même pinard, le même cinéma, les mêmes ragots sportifs, la même soumission enthousiaste aux besoins naturels, de la gueule et du cul, en referaient là-bas comme ici la même horde lourde, boueuse, titubante d'un bobard à l'autre, hâblarde toujours, trafiqueuse, malveillante, agressive entre deux paniques.

Mais puisque le malade, lui, change bien de côté dans son lit, dans la vie, on a bien le droit aussi, nous, de se chambarder d'un flanc sur l'autre, c'est tout ce qu'on peut faire et tout ce qu'on a trouvé comme défense contre son Destin. Faut pas espérer laisser sa peine nulle part en route. C'est comme une femme qui serait affreuse, la Peine, et qu'on aurait épousée. Peut-être est-ce mieux encore de finir par l'aimer un peu que de s'épuiser à la battre pendant la vie entière. Puisque c'est entendu qu'on ne peut pas l'estourbir?

This passage[2] reflects in microcosm the general thematic pattern of the novel: the compulsive journeying of Bardamu leads to disillusionment, as he realizes that the excitement of travel is an absurdity; displacement produces only sameness, for everywhere he finds the same misery and meanness. The first paragraph invokes the possibility that a change of environment might have positive results; qualification as a doctor might be a passport to a better life. But this optimistic notion is immediately defined as an illusion: men are mean and malevolent wherever you are. The third paragraph suggests ironically that life itself is inherently a form of sickness, a pathological condition. The sick person's desire to shift positions in bed, like Bardamu's urge to travel, reflects an impossible desire to escape Destiny: death (which awaits us all at the far end of the night) and the futility of human existence.

Céline's rhetoric is marked by the rhythmic force of his language and by techniques of persuasion aimed at implicating the reader. In the first paragraph, the familiar term 'vacherie' (derived from *troupeau de vaches*, a herd of cows) gives hyperbolic force to the notion of man's malevolence by suggesting an animalistic dimension. In the second paragraph, the tone becomes vituperative as the invective uses triple and quadruple repetition ('ni moins', 'même(s)') to insist on man's cupidity, stupidity and baseness. Men are reduced – echoing the connotations of 'vacherie' – to animal level, subjected as they are to their basic instincts (food, alcohol, sex). The oxymoronic 'soumission enthousiaste'/'happy subjection' suggests abject acceptance of alienation through these 'artificial paradises'. Finally, men and women are reduced to an undifferentiated 'horde' – a word that again connotes animality and denotes a large crowd of people who are lost or out of control. '[T]itubante' (from the infinitive *tituber*, to stagger) evokes drunkenness, but also confusion; the word is appropriately paired with 'bobard', suggesting the exaggerated nonsense of their wild utterances. Effects of sound, of alliteration and assonance ([b], [a], [ou]), reinforce the insistent rhythm ('music') of the long sentence beginning 'Le même'/'The same'. The shape of this sentence mimics the disoriented, lurching movements of a mass of human beings – aggressive, fearful, mindless – driven along by their instincts. The word 'paniques' (in a panic) is rich in implications: it suggests, in the context of the novel as a whole, the fear of death that figures prominently in the text.

The narrator thus progresses from the particularities of his own situation ('my . . . degree, I') to general reflections on the human condition. This corresponds to the transitions from the first person to the second person (*you*) or the impersonal third person (*one/you/we*) and from the past to the present tense; and it involves insidious appeals to the reader to identify with the narrator. In the first paragraph, the 'forcément'/'of course' invites the reader's assent, just as the repeated use of the second person invites the reader to endorse the dismal truth about human malevolence. The repetition in various ways of the same proposition is a feature of the rhetorical style; and the 'En somme'/'There's no doubt' provides a conclusive note. In the third paragraph, the 'on a bien le droit'/'we have a perfect right' and the 'nous'/'we' of the generalizing statement again seeks the reader's complicity; it is a statement about the universal condition of human beings. The rhetoric of persuasion is reinforced by the maxim-like quality of the short sentence 'Faut pas . . . route'/'No good ... along the way', which suggests a self-evident truth. The final question ('Puisque ... l'estourbir?'/'Because ... can you?'), echoing the question that ends the first paragraph, is a rhetorical ploy, inviting the reader to respond; *estourbir* is an aggressively colloquial word, as if concluding the passage with a provocation in order to underline the general provocation embodied in a form of writing that aims to assault the reader's emotions with the darkness of its vision.

Merlin Thomas writes: 'The disruptive, violent, corrosive side of Céline is what makes him a man of our century, just as Villon is a product of the Hundred Years War. But ... above all ... he was a great artist, shot through with compassion born of indignation. Original as a stylist, he makes most other narrative writers in France since 1932 look like either virtuous commercial hacks or like specialists in intellectual self-abuse' (*Louis-Ferdinand Céline*, pp. 239–40). Thomas's view that Céline is the greatest twentieth-century French novelist along with Proust is widely shared. As for Céline's influence on modern fiction, it has been immeasurable. In the United States especially, Céline's influence has been acknowledged by numerous writers, notably Charles Bukowski, William Burroughs, Joseph Heller, Jack Kerouac, Henry Miller, Thomas Pynchon, Philip Roth and Kurt Vonnegut. In France, Sartre and Queneau were strongly influenced by Céline. Sartre was bowled over by *Journey* when he read it soon after its publication, and in the light of Céline's novel he completely revised the style of the book he was working on: *La Nausée*.

Chapter 27

Sartre: writing in the world

> ...no society can complain of its intellectuals without accusing itself,
> for it has the intellectuals it makes.
>
> – Sartre, 'A Plea for Intellectuals'

When Jean-Paul Sartre (1905–1980) was arrested in 1970 for distributing seditious political literature in the streets of Paris, President de Gaulle vetoed the move to hold him in prison, reportedly saying: 'You don't put Voltaire in prison.' What he was alluding to by his comparison was that both men made themselves the radical consciences of their respective societies. Sartre – at once a philosopher, novelist, dramatist, literary critic, art critic, political theorist, political essayist and political activist – was as versatile and prolific as Voltaire, but more original. He dominated the intellectual life of the mid-twentieth century. He was the public intellectual par excellence.

Early years

The essential theme of Sartre's life and work is liberty. As a child, his rejection of authority was expressed in his rejection of his tyrannical grandfather, Charles Schweitzer, who ran a German school in Paris. He chose to become a writer precisely because his grandfather solemnly warned him against it. Sartre's brilliant account of his childhood, and of his relationship to culture and language, in *Words* (*Les Mots*, 1964) sheds much light on his later development. Sartre's father died when his son was fifteen months old, and Sartre and his mother were reintegrated into his grandfather's household, where they were both called 'the children' and brought up together almost as brother and sister. In *Words* he lays bare the forces that worked upon his consciousness a child, especially the bourgeois ideology embodied in his grandfather. The book is the judgement of the man on the child, but it is even more a judgement on a society that bred extreme forms of self-deception. Sartre presents himself as a young boy constrained to fit into an old-fashioned household and describes how he was constantly acting a part to please a dictatorial old man. At the heart of Sartre's work generally is a preoccupation with all forms of hypocrisy; playing roles, pretending to be someone or something one is not, came to represent a major crime in his eyes.

The Schweitzer family came from Alsace-Lorraine, in the north-eastern part of contemporary France, and belonged to a sternly puritanical Protestant tradition. Sartre (who later became an atheist) developed an attitude of uncompromising integrity towards the things in which he believed. This attitude marked Sartre's entire, increasingly non-conformist life. The ethics of Existentialism are informed by an austere moral attitude. In 1964 he became the only writer to decline the Nobel Prize in Literature. He felt that the Nobel Prize embodied an Establishment view of literature whose main concern was the maintenance of bourgeois values.

Sartre's years as a student (1920–29) coincided with post-First World War inflation and the beginning of the Great Depression. He became increasingly aware of social inequalities and poverty, reflected in the contrast between the people he saw in the streets (the poor and unemployed, the war veterans and the war widows and orphans) and the complacency of the bourgeoisie to which he belonged. His conversion to Marxism came after the Second World War, but its roots were laid much earlier. In 1933–34 Sartre spent a year in Berlin, studying German philosophy, in particular the doctrines of Edmund Husserl (1859–1938) and Martin Heidegger (1889–1976), which were to form the basis for his brand of Existentialism. During this year Sartre witnessed the Nazi takeover in Germany and the burning of the Reichstag; he saw at close range the growth of fascism, mass hysteria and anti-Semitism. In 1936 'Popular Fronts' came to power in both France and Spain. Almost immediately there were attempts at *coups d'état* in both countries. In France the coup, led by the neo-Fascist Action Française, proved abortive. Léon Blum's government introduced a number of significant social reforms: social security, paid holidays, the forty-hour week. Spain, however, was almost immediately engulfed in civil war. Arms and munitions were sent by the fascist countries to the right-wing forces in Spain, while the Republican Left received little help. It became a matter of faith among many left-wing writers and intellectuals to support the Spanish Republican cause. Many travelled to Spain from the United States and other parts of Europe. The so-called International Brigade included such figures as Louis Aragon, Georges Bernanos, John Dos Passos, Ilya Ehrenburg, Ernest Hemingway, Arthur Koestler, André Malraux, Pablo Neruda, George Orwell and Simone Weil. Their cause was doomed, but the symbolic political value of their commitment was immense. The Spanish Civil War ended with the victory of General Franco in 1938, while the Blum government was replaced by a right-wing government firmly convinced that Hitler would be preferable to Blum. The end of the conflict in Spain was closely followed by Hitler's march into Austria. The Second World War became inevitable.

Nausea

1938 was the year in which Sartre published *Nausea* (*La Nausée*), widely recognized as one of the most important and arresting French novels of the twentieth century. Cast in the form of a diary, the novel describes several weeks in the life of the narrator-diarist Antoine Roquentin, a historian whose projected biography of a minor eighteenth-century nobleman has led him to Bouville, a provincial seaport – a fictional transposition of Le Havre (where Sartre taught philosophy at the *lycée* between 1931 and 1936). The diary describes Roquentin's daily existence: his long days in the town library, his desultory sexual encounters with the female proprietor of the café he frequents, his fitful relations with a former girlfriend, Anny, and with someone he refers to only as the 'Autodidact', and, above all, his growing feelings of existential malaise.

Nausea expresses in compelling fictional terms some philosophical ideas about consciousness and human identity. The novel remains first and foremost a work of art, a poetic fiction about the visceral experience of alienation and absurdity; it does not have to be read in the light of theories expressed by the author elsewhere. The essential idea of the book is that *nothing justifies existence*. Roquentin painfully discovers that the world and his existence in it are *contingent* rather than *necessary*: the world has no reason to exist and neither does he. His diary reflects his efforts to describe and, if possible, elucidate his growing state of anxiety. He experiences a series of attacks of physical nausea as his new perception of the world intensifies. He feels lost in the nauseating proliferation of the world, though at the same time part of it; it seems that the world of consciousness will be engulfed by the world of things. He reaches a crisis after he contemplates the root of a chestnut tree in the town park and begins to conceptualize his feelings. He sees himself as a doomed rationalist, whose desire to understand the world with concepts and categories has collapsed; he becomes aware that all the distinctions and definitions that give intelligibility to our perceptions are merely projections of the human mind. Objects exist beyond words, beyond ideas and concepts.

> The word Absurdity is now born beneath my pen; just now, in the park, I couldn't find it, but I wasn't looking for it either, I didn't need it: I was thinking without words, *about* things, *with* things ... Without formulating anything clearly, I understood that I had found the key to Existence, the key to my Nausea, to my own life. In fact, all that I was able to grasp afterwards comes down to this fundamental aburdity.

Absurdity: another word; I am struggling against words; back there I touched the thing itself. But I want to capture the absolute nature of this absurdity here. A gesture, an event in the little coloured world of men can only be absurd in a relative sense: in relation to particular circumstances. A madman's ravings, for example, are absurd in relation to the situation in which he finds himself, but not in relation to his madness. But just now I experienced the absolute: the absolute or the absurd. That root – there was nothing in relation to which it was not absurd. Oh, how can I express that in words? Absurd: in relation to the stones, the tufts of yellow grass, the dry mud, the tree, the sky, the green benches. Absurd, irreducible; nothing – not even a profound, secret upheaval of nature – could explain it. Obviously I didn't know everything, I hadn't seen the seed sprout or the tree grow. But faced with that big gnarled paw, neither ignorance nor knowledge was important: the world of explanations and reasons is not the world of existence.

Le mot d'Absurdité naît à présent sous ma plume: tout à l'heure, au jardin, je ne l'ai pas trouvé, mais je ne le cherchais pas non plus, je n'en avais pas besoin: je pensais sans mots, *sur* les choses, *avec* les choses . . . Et sans rien formuler nettement, je comprenais que j'avais trouvé la clef de l'Existence, la clef de mes Nausées, de ma propre vie. De fait, tout ce que j'ai pu saisir ensuite se ramène à cette absurdité fondamentale. Absurdité: encore un mot; je me débats contre des mots; là-bas, je touchais la chose. Mais je voudrais fixer ici le caractère absolu de cette absurdité. Un geste, un évènement dans le petit monde colorié des hommes n'est jamais absurde que relativement: par rapport aux circonstances qui l'accompagnent. Les discours d'un fou, par exemple, sont absurdes par rapport à la situation où il se trouve mais non par rapport à son délire. Mais moi, tout à l'heure, j'ai fait l'expérience de l'absolu: l'absolu ou l'absurde. Cette racine, il n'y avait rien par rapport à quoi elle ne fût absurde. Oh! Comment pourrai-je fixer ça avec des mots? Absurde: par rapport aux cailloux, aux touffes d'herbe jaune, à la boue sèche, à l'arbre, au ciel, aux bancs verts. Absurde, irréductible; rien – pas même un délire profond et secret de la nature – ne pouvait l'expliquer. Evidemment je ne savais pas tout, je n'avais pas vu le germe se développer ni l'arbre croître. Mais devant cette grosse patte rugueuse, ni l'ignorance ni le savoir n'avaient d'importance: le monde des explications et des raisons n'est pas celui de l'existence.

Roquentin knows that he cannot avoid the question of what to do with his life, and his awareness of this fills him with horror. He is afraid of his existing self and its insistent demand for a form of justification:

My thought is *me*: that's why I can't stop. I exist because I think . . . and I can't prevent myself from thinking. At this very moment – this is terrible – if I exist, *it is because* I hate existing. It is I, *it is I* who pull myself from the nothingness to which I aspire: hatred and disgust for existence are just so many ways of *making me* exist, of thrusting me into existence. Thoughts are born behind me like a feeling of giddiness, I can feel them being born behind my head . . . If I give way, they'll come here in front, between my eyes – and I go on giving way, the thought grows and grows and here it is, huge, filling me completely and renewing my existence.

Ma pensée, c'est *moi*: voilà pourquoi je ne peux pas m'arrêter. J'existe parce que je pense . . . et je ne peux pas m'empêcher de penser. En ce moment même – c'est affreux – si j'existe, *c'est parce que* j'ai horreur d'exister. C'est moi, *c'est moi* qui me tire du néant auquel j'aspire: la haine, le dégoût d'exister, ce sont autant de manières de *me faire* exister, de m'enfoncer dans l'existence. Les pensées naissent par-derrière ma tête . . . si je cède, elles vont venir là devant, entre mes yeux – et je cède toujours, la pensée grossit, grossit et la voilà, l'immense, qui me remplit tout entier et renouvelle mon existence.

As the novel ends, Roquentin has abandoned his biography and is waiting to leave for Paris where he hopes to write another kind of book, probably a novel – for only the ordered, harmonious forms of art, he now feels, may redeem the shapelessness and emptiness of existence. Art holds out the possibility of escape from the real world of contingency into a created world of necessity.

Commitment

Despite the momentous political events of the 1930s, and his brilliant story *Childhood of a Leader* (*L'Enfance d'un chef*, included in *The Wall/Le Mur*, 1939), in which he dramatizes the psychological roots of the fascist (and anti-Semitic) mentality, Sartre showed little interest in becoming involved, as writer or citizen, in political debate. This changed with the outbreak of the Second World War in 1939. Sartre was enlisted as a reservist and sent to the front in Alsace. He was caught up in the German advance of May–June 1940 and taken prisoner, without firing a shot, on his thirty-fifth birthday: 21 June 1940. His experience as a prisoner of war made him realize that everyone was *de facto* engaged in history, whether they liked it or not. He later revealed that during his period of internment at Stalag XIID in Trier, he underwent a fundamental change of attitude and became committed to the ideal of collective action. He was released from service in March 1941 on medical grounds, and sent back to Paris, where he engaged in clandestine resistance to the Germans.

Although Roquentin experiences responsibility in a purely negative way, a strong current in *Nausea* is the satire Sartre directs at the town's bourgeoisie.

The opposition between consciousness and the external world is transposed into social terms as a conflict between the insecure individual and the massive complacency of organized bourgeois society, anatomized at length in Roquentin's visit to the Bouville art gallery. As he gazes at the portraits of several generations of the town's worthies, offensive in their frozen respectability, he feels disgust at the idea that these men were blinded by their pomposity to the 'absurdity' of the world; and he feels anger at their conviction that their right to exist included the right to govern society and use it to their own advantage.

> All square, that day as on every other day, with God and the world, these men had slipped gently into death, to go and claim the share of eternal life to which they were entitled.
> For they had a right to everything: to life, to work, to wealth, to authority, to respect, and finally to immortality.

> En règle, ce jour-là comme les autres jours, avec Dieu et avec le monde, ces hommes avaient glissé doucement dans la mort, pour aller réclamer la part de vie éternelle à laquelle ils avaient droit.
> Car ils avaient eu droit à tout: à la vie, au travail, à la richesse, au commandement, au respect, et, pour finir, à l'immortalité.

Hatred of the bourgeoisie and bourgeois values came increasingly to dominate Sartre's thought. His satire of the bourgeois of Bouville reflects in reverse the values he most wanted to promote: moral honesty, lucidity and man's capacity to take responsibility for himself.

Sartre discussed these values in a massive philosophical work, *Being and Nothingness* (*L'Être et le néant*, 1943), which developed the main themes of *Nausea*, in particular the implications of the realization that there is no 'meaning' in the world that is not imposed by the human mind. Consciousness is radically free, enabling the human subject to assert and define her/himself as an individual. Man is condemned to be free and is thereby responsible for all his actions. Acceptance of freedom gives one's life *authenticity*, genuine value; avoidance of freedom means *inauthenticity*. All the ways in which people avoid their freedom are termed *bad faith*, which consists in the conscious or unconscious belief that our behaviour is determined or justified by something external to us, by some higher authority or by other people's rules or wishes. The bourgeois in *Nausea* assume that their privileged social position is justified by notions such as 'the social order', 'respectability' and 'property'. Since it is consciousness that gives meaning to the world, there is a duel between consciousnesses, between people's different visions of themselves and the world; tension and struggle are the basis of human relationships. The corollary of freedom is the necessity of *choice*. Human reality is entirely conscious; it faces its future with the total *responsibility* of choosing what it will become. This 'becoming' is a continuous concrete process. While we cannot alter the past as we move through time, we are always free to alter its significance by a further act of choice. Choice is manifested in *action*. Man is his acts. Our free choices create the concrete situations in which others must make their free choices, and vice versa. Our choices have moral implications, for they express our view of what it is right for a human being to do in any given situation. Man is thus the architect of his own values. The plays and novels Sartre produced during the 1940s and 1950s are largely concerned with the dramatization, sometimes schematically but always accessibly, of the ways in which people try to exercise their freedom as they grapple with the ambiguities of choice both in their personal lives and in the world of politics.

After the Liberation of France in August 1944, Sartre began a life of political activism. He became committed to socialism as the only means of producing a genuinely free society. While never joining the French Communist Party, he continued to support it until the Soviet repression of the Hungarian revolt in 1956 made him break off all relations with it (while continuing to believe in Marxism). His reaction to the Soviet invasion of Czechoslovakia in August 1968 was even more violent. With the failure of the May 1968 revolt in France, he was left in despair about the future of European politics; he attacked the French Communist Party for betraying the hope which the students had created of a new, genuine revolution. His politics became increasingly radical. He concerned himself more and more with the struggles of the colonized world and, in the last decade of his life, gave his support to the European Maoist movement.

In 1945 Sartre co-founded the monthly review *Les Temps modernes* (Modern Times) with Simone de Beauvoir and Maurice Merleau-Ponty. The review became the main platform for Existentialism and for Sartre's frequent interventions in the political, social and cultural issues of the day. In 1947 he wrote a series of articles, published in book form as *What Is Literature?* (*Qu'est-ce que la littérature?*, 1948), in which he championed the idea of the 'committed writer', arguing that the writer's primary task is to further the cause of progress (identified with socialism) by making people aware of their freedom and responsibility, and by addressing the political issues of the day. Literature cannot be extricated from history or society. This notion of 'commitment' is thus the exact opposite of Roquentin's dream of a perfect aesthetic anti-world.

Sartre never stopped interrogating literature and its function. He wrote distinguished essays on Georges Bataille, Maurice Blanchot, Albert Camus, John Dos Passos, William Faulkner, André Gide, Paul Nizan and Nathalie Sarraute. He wrote critical studies of Charles Baudelaire, Jean Genet, Stéphane

Mallarmé and Gustave Flaubert. His lifelong fascination with Flaubert culminated in the early 1970s with his three-volume study, *The Family Idiot* (*L'Idiot de la famille*, 1971–72). The main reason for Sartre's preoccupation with his nineteenth-century predecessor is that the case of Flaubert embodies in a particularly acute form the 'false situation' of the writer in bourgeois society. In *What Is Literature?* Sartre denounced those nineteenth-century bourgeois writers – and Flaubert in particular – who concealed their fear of commitment behind an attitude of élitist reclusion. Flaubert's aestheticism, his immersion in a world of pure Form, thus constitutes a flagrant challenge to Sartre's belief that art is necessary action. Sartre dismissed Flaubert as 'a talented *rentier*'[1] and blamed his detachment for the repression of the Paris Commune, when 20,000 Parisians were killed by French government troops after the failure of the revolutionary uprising in the city in 1871. He meant that Flaubert, in his writing, did nothing that might have prevented the disaster (whereas Flaubert himself blamed the events of 1871 on a general failure to understand his novel *Sentimental Education*). But having chosen to study a writer as different from himself as possible, Sartre's antipathy became informed by a degree of empathy, an ambivalence to be explained by the fact that Flaubert's ironic detachment brought into sharp relief Sartre's own anxieties and frustrations as a writer. By the 1970s Sartre had lost much of his influence and was well aware that his various political activities had gone virtually nowhere. Had his own work, he wondered, made any greater impact on public life than that of the uncommitted Flaubert? Had it, any more than Flaubert's, reduced oppression and injustice in the world? There are grounds for regarding *The Family Idiot* as being obliquely autobiographical, almost self-mocking, reflecting Sartre's sense that Flaubert's 'false situation' was similar to his own, mirroring his own position as a public writer who, though committed to revolutionary action, remained an essentially marginal figure relegated (as the 3,000 pages of *The Family Idiot* themselves demonstrate) to endless word-spinning.

And yet, like Voltaire and Victor Hugo before him, Sartre's funeral attracted a vast crowd. Sartre may have been haunted by ambivalent feelings about his own work and achievement; we can say with certainty, however, that no other writer embodied so brilliantly, and across so many fields, the complexity of the modern world.

Chapter 28

Camus: a moral voice

Don't wait for The Last Judgment. It takes place every day.

– Camus, *The Fall*

When Albert Camus (1913–60) was awarded the Nobel Prize in Literature in 1957, the jury singled out for special mention the contribution he had made to illuminating 'the problems of the human conscience in our times'. Camus and Sartre were united by their common need to explore the limits and consequences of human action in an age – the war and the immediate post-war period – in which fundamental values needed to be rediscovered and reaffirmed. On the other hand, they were separated by their totally different social backgrounds and by their profoundly different attitudes to politics. Whereas Sartre, the Parisian, was a son of the bourgeoisie, received a highly privileged education and came first in the national philosophy examination (the *agrégation*), Camus was the son of European (French and Spanish) immigrants to Algeria, the French colony where he grew up in conditions of extreme poverty; and he was forced by tuberculosis to cut short his education at the University of Algiers. Whereas Sartre was a builder of grand intellectual systems, Camus was suspicious of doctrinaire thinking of any kind and distrusted abstractions that cannot be verified by personal experience.

The outsider

Camus's first publications were two slim volumes of lyrical essays, *Betwixt and Between* (*L'Envers et l'endroit*, 1937) and *Nuptials* (*Noces*, 1938). Together with his later collection of essays, *L'Eté* (*Summer*, 1954), they contain some of his best writing. Their setting is Algeria and their central theme is the contrast between the pleasures of the natural world – the sea, sun and light of the Mediterranean – and the dark realities of poverty and death. This contrast is an aspect of what, in his essay *The Myth of Sisyphus* (*Le Mythe de Sisyphe*, 1942), Camus called 'the absurd'. For Camus this meant any of three things:

a sense of human mortality (greatly heightened in the case of Camus by the shadow cast by his tubercular condition); the presence in the world of apparently arbitrary suffering and death; and the disjunction between the lack of immanent meaning in the world and the human need for sense and purpose.

The absurd is the theme of the novel *The Outsider/The Stranger* (*L'Étranger*, 1942), which tells the story of an office worker, Meursault, a white Frenchman living in Algeria who kills an Arab on a beach for no apparent reason. At the beginning of the novel he learns of his mother's death and attends her funeral. The day after the funeral he starts an affair with a girl named Marie. Later on, he gets involved with some Arabs; in the blinding light and burning heat of a beach one of the Arabs pulls a knife, the sunlight flashes on the blade, Meursault happens by chance to have a gun, and the trigger 'gives way under [his] finger'. When Meursault is charged with murder he makes no conventional plea of self-defence or accident, but says only that he killed the man 'because of the sun'. In the course of the trial witnesses are called to say how callously he behaved at his mother's funeral. The bourgeois judges pronounce him to be morally degenerate, a man 'without a soul', and he is sentenced to the guillotine.

One of the main features of *The Outsider* is the innovative use Camus makes of first-person narrative. Though written in the first person, by Meursault himself, the novel sounds more like a third-person account. The hallmark of first-person narratives is self-disclosure; but the most striking aspect of Meursault as narrator in Part 1 of *The Outsider* is his lack of self-reflection. On feelings and beliefs, he has little to say. He narrates events in a terse, impassive manner, making little attempt to comment on his experience. He reveals no emotion at the news of his mother's death, nor does he describe his feelings when he attends the vigil and the funeral, though he senses that people are questioning his behaviour. The contrast between the first-person form, which usually creates a sense of intimacy between the narrator and reader, and the distancing effect of the text, is a key aspect of *The Outsider* (though the style changes in the long final chapter, when Meursault finally expresses his thoughts). The narrative style (the laconic tone, the dominance of the *passé composé*, the use of the diary form, the absence of causal explanations) not only reinforces a general sense of disconnectedness, of living aimlessly from day to day on an immediate, physical level, but also generates a great deal of ambiguity.

The novel opens on a note of uncertainty:

> Maman died today. Or yesterday maybe, I don't know. I got a telegram from the old people's home: 'Mother passed away. Funeral tomorrow. Sincerely.' That doesn't mean anything. Perhaps it was yesterday.

210 Camus: a moral voice

> Aujourd'hui, maman est morte. Ou peut-être hier, je ne sais pas. J'ai
> reçu un télégramme de l'asile: 'Mère décédé. Enterrement demain.
> Sentiments distingués.' Cela ne veut rien dire. C'était peut-être hier.

Meursault's comment 'Perhaps it was yesterday' may suggest that the preced-
ing phrase, 'That doesn't mean anything', refers to the fact that the day of his
mother's death can't be inferred from the cryptic message. Or does the comment 'That doesn't mean anything' refer to the fact that the brevity and impersonality of the telegram, with its conventional formula ('Sincerely'), doesn't
mean anything from the point of view of human feeling – an early allusion
to the empty official language of the court? Or does the phrase 'That doesn't
mean anything' refer, more generally, to the death of Meursault's mother and
express a feeling of apathy and possible insensitivity, reflected in the flatness of
Meursault's tone?

Meursault asks his boss for two days off. His uncertainty about what he
should have said anticipates various instances of his unease with other people. He sometimes has the impression that other people are judging him in
some way. At the funeral, he's unsure how to behave. During his trial the nature
and degree of his crime are submerged in the hostility provoked by his bare
but unwavering honesty about his feelings. When asked how he felt towards
his mother, he replies that he would have preferred his mother not to die, but
all normal people have, at some time, more or less wished for the death of
those they love. Meursault often admits uncertainty and says no more than he
means. His simple, direct language is drowned by the assertive, public language
of the court. He soon has the curious impression of being an intruder at his
own trial, which he finds ridiculous. He becomes simply 'the accused' and
is told to keep quiet. His depersonalization reaches an extreme point when
his defence counsel speaks in his name, in the first person, as if replacing him
entirely. The individual is silenced. Only the public voice is heard. By this time,
of course, Meursault has realized that he is being tried less for his actual crime
than for his social attitudes. Throughout his interrogations, he is questioned
about his feelings and beliefs rather than his acts. He is condemned because
of his unconventional ideas about love and marriage, his lack of conventional
ambition and, above all, because he didn't cry at his mother's funeral. He is also
punished for not even wanting to believe in God. Society cannot understand
Meursault, finds him threatening and does not hesitate to eliminate him.

Meursault's trial and imprisonment provoke his growing self-awareness,
culminating in a dramatic outburst to the prison chaplain, followed by a sense
of calm. For the first time, he says, he opens himself to 'the benign indifference
of the world. Finding it so much like myself, like a brother really, I felt that I

had been happy and that I was happy once more' ('la tendre indifférence du monde. De l'éprouver si pareil à moi, si fraternel enfin, j'ai senti que j'avais été heureux, et que je l'étais encore'). Confronted with death, Meursault realizes the universality of his situation: all men are condemned ultimately to die. Life has no transcendent meaning, but it's all we have: the only worthwhile afterlife would be one in which life on earth, the happiness of sheer sensuous existence, could be remembered. Death, he says, makes all human experience equally unimportant and yet equally precious.

Meursault's affirmation of the inextinguishable value of life is eloquent. However, it clearly raises questions. Not only does the novel's portrayal of institutionalized society have a caricatural quality, but the type of authenticity represented by Meursault – he will not lie about his feelings – is strictly limited. An innocent murderer? A victim of the prejudices of society? The novel's textual ambiguities, as embodied in its narrative style and certain elements of the plot (why does Meursault return to the spot on the beach where he had first encountered the Arabs? Why does he fire the extra shots into the body of the Arab?), are inseparable from its moral ambiguities. By leaving open the question of how one system of values might be thought preferable to any other, the novel invites the reader to reflect on this very issue.

Morality and politics

Camus's thinking, like that of Sartre, was profoundly affected by his experience of the Second World War. He could not remain morally indifferent to historical events: the deportation of Jews, the concentration camps, mass deaths. In occupied France, he played a part, mainly as a journalist, in the Resistance. It was his daily editorials in the underground Resistance newspaper *Combat*, of which he was chief editorial writer from 1944 to 1947, that made him famous and gave him his status, at the end of the war, as an intellectual and moral leader. Not only do Camus's *Combat* articles[1] reflect an important moment in his development as a writer (he was just finishing his novel *The Plague* (*La Peste*, 1947)), but they still resonate powerfully today. What is striking about them is his independence of thought. They show him trying to think his way in the world, and becoming increasingly suspicious of the Manichean divisions of the Cold War and the ideologies of left and right. Though concerned with immediate, largely political issues, in the context of a post-war world in which so much weighed in the balance, the articles deal essentially with the same themes that inform his novels, plays and essays: freedom, justice, truth. Above all, they are marked by the strength of Camus's conviction that political choices are essentially ethical choices. He was fundamentally preoccupied with the ways in which a just order could be created out of the ruins of war, while at the same time upholding liberty. His thinking can be seen evolving from support of a revolutionary transformation of post-war society to scepticism towards the radical left alongside his fierce opposition to the reactionary right. At the same time, the post-war purge of wartime collaborators came to represent for Camus a situation in which yesterday's victims, the occupied French, were quickly becoming today's executioners. Camus's aim was to build a political culture free from violent absolutes, within which it was possible to exist as 'neither victims nor executioners'. Dialogue had to be the basis of any just political order. This explains Camus's deep respect for journalism itself and his emphasis on the political importance of the scrupulous use of language. 'The language of free men,' he wrote, 'is the language of clarity'; and clarity, he stressed, can be realized only in language able to convey the full complexity of any question.

The Plague directly reflects Camus's experience of the war and Resistance. The novel describes the outbreak of a bubonic plague in Oran, a small town in Algeria. The plague has been read as an allegory of the German occupation of France and, more generally, as a symbol of evil in the world: that is, the suffering brought upon man by uncontrollable forces such as disease or natural disaster (the plague as life) or by the behaviour of people towards others (the plague as human history). As the epidemic advances, the protagonists adopt positions ranging from exploitation of the situation for personal advantage to heroism and idealism. Rieux, the doctor (and narrator) who organizes the medical units formed to combat the plague, embodies a modest, pragmatic humanism. By his conduct, and his instinctive feeling of responsibility towards his fellows, he bears witness, Camus suggests, to the reality of moral values. This ethic of responsibility creates a sense of community among men, rooted in the realization that it is based on a belief in the dignity of human life.

The essential theme of *The Plague* – how to live in times of catastrophe – was explored at length in the philosophical and historical work, *The Rebel* (*L'Homme révolté*, 1951). This book, written at the height of the Cold War, was a critique of communism at a time when the French Communist Party was still very powerful. *The Rebel* was a plea for moderation against the extremism of right or left, and against the false promise of a future utopia: 'historicism justifies every humiliation,' wrote Camus, 'by reference to a future grandeur'. Camus attacked some aspects of Marx – his messianic tendencies and his historical determinism – and condemned the Soviet Gulag (the system of forced labour camps begun in 1919 and used by Stalin from the 1930s onwards at the cost of millions of lives). No ideological ends, Camus wrote, can justify murderous means: the moral costs are too great: 'It is better to be wrong while killing no one than to be right with mass graves.' Terror, he reminded his readers, had followed in the wake of both the French and the Russian revolutions. In effect, Camus was postulating a non-violent liberal-democratic alternative to communism. The publication of *The Rebel* infuriated Sartre, who argued that we must be prepared to get our hands dirty by using violence in the pursuit of our ultimate political goals. To condemn the Soviet prison camps was, for Sartre, to side with capitalism against communism. The famous debate that ensued in *Les Temps modernes* marked the end of Camus's friendship with Sartre. The break, announced by Sartre, was brutal and public; Camus was deeply affected by it.

During the last ten years of his life, Camus was derided by the intellectual establishment of the Left Bank for his non-PC sins. He was accused of complicity with French colonialism because of his refusal, as a French-Algerian born and bred, to take sides in the Algerian War (1954–62) and, in particular, to support the idea of Algerian independence from France. It was especially galling for Camus that the native Algerians whose plight he had highlighted as a journalist in the late 1930s, in the left-wing newspaper *Alger Républicain*, had become the cause of the Parisian intelligentsia that now vilified him. Moreover, the North African world that was now the subject of so many intellectual discussions in Paris was the world he knew (and loved) with the emotional and physical intensity of someone who had grown up within it. The left's support for Algerian nationalism and the Arab National Liberation Front he found simple-minded. As a white working-class French-Algerian, he understood that the interests of both the indigenous and the non-indigenous populations needed to be accommodated in a just solution. He continued to dream of an integrated community of Arabs and Europeans. He condemned the violence that exploded on both sides, but he was eventually rendered mute, as it were, by its degeneration into extremes and by his realization that he could do nothing to influence the situation. The sudden withdrawal of the French from Algeria, he believed, would result in a power vacuum that would plunge the country into chaos, cause economic havoc and hold back the conditions of democracy for years to come. This is precisely what happened after de Gaulle granted independence in 1961. History proved Camus right, just as it did in relation to the Soviet Union.

As a working-class Algerian who had spent the first half of his life outside France, Camus had always regarded the intellectual world of Paris as a place of exile, not a home; but during his last decade he felt increasingly isolated. His status as a public intellectual, and in some measure the public conscience of his age, weighed heavily upon him. These feelings are reflected in his last completed novel, *The Fall* (*La Chute*, 1956). The entire text takes the form of an extraordinary, virtuoso monologue delivered by Jean-Baptiste Clamence, formerly a much-admired Parisian lawyer specializing in 'noble causes'. In his private life, too, he is a model citizen, a man of infinite kindness and virtue. One day, however, he does nothing to save a girl who commits suicide by throwing herself into the Seine. From that moment on, he is tortured by guilt. He exiles himself to a bar in Amsterdam where he buttonholes customers who will listen to his confessions and confess their sins in turn. He is, he explains, a 'judge-penitent'; he judges himself once he has confessed and he will judge others when they do the same. A tour de force of ironic confessional narrative, *La Chute* is a sad, sardonic reflection on the torments and hubris of the liberal conscience. As Tony Judt has written:

> The idea of judgment – of judging oneself, being judged by others, of the passing of judgments as an act of intellectual power and of retreat/exile as an escape from such judgments – is a constant of Camus's writing from *L'Etranger* to *La Chute*, and the latter can also be read as a brilliant, dyspeptic disquisition on the forensic habits of mind of the Parisian talking classes – of 'those specialized cafés where our professional humanists sit' . . . Camus took his *own* failings as he saw them, generalized them across the spectrum of Parisian intellectual life, and then subjected them to cruel inspection and interrogation in the manner of his own intellectual enemies.
>
> (*The Burden of Responsibility*, pp. 101, 104)

On Camus's death, it was, ironically, Sartre who summed up Camus's achievement best in the obituary he wrote in *France-Observateur*, assimilating him (just as he had in his review-essay on *The Outsider* when that book first appeared) to the great tradition of French moralists that included Voltaire, Rousseau and others. The word *moraliste* in French has none of the implications of the English 'to moralize'. It denotes a writer who comments – wryly, compassionately, searchingly – on the human condition, with its infinite complexities and ironies, and whose commentary is informed not only by his sincerity and clear-sightedness but also by his own discomfort and self-questioning.

> In this century, and against the grain of History, he was the current heir of the long line of moralists whose work perhaps constitutes the most distinctive feature of French literature. His stubborn humanism, narrow and pure, austere and sensual, waged an uncertain battle against the monstrous, overwhelming events of our times. And yet, conversely, at the very heart of our age, through his unrelenting revolt, against the

Machiavellians and the golden calf of realism, he reasserted the existence of morality.

Il représentait en ce siècle, et contre l'Histoire, l'héritier actuel de cette longue lignée de moralistes dont les œuvres constituent peut-être ce qu'il y a de plus original dans les lettres françaises. Son humanisme têtu, étroit et pur, austère et sensuel, livrait un combat douteux contre les évènements massifs et difformes de ce temps. Mais, inversement, par l'opiniâtreté de ses refus, il réaffirmait, au cœur de notre époque, contre les machiavéliens, contre le veau d'or du réalisme, l'existence du fait moral.[2]

Chapter 29

Beckett: filling the silence

> We always find something, eh, Didi, to give us the impression that we exist?
>
> — Estragon, *Waiting for Godot*

The Irish-born Samuel Beckett (1906–89), though associated with the 'new novel' (see below, pp. 223–24) and the 'new theatre' of Eugène Ionesco (1912–94), Arthur Adamov (1908–70) and Jean Genet (1910–86), was a highly original writer who developed his own distinctive modes of expression in fiction and on the stage. His work has been described by J. M. Coetzee as 'philosophical comedy'. 'Beckett,' he writes, 'was an artist possessed by a vision of life without consolation or dignity or promise of grace, in the face of which our only duty – inexplicable and futile, but a duty nonetheless – is not to lie to ourselves. It was a vision to which he gave expression in language of a virile strength and intellectual subtlety that marks him as one of the great prose stylists of the twentieth century.'[1]

Finding a voice

Beckett's discovery of his literary voice came to him as a kind of revelation shortly after the Second World War. It became clear to him that he should allow his work to be created out of his pessimistic view of the world and his sombre conception of what it means to be human; it would be shaped by what he called, in his highly autobiographical play *Krapp's Last Tape* (1958), 'the dark [he had] always struggled to keep under'. It was now, in 1946, that he decided to write mainly in French, which he knew intimately (he had been a student at Trinity College, Dublin, excelling at French and Italian, and had settled in Paris in 1937). Eschewing the Joycean verbal flamboyance of his pre-war English works (*Murphy*, 1938, for example), he aimed for a more rigorous and concentrated form of writing. The now familiar adjective

216

'Beckettian' is usually used to denote 'meaning stripped down to a minimum of discourse or ornament to reveal existence as such in its full bleakness' (Luke Thurston). Instead of enacting mastery, he wanted his writing to express, he said, feelings of ignorance and impotence: the ignorance inflicted by a chaotic and directionless world; the impotence resulting from, among other things, the problem of expression itself, the difficulties involved in using language to make sense of and to communicate our experience. The very idea of artistic representation is problematized. In a series of dialogues on contemporary painting with the art critic Georges Duthuit, first published in 1949, Beckett stated that his preferred form of art expressed the artist's awareness that 'there is nothing to express, nothing with which to express, nothing from which to express, no power to express, no desire to express, together with the obligation to express'. Both Beckett and his characters are possessed by a need to express; and the paradox at the centre of his work – the yearning for expression and the conviction of its pointlessness – gives his writing its energy and its tragi-comic quality.

   The half-dozen or so years that followed Beckett's transition to French were hugely productive. He wrote a trilogy of prose texts, *Molloy* (1951), *Malone Dies* (*Malone meurt*, 1951) and *The Unnamable* (*L'Innommable*, 1953), the thirteen *Stories and Texts for Nothing* (*Nouvelles et textes pour rien*, 1955), and the two-act play that made him famous, *Waiting for Godot* (*En attendant Godot*, 1953). These works introduce the main elements of his vision and all of his most characteristic themes: incomprehension, disconnection, degeneration, identity, language. The framework of traditional narrative *à la* Balzac is removed entirely. No details of history or social setting are provided, there is no coherent plot, no omniscient narrator, no linear narrative progression and the 'characters', such as they are, are marginal specimens of humanity who exist in a void, in a wasteland or in confined spaces, with no apparent purpose for their existence in a world that is collapsing:

> I listen and the voice is of a world collapsing endlessly, a frozen world, under a faint untroubled sky, enough to see by, yes, and frozen too. And I hear it murmur that all wilts and yields, as if loaded down … For what possible end to these wastes where true light never was, nor any upright thing, nor any true foundation, but only these leaning things, forever lapsing and crumbling away, beneath a sky without memory of morning or hope of night.   (*Molloy*)

In his trilogy, Beckett explores the experience of living in a world that lacks meaning, and the question of the identity of the human self in such a world.

His texts radically question the philosophy of the subject founded by the seventeenth-century thinker René Descartes (1596–1659): *Cogito ergo sum*, I am thinking, therefore I must exist. The main focus of the texts becomes narration itself, as the various narrators attempt to capture the essence of their (self-)consciousness by telling their stories in a definitive form that will enable them to fall silent. But they fail in their quest. Each successive narrating voice shows a heightened tone of desperation and an increased level of physical disability. Molloy sets off on a bicycle, gets lost, regresses to crutches, then to crawling, and finally to complete immobility. Malone, dying, ruminates as he writes strange, confused stories in a room. The voice in the third part of the trilogy is that of someone who is unnamable, a barely human creature without memory or any capacity for coherent thought. All these monologuers have is words, which ultimately fail them. They are condemned, like the nameless speaker in *The Unnamable*, to carry on speaking, to try to make sense of things that remain forever enigmatic:

> The fact would seem to be, if in my situation one may speak of facts, not only that I shall have to speak of things of which I cannot speak, but also, which is even more interesting, but also that I, which is if possible even more interesting, that I shall have to, I forget, no matter. And at the same time I am obliged to speak. I shall never be silent. Never.
>
> (*The Unnamable*)

In his plays as in his fiction, Beckett created compelling drama by getting rid of the traditional elements of plot, setting and character. There is indeed a high degree of convergence between his plays and his fiction in terms of both style and theme. *Waiting for Godot*, with its depiction of two tramps waiting for someone who never shows up, represents man's state of metaphysical suspension: his predicament of perpetual uncertainty. In later plays, Beckett created indelible images for the experience of waiting, wondering, remembering, decaying: Hamm's legless parents, Nag and Nell, living in dustbins in *Endgame* (*Fin de partie*, 1957); Krapp listening obsessively to recordings made by his younger self on an old tape recorder in *Krapp's Last Tape* (*La Dernière Bande*, 1959); Winnie, buried in sand, first up to her waist, then up to her neck, in *Happy Days* (*Oh les beaux jours*, 1963), prattling away to her husband, Willy; and a husband, wife and mistress encased in funeral urns in *Play* (*Comédie*, 1963). Like his prose works, his dramatic texts grew shorter and shorter, more and more condensed, coming increasingly to resemble the monologues of his fiction, with only one speaker, sometimes only one actor not speaking but simply listening to a disembodied voice. In the mesmeric *Not I* (1972), the speaker is simply a 'Mouth', gabbling out memories to a silent

'Auditor'. Gabriel Josipovici, in his introduction to the novel trilogy, aptly observes that: 'Beckett returns to an oral literature … an art that demands to be spoken by the reader, the words formed in the mouth, the rhythms activated in the body.' Imperative to Beckett in performances of his dramatic work were quality of voice and observation of rhythm, the latter meticulously signalled through punctuation and extensive directorial notes. His preferred actors – Jack MacGowran, Patrick Magee, David Warrilow, Billie Whitelaw, for all of whom he wrote individual pieces – had arrestingly expressive voices and a natural feel for the precisely patterned rhythms and repetitions (and silences) of his texts, which became increasingly like musical compositions, intense and often moving.

Although Beckett's world is dark, it is filled with humour, a humour of limit, incapacity and parody. The comic rituals, for example, of the two tramps in *Godot*; Lucky's crazed monologue in the same play, a parodic disarticulation of human intellectual pretensions; Winnie's cheerful chatter in the face of her progressive entombment in *Happy Days*; Molloy's complex stratagems – a parody of the human desire for order – for keeping track of his 'sucking-stones'. Having gone to the seaside, Molloy gathers a store of pebbles, which he calls stones. He wants to suck them all in order – 'turn and turn about', as he puts it. He therefore needs to keep track of each of them as he moves them around his person.

> I had sixteen stones, four in each of my four pockets these being the two pockets of my trousers and the two pockets of my greatcoat. Taking a stone from the right pocket of my greatcoat, and putting it in my mouth, I replaced it in the right pocket of my greatcoat by a stone from the right pocket of my trousers, which I replaced by a stone from the left pocket of my trousers, which I replaced by a stone from the left pocket of my greatcoat, which I replaced by the stone which was in my mouth, as soon as I had finished sucking it. Thus there were still four stones in each of my four pockets, but not quite the same stones. And when the desire to suck took hold of me again, I drew again on the right pocket of my greatcoat, certain of not taking the same stone as the last time. And while I sucked it I rearranged the other stones in the way I have just described. And so on.

But he soon realizes that the four stones circulating might always be the same four, and so he is forced to reflect (hilariously, over several pages) on other methods. Transfer the stones four by four? Increase the number of his pockets? Eventually he comes to the conclusion that he will have to keep all the unsucked stones on one side, shifting them over to the other, one by one, after sucking.

He is thus put off balance for considerable periods as he feels the weight of the stones dragging him to the right or the left. This is uncomfortable and frustrating, and in an access of annoyance he finally gives up his attempt to achieve complete order, with everything in its correct place, and throws away all the stones but one, 'which I kept now in one pocket, now in another, and which of course I soon lost, or threw away, or gave away, or swallowed'.

Waiting for Godot

Two grubby individuals, Vladimir (Didi) and Estragon (Gogo), are waiting on a bare country road, next to a solitary tree, for someone called Godot, about whom we learn nothing. If Godot comes, they will be saved, or at least their situation will be improved. Another strange couple arrive in the form of Pozzo and, in the noose of Pozzo's rope, Lucky: master and slave. In the first act these two newcomers are highly voluble (though only once, spectacularly, in the case of Lucky), but when they reappear in the second act Pozzo is blind and Lucky completely dumb. Godot does not come, but at the end of each act, a boy appears to tell Didi and Gogo that he will come the next day. 'Nothing happens, twice', according to a much-quoted phrase used to characterize the play. Although the characters are caught up in a cycle of repetition, this statement is not entirely true, for they are also subject to a seemingly irresistible process of degeneration. Dereliction: the use of tramp-figures to represent the human condition ('at this place, at this moment of time, all mankind is us, whether we like it or not', says Vladimir in Act II) reinforces the play's strong elements of parody, with its demystification of the humanist idea of the dignity and nobility of Man.

When Pozzo and Lucky are on stage in Act I, a motif of the four characters' interaction is their cruelty towards each other: above all that of Pozzo towards Lucky, but also that of Lucky towards Estragon, whom Lucky kicks violently in the shins, and of Estragon, who retaliates by spitting on Lucky. However, their cruelty is arbitrary, their behaviour incoherent. Their utterances are empty of meaning ('It's a good sign', 'It's true that the population has increased') and the attitudes they adopt can be contradictory: Estragon expresses sympathy for Lucky at one moment and then equal sympathy for Pozzo, who immediately derides what he himself has just said ('I don't remember what it was, but you may be sure there wasn't a word of truth in it'). The characters have no psycho-logical density and embody no discernible set of values. The differences between them serve, however, to keep the whole game going. As Vladimir laconically notes after Pozzo and Lucky have departed: 'That passed the time.' Moreover, the *clochards*, with their baggy coats, bowler hats and boots, are clowns who have their own ways of making the time pass more quickly, a feature of their existence to which our attention is drawn through their lugubrious reference ('Charming evening we're having') to various forms of popular entertainment: the pantomime, the music-hall, the circus. The function of Didi and Gogo as clowns – indeed, as clowns playing clowns – reinforces the senses in which the play is a 'tragi-comedy', as designated by Beckett in the play's subtitle. Humour is not a way out of tragedy, but an ironically appropriate component of it: a further degradation. Indeed, 'tragedy', writes Terry Eagleton, 'is too highbrow, portentous a term for the deflation and debunkery of Beckett's work'.[2] But a tragic dimension lives on, as Eagleton suggests, 'in the grief which springs from knowing that we can no longer even bestow a dignified title on our wretchedness, view it as part of some predestined order, or discern in its very terror the shadow of transcendence'.[3] Pathos – 'It's awful,' says Estragon – lies in the difficulty of *being*, of being in the world and not knowing why. It lies in the very experience of waiting, which the play represents and which is the source of its comedy and distinctive tone. The theatrical originality of *Godot*, as Leo Bersani and Ulysse Dutoit have stressed, lies in its dramatization of the question of how to pass the time, given the absence of God: 'waiting for drama has become the object of dramatic representation'.[4] The play's particular fascination resides in the tension between its 'serious' themes (dependency, exploitation, physical suffering, the burden of existence) and the buffoonery of language and knockabout farce. Estragon and Vladimir engage in comedy routines familiar to anyone who has been to the circus or knows the movies of Laurel and Hardy or the Marx Brothers: trousers that fall down, characters who fall over, a preoccupation with feet and boots, a game of hat-swapping, pointless patter about carrots and radishes. Above all, they divert themselves with cross-talk, with rapid one-line exchanges that are constantly repeated, get nowhere, go round in circles:

> VLADIMIR: You must be happy too, deep down, if only you knew it.
> ESTRAGON: Happy about what?
> VLADIMIR: To be back with me again.
> ESTRAGON: Would you say so?
> VLADIMIR: Say you are, even if it's not true.
> ESTRAGON: What am I to say?
> VLADIMIR: Say, I'm happy.
> ESTRAGON: I am happy.
> VLADIMIR: So am I.

ESTRAGON: So am I.

VLADIMIR: We are happy.

ESTRAGON: We are happy (*silence*). What do we do now, now that we're happy?

VLADIMIR: Wait for Godot.

They carry on waiting, filling the silence with their words, as Beckett carried on, doubting and struggling with language, throughout his life.

Chapter 30

French literature into the twenty-first century

To Write: An Intransitive Verb?

– Roland Barthes

It becomes increasingly difficult, the closer we get to the present day, to have a clear sense of the enduring importance particular writers might acquire. In this chapter, which is organized in a loosely chronological manner, I will focus less on individual writers and texts, and more – though still highlighting emblematic figures – on some of the main currents of French literature since the middle of the twentieth century: formal experimentation, the use of traditional narrative forms for subversive purposes, writing by women, the rise of autobiography and the emergence of francophone writing; finally, I will discuss some significant figures in contemporary fiction.

New novel, new criticism

The 1950s and 1960s saw a wave of experimentation in French literature. Rejecting Sartre's advocacy of a 'committed', politically grounded art, writers reaffirmed art's self-sufficiency. Experiment in the field of narrative fiction reflected feelings of scepticism towards the conventions of the traditional realist novel established in the nineteenth century. A variety of novelists – notably Alain Robbe-Grillet (1922–2008), Michel Butor (b. 1926) and Nathalie Sarraute (1900–99) – came to be known as 'New Novelists'. Although very different from each other, they all argued that nineteenth-century conventions like the omniscient narrator, linear plots and neat narrative resolutions give a false implication of the coherence and intelligibility of the world; and they questioned the presentation of characters in monolithic, well-defined terms on the grounds that such an approach distorts and oversimplifies human experience. Our lives, they wrote, do not follow strict storylines, with events and experiences unfolding naturally; and to suggest that we know fully what we, let alone other people, are thinking at any given moment is unrealistic. It was argued, most notably by Sarraute in *The Age of Suspicion* (*L'Ère du soupçon*, 1950) and Robbe-Grillet in *For a New Novel* (*Pour un nouveau roman*, 1963), that to represent the world as muddled, experience as discontinuous and characters as opaque is more true to life, and hence more realistic, than traditional fiction.

In place of the omniscient narrator of the Balzacian novel, all-knowing and ever-present, the New Novel presents narrative voices that are limited and subject to uncertainty (especially in the novels of Robbe-Grillet); the portrayal of character in terms of psychological depth and coherence is replaced by an evocation of the fragmented, unpredictable impulses that flow beneath the surface of our conversation (especially in the novels of Sarraute); the kind of time we encounter in a New Novel is not that of a chronological, purposeful plot, but one full of gaps and repetitions, with events narrated out of order, corresponding to patterns of memory and subjective experience (this is especially the case in the novels of Claude Simon (1913–2005) and in Butor's *Passing Time* (*L'Emploi du temps*, 1956)); and the plots of these novels often focus on an enigma or some kind of mystery (Robbe-Grillet's novel *The Erasers* (*Les Gommes*, 1953) is actually cast in the form of a detective novel, in which the detective is trying to find the murderer in a crime that has not yet occurred, only to discover that he himself is fated to become the murderer). Faced with texts that resist easy interpretation, the reader is invited to become an active participant in the very processes of the writing. The New Novel brings us face to face, so to speak, with our own creative role as narrators of our own lives. Whereas the traditional novel always referred ultimately to an external centre of meaning, the practitioners of the New Novel intended, through their practice of writing, to probe the workings of the imagination and to make the reader realize that the text is what happens in his mind; moreover, they maintained that to create a text which is not validated by any external system of reference is to represent the truth of the world and that to understand this is the benefit the reader may derive from their texts. Thus one of the major functions of the New Novel was to militate against our tendency to take the world we live in as a natural world in which things happen as they do simply because 'that's the way things are'.

One of the greatest proponents of the New Novel was the critic and essayist Roland Barthes (1915–80), a key figure in what came to be called the 'New Criticism' (*la nouvelle critique*) in France. For Barthes, the traditional realist novel is marked by its philosophical innocence. First, there is no 'real' world independent of our perceptions of it; what is regarded as 'reality' at any given moment is culturally, not naturally produced and is therefore not something which is simply 'given'. Second, this construction of reality is produced by language, which for Barthes is not a simple vehicle for expressing reality but a way of organizing the world. The shift in literary consciousness which is generally termed 'modernism' is marked by a conception of language as the very means through which the real is produced or real-ized. Barthes argued that traditional realism, by implying that the writer can unproblematically transcribe reality, completely falsifies the relationship between words and things. What the realist novelist is actually doing, he wrote, is voicing his own society's system of intelligibility – that is, its own relative conception of what may be considered 'realistic'. By obscuring the artificiality of his writing, he is articulating what Barthes called the *doxa*, by which he meant the whole body of conventional notions that shape a society's views of reality and are presented as being somehow inscribed into the natural order of things. According to this view, the realist novel becomes a powerful instrument for the *doxa* and is thus conservative in that it reinforces the status quo. Barthes made a crucial distinction between what he called 'readerly' and 'writerly' texts. The 'readerly' (or realist) text is based on logical, linear progression, adds up to an integrated whole and requires nothing more than that the reader should passively consume it. The 'writerly' (or modernist) text, unconstrained by representational considerations, makes us not consumers but producers, because we have to choose (virtually to 'write') what happens for ourselves; we construct meanings in the text as we read. Barthes disliked traditional realism because of its transitive nature, its concern with social and historical reality; he admired 'writerly' texts, which turn the entire field of the writer into writing itself. Hence his enthusiasm for the New Novel, which was characterized by one of its exponents and champions, Jean Ricardou (b. 1932), as 'no longer the writing of an adventure but the adventure of writing'.[1]

The writings of Barthes, and the literary experimentation of the 1950s and later, are part of a broad context of intellectual experiment – or rather, iconoclasm. Barthes was one of the most influential figures in 'structuralism', a movement that draws attention to means of representation by focusing on the ways in which meanings are mediated. Structuralism makes us more aware of the contingent nature of literary representations and encourages us to consider them as ideological constructions rather than empirical reflections of reality. Barthes argued for the importance of 'critical theory' in opposition to traditional academic criticism in France, which tended to interpret works in the light of the writer's life and his or her stated or purported intentions. In a famous polemical essay of 1968 entitled 'The Death of the Author' ('La Mort de l'auteur') Barthes attacked the method of reading that relies on aspects of the author's biographical identity – political views, historical context, psychology, etc. – to extract meaning from a literary work. Texts must be separated from their creators, he argued, in order to liberate them from interpretative tyranny. Every piece of writing is many-layered, containing meanings drawn from 'innumerable centres of culture', rather than from one person's individual experience. The essential meanings of a work depend on the impressions of its successive readers, not on any authority of its author. As Barthes put it: 'the birth of the reader has as its price the death of the author'.

A return to tradition

The experimental writing of the New Novelists found limited favour with the reading public. Readers warmed immediately, however, to Michel Tournier (b. 1924), whose novels were welcomed as restoring to French literature the human and philosophical content many felt it had lost since the heyday of Sartre and Camus. 'My aim,' Tournier wrote in his autobiographical essay *The Wind Spirit* (*Le Vent Paraclet*, 1977), 'is not to innovate in terms of form, but to use the most traditional, conservative and reassuring of forms to explore a content that possesses none of these qualities' ('Mon propos n'est pas d'innover dans la forme, mais de faire passer au contraire dans une forme aussi traditionnelle, préservée et rassurante que possible une matière ne possédant aucune de ces qualités'). Nineteenth-century narrative procedures (character, plot, description) are used by Tournier in fictions that comment on the contemporary world, challenge accepted values and do so through provocative rewritings of certain myths. A myth is defined by Tournier as being, among other things, 'a story everybody knows'; and a mythological character, he says, is 'one who is of relevance to all humanity, because he or she embodies one of the great human problems: for instance, Tristan and Isolde represent passion, Don Juan eroticism, Robinson Crusoe solitude, the Ogre war, and so on' ('Talking Shop', in Worton (ed.), *Michel Tournier*, pp. 191–92).

Tournier's most celebrated novel is *The Erl-King*, also known as *The Ogre* (*Le Roi des Aulnes*, 1970). This novel (which won the Prix Goncourt by the first unanimous vote since the award began in 1903) combines myth, fable and allegory in its exploration of the phenomenon of Nazism, figured in the journey of a motor mechanic, Abel Tiffauges, from his little garage in Paris to Hermann Göring's palatial hunting lodge at Rominten, in the heart of Nazi Germany. I will focus, however, on Tournier's first, widely admired novel, *Friday or the Other Island* (*Vendredi ou les limbes du Pacifique*, 1967) – a rewriting of Daniel Defoe's *Robinson Crusoe* (1719)[2] that introduces many of the large philosophical and social themes around which much of his subsequent work revolves. In

Tournier's retelling of the story of Crusoe, the hierarchical relationship between Crusoe and Friday (Western man and the native whom he makes his slave) is inverted. In *Friday* it is Crusoe, reduced to a state of spiritual destitution by his isolation, who is saved by his encounter with the so-called primitive. Whereas Defoe's novel is aimed at showing the triumph of culture over nature and is an apology for colonialism and capitalism, Tournier's novel brings into question the whole concept of 'civilization'. Friday does not arrive, however, until the middle of the novel. The early chapters show Crusoe falling into semi-madness, and then, to maintain his mental balance, attempting to recreate on his island the forms and structures – the order – of the culture he has left behind: surveying the island, building a dwelling, cultivating the land, creating a water clock, writing out a system of government (complete with penal code), constructing a Conservatory of Weights and Measures, a Palace of Justice and a religious meeting house, and making plans for the island to become a fortified state (with him assuming the rank of general) in the event of an attack. The omniscient third-person narrative is interspersed with extracts from Crusoe's 'Journal', which begins to show him grappling with fundamental questions of meaning and identity: the existence of God, the function of religion, the nature of morality, what it means to be human, the role of others and of society in forming one's sense of the world and one's own self, how to maintain one's humanity in a state of solitude. Crusoe concludes that his mental journey has taken him to 'a place suspended between heaven and hell, in limbo' ('un lieu suspendu entre ciel et enfers, dans les limbes'). The novel's subtitle in French is, indeed, 'The Limbo . . . ' – suggesting an indeterminate sense of identity as well as a position of marginality.

It is at this point, with Crusoe reduced to a kind of tabula rasa of existence, that Friday appears on the scene. Gradually, in his spontaneity and essential *difference*, he guides Crusoe out of his solipsistic limbo, initiating him into a new, individualistic mode of being. Crusoe, abandoning his Western obsession with order and 'progress', enters a new world of innocence. He learns from Friday how to experience life *naturally*. He begins to live like a savage, enjoying his natural surroundings rather than struggling against them, savouring the pleasures of the body and the poetry of air and sun, converting work into play and allowing his imagination to enrich his life. Many years later a British ship stops at the island for water, offering Crusoe the possibility of leaving. But he has become so marked by his 'solar metamorphosis', and so disenchanted with the utilitarianism and conformity of his own civilization, that he decides to stay. Friday, on the other hand, is fascinated by the ship and joins the crew. Crusoe is not left alone, however, for a cabin boy, unhappy with his life on the ship, has taken refuge on the island. Crusoe, delighted, names him 'Thursday':

'Jeudi' in the original French, 'Sunday' in the English translation; in both cases the name refers to 'the day of our master, the Sun'.[3]

Literature as play

The novel form was further reinvigorated, in spectacular fashion, by Georges Perec (1936–82), the most brilliant member of the OULIPO group (Workshop for Potential Literature; Ouvroir de Littérature Potentielle) founded in 1960 by the writer Raymond Queneau (1903–76) and the mathematician-writer François Le Lionnais (1901–84). This group was devoted to experimentation with literary form, especially the exploration of how formal constraints may be used to stimulate creativity and to generate texts. Restrictive forms with which they played included palindromes (a word, sentence or number that reads the same backward or forward), snowballs (a series of words each of which is one letter longer than its predecessor), isograms (in which no letter appears more than once), tautograms (in which all words begin with the same letter) and lipograms (texts that exclude one or more letters). Perec composed a 312-page novel, *La Disparition* (1969), that made no use whatever of the letter *e*. (The novel has been brilliantly translated into *e*-less English by Gilbert Adair: *A Void*, 1994.) This renewal of interest in literature as play converged with the fascination of contemporary critical theory with language and the ways in which we are 'spoken' by language almost as much as we speak it.

Queneau had been writing novels and poetry since the 1930s, but did not become widely known until *Zazie in the Metro* (*Zazie dans le métro*, 1959). In 1947, after attending a concert performance of Bach's 'Art of Fugue', he decided to attempt something similar – an exercise in stylistic variations – with language. The result was one of the jewels of twentieth-century French literature: *Exercises in Style* (*Exercises de style*, 1947). He takes two banal incidents – a man gets on a bus, complains of being pushed and starts an argument; later he is seen talking to a friend about putting an extra button on his overcoat – and recounts them in ninety-nine different ways. Each of the ninety-nine sections is given a simple title – 'Hesitation', 'Official Letter', 'Noble', 'Cockney', 'Comedy', 'Dog Latin', 'Abusive', etc. 'Double Entry' starts thus: 'Towards the middle of the day and at midday I happened to be on and got on the platform and the balcony at the back of an S-line and of a Contrescarpe-Champerret bus and passenger transport vehicle which was packed and to all intents and purposes full. I saw and noticed a young man and an old adolescent who was rather ridiculous and pretty grotesque . . . ' 'Cockney' begins: 'So A'm stand'n' n' ahtsoider vis frog bus when A sees vis young Froggy bloke, caw bloimey, A finks, f'at ain't ve most funniest look'n' geezer wot ever A claps eyes on' (trans. Barbara Wright). And so on. Various registers and literary styles are matched by different forms ranging from Japanese haikus to alexandrines, from a sonnet to a set of exclamations. The book is, in an obvious sense, pure play, a celebration of the infinite plasticity of language. More seriously, it enacts a point about the relationship between language and meaning, form and content, implying that the form in which a text or utterance is cast is never simply a vehicle for content, but, as Flaubert suggested (see above, pp. 123–24) always expresses meaning in itself. There is no such thing as a stylistically neutral text. As the *Exercises* demonstrate, even the simplest, most inconsequential piece of writing carries marks of style that have strong expressive potential; and recognizing that capacity can be immense fun.

Like Queneau, Perec was a writer of great wit and inventiveness. His most celebrated work is his 700-page novel *Life: A User's Manual* (*La Vie mode d'emploi*, 1978; henceforth *Life*). Constructed in the manner of a huge jigsaw puzzle, it focuses on a large Parisian apartment building ten storeys high by ten rooms wide, suggesting a chessboard. The successive chapters describe in great detail each room of each resident, in a special order determined by a 'knight's tour', that is, the route a knight would have to take to visit every square only once. A further patterning device, a complicated mathematical algorithm, is used to determine the forty-two constituent elements (characters, objects, situations, etc.) of each minutely described room. Oulipian in its compositional virtuosity, *Life* is Balzacian in its encyclopaedic range and taxonomic richness. The novel teems with descriptions, characters and their interrelated stories. One story stands out: that of Percival Bartlebooth, an eccentric English millionaire who organizes his entire life round a vast artistic project, 'an arbitrary constrained programme with no purpose outside its own completion'. For ten years he studies the art of watercolour painting; for the next twenty years he travels the world, painting a seascape in a different port every two weeks; each painting is sent back to Paris, where it is glued to a wooden board and turned into a jigsaw puzzle by a master craftsman named Gaspard Winckler; 500 puzzles thus await Bartlebooth on his return, and he devotes another twenty years to piecing them together, again one every two weeks; when each puzzle is solved, he sends it back to the port city where it was painted, and there it is dipped in the water until nothing remains but the original blank paper. But Bartlebooth's project is left incomplete, for he dies of a heart attack as he is trying to fill in the last blank space in the four hundred and thirty-ninth puzzle; the space, moreover, has the perfect shape of an X, whereas the piece Bartlebooth is clutching as he dies is shaped like a W.

Perec's fascination with the idea of writing as a game is postmodernist in its emphasis on the self-reflexive dimensions of texts, but his exploitation of literary play and the motifs of art, absence and incompletion in his work have a deeply serious aspect that is rooted in his own life. His parents, immigrant Jews of Polish origin, were both killed during the war. His father died while serving in the army in 1940, and his mother was deported to Auschwitz in 1943, traumatic events to which his work constantly alludes in the most oblique ways. As Harry Mathews has written, in a long and insightful review of *Life*:

> Autobiography, or at least concern with autobiography, underlies much of Perec's writing, even in those works in which it is least obvious... While *La Disparition* and *Life: A User's Manual* are not overtly autobiographical, I think they can be read, among other ways, as products of Perec's preoccupation with autobiography or, perhaps more accurately, of his obsession with the autobiography he felt he could never write... Many of us who are not orphans have had the experience of literature as 'family', even if we can only guess at its intensity in Perec's case. However, the experience suggests also one origin of Perec's desire to write: since the sense of loss and of being lost is inexpressible, what can you say in its place? How can you say anything at all? Instead of struggling to find an answer to these questions, Perec sidestepped them, by becoming what used to be called a formalist, ignoring history, looking for things to do inside language, inside writing. Instead of trying to find words to describe the world, he tried to invent interesting ways to use words in their own right.[4]

What Perec received from the post-war French government, in relation to his mother's death, was a 'certificate of disappearance' (an 'Acte de Disparition') – a term reflected in the title and composition of his e-less novel *La Disparition*. The letter *e* in French is pronounced as 'eux' ('them'), and when Perec dedicated his *W, or the Memory of Childhood* (*W ou le souvenir d'enfance*, 1975) 'To E', he admitted later to a cousin that he really meant Esther, his mother, and 'them'. Like Bartlebooth, Perec was haunted by the existential reality of incompletion, the unsolvable puzzle of his own loss. Art is a defence against the void, but (as Beckett also believed) it is temporary and limited, a fact ironically reflected in the circularity of Bartlebooth's grand scheme: 'his aim was for nothing, nothing at all, to subsist, for nothing but the void to emerge from it, for only the immaculate whiteness of a blank to remain, only the gratuitous perfection of a project entirely devoid of utility'.

Duras and other women writers

The most significant general development in French literature in the second half of the twentieth century was the growth of writing by women. Simone de Beauvoir's *The Second Sex* (*Le Deuxième Sexe*, 1949) and *Memoirs of a Dutiful Daughter* (*Mémoires d'une jeune fille rangée*, 1958) were seminal. Female autobiography and autobiographical fiction, focusing especially on sexuality, the family and the situation of women, became popular. *La Bâtarde* (1964), a memoir by Violette Leduc, a protégée of de Beauvoir, was a bestseller. *The Words to Say It* (*Les Mots pour le dire*, 1975), an autobiographical fiction by Marie Cardinal, recounts a long course of psychonanalysis by which the author came to terms with herself, her past and her mother. Annie Ernaux (b. 1940), the daughter of working-class parents, addresses questions of social class in novels such as *A Frozen Woman* (*La Femme gelée*, 1981), *A Man's Place* (*La Place*, 1983) and *A Woman's Story* (*Une Femme*, 1988). Beyond autobiographical and broadly realist writing, the most important type of women's writing was what became known as *écriture féminine* (often translated as 'writing the body'). An interest in this type of writing emerged from the feminist movement of the 1970s, and was theorized by such figures as Luce Irigaray (b. 1930), Hélène Cixous (b. 1937) and Julia Kristeva (b. 1941). Key texts are Irigaray's *This Sex Which Is Not One* (*Ce sexe qui n'en est pas un*, 1977) and Cixous's *The Newly Born Woman* (*La Jeune Née*, 1975) and 'The Laugh of the Medusa' ('Le Rire de la méduse', 1975), which argued that Western thought, including language, has always claimed universal status for what are in fact male perspectives, and has thus silenced and marginalized the female. Women, it was argued, must develop their own writing practices, and in so doing celebrate their power of disruption. In particular, they must seek to express female experience by finding a new language to express woman's relationship to her body. These ideas were brought to a wide audience by Annie Leclerc in her bestselling essay *Woman's Word* (*Parole de femme*, 1974).[5] Works taken as examples of *écriture féminine* include Monique Wittig's *The Lesbian Body* (*Le Corps lesbien*, 1973), Chantal Chawaf's *Mother Love, Mother Earth* (*Retable*, 1974) and *Redemption* (*Rédemption*, 1988), Jeanne Hyvrard's *Mother Death* (*Mère la mort*, 1976) and *The Dead Girl in a Lace Dress* (*La Jeune Morte en robe de dentelle*, 1990), and Cixous's own *The Book of Promethea* (*Le Livre de Prométhéa*, 1983).

France's most celebrated woman writer of the second half of the twentieth century was Marguerite Duras (1914–96). Attempts have been made to claim Duras's style of writing as *écriture féminine*, though she herself resisted such identification. The spectacular success of *The Lover*, trans. Barbara Bray (*L'Amant*, 1984), brought her to the attention of a mass audience. She had been writing fiction, however, since the 1940s, and by the end of her career had produced over fifty novels, plays and films. Her recurring themes – which all touch on female experience – are: desire and its disruptive force, trauma, transgression, madness, violence and death. A distinctive Durassian voice emerged with short, spare texts such as *The Square* (*Le Square*, 1955) and *Moderato cantabile* (1958), in which traditional characterization and plot are replaced by a narrative style that explores human experience through blanks, silences and ellipses – disrupting narrative coherence and expressing the enigmatic nature of the story being told. *Moderato cantabile* centres on a series of encounters between two people who share a fascination with a recent *crime passionnel* and appear to re-enact the murder in fantasized form. *The Ravishing of Lol V. Stein* (*Le Ravissement de Lol V. Stein*, 1964) represents a further stage of formal experimentation with structure and perspective. Focused on the mental disturbance of the protagonist after her fiancé leaves her for another woman, this novel stages a loss of identity, the fragmentation of the feminine psyche, through various forms of narrative dislocation.

The narrator of *The Lover* is a woman in her sixties who is looking back at a period in her adolescence and considering its emotional consequences for her. The formation of her personality is explored in the light of her memories of complex family relationships (especially her mother's 'madness'), her awakening sexuality and her experience as the child of a poor white family in a colonial country. The setting is French Indo-China (now Vietnam, where Duras herself was born and grew up). Duras's parents had taken advantage of a government incentive scheme to emigrate there, but her father was forced to return to France for health reasons and died. Her mother was left in Saigon to raise her daughter and two elder sons, supposedly on the proceeds of a piece of farmland (the incentive) that was flooded every year and thus became unprofitable. Duras's mother, unaware that they had needed to bribe the local officials to obtain decent land, spent the rest of her life locked in dispute with the authorities. Her children, neglected and brought up in poverty, are victims of this situation.

Autobiography and fiction are hardly separable in *The Lover*. To be different from her oppressive mother, the young protagonist starts to wear gold lamé shoes and a man's felt hat. In so doing, she sees herself 'as another, as another would be seen, outside myself, available to all, available to all eyes, in circulation for cities, journeys, desire' ('comme une autre, comme une autre serait vue, au-dehors, mise à la disposition de tous, mise à la disposition de tous les regards, mise dans la circulation des villes, des routes, du désir'). Soon afterwards, her desire to be different, accompanied by her new sense of herself as an object of desire, finds another outlet: at the age of fifteen, while crossing the Mekong river on a ferry, she meets a rich Chinese man in his late twenties and begins a passionate affair with him. The intensity of her desire is heightened by the fact that he is Oriental – exotic and forbidden. Her mother and brothers know about the affair, but do not acknowledge or discuss it. Sometimes the nameless lover takes them for a meal, but is ignored. The affair lasts for eighteen months and ends when the girl leaves for France. She does not hear from the man until many years later when he comes to Paris with his wife and telephones her, saying that he still loves her and always will. The story ends there.

The theme of sexual desire is closely related to the author-narrator's ambivalent relationship with her mother, a relationship at least as important as that with the Chinese lover. The 'madness' of the mother (who both colludes with her daughter in her affair and hysterically denounces her as a prostitute) represents the tensions of her position as a poor white widow in a patriarchal, colonial society, as well as the tensions that inform her daughter's feelings towards her (love mixed with deep resentment at her stifling influence and her inability ever to be, herself, a subject of desire). The girl's affair is an act of rebellion and expresses a wish for independence. But the mother's presence is hauntingly persistent: when the girl first makes love, in the Chinese quarter of Cholon, her mother is present in her thoughts and in her conversation. It is as if the girl wishes to incorporate her mother (who 'never knew pleasure'/'n'a jamais connu la jouissance') into her world of desire – to effect a kind of fusion with her while escaping from her through her scandalous affair. The intensity of the text corresponds in some measure to the intensity of the various feelings evoked – feelings that define her family history and seem beyond understanding but nonetheless contribute very powerfully to the story of her life.

The telling of the story is mesmerizing; and its fascination lies precisely in the manner of its telling, in the writing itself, rather than in its basic content as a story of sexual initiation and transgression. *The Lover* is no ordinary work of autobiography. Near the beginning of her text, Duras states: 'The story of my life doesn't exist. It doesn't exist. There is never a centre. No path, no line. There are great spaces where you make people believe there was someone. But it's not true, there was no one' ('L'histoire de ma vie n'existe pas. Ça n'existe pas. Il n'y a jamais de centre. Pas de chemin, pas de ligne. Il y a de vastes endroits où l'on fait croire qu'il y avait quelqu'un, ce n'est pas vrai, il n'y avait personne'). The past has no fixed form; life has no definitive, linear pattern that can be transparently represented. An illusion of continuity might be given, but it would be false. The discontinuity and mystery of the past and of life can only be expressed through texts which, like *The Lover*, are fragmentary, non-linear, elliptical, poetic. The narrator represents her past self sometimes in the first person, sometimes (like a fictional character) in the third, and often uses the present tense to describe the past ('So, I'm fifteen and a half'). She also uses constantly shifting perspectives in a manner reminiscent of the cinema, cutting backwards and forwards like a film director. Shifts of perspective imply shifts of identity – desire as 'a constant negation and displacement of all fixities' (Sheringham, *French Autobiography*, p. 319). The two main perspectives or voices – that of the narrating self and that of the fifteen-year-old girl – interact and converge. The girl moves towards sexual knowledge, womanhood, independence, a life as a writer (the symbolic value of her journey across the river, and finally across the sea, is clear). The present was already implicit in the past, while the emotions of the past flood the present. The narrator's quest to reconstitute her past reflects her desire to locate the origins of her desire to write; and, through her efforts to recount her memories and imagine her younger self, it embodies the endless, renewable process of recreation and reinvention, the work of fantasy, that for Duras defines the act of writing: autobiography, in that sense, as fiction.

Autobiography/autofiction

Duras's *The Lover*, with its ambiguous blend of autobiography and fictional narrative, was symptomatic of an upsurge of interest in forms of 'life writing' from the 1970s onwards; while feminist theory, with its emphasis on the gendered, embodied subject, has contributed powerfully to a renewed focus on subjective reality and the forces that constitute it.

Some remarkable works of autobiography had already been produced by writers associated with Existentialism. Exploring the possibilities and limits of human agency, these works included Jean Genet's *The Thief's Journal* (*Jounal du voleur*, 1948) as well as Simone de Beavoir's *Memoirs of a Dutiful Daughter* (*Mémoires d'une jeune fille rangée*, 1958) and Violette Leduc's *La Bâtarde* (1964). Sartre explored the existentialist themes of choice, freedom and responsibility in his biographical studies of Baudelaire (*Baudelaire*, 1946), Genet (*Saint Genet: Actor and Martyr/Saint Genet, comédien et martyr*, 1952) and Flaubert (*The Idiot of the Family/L'Idiot de la famille*, 1971–72). He turned his attention to himself in his beguiling and penetrating study of his own childhood, *Words* (*Les Mots*, 1963). The artfully constructed narrative is built on the interplay between two perspectives – that of the boy of 1911–14 and the man of 1963.

Two groundbreaking experiments in autobiography appeared in 1975: Roland Barthes's *Roland Barthes by Roland Barthes* (*Roland Barthes par Roland Barthes*) and Georges Perec's *W, or the Memory of Childhood* (*W ou le souvenir d'enfance*). Composed of alphabetically ordered fragments, Barthes's text uses a narrative voice that moves between the first and third persons and mixes these with photographs, drawings, critical analysis and personal confession. Susan Sontag, writing in 1981, commented:

> Barthes is the latest major participant in the great national literary project, inaugurated by Montaigne: the self as vocation, life as a reading of the self. The enterprise construes the self as the locus of all possibilities, avid, unafraid of contradiction (nothing need be lost, everything may be gained), and the exercise of consciousness as a life's highest aim, because only by becoming fully conscious may one be fully free. The distinctive French utopian tradition is this vision of reality redeemed, recovered, transcended by consciousness; a vision of the life of the mind as a life of desire, of full intelligence and pleasure – so different from, say, the traditions of high seriousness of German and Russian literature.
>
> (Sontag, introduction to *Barthes*, pp. xxxiii–xxxiv)

Perec's novel consists of alternating chapters of autobiography, focused on the author's attempt to sift through his memories of childhood, and a reconstructed fictional story written when Perec was an adolescent. It slowly becomes clear that the intertwining of these narratives reflects the author's confrontation with the fact of his mother's disappearance into the concentration camp at Auschwitz. As Michael Sheringham puts it, 'the writing of memory becomes (to use Perec's own terms . . .) an *encrage*, an inking, which provides an *ancrage*, an anchorage – a place of inscription for the traces of a scandalous absence which writing cannot redeem but whose place it can mark forever' (*French Autobiography*, p. 326).

Multi-generic or multi-focal forms of autobiography began to appear in increasing numbers. Outstanding examples were *Livret de famille* (1977) by Patrick Modiano (b. 1945), *Childhood* (*Enfance*, 1983) by Nathalie Sarraute (1900–99) and *Small Lives* (*Vies minuscules*, 1984) by Pierre Michon (b. 1945). The term 'autofiction', coined by the writer and critic Serge Doubrovsky (b. 1928), quickly gained currency (though it should be noted that Sartre had suggested that *Words* is as much a novel as an autobiography; while Barthes, at the beginning of *Roland Barthes. . .* , had declared: 'All this must be considered as being spoken by a fictional character'; and the interaction between fact and fiction is the very essence of Perec's *W*). The term 'autofiction' is highly resonant, for it not only denotes a new form of writing, blurring (and playing with) the borders between autobiography and fiction, but also draws attention to a fundamental aspect of the entire genre of autobiography: its nature as a narrative process. What is important in autobiography, as Philippe Lejeune and Michael Sheringham have shown in their excellent critical studies, is not a quest for some kind of 'truth' about our past, but the act of narration itself – the dynamics at work in the writer's relationship to his or her past.

Autofiction, which implicitly (and explicitly) recognizes that the autobiographical self is a textual construct, is highly popular among both writers and readers, and is regarded by many as the most important mode of writing in contemporary French literature. Reasons for its appeal have been well described by Johnnie Gratton:

> Our contemporary models of the refigured subject emphasize the
> uncertainties informing selfhood, identity, experience, and memory,
> and contemporary writers have responded to these models by producing
> more conjectural and conditional forms of autobiographical writing in
> which a pervasive sense of disquiet, encompassing questions of genre,
> gender, and self, is assumed as both an aesthetic resource and an ethical
> safeguard. Fictionality is thus invoked by the vigilant autobiographer
> not only to assert the power of the imagination but equally to concede
> the limits of re-imagination.[6]

Prominent exponents of autofiction, besides Serge Doubrovsky, include Pierre Bergounioux (b. 1949), Christine Angot (b. 1959), Camille Laurens (b. 1957) and, perhaps most notably, Hervé Guibert (1955–91) and Annie Ernaux (b. 1940). The author of nineteen books, Guibert wrote about his life as a gay man, and he played a considerable role in changing French public attitudes towards AIDS by describing his own terminal experience of it in *To the Friend Who Did Not Save My Life* (*À l'ami qui ne m'a pas sauvé la vie*, 1990).

Francophone writing

Francophone literature is the subject of a separate volume in the present series (*The Cambridge Introduction to Francophone Literature* by Patrick Corcoran), and I will treat it only very briefly here.

It is significant that the new version of *The Oxford Companion to French Literature* (edited by Sir Paul Harvey and J. E. Heseltine, 1959) was entitled *The New Oxford Companion to Literature in French* (edited by Peter France, 1995). This change reflects the development over the last few decades of a whole new field, 'Francophone studies'. *Francophonie* is, of course, largely a legacy of colonialism. The term is commonly used to denote French-speakers outside France (they slightly outnumber those within France itself) and organized efforts to strengthen their numbers. Francophone literature is vast and very diverse, as indicated in part by its sheer extent across the globe: Belgium, Luxembourg, Monaco, Switzerland, North Africa (Algeria, Morocco, Tunisia), Sub-Saharan Africa, Quebec, the Caribbean (Martinique, Guadeloupe, French Guyana), Haiti, the Middle East, the Indian Ocean (Mauritius, Réunion, Madagascar), Southeast Asia (Vietnam, Laos, Cambodia) and the South Pacific (French Polynesia, New Caledonia, Vanuatu). Before we even leave France, there are the migrant narratives of so-called *Beur* writers (that is, writers of North African extraction, particularly Algerian, born in France; 'Beur' is a modified inversion of 'Arabe'): writers such as Mehdi Charef (b. 1952) and Azouz Begag (b. 1957), who have written autobiographical fictions about their experiences growing up as members of an ethnic minority living on the margin of French society. Widely admired writers born in French-speaking countries outside France include pioneering figures like Léopold Sédar Senghor (1906–2001, Senegal), Aimé Césaire (1913–2008, Martinique), Anne Hébert (1916–2000, Quebec), Albert Memmi (b. 1920, Tunisia), Mohammed Dib (1920–2003, Algeria), Ousmane Sembène (1923–2007, Senegal), Frantz Fanon (1925–61, Martinique), Driss Chraïbi (1926–2007, Morocco), Ahmadou Kourouma (1927–2003, Ivory Coast) and Édouard Glissant (1928–2011, Martinique), and later writers such as Maryse Condé (b. 1937, Guadeloupe), Assia Djebar (b. 1939, Algeria), Rachid Boudjedra (b. 1941, Algeria), V. Y. Mudimbe (b. 1941, Belgian Congo), Tahar Ben Jelloun (b. 1944, Morocco), Amin Maalouf (b. 1949, Lebanon), Raphaël Confiant (b. 1951, Martinique) and Patrick Chamoiseau (b. 1953, Martinique). Despite the diversity of these writers, common themes focus on questions of national, cultural and personal identity in the context of colonialism, postcolonialism and, latterly, globalization.

One emblematic figure is Tahar Ben Jelloun. The son of a Fez shopkeeper, he began to attract a wide audience with *The Sand Child* (*L'Enfant de sable*, 1985), the story of an Arab girl raised as a boy by a father determined to have a male heir. The sequel, *The Sacred Night* (*La Nuit sacrée*, 1987), describes her release from the bondage of her false gender and her rediscovery of her female identity. Ben Jelloun uses a hallucinatory, poetic, multivocal style (that clearly owes much to Arab oral traditions of storytelling) to critique the condition of women in contemporary Muslim societies. *The Sacred Night* was awarded the Prix Goncourt, France's most prestigious literary prize. Ben Jelloun was the first North African novelist to be thus honoured.[7] Later novels include Silent *Day in Tangier* (*Jour de silence à Tanger*, 1990), about a dying old man sifting through his memories, and *With Downcast Eyes* (*Les Yeux baissés*, 1991), about a young Moroccan (Berber) girl who moves to Paris and struggles to reconcile her two cultures. *This Blinding Absence of Light* (*Cette aveuglante absence de lumière*, 2000), a narrative based on the testimony of a former inmate at Tazmamart, the notorious desert concentration camps in which King Hassan II of Morocco (1929–99) held political prisoners in underground cells, won the International IMPAC Dublin Literary Award in 2004. Ben Jelloun has also written a great deal of provocative non-fiction, especially his quasi-journalistic *French Hospitality* (*Hospitalité française*, 1984), an account of racism and xenophobia in contemporary France, and *Racism Explained to My Daughter* (*Le Racisme expliqué à ma fille*, 1998), written in an accessible question-and-answer format. This format was repeated in *Islam Explained* (*L'Islam expliqué aux enfants*, 2002), produced in response to the anti-Muslim sentiment unleashed by the 11 September 2001 attacks in the United States. Ben Jelloun's aim in this book was to combat ignorance about the Muslim and Arab worlds by explaining the origins and main tenets of Islam and stressing its humanist values.

The development of francophone studies is seen by many as highly enriching inasmuch as, along with other forces, it has obliged the discipline of French studies to broaden and renegotiate its scope in ways appropriate to the modern world. New approaches, adopting a global understanding of language, literature and culture, question established assumptions about the stability or autonomy of national cultures and foreground instead what Charles Forsdick has called 'modes of mobility and contact'[8] – the interaction of cultures, plural notions of identity, the presence of the French language across borders and frontiers.

French fiction today

Contemporary French fiction is remarkably rich, though one would not think so judging from the small number of works in translation. A list of significant French-language writers born in the main after 1945 would include Pierre Alféri, Pierre Bergounioux, François Bon, Olivier Cadiot, Éric Chevillard, Didier Daeninckx, Marie Darrieusecq, Jean Echenoz, Annie Ernaux, Hélène Lenoir, Gérard Macé, Patrick Modiano (winner of the Nobel Prize in Literature, 2014), Laurent Mauvignier, Pierre Michon, Richard Millet, Marie NDiaye, Christian Oster, Pascal Quignard, Jacques Roubaud, Jean Rouaud, Lydie Salvayre, Jean-Philippe Toussaint and Antoine Volodine. I can do no more here than gesture towards this rich field. I will do so by evoking the work of three winners of the Prix Goncourt: Jean Echenoz (b. 1947), who won with *Je m'en vais* in 1999 (translated by Guido Waldman as *I'm Off* and by Mark Polizzotti as *I'm Gone*); Marie NDiaye (b. 1967), who won in 2009 with *Trois femmes puissantes* (*Three Strong Women*, translated by John Fletcher);

and Michel Houellebecq (b. 1956), whose *La Carte et le Territoire* (*The Map and the Territory*, translated by Gavin Bowd) won the prize in 2010.

It has often been remarked that the profoundly ironic narrative style of Jean Echenoz makes him a perfect representative of the 'postmodern' sensibility.[9] He is known for his comic pastiches of traditional genre fiction, mainly the crime novel, the adventure novel and the spy thriller, or combinations thereof. *I'm Off* is entirely typical. The novel begins with the words 'I'm off' as womanizing art dealer Félix Ferrer leaves his wife and sets off into an unknown future. His business is faltering and his ears prick up when his dishevelled assistant, Delahaye, tells him about a vessel with a cargo of priceless Inuit art, which became trapped in the ice forty years earlier. Delahaye suddenly dies and Ferrer attends his funeral. He then travels by icebreaker, helicopter and dog-sled to the Arctic Circle, finds the vessel and its antiquities and returns to Paris with the treasure. But ill-luck strikes: he suffers a severe heart attack (from which he recovers), the loss of several lovers and the theft of the precious artefacts before he can insure them. We meet a suave, sinister character called Baumgartner, who has masterminded the theft and disposes of his accomplice in a farcically chilling manner (the latter vainly accusing him, as a last resort, of behaving as if in a soap opera). Ferrer catches up with the villain and recognizes him as the 'dead' Delahaye. The plot is foiled. Finally, on New Year's Eve, almost a year after he began his adventures, Ferrer decides to visit his wife. The apartment where they used to live is now occupied by strangers. Invited into their party, he says characteristically that he'll only stay a moment: 'Just a quick one then I'm off.'

The fast-moving but absurd plot eventually peters out, though its twists and turns make for rollicking entertainment. But the real attraction of the novel, and its defining element, is its playful narrative voice. It is no surprise that Echenoz has been compared to Raymond Queneau. The narrating voice speaks with a droll, deadpan wit. Laconic observations on contemporary life are combined with tongue-in-cheek play with narrative conventions, creating a pleasurable complicity between narrator and reader: 'But had [Ferrer] been told that each one of the three people gathered in his flat this evening was about to disappear in his or her own way before the month was out, not excluding himself, he would have been considerably alarmed'; 'Personally this man Baumgartner's beginning to get up my nose'; 'Let's keep moving forward, and faster'. And there is a comic focus on inconsequentiality. For instance, we are told more about Ferrer's discomfiture with ill-fitting socks than about his inner life; we learn little about the reasons for his problems with women, but a great deal about his efforts to rid his apartment of the obnoxious smell of a girlfriend's perfume. The inconsequential is matched by the incidental: frequent, seemingly irrelevant descriptions of objects and clothes, the accessories the characters wear, the cars they drive, the décor of their apartments – in sum, the way they (and we) live now, among the glossy surfaces of urban life. As Simon Kemp has commented: 'Echenoz [undermines] the novel as we expect it to function, turning away from the linear progress of the plot into the side roads of curiosity. What we discover down these side roads, however, is not just a metafictional critique of traditional storytelling, but an incisive portrait of our shallow, image-ridden society and the busy, empty lives we live within it' (*French Fiction into the Twenty-First Century*, p. 129).

Marie NDiaye published her first novel at the age of seventeen and built up a considerable body of work (including plays, short stories and a film script) before winning the Prix Femina for her novel *Rosie Carpe* (2001) and the Goncourt for *Trois femmes puissantes* (2009). In 2013 she was shortlisted for the International Man Booker Prize. Her fictional world is highly original. It is marked by the mixture of fable and realism, its use of fantasy in everyday contexts, dreamlike atmospheres, striking visual imagery, ambiguities of narrative perspective and a compelling prose style characterized by complex syntactical structures. *Three Strong Women* is composed of three loosely connected stories. The first takes place in Dakar and focuses on the fraught relationship between a selfish Senegalese man and Norah, the half-French daughter, now a lawyer, he abandoned years before and whom he has summoned from her home in France to help him resolve a catastrophic family situation. The second is set in rural south-west France and evokes the paranoid thoughts and feelings of Rudy, a Frenchman whose marriage to a Senegalese woman, whom he brought to France from Dakar, is falling apart. The final section tells the story of Khady Demba, a Senegalese woman made destitute by the death of her husband and who finds herself prostituted, raped and, finally, killed as she attempts to join the army of clandestine migrants seeking to make their way to Europe. The French title of the novel has an ironic dimension that is lost in the English version, for the women in these stories (the second of which is narrated from a man's perspective) are all relatively powerless. They grow in awareness, but they are all damaged, victims of father, husband or other family members.

Born to a French mother and a Senegalese father, but brought up and educated entirely in France, NDiaye is sometimes stereotyped as being representative of the French African diaspora or multicultural France. She has stressed, however, that she never knew her father, who returned to Senegal when she was one year old, and that she makes no claim to biculturalism. The 'African' stereotype has been reinforced by the ways in which *Three Strong Women* was marketed.[10] Questions of ethnicity are treated both directly and indirectly in

NDiaye's work, but her recurrent themes are abandonment, difference, alterity and exclusion of various kinds, not always ethnic: exclusion from one's family, society or community, and the conflicts and violent feelings that are often involved, together with the corresponding desire for acknowledgement and acceptance. The politics of family life interact with broader issues that concern society as a whole.

For Michel Houellebecq – the most famous and the most controversial living French writer – the verb 'to write' is definitely transitive. He has noted several times in interviews that he counts himself in the tradition of French writers like Balzac, who ask questions of the contemporary world. He is, he says, 'a realist who exaggerates a little', and comments: 'I've always liked Balzac's very insulting statement that the only purpose of the novel is to show the disasters produced by the changing of values. He's exaggerating in an amusing way. But that's what I do: I show the disasters produced by the liberalization of values.'[11] The problem of liberalism is articulated by the narrator of *Whatever* (*L'Extension du domaine de la lutte*, 1994), Houellebecq's first novel, in a passage that gives the volume its French title: 'In a totally liberal economic system certain people accumulate considerable fortunes; others stagnate in unemployment and misery. In a totally liberal sexual system certain people have a varied and exciting erotic life; others are reduced to masturbation and solitude. Sexual liberalism [like economic liberalism] is . . . an extension of the domain of the struggle.' The narrator, a morally torpid thirty-year-old IT consultant, comments cynically on the miserable lives of his colleagues and clients, who, like himself, are sucked into 'the struggle' by the prevailing ethos of competition, which continually stimulates desire while leaving everyone gasping for more. Houellebecq focuses on the sexual underclass, the 'losers' who do not have the looks or the personality to 'score' and who consequently live lives of desperation and loneliness. *Whatever* describes a morbidly atomized world of sad, disconnected individuals.

Atomised (*Les Particules élémentaires*, 1999) tells the story of Bruno and Michel, two half-brothers abandoned in childhood by their narcissistic hippie mother. Both are psychologically disturbed. Like the protagonists of Flaubert's *Sentimental Education*, they represent a generation, evoking the 'moral history' (as Flaubert described his novel) of France over the last few decades. They embody the post-1968 generation, now living with the sins, so to speak, of their fathers and mothers – for it is the permissive generation of the 1960s that Houellebecq blames for promoting a society based on unfettered individualism. The search for sexual freedom has become a form of enslavement; the liberal values of the sixties have led to a mood of moral and cultural emptiness, endless anomie. Bruno is obsessed with sex and pornography, but does not have a body beautiful enough to ensure success in the market economy. He lives in a state of sexual frenzy and frustration, but cannot hide his need for love. He abandons, however, the one woman who loves him when she becomes a paraplegic after breaking her back while taking part in an orgy with Bruno. She commits suicide and Bruno ends up checking himself into a psychiatric hospital, where he plans to live on a regimen of libido-killing drugs. Michel, on the other hand, has no sex drive nor, indeed, any emotional life, having been deadened by the trauma of his abandonment. He becomes an eminent molecular biologist working in the field of genetic engineering. Eventually he withdraws from society and disappears, though not without leaving a blueprint for a new species of human clones – a discovery that will liberate mankind from the burden of individuality and the need to rely on sex for reproduction. In a final twist, it is revealed that the book's narrator is himself a clone and the novel we have been reading is a history of the last days of the human race.

Houellebecq's novels – a compelling mixture of sociological burlesque, dystopian fantasy, sardonic wit and essayistic commentary – are portraits of a world gone wrong. Little wonder that not everyone likes what they see reflected in these portraits. Houellebecq has been attacked as a pornographer, a sexist, a reactionary and a nihilist; and admired as the most devastating chronicler of our age. His reputation as a *provocateur* was consolidated by his latest novel, *Submission* (*Soumission*), which was published on the same day, 7 January 2015, as the murderous attack on the Paris offices of the satirical magazine *Charlie Hebdo*. This novel, described by Houellebecq as 'political fiction', is set in 2022 and imagines the old left and right parties joining forces to support the leader of a (fictional) Islamic Party for President, accepting the imposition of Sharia law in France in order to forestall the victory of the far-right candidate of the Front National.

Notes

Preface

1 For a challenging discussion of some of these issues in relation to the practice of literary criticism within the academy, especially its retreat from aesthetics (i.e. the study of how individuals respond to art with their senses and emotions), see Lindsay Waters, 'Literary Aesthetics: the Very Idea', *The Chronicle of Higher Education*, 16 December 2005. Waters (who is executive director for the humanities at Harvard University Press) writes: 'Ever since it became professional and, for the most part, lost touch with the readers who have fostered the little-magazine criticism that reaches back to *The Spectator*, today's academic scholarship has become separated from its grounding: it is no longer connected to the very medium that gave it rise, literature.' See also Malcolm Bowie, 'The Fate of Pleasure: An Update', *German Life and Letters*, 63: 3 (July 2009), 252–54. Bowie writes: 'However we define pleasure, we have lost contact with it over the two centuries since the French Revolution, at least in so far as the quest for pleasure informs our notions of *why art matters*' (p. 252).
2 Harold Bloom, *The Anatomy of Influence* (New Haven, Conn., and London: Yale University Press, 2011), p. x.

Chronology

1 For an admirable book-length reference guide, see Ian Littlewood, *France: The Rough Guide Chronicle* (London: Rough Guides, 2002).

1 Villon: a dying man

1 Simon Gaunt, *Retelling the Tale: An Introduction to Medieval French Literature* (London: Duckworth, 2001), p. 149. Gaunt's book is an accessible commentary on, and embodiment of, the new critical approaches to French medieval texts. See also Simon Gaunt and Sarah Kay (eds.), *The Cambridge Companion to Medieval French Literature* (Cambridge University Press, 2008), and Sharon Kinoshita, 'What's Up in French Medieval Studies?', *Australian Journal of French Studies*, 46: 3 (2009), 169–77.

2 François Villon, *Poems*, trans. David Georgi (Evanston, Ill.: Northwestern University Press, 2012), p. xviii.

3 The name comes from the title of Paul Verlaine's collection of essays on Mallarmé, Rimbaud and other French poets, *Les Poètes maudits* (1884).

4 John Fox, *The Poetry of Villon* (London: Thomas Nelson, 1962), p. xx.

2 Rabelais: the uses of laughter

1 Milan Kundera, *Encounter* (London: Faber & Faber; New York: HarperCollins, 2010), p. 63.

2 Gérard Defaux, 'Rabelais and the Monsters of Antiphysis', *Modern Language Notes*, 110 (1995), 1017–42 (p. 1027).

3 It should be borne in mind that the printing press was in Rabelais's time a relatively recent invention: its invention is credited to the German printer Johannes Gutenberg in 1450; the first French press was established in Paris in 1470.

4 This argument has been forcefully propounded by Gabriel Josipovici, who believes that the origins of Modernism ('art arriving at a consciousness of its own limits and responsibilities') can be sought not in the nineteenth century, with the beginnings of industrialization, but in the early sixteenth century, in the work of Rabelais and Cervantes. See Further reading, and also *What Ever Happened to Modernism?* (New Haven, Conn., and London: Yale University Press, 2010). Terence Cave, in his brilliant book *The Cornucopian Text*, has analysed problems of writing in the French Renaissance more broadly, arguing that the works of Rabelais, like those of other French Renaissance writers, 'are characteristically reflexive, dialogic, open-ended', and that 'the striking feature of sixteenth-century French literature is the eruption of explicit self-awareness at the very heart of major texts' (pp. 182, 330).

5 Stephen Greenblatt, *Learning to Curse: Essays in Early Modern Culture* (New York and London: Routledge, 2007 [1990]), p. 87.

3 Montaigne: self-portrait

1 For an excellent cultural history of the period, see William J. Bouwsma, *The Waning of the Renaissance, 1550–1640* (New Haven, Conn., and London: Yale University Press, 2000).

2 This passage is the object of distinguished analyses by Erich Auerbach and Frank P. Bowman: see Further reading.

4 Corneille: heroes and kings

1 Arnold Hauser, *The Social History of Art*, vol. II (London: Routledge, 1999 [1951]), p. 178.

5 Racine: in the labyrinth

1 Charles Mauron, *L'Inconscient dans l'œuvre et la vie de Jean Racine* (Paris: Corti, 1969).
2 Terry Eagleton, *Sweet Violence: The Idea of the Tragic* (Oxford: Blackwell, 2003), p. 147.

6 Molière: new forms of comedy

1 Jacques Guicharnaud, 'Introduction', *Molière: A Collection of Critical Essays*, ed. Jacques Guicharnaud (Englewood Cliffs, NJ: Prentice-Hall, 1964), p. 7.
2 See the entry on *Honnêteté* in *The New Oxford Companion to Literature in French*, ed. Peter France (Oxford University Press), pp. 389–90. See also Peter France, *Politeness and its Discontents: Problems in French Classical Culture* (Cambridge University Press, 1992).
3 Terence Cave, in *A Short History of French Literature*, ed. Sarah Kay, Terence Cave and Malcolm Bowie (Oxford University Press, 2003), pp. 168–69.

7 La Fontaine: the power of fables/fables of power

1 These *Contes* tended to be dismissed over the years as being merely scabrous. A case for their revaluation is strongly argued by John C. Lapp in his *The Esthetics of Negligence: La Fontaine's 'Contes'* (Cambridge University Press, 1971).
2 The Roman numeral refers to the Book, the Arabic to the fable.
3 See Ross Chambers, *Room for Maneuver: Reading (the) Oppositional (in) Narrative* (University of Chicago Press, 1991), pp. 49–50. See pp. 47–55 for an extended analysis of the fable.

9 Voltaire: the case for tolerance

1 Isaiah Berlin, *Against the Current: Essays in the History of Ideas* (Oxford: Clarendon Press, 1991), p. 88.

10 Rousseau: man of feeling

1 For example: Rousseau's notion of the primacy of the General Will is described by Isaiah Berlin as a form of 'enlightened despotism' and as 'one of the most powerful and dangerous arguments in the entire history of human thought' (Isaiah Berlin, *Political Ideas in the Romantic Age* (London: Chatto & Windus, 2006), p. 124).

2 David Lodge, *Write On: Occasional Essays '65–'85* (London: Secker & Warburg, 1986), p. 121.

11 Diderot: the enlightened sceptic

1 *Dialogic*: 'Characterized or constituted by the interactive, responsive nature of dialogue rather than by the single-mindedness of monologue' (Baldick, *Oxford Dictionary of Literary Terms*). The concept of dialogism was developed by the Russian literary theorist Mikhail Bakhtin (1895–1975).
2 Jean Starobinski, 'The Man Who Told Secrets', *New York Review of Books*, 22 March 1973.
3 *Narratee*: 'the imagined person whom the narrator is assumed to be addressing in a given narrative. The narratee is a notional figure within the space of the text itself, and is thus not to be confused with the actual reader' (Baldick, *Oxford Dictionary of Literary Terms*).

12 Laclos: dangerous liaisons

1 Peter Gay, *The Party of Humanity: Studies in the French Enlightenment* (London: Weidenfeld & Nicolson, 1964), p. 146.
2 From the late sixteenth century to the end of the seventeenth century, the term 'libertine' connoted freethinking – the philosophical rejection of traditional moral and religious values. By the middle of the eighteenth century, the term was used primarily to designate debauched behaviour. See the entry *Libertin* by Ian Maclean in *The New Oxford Companion to Literature in French*, edited by Peter France.
3 Martin Turnell, *The Novel in France* (Harmondsworth: Penguin, 1962), p. 87. (Originally published by Hamish Hamilton, 1950.)

14 Balzac: '*All is true*'

1 Victor Brombert, *The Hidden Reader: Stendhal, Balzac, Hugo, Baudelaire, Flaubert* (Cambridge, Mass.: Harvard University Press, 1988), p. 21.
2 Christopher Prendergast and Peter Brooks (see Further reading) have brought out extremely well Balzac's creative use of the conventions of melodrama to articulate a vision of social instability and disintegration.

15 Hugo: the divine stenographer

1 For an excellent discussion of the public writer in the context of French literary culture from the Ancien Régime to the present, see Priscilla Parkhurst Clark, *Literary France:*

The Making of a Culture (Berkeley, Los Angeles, London: University of California Press, 1987*)*.

2 'Romanticism: A sweeping but indispensable modern term applied to the profound shift in Western attitudes to art and human creativity that dominated much of European culture in the first half of the 19th century... [The] chief emphasis of the Romantic Movement was upon freedom of individual self-expression... Rejecting the ordered rationality of the Enlightenment as mechanical, impersonal, and artificial, the Romantics turned to the emotional directness of personal experience and to the boundlessness of individual imagination and aspiration. Increasingly independent of the declining system of aristocratic patronage, they saw themselves as free agents expressing their own imaginative truths; several found admirers ready to hero-worship the artist as a genius or prophet. The restrained balance valued in 18th-century culture was abandoned in favour of emotional intensity, often taken to extremes of rapture, nostalgia (for childhood or the past), horror, melancholy, or sentimentality. Some... Romantic writers cultivated the appeal of the exotic, the bizarre, or the macabre; almost all showed a new interest in the irrational realms of dream and delirium or of folk superstition and legend. The creative imagination occupied the centre of Romantic views on art, which replaced the "mechanical" rules of conventional form with an "organic" principle of natural growth and free development' (Baldick, *Oxford Dictionary of Literary Terms*, p. 294).

3 See especially Victor Brombert, *Victor Hugo and the Visionary Novel* (Cambridge, Mass.: Harvard University Press, 1984).

4 Simon Leys, *The Angel and the Octopus* (Sydney: Duffy & Snellgrove, 1999), p. 111.

19 Huysmans: against nature

1 Positivism is a philosophical system that recognizes only that which can be scientifically verified or which is capable of logical or mathematical proof. It therefore rejects all metaphysical speculation. The founder of the doctrine of positivism, and a founder of the discipline of sociology, was Auguste Comte (1798–1857).

20 Mallarmé: the magic of words

1 'Crise de vers' is one of Mallarmé's most important statements of his poetic principles. It is reproduced in translation in Rosemary Lloyd's *Mallarmé: The Poet and his Circle*, pp. 227–33.

2 George Steiner, *On Difficulty* (New York and Oxford: Oxford University Press, 1980), p. 42.

3 Jules Huret, 'Interview with Stéphane Mallarmé (1891)', in *Symbolist Art Theories: A Critical Anthology*, ed. Henri Dorra (Berkeley, Los Angeles, London: University of California Press, 1994), pp. 139–42.

4 Bowie comments on the poem in *Mallarmé and the Art of Being Difficult*, pp. 10–13.
5 James R. Lawler, 'A Reading of Mallarmé's "Le Vierge, le Vivace et le bel Aujourd'hui . . . "', *AUMLA* (*Journal of the Australasian Universities Language and Literature Association*), 9 (1958), 78–83 (p. 81).

21 Rimbaud: somebody else

1 Leo Bersani, *A Future for Astyanax: Character and Desire in Literature* (Boston and Toronto: Little, Brown and Co., 1976), p. 230. ('Rimbaud's Simplicity', pp. 230–58.)

22 Proust: the self, time and art

1 Malcolm Bradbury, *The Modern World: Ten Great Writers* (London: Penguin, 1988), p. 152.

24 Apollinaire: impresario of the new

1 Hughes, *The Shock of the New*, pp. 9, 15. 'Il faut être absolument moderne' ('One must be absolutely modern') is a statement of Rimbaud's in his *A Season in Hell*.
2 Martin Sorrell, BBC Radio 3 Essay, 9 January 2013: *Paris 1913: Alcools*.

25 Breton & Company: Surrealism

1 For an absorbing study of the relationship between dreams and artistic expression, see A. Alvarez, *Night: An Exploration of Night Life, Night Language, Sleep and Dreams* (London: Vintage; New York: Norton, 1996).
2 Walter Benjamin, *The Arcades Project*, trans. Howard Eiland and Kevin McLaughlin (Cambridge, Mass., and London: The Belknap Press of Harvard University Press, 1999), p. 883.
3 Alvarez, *Night*, pp. 206–7.

26 Céline: night journey

1 The most sustained expression of Céline's views on style and on his own writing is *Conversations with Professor Y* (*Entretiens avec le professeur Y*).
2 For a detailed sequential analysis of the passage, see Marie-Annick Gervais-Zaninger, *L'explication de texte en littérature* (Paris: Hermann, 2006), pp. 207–26.

27 Sartre: writing in the world

1 A person with a comfortable private income and who has no need to work for a living, i.e. an embodiment of bourgeois parasitism.

28 Camus: a moral voice

1 All of Camus's writings for the newspaper during this period – 165 pieces in all – have been made available to English readers in *Camus at "Combat": Writing 1944–1947*, ed. Jacqueline Lévi-Valensi, with a foreword by David Carroll (Princeton University Press, 2006).
2 Jean-Paul Sartre, *Portraits*, trans. Chris Turner (New York: Seagull Press, 2009), 173–78. The French original, *Situations IV*, was published by Gallimard in 1964.

29 Beckett: filling the silence

1 Introduction to volume IV of the Grove Centenary Edition of Beckett's works.
2 Terry Eagleton, *Sweet Violence: The Idea of the Tragic* (Oxford: Blackwell, 2003), pp. 65, 67.
3 Eagleton, *Sweet Violence*, pp. 68–69.
4 Leo Bersani and Ulysse Dutoit, *Arts of Impoverishment: Beckett, Rothko, Resnais* (Cambridge, Mass.: Harvard University Press, 1993), p. 29.

30 French literature into the twenty-first century

1 For a critique of Barthes's position, and a searching general study of mimesis in the light of contemporary critical theory, see Christopher Prendergast, *The Order of Mimesis* (Cambridge University Press, 1986). See also *Realism Revisited*, special issue of *Romance Studies*, 30: 3–4 (July 2012).
2 Daniel Defoe (1660–1731) was an English novelist and chronicler whose most celebrated works are *Robinson Crusoe* (1719), *Moll Flanders* (1722) and *A Journal of the Plague Year* (1722).
3 Etymologically, 'jeudi' in French derives from the Latin *iovis dies*, the day of Jove or Jupiter (king of the gods, ruler of heaven and earth).
4 Harry Mathews, 'That Ephemeral Thing', *New York Review of Books*, 16 June 1988.
5 Extracts from Leclerc's essay are included in Claire Duchen (ed.), *French Connections: Voices from the Women's Movement in France* (London: Hutchinson, 1987), pp. 58–63. Cixoux's 'The Laugh of the Medusa' is included in Elaine Marks and Isabelle de Courtivron (eds.), *New French Feminisms: An Anthology* (Brighton: Harvester Press, 1981), pp. 245–64.

6 Johnnie Gratton, 'Autobiography', in Christopher John Murray (ed.), *Encyclopedia of Modern French Thought* (New York and London: Fitzroy Dearborn, 2004), pp. 28–31 (p. 31).

7 Antonine Maillet, an Acadian novelist, had won the prize in 1979 for *Pélagie: The Return to Acadie* (*Pélagie la Charette*), while Patrick Chamoiseau was to win it in 1992 for *Texaco* (*Texaco*) and Amin Maalouf in 1993 for *The Rock of Tanios* (*Le Rocher de Tanios*). Andreï Makine, a Russian-born author who settled in France in 1987 at the age of thirty, won in 1995 for *Dreams of My Russian Summers* (*Le Testament français*); Atiq Rahimi, an Afghan-born writer and filmmaker who relocated to France in 1985 in his early twenties, won in 2008 for *The Patience Stone* (*Syngue Sabour*).

8 Charles Forsdick, 'Mobilising French Studies', *Australian Journal of French Studies*, 48: 1 (2011), 88–103 (p. 97). This article was reprinted with a preface by Forsdick in *AJFS*, 51: 2/3 (2014), 250–68.

9 'As applied to literature and other arts, the term [postmodernism] is notoriously ambiguous, implying either that modernism has been superseded or that it has continued into a new phase. Postmodernism may be seen as a continuation of modernism's alienated mood and disorienting techniques and at the same time as an abandonment of its determined quest for artistic coherence in a fragmented world: in very crude terms, where a modernist artist or writer would try to wrest a meaning from the world through myth, symbol, or formal complexity, the postmodernist greets the absurd or meaningless confusion of contemporary existence with a certain numbed or flippant indifference, favouring self-consciously "depthless" works of fabulation, pastiche, *bricolage*, or aleatory disconnection' (Baldick, *Oxford Dictionary of Literary Terms*, p. 266).

10 See Andrew Asibong, 'The Spectacle of Marie NDiaye's *Trois Femmes Puissantes*', *Australian Journal of French Studies*, 50: 3 (2013), 385–98.

11 *Paris Review*, 194 (Fall 2010).

Further reading

Histories, guides, companions, etc.

Birkett, Jennifer, and James Kearns, *A Guide to French Literature from Early Modern to Postmodern* (Basingstoke: Macmillan, 1997).

Burgwinkle, William, Nicholas Hammond and Emma Wilson (eds.), *The Cambridge History of French Literature* (Cambridge University Press, 2011).

Charlton, D. G. (ed.), *France: A Companion to French Studies* (London: Methuen, 1972). Published in five separate volumes in 1974: *French History and Society* by Roger Mettam and Douglas Johnson; *French Thought since 1600* by D. C. Potts and D. G. Charlton; *French Literature from 1600 to the present* by W. D. Howarth, Henri M. Peyre and John Cruickshank; *French Art and Music* by Anthony Blunt and Edward Lockspeiser; *Contemporary France: Politics, Society and Institutions* by Jean Blondel.

Clark, Carol, *French Literature: A Beginner's Guide* (Oxford: Oneworld Publications, 2011).

Coward, David, *A History of French Literature: From 'Chanson de geste' to Cinema* (Oxford: Blackwell, 2002).

Cruickshank, John (ed.), *French Literature and its Background*, 6 vols. (Oxford University Press, 1968–70).

Finch, Alison, *French Literature: A Cultural History* (Cambridge: Polity Press, 2010).

Forbes, Jill, and Michael Kelly (eds.), *French Cultural Studies: An Introduction* (Oxford University Press, 1995).

Gaunt, Simon, and Sarah Kay (eds.), *The Cambridge Companion to Medieval French Literature* (Cambridge University Press, 2008).

Hewitt, Nicholas (ed.), *The Cambridge Companion to Modern French Culture* (Cambridge University Press, 2003).

Hollier, Denis (ed.), *A New History of French Literature* (Cambridge, Mass., and London: Harvard University Press, 1989).

Kay, Sarah, Terence Cave and Malcolm Bowie, *A Short History of French Literature* (Oxford University Press, 2003).

Lyons, John D., *French Literature: A Very Short Introduction* (Oxford University Press, 2010).

New Readings: Introductions to European Literature and Culture (London:
  Bloomsbury; originally published by Duckworth):
  Best, Victoria, *An Introduction to Twentieth-Century French Literature* (2002).
  Farrant, Tim, *An Introduction to Nineteenth-Century French Literature*
    (2007).
  Gaunt, Simon, *Retelling the Tale: An Introduction to French Medieval
    Literature* (2001).
  Hammond, Nicholas, *Creative Tensions: An Introduction to
    Seventeenth-Century French Literature* (1997).
  Kenny, Neil, *An Introduction to Sixteenth-Century French Literature and
    Thought: Other Times, Other Places* (2008).
  Leigh, John, *The Search for Enlightenment: An Introduction to
    Eighteenth-Century French Writing* (1999).
Prendergast, Christopher (ed.), *A History of Modern French Literature, 1500–2000*
  (Princeton University Press, 2015).
Robinson, Christopher, *French Literature in the Nineteenth Century* (Newton
  Abbot: David & Charles, 1978).
  French Literature in the Twentieth Century (Newton Abbot: David & Charles,
    1980).
Unwin, Timothy (ed.), *The French Novel: From 1800 to the Present* (Cambridge
  University Press, 1997).
Worth-Stylianou, Valerie (ed.), *Cassell Guide to Literature in French* (London:
  Cassell, 1996).

Reference works

Baldick, Chris, *The Oxford Dictionary of Literary Terms* (Oxford University Press,
  1990).
Childs, Peter, and Roger Fowler (eds.), *The Routledge Dictionary of Literary Terms*
  (London and New York: Routledge, 2006).
Flower, John (ed.), *Historical Dictionary of French Literature* (Lanham, Toronto,
  Plymouth: Scarecrow Press, 2013).
France, Peter (ed.), *The New Oxford Companion to Literature in French* (Oxford:
  Clarendon Press, 1995).
Hughes, Alex, and Keith Reader (eds.), *Encyclopedia of Contemporary French
  Culture* (London and New York: Routledge, 1998).
Kelly, Michael (ed.), *French Culture and Society: The Essentials* (London: Arnold,
  2001).

Background

Jones, Colin, *The Cambridge Illustrated History of France* (Cambridge University
  Press, 1999).
Littlewood, Ian, *France: The Rough Guide Chronicle* (London: Rough Guides,
  2002).

1 Villon: a dying man

Criticism

Armstrong, Adrian, 'The Testament of François Villon', in Simon Gaunt and
 Sarah Kay (eds.), *The Cambridge Companion to Medieval French
 Literature* (Cambridge University Press, 2008), pp. 63–76.
Clemens, Justin, 'Testimony, Theory, Testament: On Translating François Villon',
 The AALITRA Review: A Journal of Literary Translation, 6 (2013), 5–21.
 Website: http://aalitra.org.au
Fein, David A., *François Villon Revisited* (New York: Twayne, 1997).
Freeman, Michael, *François Villon in his Works: The Villain's Tale* (Amsterdam:
 Rodopi, 2000).
Hunt, Tony, *Villon's Last Will: Language and Authority in the Testament* (Oxford
 University Press, 1996).
Regalado, Nancy Freeman, '*I the Scholar François Villon*', in Denis Hollier (ed.), *A
 New History of French Literature* (Cambridge, Mass., and London:
 Harvard University Press, 1989), pp. 118–24.
Taylor, Jane, *The Poetry of François Villon* (Cambridge University Press, 2001).

Translations

Clemens, Justin, *Villain* (Melbourne: Hunter Publishers, 2009). Contains
 translations of 'Ballad of Olde-Time Ladies', 'Ballad of Olde-Time Lords',
 'Lament of the Beautiful Helmet-Seller', 'The Beautiful Helmet-Seller to
 Good-Time Girls', 'Double Ballade', 'Ballad of Fried Tongues', 'Ballad of
 Parisiennes', 'Ballad of Fat Margot' and 'Ballad of the Hanged'.
Lowell, Robert, *Imitations* (New York: Farrar, Straus and Giroux, 1961). Contains
 twenty stanzas from *The Testament* together with 'Ballad for the Dead
 Ladies', 'The Old Lady's Lament for her Youth', 'Villon's Prayer for his
 Mother to Say to the Virgin' and 'Villon's Epitaph'.
Villon, François, *Complete Poems*, ed. with English translation and commentary
 by Barbara Sargent-Baur (Toronto, Buffalo, London: University of
 Toronto Press, 1994).
 Poems, trans. David Georgi (Evanston, Ill.: Northwestern University Press,
 2012). A bilingual edition.

2 Rabelais: the uses of laughter

Criticism

Auerbach, Erich, *Mimesis: The Representation of Reality in Western Literature*,
 trans. Willard R. Trask (Princeton University Press, 1953). (Chapter 11,
 'The World in Pantagruel's Mouth', pp. 262–84.)
Bakhtin, Mikhail, *Rabelais and his World*, trans. Hélène Iswolsky (Bloomington:
 Indiana University Press, 1984; originally published Moscow, 1965).

Bowen, Barbara C., *Enter Rabelais, Laughing* (Nashville: Vanderbilt University Press, 1998).

Cave, Terence, *The Cornucopian Text: Problems of Writing in the French Renaissance* (Oxford and New York: Oxford University Press, 1979), especially chapter 7 ('Rabelais').

Clark, Carol, *The Vulgar Rabelais* (Glasgow: Pressgang Publishers, 1984).

Coleman, Dorothy Gabe, *Rabelais: A Critical Study in Prose Fiction* (Cambridge University Press, 1971).

Greene, Thomas M., *Rabelais: A Study in Comic Courage* (Englewood Cliffs, NJ: Prentice-Hall, Inc., 1970).

Hall, Kathleen M., *Rabelais: 'Pantagruel' and 'Gargantua'* (London: Grant & Cutler, 1991).

Jeanneret, Michel, *A Feast of Words: Banquets and Table Talk in the Renaissance*, trans. Jeremy Whiteley and Emma Hughes (London: Polity Press, 1991; originally published in French, 1987).

Josipovici, Gabriel, 'Rabelais: Language and Laughter', in *The World and the Book: A Study of Modern Fiction*, 2nd edn (London: Macmillan, 1979), pp. 100–21.

O'Brien, John (ed.), *The Cambridge Companion to Rabelais* (Cambridge University Press, 2011).

Reeser, Todd W., and Floyd Gray (eds.), *Approaches to Teaching the Works of François Rabelais* (New York: MLA, 2011).

Screech, Michael, *Rabelais* (London: Duckworth; Ithaca, NY: Cornell University Press, 1979).

Translations

Rabelais, François, *Gargantua*, trans. Andrew Brown (London: Hesperus, 2003).

Gargantua and Pantagruel, trans. Sir Thomas Urquhart and Pierre Le Motteux, intro. by Terence Cave, Everyman's Library (London: David Campbell, 1994). A modern reprint of a seventeenth-century translation.

Gargantua and Pantagruel, trans. Sir Thomas Urquhart and Pierre Le Motteux, intro. by Richard Cooper, Wordsworth Classics of World Literature (Ware: Wordsworth, 1999). (As above.)

Gargantua and Pantagruel, trans. and ed. M. A. Screech (London: Penguin Books, 2006).

Gargantua and Pantagruel, trans. Burton Raffel (New York: Norton, 1990).

Pantagruel, trans. Andrew Brown (London: Hesperus, 2003).

3 Montaigne: self-portrait

Criticism

Auerbach, Erich, *Mimesis: The Representation of Reality in Western Literature*, trans. Willard R. Trask (Princeton University Press, 1953). ('L'Humaine Condition', pp. 285–311.)

Bakewell, Sarah, *How to Live: A Life of Montaigne in One Question and Twenty Attempts at an Answer* (London: Chatto & Windus, 2010).

Bloom, Harold, *The Western Canon* (New York: Harcourt Brace, 1994), pp. 147–58.

Bowman, Frank P., 'Montaigne: *Du Repentir, Essais*, Book III, Chapter 2', in Peter H. Nurse (ed.), *The Art of Criticism: Essays in French Literary Analysis* (Edinburgh University Press, 1969), pp. 41–56.

Montaigne: Essays (London: Edward Arnold, 1965).

Burke, Peter, *Montaigne* (Oxford University Press, 1981).

Cave, Terence, *How to Read Montaigne* (London: Granta Books, 2007).

Coleman, Dorothy Gabe, *Montaigne's 'Essais'* (London: Allen & Unwin, 1987).

Frampton, Saul, *When I Am Playing With My Cat, How Do I Know She Is Not Playing With Me?: Montaigne and Being in Touch With Life* (London: Faber & Faber, 2011).

Friedrich, Hugo, *Montaigne*, ed. Philippe Desan, trans. Dawn Eng (Berkeley: University of California Press, 1991; originally published in German, 1949).

Henry, Patrick (ed.), *Approaches to Teaching Montaigne's Essays* (New York: MLA, 1994).

Langer, Ullrich (ed.), *The Cambridge Companion to Montaigne* (Cambridge University Press, 2005).

Regosin, Richard L., *The Matter of My Book: Montaigne's 'Essais' as the Book of the Self* (Berkeley: University of California Press, 1977).

Sayce, Richard, *The Essays of Montaigne: A Critical Exploration* (London: Weidenfeld & Nicolson, 1972).

Screech, M. A., *Montaigne and Melancholy: The Wisdom of the Essays*, new edn (London: Duckworth; New York: Rowman & Littlefield, 2000)

Starobinski, Jean, *Montaigne in Motion*, trans. Arthur Goldhammer (University of Chicago Press, 1985). French original: *Montaigne en mouvement*, 1982.

Woolf, Virginia, 'Montaigne', in A. McNeillie (ed.), *The Essays of Virginia Woolf* (London: Hogarth, 1986), IV, pp. 71–81.

Translations

Frame, Donald, *The Complete Works of Montaigne* (London: Everyman's Library, 2003; originally published Stanford University Press, 1943).

Screech, M. A., *The Complete Essays of Michel de Montaigne*, new edn (London: Penguin, 2004; originally published London: Allen Lane, 1991).

The Essays: A Selection (London: Penguin, 2004).

4 Corneille: heroes and kings

Criticism

Bénichou, Paul, *Man and Ethics: Studies in French Classicism*, trans. Elizabeth Hughes (Garden City, NY: Doubleday & Company, 1971), pp. 1–74. French original: *Morales du Grand Siècle*, 1948.

Clarke, David, *Pierre Corneille: Poetics and Political Drama under Louis XIII* (Cambridge University Press, 1992).

Greenberg, Mitchell, *Corneille, Classicism and the Ruses of Symmetry* (Cambridge University Press, 1986).

Subjectivity and Subjugation in Seventeenth-Century Drama and Prose: The Family Romance of French Classicism (Cambridge University Press, 1992). ('The Grateful Dead: Corneille's Tragedy and the Subject of History', pp. 48–64.)

Howarth, W. D., *Corneille: 'Le Cid'* (London: Grant & Cutler, 1988).

Ibbett, Katherine, *The Style of the State in French Theater, 1630–1660: Neoclassicism and Government* (London: Ashgate, 2009).

Knight, R. C., *Corneille: 'Horace'* (London: Grant & Cutler, 1981).

Lyons, John D., *Kingdom of Disorder: The Theory of Tragedy in Classical France* (West Lafayette, Ind.: Purdue University Press, 1999).

The Tragedy of Origins: Pierre Corneille and Historical Perspective (Stanford University Press, 1996).

Translations

Corneille, Pierre, *Le Cid and The Liar*, trans. Richard Wilbur (Boston and New York: Houghton Mifflin Harcourt, 2009).

The Cid/Cinna/The Theatrical Illusion, trans. and intro. John Cairncross (Harmondsworth: Penguin Books, 1975).

Horace, trans. Alan Brownjohn, intro. David Clarke (London: Angel Books, 1997).

Three Plays: Le Cid, Cinna, Polyeuct, trans. Norel Clarke (Bath: Absolute Classics, 1993).

5 Racine: in the labyrinth

Criticism/critical editions

Barthes, Roland, *On Racine*, trans. Richard Howard (New York: Hill & Wang, 1964; Oxford: Blackwell, 1992). French original: *Sur Racine* (Paris: Seuil, 1963).

Bénichou, Paul, *Man and Ethics: Studies in French Classicism*, trans. Elizabeth Hughes (Garden City, NY: Doubleday, 1971). French original: *Morales du Grand Siècle* (Paris: Gallimard, 1948).

Butler, Philip, *A Student's Guide to Racine* (London: Heinemann, 1974).

Campbell, John, *Questioning Racinian Tragedy* (Chapel Hill: University of North Carolina Press, 2005).

De Mourgues, Odette, *Racine; or, The Triumph of Relevance* (Cambridge University Press, 1967).

France, Peter, *Racine's Rhetoric* (Oxford: Clarendon Press, 1965).

Goldmann, Lucien, *The Hidden God: A Study of Tragic Vision in the 'Pensées' of Pascal and the Tragedies of Racine*, trans. Philip Thody (London: Routledge, 1964). French original: *Le Dieu caché*, 1955.

Goodkin, Richard E., 'Neoclassical Dramatic Theory in Seventeenth-Century France', in Rebecca Bushnell (ed.), *A Companion to Tragedy* (Oxford: Blackwell, 2005), pp. 373–92.

Greenberg, Mitchell, 'French Neoclassical Tragedy: Corneille/Racine', in Rebecca Bushnell (ed.), *A Companion to Tragedy* (Oxford: Blackwell, 2005), pp. 393–410.

Hawcroft, Michael, *Word as Action: Racine, Rhetoric and Theatrical Language* (Oxford: Clarendon Press, 1992).

James, Edward, and Gillian Jondorf, *Racine: 'Phèdre'* (Cambridge University Press, 1994).

Lapp, J. C., *Aspects of Racinian Tragedy* (University of Toronto Press, 1955; reissued 1978).

Maskell, David, *Racine: A Theatrical Reading* (Oxford University Press, 1991).

Parish, Richard, *Racine: The Limits of Tragedy* (Tübingen: PFSCL, Biblio-17, 1993).

Phillips, Henry, *Racine: Language and Theatre* (Durham University Press, 1994).

Racine: 'Phèdre', ed. with intro., commentary and notes by Richard Parish (Bristol Classical Press, 1996).

Short, J. P., *Racine: 'Phèdre'* (London: Grant & Cutler, 1983).

Spitzer, Leo, 'Racine's Classical Piano' and 'The "Récit de Théramène" in Racine's *Phèdre*', in David Bellos (ed.), *Leo Spitzer: Essays on Seventeenth-Century French Literature* (Cambridge University Press, 1983), pp. 1–113, 209–51.

Steiner, George, *The Death of Tragedy* (New York: Knopf, 1961; Oxford University Press, 1980; New Haven, Conn., and London: Yale University Press, 1996).

Yarrow, P. J., *Racine* (Oxford: Blackwell, 1978).

Translations

For a useful discussion of issues involved and the fortunes of Racine in English translation, see Patrick Swinden, 'Translating Racine', *Comparative Literature*, 49: 3 (1997), 209–26.

Racine, Jean, *Andromache*, trans. Richard Wilbur (New York: Harcourt Brace, 1984) and *Phaedra*, trans. Richard Wilbur (New York: Harcourt Brace, 1987).

Britannicus, Phaedra, Athalia, trans. C. H. Sisson (Oxford University Press, 1987).

Iphigenia, Phaedra, Athaliah, trans. John Cairncross (Harmondsworth: Penguin, 1963) and *Andromache, Britannicus, Berenice*, trans. John Cairncross (Harmondsworth: Penguin, 1967).

Phaedra, trans. Robert Lowell (London: Faber & Faber, 1963).
Phedra, trans. Julie Rose (London: Nick Hern Books, 2001).
Phèdre, trans. Ted Hughes (London: Faber & Faber, 1998).
Three Plays, trans. Tim Chilcott, with an intro. and notes by Michael
    Hawcroft (London: Wordsworth Classics, 2000). Bilingual edition of
    Andromache, Phaedra and *Athalia*.

6 Molière: new forms of comedy

Criticism/critical editions

Bradby, David, and Andrew Calder (eds.), *The Cambridge Companion to Molière*
    (Cambridge University Press, 2006).
Gaines, James F., and Michael S. Koppisch, *Approaches to Teaching Molière's
    'Tartuffe' and Other Plays* (New York: MLA, 1995).
Howarth, W. D., *Molière: A Playwright and his Audience* (Cambridge University
    Press, 1982).
Molière: 'Le Bourgeois gentilhomme', ed. with an intro. by H. Gaston Hall
    (University of London Press, 1966).
Molière: 'Le Misanthrope', ed. with an intro. and commentary by Jonathan
    Mallinson (London: Bristol Classical Press, 1996).
Molière: 'Le Tartuffe', ed. with an intro. and notes by Richard Parish (London:
    Bristol Classical Press, 1998).
Moore, W. G., *Molière: A New Criticism* (Oxford: Clarendon Press, 1949).
Norman, Larry F., 'Seventeenth-Century Comedy', in William Burgwinkle,
    Nicholas Hammond and Emma Wilson (eds.), *The Cambridge History of
    French Literature* (Cambridge University Press, 2011), pp. 274–83.
Nurse, Peter, *Molière and the Comic Spirit* (Geneva: Droz, 1991).

Individual plays

Broome, J. H., *Molière: 'L'École des femmes' and 'Le Misanthrope'* (London: Grant
    & Cutler, 1982; repr. with corrections 1993).
Hall, H. Gaston, *Molière's 'Le Bourgeois Gentilhomme': Context and Stagecraft*
    (University of Durham, Durham Modern Languages Series, 1990).
Molière: 'Tartuffe' (London: Edward Arnold, 1960).
Mallinson, G. J., *Molière: 'L'Avare'* (London: Grant & Cutler, 1988).
Peacock, Noel, *Molière: 'L'École des femmes'* (University of Glasgow French and
    German Publications, 1989).
Whitton, David, *Molière: 'Le Bourgeois Gentilhomme'* (London: Grant & Cutler,
    1992).
Molière: 'Le Misanthrope' (University of Glasgow French and German
    Publications, 1991).

Translations

The verse plays of Molière are traditionally translated either into prose or into rhymed iambic pentameter. As Christopher Hampton has commented, the characteristics of the French language, especially the fact that it has a much more rigid and defined phonetic structure than English, mean that 'finding a rhyme is infinitely simpler and more natural in French than it can ever be in English. There have been a number of admirable rhyming translations of Molière: but the ingenuity they demand cannot avoid drawing attention to itself, somewhat at the expense of the line of the play as a whole.' I agree with Hampton's assessment that it is 'logical to translate a play written in Alexandrines, the form naturally adopted by dramatists in the golden age of French theatre, into the form adopted equally naturally by English dramatists in their golden age: namely blank verse.' Hampton has put his views into practice in his own admirable translation of *Tartuffe*.

Molière, *Don Juan and Other Plays*, trans. George Graveley and Ian Maclean, ed. Ian Maclean (Oxford University Press, 1989 and 1998).
  The Misanthrope and Tartuffe, trans. Richard Wilbur (New York: Harcourt Brace, 1993; originally published 1965).
  The Misanthrope, Tartuffe and Other Plays, trans. and ed. Maya Slater (Oxford University Press, 2001 and 2008).
  The Misanthrope and Other Plays, trans. John Wood and David Coward, ed. David Coward (London: Penguin Books, 2000).
  The Miser and Other Plays, trans. John Wood and David Coward, ed. David Coward (London: Penguin Books, 2000).
  Molière's 'Tartuffe', trans. Christopher Hampton (London: Faber & Faber, 1984).
  Molière's 'Tartuffe', trans. Constance Congdon, ed. Constance Congdon and Virginia Scott (New York and London: Norton, 2009). Contains much useful background and critical material, including Molière's petitions to the King and his 1669 preface to the published version of the play.
  Molière: 'The Misanthrope', trans. Tony Harrison (New York: Samuel French, 1973).

7 La Fontaine: the power of fables/fables of power

Criticism

Biard, Jean Dominique, *The Style of La Fontaine's Fables* (Oxford: Blackwell, 1966).
Calder, Andrew, *The Fables of La Fontaine: Wisdom Brought Down to Earth* (Geneva: Droz, 2001).
Chambers, Ross, *Room for Maneuver: Reading (the) Oppositional (in) Narrative* (University of Chicago Press, 1991), pp. 47–101.

Danner, Richard, *Patterns of Irony in the 'Fables' of La Fontaine* (Athens: Ohio University Press, 1985).

De Mourgues, Odette, *La Fontaine: Fables* (London: Edward Arnold, 1960).

Fumaroli, Marc, *The Poet and the King: Jean de La Fontaine and his Century*, trans. Jean Marie Todd (University of Notre Dame Press, 2002). French original: *Le Poète et le roi*, 1997.

Rubin, David Lee, *A Pact with Silence: Art and Thought in the Fables of Jean de La Fontaine* (Columbus: Ohio State University Press, 1991).

Slater, Maya, *The Craft of La Fontaine* (London: Athlone Press, 2000).

Sweetser, Marie-Odile, *La Fontaine* (Boston: Twayne, 1987).

Translations/editions

La Fontaine, Jean de, *The Complete Fables of La Fontaine*, trans. Norman Spector (Evanston, Ill.: Northwestern University Press, 1989).

Fables, trans. Gordon Pirie, intro. by Robert Chandler (London: Hesperus, 2008). With French text.

The Fables, trans. Elizur Wright (London: Bloomsbury, 1987; originally published by Jupiter Books, 1975). A handsome edition with illustrations by Gustave Doré. With French text.

Selected Fables, trans. Christopher Betts (Oxford University Press, 2014). With illustrations by Gustave Doré.

Selected Fables, trans. James Michie, intro. by Geoffrey Grigson (London: Penguin Books, 2006; originally published London: Allen Lane, 1979).

8 Madame de Lafayette: the birth of the modern novel

Criticism

Beasley, Faith E., and Katharine Ann Jensen (eds.), *Approaches to Teaching Lafayette's 'The Princess of Clèves'* (New York: MLA, 1998).

Brink, André, 'Courtly Love, Private Anguish: Madame de Lafayette: *La Princesse de Clèves*', in *The Novel: Language and Narrative from Cervantes to Calvino* (London: Palgrave Macmillan, 1997; New York University Press, 1998), pp. 46–64.

DeJean, Joan E., *Tender Geographies: Women and the Origins of the Novel in France* (New York: Columbia University Press, 1993), esp. pp. 94–126.

DiPiero, Thomas, 'A Discourse of One's Own: *La Princesse de Clèves*', in *Dangerous Truths and Criminal Passions: the Evolution of the French Novel, 1569–1791* (Stanford University Press, 1992), pp. 194–226.

Howarth, W. D., 'Mme de Lafayette (1634–93)', in *Life and Letters in France: The Seventeenth Century* (London and Edinburgh: Nelson, 1965), pp. 123–33.

Miller, Nancy K., *Subject to Change: Reading Feminist Writing* (New York: Columbia University Press, 1988). (Chapter 1: 'Emphasis Added: Plots and Plausibilities in Women's Fictions'.)

Raitt, Janet, *Madame de Lafayette and 'La Princesse de Clèves'* (London: Harrap, 1971).

Scott, J. W., *Madame de Lafayette: 'La Princesse de Clèves'* (London: Grant & Cutler, 1983).

Translations/editions

de Lafayette, Marie-Madeleine, *The Princesse de Clèves*, trans. with an intro. and notes by Terence Cave (Oxford University Press, 1992). The introduction is excellent and the notes extremely useful.

The Princess of Clèves, ed. and with a revised translation by John D. Lyons (New York: Norton, 1994). Contains a substantial anthology of contemporary reactions and modern criticism.

9 Voltaire: the case for tolerance

Criticism

Cronk, Nicholas (ed.), *The Cambridge Companion to Voltaire* (Cambridge University Press, 2009).

Davidson, Ian, *Voltaire in Exile* (London: Atlantic Books, 2004).

Voltaire: A Life (London: Profile Books, 2010).

Fletcher, Dennis, *Voltaire: 'Lettres Philosophiques'* (London: Grant & Cutler, 1986).

Gray, John, *Voltaire* (London: Phoenix, 1998).

Howells, Robin, *Disabled Powers: A Reading of Voltaire's 'Contes'* (Amsterdam: Rodopi, 1993).

Mason, Haydn, *'Candide': Optimism Demolished* (New York: Twayne, 1992).

Voltaire (London: Hutchinson, 1975).

Pearson, Roger, *The Fables of Reason: A Study of Voltaire's 'Contes Philosophiques'* (Oxford: Clarendon Press, 1993).

Voltaire Almighty: A Life in Pursuit of Freedom (London: Bloomsbury, 2005).

Todd, Christopher, *Voltaire: 'Dictionnaire Philosophique'* (London: Grant & Cutler, 1980).

Waldinger, Renée (ed.), *Approaches to Teaching Voltaire's 'Candide'* (New York: MLA, 1987).

Williams, David, *Voltaire: 'Candide'* (London: Grant & Cutler, 1997).

On the Enlightenment

Brewer, Daniel, *The Enlightenment Past: Reconstructing Eighteenth-Century French Thought* (Cambridge University Press, 2008).

Gay, Peter, *The Enlightenment: An Interpretation*, 2 vols. (New York: Knopf, 1966–69).
 (ed.), *The Enlightenment: A Comprehensive Anthology*, rev. edn (New York: Simon, 1985).
Hampson, Norman, *The Enlightenment*, new edn (London: Penguin, 1990).
Israel, Jonathan, *Enlightenment Contested: Philosophy, Modernity, and the Emancipation of Man, 1670–1752* (Oxford University Press, 2006).
Spencer, Lloyd, and Andrzej Krauze, *Introducing the Enlightenment* (New York: Totem Books, 1997; Cambridge: Icon Books, 2000).
Yolton, John, Roy Porter, Pat Rogers and Barbara Stafford (eds.), *The Blackwell Companion to the Enlightenment* (Oxford: Blackwell, 1991).

Translations

Voltaire, *Candide and Other Stories*, trans. with an intro. and notes by Roger Pearson (Oxford University Press, 1990; new edn 2006).
 Candide, trans. and ed. Robert M. Adams, 2nd edn (New York: Norton, 1991). Includes a wide selection of criticism and background material.
 Candide, trans. Theo Cuffe, with an afterword by Michael Wood (London: Penguin, 2005).
 Candide, trans. and ed. Peter Gay (New York: St Martin's, 1963). A bilingual edition.
 Candide, trans., ed. and with an intro. by Daniel Gordon (Boston and New York: Bedford/St Martin's, 1999).
 Candide, Zadig and Selected Stories, trans. Donald M. Frame, intro. by John Iverson, afterword by Thaisa Frank (New York: Signet Classics, 2009 [1961])
 Letters Concerning the English Nation, ed. Nicholas Cronk (Oxford University Press, 1994; rev. edn 2005).
 Letters on England, trans. Leonard Tancock (Harmondsworth: Penguin, 1980).
 Micromégas and Other Short Fictions, trans. Theo Cuffe, ed. Haydn Mason (London: Penguin, 2002).
 Philosophical Dictionary, trans. Theodore Besterman (London: Penguin, 1972).
 Philosophical Letters, trans. Prudence L. Steiner, ed. John Leigh (London: Hackett, 2007).
 Political Writings, trans. and ed. David Williams (Cambridge University Press, 1994).
 Treatise on Tolerance and Other Writings, trans. Brian Masters, ed. Simon Harvey (Cambridge University Press, 2000).

10 Rousseau: man of feeling

Criticism

Bloom, Harold (ed.), *Jean-Jacques Rousseau* (New York: Chelsea House, 1991).

Damrosch, Leo, *Jean-Jacques Rousseau: Restless Genius* (New York: Houghton Mifflin, 2005).

France, Peter, *Rousseau: 'Confessions'* (Cambridge University Press, 1987).

Gauthier, David, *Rousseau: The Sentiment of Existence* (Cambridge University Press, 2006).

Howells, R. J., *Rousseau: 'La Nouvelle Héloïse'* (London: Grant & Cutler, 1987).

O'Neill, John C., and Ourida Mostefai (eds.), *Approaches to Teaching Rousseau's 'Confessions' and 'Reveries of the Solitary Walker'* (New York: MLA, 2003).

Porter, Dennis, *Rousseau's Legacy: Emergence and Eclipse of the Writer in France* (Oxford University Press, 1995), pp. 22–70.

Riley, Patrick (ed.), *The Cambridge Companion to Rousseau* (Cambridge University Press, 2001).

Sheringham, Michael, *French Autobiography: Devices and Desires – Rousseau to Perec* (Oxford: Clarendon Press, 1993). ('Rousseau and the Chains of Narrative', pp. 31–66.)

Starobinski, Jean, *Jean-Jacques Rousseau: Transparency and Obstruction*, trans. Arnold Goldhammer (University of Chicago Press, 1988). French original: *Jean-Jacques Rousseau, la transparence et l'obstacle*, 2nd edn, 1971.

Tanner, Tony, *Adultery in the Novel: Contract and Transgression* (Baltimore and London: Johns Hopkins University Press, 1979). ('Rousseau's *La Nouvelle Héloïse*', pp. 113–78.)

Wokler, Robert, *Rousseau* (Oxford University Press, 1995).

Translations/editions

Rousseau, Jean-Jacques, *Confessions*, trans. Angela Scholar, ed. Patrick Coleman (Oxford University Press, 2000).

The *'Confessions'*, trans. Christopher Kelly, ed. Christopher Kelly, Roger D. Masters and Peter G. Stillman (Hanover, NH: University Press of New England, 1995).

'The Discourses' and Other Early Political Writings, ed. and trans. Victor Gourevitch (Cambridge University Press, 1997).

Discourse on the Origins of Inequality, trans. Franklin Philip, ed. Patrick Coleman (Oxford University Press, 2009; originally published 1994).

Julie, or the New Heloise, trans. and ed. Philip Stewart and Jean Vaché (Hanover, NH: University Press of New England, 1997).

Reveries of The Solitary Walker, trans. with an intro. by Peter France (Harmondsworth: Penguin, 1979).

The Social Contract, trans. and ed. Christopher Betts (Oxford University Press, 2008; originally published 1994).

'The Social Contract' and Other Later Political Writings, ed. and trans. Victor Gourevitch (Cambridge University Press, 1997).

11 Diderot: the enlightened sceptic

Criticism

Alter, Robert, *Partial Magic: The Novel as a Self-Conscious Genre* (Berkeley, Los Angeles and London: University of California Press, 1975). ('Diderot's *Jacques*: This Is and Is Not a Story', pp. 57–83.)

Bremner, Geoffrey, *Diderot: 'Jacques le Fataliste'* (London: Grant & Cutler, 1985).
Order and Chance: The Pattern of Diderot's Thought (Cambridge University Press, 1983).

Brink, André, *The Novel: Language and Narrative from Cervantes to Calvino* (New York University Press, 1998). ('The Dialogic Pact – Denis Diderot: *Jacques the Fatalist and His Master*', pp. 86–103.)

Fellows, Otis, *Diderot*, rev. edn (Boston: Twayne, 1989).

Fowler, James (ed.), *New Essays on Diderot* (Cambridge University Press, 2011).

France, Peter, *Diderot* (Oxford University Press, 1982).

Furbank, P. N., *Diderot: A Critical Biography* (London: Secker and Warburg; New York: Knopf, 1992; Faber & Faber, 2008).

See also Malcolm Bradbury's novel *To The Hermitage* (London: Picador, 2000), which, like *Jacques the Fatalist*, is a reflection on novel-writing and the state of contemporary culture, and recreates Diderot's journey to Russia as a vehicle for this.

Translations/editions

Diderot, Denis, *Diderot on Art*, ed. and trans. John Goodman, 2 vols. (New Haven, Conn., and London: Yale University Press, 1995).
Diderot: Political Writings, ed. and trans. John Hope Mason and Robert Wokler (Cambridge University Press, 1992).
Diderot's Letters to Sophie Volland: A Selection, ed. and trans. Peter France (Oxford University Press, 1972).
Jacques the Fatalist, ed. and trans. David Coward (Oxford University Press, 1999).
Jacques the Fatalist and his Master, ed. and trans. Michael Henry (Harmondsworth: Penguin, 1986).
The Paradox of Acting, trans. Walter Herries Pollock (New York: Kessinger Publishing, 2007 [1957]).
Rameau's Nephew and First Satire, ed. Nicholas Cronk, trans. Margaret Mauldon (Oxford University Press, 2008).
This Is not a Story and Other Stories, ed. and trans. P. N. Furbank (Oxford University Press, 1993).

12 Laclos: dangerous liaisons

Criticism

Brooks, Peter, *The Novel of Worldliness* (Princeton University Press, 1969), pp. 172–218.

Byrne, Patrick, *'Les Liaisons Dangereuses': A Study of Motive and Moral* (University of Glasgow French & German Publications, 1989).

Davies, Simon, *Laclos: 'Les Liaisons dangereuses'* (London: Grant & Cutler, 1987).

DeJean, Joan, *Literary Fortifications: Rousseau, Laclos, Sade* (Princeton University Press, 1984), pp. 214–31.

Rosbottom, Ronald C., *Choderlos de Laclos* (Boston: Twayne, 1978).

Translations

Laclos, *Dangerous Liaisons*, trans. Helen Constantine (London: Penguin, 2007).

Laclos, *Les Liaisons dangereuses*, trans. Douglas Parmée (Oxford University Press, 1995). This edition has an excellent introduction by David Coward.

Film version

There is a fine film version of *Dangerous Liaisons*, directed by Stephen Frears (1988). The screenplay is by Christopher Hampton, whose theatrical adaptation of the novel – *Les Liaisons dangereuses* – was first produced by the Royal Shakespeare Company in 1985.

13 Stendhal: the pursuit of happiness

Criticism

Auerbach, Erich, *Mimesis: The Representation of Reality in Western Literature*, trans. Willard R. Trask (Princeton University Press, 1953). ('In the Hôtel de la Mole', pp. 454–92.)

Bolster, Richard, *Stendhal: 'Le Rouge et le Noir'* (London: Grant & Cutler, 1994).

Brombert, Victor, *Stendhal: Fiction and the Themes of Freedom* (New York: Random House, 1968).

    (ed.), *Stendhal: A Collection of Critical Essays* (Englewood Cliffs, NJ: Prentice-Hall, 1962).

Brooks, Peter, *The Novel of Worldliness* (Princeton University Press, 1969). ('Stendhal and the Styles of Worldliness', pp. 219–88.)

    Reading for the Plot: Design and Intention in Narrative (New York: Knopf, 1984). ('The Novel and the Guillotine; or, Fathers and Sons in *Le Rouge et le Noir*', pp. 62–89.)

De la Motte, Dean, and Stirling Haig (eds.), *Approaches to Teaching Stendhal's 'The Red and the Black'* (New York: MLA, 1999).

Finch, Alison, *Stendhal: 'La Chartreuse de Parme'* (London: Edward Arnold, 1984).

Genette, Gérard, *Figures of Literary Discourse* (New York: Columbia University Press, 1982). ('Stendhal', pp. 147–82.)

Girard, René, *Deceit, Desire, and the Novel* (Baltimore: Johns Hopkins University Press, 1965). ('Triangular Desire', pp. 503–21.)

Haig, Stirling, *Stendhal: 'The Red and the Black'* (Cambridge University Press, 1989).

Humphries, Jefferson, *'The Red and the Black': Mimetic Desire and the Myth of Celebrity* (Boston: Twayne, 1991).

Jefferson, Ann, *Reading Realism in Stendhal* (Cambridge University Press, 1988).

Stendhal: 'La Chartreuse de Parme' (London: Grant & Cutler, 2003).

Moretti, Franco, *The Way of the World: The 'Bildungsroman' in European Culture* (London: Verso, 1987), pp. 75–94 and *passim*.

Pearson, Roger, *Stendhal's Violin: A Novelist and his Reader* (Oxford: Clarendon Press, 1988).

(ed.), *Stendhal: 'The Red and the Black' and 'The Charterhouse of Parma'* (London and New York: Longman, 1994).

Petrey, Sandy, *Realism and Revolution* (Ithaca, NY: Cornell University Press, 1988), pp. 123–62.

Talbot, Emile, *Stendhal Revisited* (New York: Twayne, 1993).

Wood, Michael, *Stendhal* (London: Elek, 1971).

Translations/editions

The major novels are available in Oxford World's Classics and Penguin Books. In addition, the following are excellent:

The Charterhouse of Parma, trans. Richard Howard (New York: Random House, The Modern Library, 1999; London: Picador, 2002).

The Life of Henry Brulard, trans. and with an intro. by John Sturrock (New York Review of Books, 1995).

The Red and the Black, ed. Ann Jefferson, based on a translation by C. K. Scott Moncrieff (London: J. M. Dent, Everyman's Library, 1997).

14 Balzac: 'All Is true'

Criticism

Auerbach, Erich, *Mimesis: The Representation of Reality in Western Literature*, trans. Willard R. Trask (Princeton University Press, 1953), pp. 468–82.

Bellos, David, *Balzac: 'Old Goriot'* (Cambridge University Press, 1987).

Bolster, Richard, *Balzac: 'Le Père Goriot'* (London: Grant & Cutler, 2000).

Brooks, Peter, *The Melodramatic Imagination: Balzac, Henry James, and the Mode of Excess* (New Haven, Conn., and London: Yale University Press, 1976).

Realist Vision (New Haven, Conn., and London: Yale University Press, 2005). ('Balzac Invents the Nineteenth Century', pp. 21–39.)

Ginsburg, Michal Peled (ed.), *Approaches to Teaching Balzac's 'Old Goriot'* (New York: MLA, 2000).

Harvey, David, *Paris, Capital of Modernity* (New York and London: Routledge, 2003). ('The Myths of Modernity: Balzac's Paris', pp. 23–57.)

Kanes, Martin, *Père Goriot: Anatomy of a Troubled World* (New York: Twayne, 1993).

(ed.), *Critical Essays on Honoré de Balzac* (Boston: G. K. Hall, 1990).

Lock, Peter W., *Balzac: 'Le Père Goriot'* (London: Edward Arnold, 1967).

Prendergast, Christopher, *Balzac: Fiction and Melodrama* (London: Edward Arnold, 1978).

Robb, Graham, *Balzac: A Biography* (London: Picador, 2000 [1994]; New York: Norton, 1995).

Stowe, William W., *Balzac, James, and the Realistic Novel* (Princeton University Press, 1983).

Tilby, Michael, 'Honoré de Balzac (1799–1850)', in Michael Bell (ed.), *The Cambridge Companion to European Novelists* (Cambridge University Press, 2012), pp. 192–208.

Tilby, Michael (ed.), *Balzac* (London: Longman, 1995).

Translations/editions

Balzac, Honoré de, *Old Man Goriot*, trans. Olivia McCannon, intro. by Graham Robb (London: Penguin, 2011).

Père Goriot, trans. Henry Reed, intro. by Peter Brooks (New York: New American Library, Signet Classics, 2004 [1962]).

Père Goriot, trans. Burton Raffel, ed. Peter Brooks (New York: Norton, 1994). Includes a selection of twentieth-century criticism and responses by contemporaries and other novelists.

15 Hugo: the divine stenographer

Criticism

Brombert, Victor, *Victor Hugo and the Visionary Novel* (Cambridge, Mass.: Harvard University Press, 1984).

Clark, Priscilla Parkhurst, *Literary France: The Making of a Culture* (Berkeley, Los Angeles, London: University of California Press, 1987), pp. 145–58.

Grossman, Kathryn, *The Early Novels of Victor Hugo: Towards a Poetics of Harmony* (Geneva: Droz, 1986).

'Les Misérables': Conversion, Revolution, Redemption (New York: Twayne, 1996).

Grossman, Kathryn, and Bradley Stephens (eds.), *'Les Misérables' and its Afterlives: Between Page, Stage and Screen* (London: Ashgate, 2015).

Howarth, W. D., *Sublime and Grotesque: A Study of French Romantic Drama* (London: Harrap, 1975).

Killick, Rachel, *Hugo: 'Notre-Dame de Paris'* (Glasgow Introductory Guides to French Literature, 1994).

Nash, Suzanne, *'Les Contemplations' of Victor Hugo: An Allegory of the Creative Process* (Princeton University Press, 1976).

Porter, Laurence M., *Victor Hugo* (New York: Twayne, 1999).

Robb, Graham, *Victor Hugo* (London: Picador; New York: Norton, 1997).
Rose, Julie, 'The Art of Hearing the Voice', in Brian Nelson and Brigid Maher
    (eds.), *Perspectives on Literature and Translation* (New York: Routledge,
    2013), pp. 13–30.
Stephens, Bradley, *Victor Hugo, Jean-Paul Sartre, and the Liability of Liberty*
    (Oxford: Legenda, 2011).
Vargas Llosa, Mario, *The Temptation of the Impossible: Victor Hugo and 'Les
    Misérables'* (Princeton University Press, 2007).
Wren, Keith, *Hugo: 'Hernani' and 'Ruy Blas'* (London: Grant & Cutler, 1982).

Translations/editions

There are many translations/editions of Hugo's work, but they are uneven in
quality. The items below are particularly recommended.

Hugo, Victor, *Four Plays: 'Hernani', 'Marion de Lorme', 'Lucrece Borgia', 'Ruy
    Blas'*, trans. John Golder, Richard Hand and William Driver Howarth,
    ed. with an intro. by Claude Schumacher (London: Methuen, 2004).
Les Misérables, trans. Julie Rose (New York and London: Random House,
    2008).
Notre-Dame de Paris, trans. and ed. A. J. Krailsheimer (Oxford University
    Press, 1993).
Notre-Dame de Paris, trans. with an intro. by John Sturrock (London:
    Penguin Books, 2004 [1978]).
Selected Poetry, trans. with an intro. by Stephen Monte (London: Carcanet
    Press, 2001).
Selected Poems, trans. E. H. and A. M. Blackmore (University of Chicago
    Press, 2004 [1980]).
The Wretched, trans. Christine Donougher (London: Penguin, 2013).

16 Baudelaire: the streets of Paris

Criticism

Benjamin, Walter, *The Writer of Modern Life*, ed. Michael Jennings, trans.
    Howard Eiland, Edmund Jephcott, Rodney Livingstone and Harry Zohn
    (Cambridge, Mass.: Harvard University Press, 2006).
Burton, Richard D. E., *Baudelaire and the Second Republic: Writing and
    Revolution* (Oxford: Clarendon Press, 1991).
Baudelaire in 1859: A Study in the Sources of Poetic Creativity (Cambridge
    University Press, 1988).
The Context of Baudelaire's 'Le Cygne' (University of Durham, Durham
    Modern Language Series, 1980).
Chambers, Ross, *Loiterature* (Lincoln: University of Nebraska Press, 1999), esp.
    pp. 215–49.

The Writing of Melancholy: Modes of Opposition in Early French Modernism,
trans. Mary Seidman Trouille (Chicago and London: University of
Chicago Press, 1993), esp. pp. 153–73. French original: *Mélancolie et
opposition: Les débuts du modernisme en France*, 1987.
Chesters, Graham, *Baudelaire and the Poetics of Craft* (Cambridge University
Press, 1988).
Fairlie, Alison, *Baudelaire: 'Les Fleurs du Mal'* (London: Edward Arnold, 1960).
Leakey, F. W., *Baudelaire: 'Les Fleurs du Mal'* (Cambridge University Press,
1992).
Lloyd, Rosemary, *Charles Baudelaire* (London: Reaktion Books, 2008).
(ed.), *The Cambridge Companion to Baudelaire* (Cambridge University Press,
2005).
Porter, Laurence M. (ed.), *Approaches to Teaching Baudelaire's 'Flowers of Evil'*
(New York: MLA, 2000).
Prendergast, Christopher, *Paris and the Nineteenth Century* (Oxford: Blackwell,
1992), pp. 36–40, 59–66, 126–63, 177–81.
Thompson, William J. (ed.), *Understanding 'Les Fleurs du Mal'* (Nashville, Tenn.:
Vanderbilt University Press, 1997).

Translations/editions

Baudelaire, Charles, *Charles Baudelaire: Complete Poems*, trans. Walter Martin
(Manchester: Carcanet, 1997).
Charles Baudelaire: Selected Poems from 'Les Fleurs du Mal', trans. Jan Owen
(Todmorden, UK: Arc Publications, 2015).
Charles Baudelaire: Selected Poems from 'Les Fleurs du Mal', trans. Norman R.
Shapiro (University of Chicago Press, 1998).
The Flowers of Evil, trans. James McGowan (Oxford University Press,
1993).
Intimate Journals, trans. Norman Cameron (New York: Syrens, 1995).
Les Fleurs du Mal, trans. Richard Howard (Boston: David R. Godine,
1982).
On Wine and Hashish, trans. Andrew Brown (London: Hesperus, 2002).
The Painter of Modern Life, trans. Jonathan Mayne (London: Phaidon, 1964)
and *Art in Paris 1845–1862*, trans. Jonathan Mayne (London: Phaidon,
1965).
Paris Spleen, trans. Martin Sorrell (London: Oneworld Classics, 2010).
Paris Spleen and La Fanfarlo, trans., with intro. and notes, by Raymond N.
MacKenzie (Indianapolis: Hackett, 2008).
The Parisian Prowler, trans. Edward Kaplan, 2nd edn with a new preface
(Athens: University of Georgia Press, 1997).
The Prose Poems and 'La Fanfarlo', ed. and trans. Rosemary Lloyd (Oxford
University Press, 1991).
Salon de 1846, ed. David Kelley (Oxford University Press, 1975).
Selected Poems, trans. with an intro. by Carol Clark (London: Penguin,
1995).

Selected Letters of Charles Baudelaire, trans. and ed. Rosemary Lloyd (University of Chicago Press, 1986).
Baudelaire in English, ed. Carol Clark and Robert Sykes (Harmondsworth: Penguin, 1997).

17 Flaubert: the narrator vanishes

Criticism

Brombert, Victor, *The Novels of Flaubert: A Study of Themes and Techniques* (Princeton University Press, 1966).

Brooks, Peter, 'Retrospective Lust, or Flaubert's Perversities', in *Reading for the Plot: Design and Intention in Narrative* (Oxford University Press, 1984). (*On Sentimental Education*, pp. 171–215.)

Culler, Jonathan, *Flaubert: The Uses of Uncertainty* (London: Elek; Ithaca, NY: Cornell University Press, 1974; rev. edn, 1985).

Dupee, F. W., 'Flaubert and *The Sentimental Education*', in *The King of the Cats and Other Remarks on Writers and Writing*, 2nd edn (University of Chicago Press, 1984), pp. 329–63. (First published in the *New York Review of Books*, April 22, 1971.)

Fairlie, Alison, 'Some Patterns of Suggestion in *L'Education Sentimentale*', in Malcolm Bowie (ed.), *Imagination and Language: Collected Essays on Constant, Baudelaire, Nerval and Flaubert* (Cambridge University Press, 1981), pp. 379–407.

Heath, Stephen, *Gustave Flaubert: 'Madame Bovary'* (Cambridge University Press, 1992).

Knight, Diana, *Flaubert's Characters: The Language of Illusion* (Cambridge University Press, 1985).

Lloyd, Rosemary, *Madame Bovary* (London: Unwin Hyman, 1990).

Prendergast, Christopher, *Paris and the Nineteenth Century* (Oxford: Blackwell, 1992). (On *Sentimental Education*, pp. 111–25.)

Tanner, Tony, 'Flaubert's Madame Bovary', in *Adultery in the Novel: Contract and Transgression* (Baltimore and London: Johns Hopkins University Press, 1999), pp. 233–367.

Paulson, William, '*Sentimental Education*': *The Complexity of Disenchantment* (New York: Twayne, 1992).

Unwin, Timothy, 'Flaubert: Realism and Aestheticism', in Michael Bell (ed.), *The Cambridge Companion to European Novelists* (Cambridge University Press, 2012), pp. 244–58.

(ed.), *The Cambridge Companion to Flaubert* (Cambridge University Press, 2004).

Translations

Flaubert, Gustave, *Madame Bovary*, trans. Lydia Davis (New York and London: Viking Penguin, 2010). There have been more than twenty translations of *Madame Bovary*. Davis's is one of the best recent versions.

The Letters of Gustave Flaubert, trans. Francis Steegmuller (London: Picador, 2001). The letters Flaubert wrote during the five years (1851–56) he devoted to the composition of *Madame Bovary* are richly informative in relation to his vision of art and literature.

Sentimental Education, trans. Robert Baldick, revised with an intro. and notes by Geoffrey Wall (London: Penguin, 2004; originally published 1964).

18 Zola: the poetry of the real

Criticism

Baguley, David, *Emile Zola: 'L'Assommoir'* (Cambridge University Press, 1992).
  Naturalist Fiction: The Entropic Vision (Cambridge University Press, 1990).
  (ed.), *Critical Essays on Emile Zola* (Boston: G. K. Hall, 1986).
Hemmings, F. W. J., *Emile Zola*, 2nd edn (Oxford: Clarendon Press, 1966).
Minogue, Valerie, *Zola: 'L'Assommoir'* (London: Grant & Cutler, 1991).
Mitterand, Henri, *Emile Zola: Fiction and Modernity*, trans. M. Lebron and D. Baguley (London: The Emile Zola Society, 2001).
Nelson, Brian, 'Émile Zola (1840–1902)', in Michael Bell (ed.), *The Cambridge Companion to European Novelists* (Cambridge University Press, 2012), pp. 294–309.
  Zola and the Bourgeoisie: A Study of Themes and Techniques in 'Les Rougon-Macquart' (London: Macmillan, 1983).
  (ed.), *The Cambridge Companion to Zola* (Cambridge University Press, 2007).
Smethurst, Colin, *Emile Zola: 'Germinal'* (London: Edward Arnold, 1974; repr. University of Glasgow French and German Publications, 1996).
Wilson, Angus, *Emile Zola: An Introductory Study of his Novels* (London: Secker & Warburg, 1964 [1953]).

Translations

Nearly all Zola's novels, including all twenty volumes in the Rougon-Macquart cycle, have been translated into English. Those published by Oxford University Press (Oxford World's Classics) and Penguin Books are especially recommended. A notable recent translation of *Germinal* is that by Raymond N. MacKenzie, with an introduction by David Baguley (Indianapolis, Ind.: Hackett, 2011). Reprints of late nineteenth-century translations, sometimes presented as new publishing ventures, are best avoided.

19 Huysmans: against nature

Criticism

Birkett, Jennifer, *The Sins of the Fathers: Decadence in France 1870–1914* (London and New York: Quartet Books, 1986). ('Consuming Passions: J.-K. Huysmans', pp. 61–97.)

Brombert, Victor, *The Romantic Prison: The French Tradition* (Princeton University Press, 1978). ('Huysmans: The Prison House of Decadence', pp. 149–70.)

Hustvedt, Asti (ed.), *The Decadent Reader: Fiction, Fantasy and Perversion from 'Fin de Siècle' France* (New York: Zone Books, 1998).

Lloyd, Christopher, *J.-K. Huysmans and the 'Fin-de-Siècle' Novel* (Edinburgh University Press, 1990).

McGuinness, Patrick (ed.), *Symbolism, Decadence and the 'Fin de Siècle': French and European Perspectives* (University of Exeter Press, 2000).

Pierrot, Jean, *The Decadent Imagination 1880–1900* (University of Chicago Press, 1981).

Porter, Laurence M., 'Decadence and the Fin-de-Siècle Novel', in *The Cambridge Companion to the French Novel* (Cambridge University Press, 1997), pp. 93–110.

Weir, David, *Decadence and the Making of Modernism* (Amherst: University of Massachusetts Press, 1995).

Williams, Rosalind H., *Dream Worlds: Mass Consumption in Late Nineteenth-Century France* (Berkeley, Los Angeles and London: University of California Press, 1991). ('The Dandies and Elitist Consumption', pp. 107–53.)

Translations

Huysmans, Joris-Karl, *Against Nature*, trans. Robert Baldick, ed. Patrick McGuinness (London: Penguin, 2003).

Against Nature, trans. Margaret Mauldon, ed. Nicholas White (Oxford University Press, 1998).

The Road from Decadence: From Brothel to Cloister. Selected Letters of J.-K. Huysmans, trans. Barbara Beaumont (London: Athlone, 1989).

20 Mallarmé: the magic of words

Criticism

Bowie, Malcolm, *Mallarmé and the Art of Being Difficult* (Cambridge University Press, 1978).

Cohn, Robert Greer, *Toward the Poems of Mallarmé* (Berkeley: University of California Press, 1965).

Lloyd, Rosemary, *Mallarmé: 'Poésies'* (London: Grant & Cutler, 1984).

Mallarmé: The Poet and his Circle (Ithaca, NY, and London: Cornell University Press, 1999).

Pearson, Roger, *Mallarmé and Circumstance: The Translation of Silence* (Oxford University Press, 2004).

Stéphane Mallarmé (London: Reaktion Books, 2010).

Unfolding Mallarmé: The Development of a Poetic Art (Oxford University Press, 1996).

Robb, Graham, *Unlocking Mallarmé* (New Haven, Conn., and London: Yale University Press, 1996).

Translations

Mallarmé, Stéphane, *Collected Poems*, trans. with a commentary by Henry Weinfield (Berkeley, Los Angeles, London: University of California Press, 1994).

Collected Poems and Other Verse, trans. E. H. Blackmore and A. M. Blackmore, intro. by Elizabeth McCombie (Oxford University Press, 2006).

The Meaning of Mallarmé. Bilingual edition of *Poésies* and *Un coup de dés jamais n'abolira le hasard*, trans. and intro. by Charles Chadwick (Aberdeen: Scottish Cultural Press, 1996).

The Poems in Verse, trans. with notes by Peter Manson (Miami University Press, 2012).

Selected Letters, ed. and trans. Rosemary Lloyd (University of Chicago Press, 1988).

21 Rimbaud: somebody else

Criticism

Bonnefoy, Yves, *Rimbaud*, trans. Paul Schmidt (New York: Harper & Row, 1973).

Hackett, Cecil A., *Rimbaud: A Critical Introduction* (Cambridge University Press, 1981).

Little, Roger, *Rimbaud: 'Illuminations'* (London: Grant & Cutler Ltd, 1983).

Nicholl, Charles, *Somebody Else: Arthur Rimbaud in Africa 1880–1891* (London: Jonathan Cape, 1997).

Robb, Graham, *Rimbaud* (London: Picador, 2000; paperback edn 2001).

Ross, Kristin, *The Emergence of Social Space: Rimbaud and the Paris Commune* (Minneapolis: University of Minnesota Press, 1988).

Wilson, Edmund, *Axel's Castle* (London: Collins, The Fontana Library, 1961; originally published New York: Scribner's, 1931). ('Axel and Rimbaud', pp. 205–35.)

Translations/editions

Rimbaud, Arthur, *Collected Poems*, trans. with an intro. and notes by Martin Sorrell (Oxford University Press, 2001). Includes parallel French text.

Illuminations, ed. Nick Osmond (London: Athlone, 1976).

Rimbaud Complete, vol. I: *Poetry and Prose*; vol. II: *'I Promise to Be Good':*
　　The Letters of Arthur Rimbaud, trans., ed. and with an intro. by Wyatt
　　Mason (New York: Random House, 2002 and 2003).
A Season in Hell and Illuminations, trans. Mark Treharne (London: Dent,
　　1998).
Selected Poems and Letters, trans. with an intro. and notes by Jeremy Harding
　　and John Sturrock (London: Penguin, 2004).

22 Proust: the self, time and art

Criticism

Bales, Richard, *Proust: 'A la recherché du temps perdu'* (London: Grant & Cutler,
　　1995).
　　(ed.), *The Cambridge Companion to Proust* (Cambridge University Press,
　　2001).
Bersani, Leo, *Marcel Proust: the Fictions of Life and of Art*, 2nd edn (New York and
　　London: Oxford University Press, 2013 [1965]).
Bowie, Malcolm, *Proust Among the Stars* (London: HarperCollins, 1998).
Ellison, David, *A Reader's Guide to Proust's 'In Search of Lost Time'* (Cambridge
　　University Press, 2010).
Landy, Joshua, *Philosophy and Fiction: Self, Deception, and Knowledge in Proust*
　　(Oxford University Press, 2004).
Minogue, Valerie, *Proust: 'Du côté de chez Swann'* (London: Edward Arnold,
　　1973).
Prendergast, Christopher, *Mirages and Mad Beliefs: Proust the Skeptic* (Princeton
　　University Press, 2013).
Schmid, Marion, 'Marcel Proust (1871–1922): A Modernist Novel of Time', in
　　Michael Bell (ed.), *The Cambridge Companion to European Novelists*
　　(Cambridge University Press, 2012), pp. 327–42.
Shattuck, Roger, *Proust's Way: A Field Guide to 'In Search of Lost Time'* (New York:
　　W. W. Norton, 2001).
Tadié, Jean-Yves, *Marcel Proust: A Life*, trans. Euan Cameron (London and New
　　York: Penguin, 2000; originally published in French in 1996).
Watt, Adam, *The Cambridge Introduction to Marcel Proust* (Cambridge University
　　Press, 2011).
　　Marcel Proust (London: Reaktion Books, 2013).
　　(ed.), *Marcel Proust in Context* (Cambridge University Press, 2013).

Translations/editions

In Search of Lost Time (General Editor: Christopher Prendergast), trans. Lydia
Davis (*The Way by Swann's/Du côté de chez Swann*), James Grieve (*In the Shadow
of Young Girls in Flower/À l'ombre des jeunes filles en fleurs*), Mark Treharne (*The
Guermantes Way/Le Côté de Guermantes*), John Sturrock (*Sodom and Gomorrah/*

Sodome et Gomorrhe), Carol Clark (*The Prisoner/La Prisonnière*), Peter Collier (*The Fugitive/Albertine disparue*) and Ian Patterson (*Finding Time Again/Le Temps retrouvé*) (London: Allen Lane, 2002). The first four volumes have been published in New York by Viking, 2003–2004.

   In Search of Lost Time, trans. C. K. Scott-Moncrieff, Terence Kilmartin and Andreas Mayor (*Time Regained*), revised by D. J. Enright (London: Chatto and Windus; New York: The Modern Library, 1992).

   Swann's Way, ed. Susanna Lee (New York: W. W. Norton, 2013). Includes an Editor's Introduction as well as much critical material – contemporary reviews and commentary, plus fourteen essays reprinted or excerpted from important critical works.

23 Jarry: the art of provocation

Criticism

Beaumont, Keith, *Alfred Jarry: A Critical and Biographical Study* (Leicester University Press, 1984).

   Jarry: 'Ubu roi' (London: Grant & Cutler, 1987).

Blackadder, Neil, 'Merdre! Performing Filth in the Bourgeois Public Sphere', in William A. Cohen and Ryan Johnson (eds.), *Filth: Dirt, Disgust, and Modern Life* (Minneapolis: University of Minnesota Press, 2005), pp. 182–200.

Brotchie, Alastair, *Alfred Jarry: A Pataphysical Life* (Cambridge, Mass.: MIT Press, 2011).

Esslin, Martin, *The Theatre of the Absurd*, 3rd edn (London: Methuen, 2001).

Fell, Jill, *Alfred Jarry* (London: Reaktion Books, 2010).

   Alfred Jarry: An Imagination in Revolt (Madison & Teaneck: Fairleigh Dickinson University Press, 2005).

Labelle, Maurice, *Alfred Jarry, Nihilism and the Theatre of the Absurd* (New York University Press, 1980).

Schumacher, Claude, *Alfred Jarry and Guillaume Apollinaire* (Basingstoke: Macmillan, 1985).

Seigel, Jerrold, *Bohemian Paris: Culture, Politics, and the Boundaries of Bourgeois Life, 1830–1930* (New York: Viking Penguin, 1986), pp. 310–22.

Shattuck, Roger, *The Banquet Years: The Origins of the Avant-Garde in France, 1885 to World War 1* (London: Jonathan Cape, 1969). ('Alfred Jarry, 1873–1907', pp. 187–251.) An expanded and revised version of a volume originally published in 1955.

Stillman, Linda, *Alfred Jarry* (Boston: Twayne, 1984).

Translations

Jarry, Alfred, *The Supermale*, trans. Ralph Gladstone and Barbara Wright (New York: New Directions, 1964).

The Ubu Plays, trans. Cyril Connolly and Simon Watson Taylor (New York: Grove Press, 1968).

The Ubu Plays, trans. Kenneth McLeish (London: Nick Hern Books, 1997).

Ubu roi, trans. Barbara Wright (London: Gaberbocchus, 1951; New York: New Directions, 1961).

Ubu the King, in *Three Pre-Surrealist Plays*, trans. Maya Slater, new edn (Oxford University Press, 1997).

Shattuck, Roger, and Simon Watson Taylor (eds.), *Selected Works of Alfred Jarry* (London: Methuen, 1965).

24 Apollinaire: impresario of the new

Criticism

Breunig, LeRoy C., *Guillaume Apollinaire* (New York and London: Columbia University Press, 1969).

Davies, Margaret, *Apollinaire* (Edinburgh and London: Oliver and Boyd, 1964).

Kelley, David, 'Defeat and Rebirth: The City Poetry of Apollinaire', in Edward Timms and David Kelley (eds.), *Unreal City: Urban Experience in Modern European Literature and Art* (Manchester University Press, 1985), pp. 80–96.

Little, Roger, *Guillaume Apollinaire* (London: Athlone Press, 1976).

Mathews, Timothy, *Reading Apollinaire: Theories of Poetic Language* (Manchester University Press, 1990).

Read, Peter, *Picasso and Apollinaire: The Persistence of Memory* (Berkeley, Los Angeles, London: University of California Press, 2008).

Shattuck, Roger, *The Banquet Years: The Origins of the Avant-Garde in France, 1885 to World War 1* (London: Jonathan Cape, 1969). ('Guillaume Apollinaire, 1880–1918', pp. 253–322.) An expanded and revised version of a volume originally published in 1955.

Translations/editions

Apollinaire, Guillaume, *Alcools*, ed. A. E. Pilkington (Oxford: Blackwell, 1970; London: Bristol Classical Press, 1993).

Alcools, ed. Garnet Rees (London: Athlone Press, 1975).

Alcools, ed. A. E. Pilkington (Oxford: Blackwell, 1970; London: Bristol Classical Press, 1993).

Apollinaire on Art: Essays and Reviews 1902–1918, ed. LeRoy C. Breunig with a new foreword by Roger Shattuck, trans. Susan Suleiman (Boston: MFA Publications, 2001).

Calligrammes: Poems of Peace and War (1913–1916), trans. Anne Hyde Greet, with an intro. by S. I. Lockerbie and commentary by Anne Hyde Greet and S. I. Lockerbie (Berkeley, Los Angeles, London: University of California Press, 1980).

The Cubist Painters, trans. Peter Read (Forest Row, East Sussex: Artists Bookworks, 2002).

Selected Poems, trans. Olivier Bernard (London: Anvil Press Poetry Ltd, 2004; originally published by Penguin Books 1965).

Selected Writings of Guillaume Apollinaire, trans. with a critical intro. by Roger Shattuck (New York: New Directions, 1971).

25 Breton & Company: Surrealism

Criticism

Ades, Dawn, *Dada and Surrealism Reviewed* (London: Arts Council of Great Britain, 1978).

Brandon, Ruth, *Surreal Lives: The Surrealists, 1917–1945* (London: Macmillan, 1999).

Cardinal, Roger, *Breton: 'Nadja'* (London: Grant & Cutler, 1987).

Cardinal, Roger, and Robert Stuart Short, *Surrealism: Permanent Revelation* (London: Studio Vista; New York: Dutton, 1970).

Caws, Mary Ann, *The Poetry of Dada and Surrealism: Aragon, Breton, Tzara, Eluard, and Desnos* (Princeton University Press, 1971).

Collier, Peter, 'Surrealist City Narrative: Breton and Aragon', in Edward Timms and David Kelley (eds.), *Unreal City: Urban Experience in Modern European Literature and Art* (Manchester University Press, 1985), pp. 214–28.

Higonnet, Patrice, *Paris: Capital of the World*, trans. Arthur Goldhammer (Cambridge, Mass.: The Belknap Press of Harvard University Press, 2002). ('The Surrealists' Quest', pp. 374–97.)

Hopkins, David, *Dada and Surrealism: A Very Short Introduction* (Oxford University Press, 2004).

Nadeau, Maurice, *The History of Surrealism*, trans. Richard Howard, intro. by Roger Shattuck (Cambridge, Mass.: The Belknap Press of Harvard University Press, 1989). French original: *Histoire du Surréalisme*, 1944.

Polizzotti, Mark, *Revolution of the Mind: The Life of André Breton* (New York: Farrar, Straus and Giroux; London: Bloomsbury, 1995).

Sheringham, Michael, 'City Space, Mental Space, Poetic Space: Paris in Breton, Benjamin and Réda', in Michael Sheringham (ed.), *Parisian Fields* (London: Reaktion Books, 1996), pp. 85–114 (see esp. pp. 88–97).

Everyday Life: Theories and Practices from Surrealism to the Present (Oxford University Press, 2006). ('Surrealism and the Everyday', pp. 59–94.)

Short, Robert, *Dada and Surrealism* (London: Octopus Books, 1980).

Translations

Aragon, Louis, *Paris Peasant*, trans. Simon Watson Taylor (London: Cape, 1971).

Breton, André, *André Breton: Selections*, ed. with an intro. by Mark Polizzotti (Berkeley: University of California Press, 2003).

Communicating Vessels, trans. Mary Ann Caws and Geoffrey T. Harris (Lincoln: University of Nebraska Press, 1997).
Mad Love, trans. with an intro. and notes by Mary Ann Caws (Lincoln: University of Nebraska Press, 1988).
Manifestoes of Surrealism, new edn, trans. Richard Seaver and Helen R. Lane (Ann Arbor: University of Michigan Press, 1969).
Nadja, trans. Richard Howard, intro. by Mark Polizzotti (Harmondsworth: Penguin, 1999; translation originally published New York: Grove Press, 1960).
Poems of André Breton: A Bilingual Anthology, trans. Jean-Pierre Cauvin and Mary Ann Caws (Boston: Black Widow Press, 2006).
Breton, André and Philippe Soupault, *Magnetic Fields*, trans. David Gascoyne (London: Atlas Press, 1985).
Éluard, Paul, *Capital of Pain*, trans. Mary Ann Caws, Patricia Ann Terry and Nancy Kline (Boston: Black Widow Press, 2006).

26 Céline: night journey

Criticism

Buckley, William K. (ed.), *Critical Essays on Louis-Ferdinand Céline* (Boston: G. K. Hall, 1988).
Hewitt, Nicholas, *The Golden Age of Louis-Ferdinand Céline* (Atlanta, Ga.: Berg, 1987).
The Life of Céline (Oxford: Blackwell, 1999).
Kaplan, Alice, and Philippe Roussin (eds.), *Céline, USA* (Durham, NC: Duke University Press, 1994).
Noble, Ian, *Language and Narration in Céline's Writing: The Challenge of Disorder* (London: Macmillan, 1987).
Scullion, Rosemarie, Philip H. Solomon and Thomas C. Spear (eds.), *Céline and the Politics of Difference* (Hanover and London: University Press of New England, 1995).
Solomon, Philip H., *Understanding Céline* (Columbia: University of South Carolina Press, 1992).
Sturrock, John, *Céline: 'Journey to the End of the Night'* (Cambridge University Press, 1990).
Thomas, Merlin, *Louis-Ferdinand Céline* (London: Faber & Faber; New York: New Directions, 1979).
Vitoux, Frédéric, *Céline: A Biography*, trans. Jesse Browner (New York: Paragon House, 1992; originally published in French in 1988).

Translations

Céline, Louis-Ferdinand, *Cannon-Fodder*, trans. K. De Coninck and B. Childish (Rochester, UK: Hangman Books, 1988).

Castle to Castle, trans. Ralph Manheim (Champaign, Ill.: Dalkey Archive Press, 1997). Translation first published 1968.

Conversations with Professor Y, trans. Stanford Luce (Champaign, Ill.: Dalkey Archive Press, 2006). Translation first published 1986.

Death on the Installment Plan, trans. Ralph Manheim (New York: New Directions, 1971). Published in UK as *Death on Credit* (London: Oneworld Classics, 2009). Translation first published 1966.

Fable for Another Time, trans. Mary Hudson (Lincoln: University of Nebraska Press, 2003).

Guignol's Band, trans. Bernard Frechtman and Jack T. Nile (London: Alma Books, 2012). Translation first published 1954.

Journey to the End of the Night, trans. Ralph Manheim (New York: New Directions, 2006; London: Alma Classics, 2012). Translation first published 1966.

London Bridge, trans. Dominic Di Bernardi (Champaign, Ill.: Dalkey Archive Press, 2006; London: Alma Books, 2012).

Normance, trans. Marlon Jones (Champaign, Ill.: Dalkey Archive Press, 2009).

North, trans. Ralph Manheim (Champaign, Ill.: Dalkey Archive Press, 1996). Translation first published 1972.

Rigadoon, trans. Ralph Manheim (Champaign, Ill.: Dalkey Archive Press, 2009). Translation first published 1974.

27 Sartre: writing in the world

Criticism

Brosman, Catharine Savage, *Jean-Paul Sartre* (Boston: Twayne, 1983).

Clark, Priscilla Parkhurst, *Literary France: The Making of a Culture* (Berkeley and Los Angeles: University of California Press, 1987). ('The Writer as Intellectual Hero', pp. 159–91.)

Cohen-Solal, Annie, *Sartre: A Life* (New York: Random House; London: Heinemann, 1987; originally published in French in 1985).

Drake, David, *Sartre* (London: Haus Publishing, 2005).

Goldthorpe, Rhiannon, *Sartre: Literature and Theory* (Cambridge University Press, 1984).

Howells, Christina, *Sartre: The Necessity of Freedom* (Cambridge University Press, 1988).

   (ed.), *The Cambridge Companion to Sartre* (Cambridge University Press, 1992).

Judt, Tony, *Past Imperfect: French Intellectuals, 1944–1956* (Berkeley: University of California Press, 1992).

Leak, Andrew, *Jean-Paul Sartre* (London: Reaktion Books, 2006).

Thody, Philip, *Jean-Paul Sartre* (London: Macmillan, 1992).

Thody, Philip, and Howard Read, *Introducing Sartre* (Cambridge: Icon Books, 1999).

Translations

Novels and short stories
Sartre, Jean-Paul, *Nausea*, trans. Robert Baldick, intro. by James Wood (London: Penguin, 2000).
   The Wall (Intimacy) and Other Stories, trans. Lloyd Alexander (New York: New Directions, 1969). (*Le Mur*, 1939.)
   The Age of Reason, trans. Eric Sutton (London: Penguin, 2005). (*L'Âge de raison*, 1945.)
   The Reprieve, trans. Eric Sutton (London: Penguin, 2001). (*Le Sursis*, 1945.)
   Iron in the Soul, trans. Gerard Hopkins (London: Penguin, 2008). (*La Mort dans l'âme*, 1949.)
   The three novels immediately above were part of an unfinished series entitled *The Paths to Freedom* (*Les Chemins de la liberté*).

Plays
   Altona and Other Plays: Altona, Men without Shadows, The Flies, trans. Sylvia Leeson (London: Penguin, 1989). (*Les Séquestrés d'Altona*, 1959; *Morts sans sépulture*, 1946; *Les Mouches*, 1943.)
   Huis Clos and Other Plays: The Respectable Prostitute, Lucifer and the Lord, Huis Clos, trans. Kitty Black and Stuart Gilbert (London: Penguin, 2000). (*La Putain respectueuse*, 1946; *Le Diable et le Bon Dieu*, 1951; *Huis clos*, 1944.)
   No Exit and Three Other Plays: The Flies, Dirty Hands, The Respectable Prostitute, trans. Stuart Gilbert (New York: Vintage, 1989).

Philosophy, politics
   Being and Nothingness, trans. Hazel Barnes (London: Routledge, 1958).
   Existentialism Is a Humanism, trans. Carol Macomber, intro. by Annie Cohen-Solal, preface and notes by Arlette Elkaïm-Sartre (New Haven, Conn.: Yale University Press, 2007). (*L'Existentialisme est un humanisme*, 1946.)
Jean-Paul Sartre, *Basic Writings*, ed. Stephen Priest (London and New York: Routledge, 2001).
   Modern Times: Selected Non-Fiction, trans. Robin Buss, ed. with an intro. by Geoffrey Wall (London: Penguin, 2000).
   War Diaries: Notebooks from a Phoney War 1939–40, trans. Quentin Hoare (London: Verso, 1984). (*Les Carnets de la drôle de guerre*, 1983.)

Literary criticism, biography
   The Family Idiot: Gustave Flaubert 1821–1857, trans. Carol Cosman, 5 vols. (University of Chicago Press, 1981–93).
   What Is Literature? and Other Essays, intro. by Steven Ungar (Cambridge, Mass.: Harvard University Press, 1988).

Autobiography
  Words, trans. Irene Clephane (London: Penguin, 2000).

28 Camus: a moral voice

Criticism

Banks, G. V., *Camus: 'L'Etranger'* (University of Glasgow French and German Publications, 1992; originally published London: Arnold, 1976).

Bloom, Harold (ed.), *Albert Camus: Modern Critical Views* (Philadelphia: Chelsea House, 1989).

  (ed.), *Albert Camus's 'The Stranger'* (Philadelphia: Chelsea House, 2001).

Carroll, David, *Albert Camus the Algerian* (New York: Columbia University Press, 2007).

Ellison, David R., *Understanding Albert Camus* (Columbia: University of South Carolina Press, 1990).

Foley, John, *Albert Camus: From the Absurd to Revolt* (Stocksfield: Acumen, 2008).

Hughes, Edward J., *Albert Camus: 'Le Premier Homme'/'La Peste'* (University of Glasgow French and German Publications, 1995).

  (ed.), *The Cambridge Companion to Camus* (Cambridge University Press, 2007).

Jones, Rosemarie, *Camus: 'L'Etranger' and 'La Chute'* (London: Grant & Cutler, 1994).

Judt, Tony, *The Burden of Responsibility: Blum, Camus, Aron, and the French Twentieth Century* (University of Chicago Press, 1998). ('The Reluctant Moralist: Albert Camus and the Discomforts of Ambivalence', pp. 87–135.)

McCarthy, Patrick, *Camus: 'The Stranger'* (Cambridge University Press, 1988; 2nd edn 2005).

Showalter, English, Jr, *'The Stranger': Humanity and the Absurd* (Boston: Twayne, 1989).

Sprintzen, David, *Camus: A Critical Examination* (Philadelphia: Temple University Press, 1988).

Williams, James S., *Camus: 'La Peste'* (London: Grant & Cutler, 2000).

Zaretsky, Robert, *Albert Camus: Elements of a Life* (Ithaca, NY: Cornell University Press, 2010).

Translations

Camus, Albert, *American Journals*, trans. Hugh Levick (New York: Paragon House, 1987; London: Hamish Hamilton, 1989).

  Between Hell and Reason, trans. Alexandre de Gramont (London: University Press of New England, 1991).

  Caligula and Other Plays: Caligula, Cross Purpose, The Just, The Possessed, trans. Stuart Gilbert (London: Penguin, 1984).

Exile and the Kingdom, trans. Justin O'Brien (London: Penguin, 2002 [1962]).
The Fall, trans. Justin O'Brien (London: Penguin, 2000 [1963]).
The First Man, trans. David Hapgood (London: Penguin, 1996).
A Happy Death, trans. Richard Howard (London: Penguin, 2002 [1973]).
Lyrical and Critical Essays, ed. Philip Thody, trans. Ellen Conroy Kennedy
    (New York: Vintage; London: Hamish Hamilton, 1967).
The Myth of Sisyphus, trans. Justin O'Brien (London: Penguin, 2000 [1975]).
The Outsider, trans. Joseph Laredo (London: Penguin, 2000 [1983]); *The
    Outsider*, trans. Sandra Smith (London: Penguin, 2012); also translated
    as *The Stranger*, trans. Matthew Ward (New York: Knopf, 1988).
The Plague, trans. Robin Buss, with an intro. by Tony Judt (London: Penguin,
    2006).
The Rebel, trans. Anthony Bower (London: Penguin, 1971). Repr. with an
    intro. by Olivier Todd (London: Penguin, 2000).
Resistance, Rebellion, and Death (partial translation of *Actuelles I, II* and *III*),
    trans. Justin O'Brien (London: Hamish Hamilton, 1961).
Selected Essays and Notebooks, trans. Philip Thody (London: Penguin, 1979).
Selected Political Writings, trans. and ed. Jonathan H. King (London:
    Methuen, 1981).
Youthful Writings, trans. Ellen Conroy Kennedy with an introductory essay
    by Paul Viallaneix (New York: Knopf, 1976).
Notebooks, 1935–1942, trans. Philip Thody (New York: Knopf, 1963).
Notebooks, 1942–1951, trans. Justin O'Brien (New York: Knopf, 1966; New
    York: Marlowe and Company, 1995).
Notebooks, 1951–1959, trans. Ryan Bloom (Chicago: Ivan R. Dee, 2008).

29 Beckett: filling the silence

Bibliography

Luke Thurston has produced a very useful selective and annotated
bibliography ('Samuel Beckett') in the Oxford Bibliographies Online series (www.
oxfordbibliographies.com).

Database

The Samuel Beckett On-line Resources and Links Page (samuel-beckett.net)

Criticism

Ackerley, C. J., and S. E. Gontarski (eds.), *The Faber Companion to Samuel Beckett*
    (London: Faber & Faber, 2006). US edition published as *The Grove
    Companion to Samuel Beckett* (New York: Grove Press, 2004).
Alvarez, A., *Samuel Beckett* (London: Fontana/Collins, 1973).
Bradby, David, *Beckett: 'Waiting for Godot'* (Cambridge University Press, 2001).
Cohn, Ruby, *A Beckett Canon* (Ann Arbor: University of Michigan Press, 2001).

Connor, Steven, *'Waiting for Godot' and 'Endgame'*, New Casebooks (London: Palgrave Macmillan, 1992).

Esslin, Martin, *The Theatre of the Absurd*, 3rd edn (London: Methuen, 2001). ('Samuel Beckett: The Search for the Self', pp. 29–91.)

Graver, Lawrence, *Beckett: 'Waiting for Godot'. A Student Guide*, 2nd edn (Cambridge University Press, 2004).

Graver, Lawrence, and Raymond Federman (eds.), *Samuel Beckett: The Critical Heritage* (London: Routledge and Kegan Paul, 1979).

Hill, Leslie, 'Samuel Beckett (1906–1989): Language, Narrative, Authority', in Michael Bell (ed.), *The Cambridge Companion to European Novelists* (Cambridge University Press, 2012), pp. 394–409.

Kenner, Hugh, *A Reader's Guide to Samuel Beckett* (London: Thames & Hudson, 1973; repr. Syracuse University Press, 1996).

Samuel Beckett: A Critical Study (London: John Calder, 1961).

Little, J. P., *Beckett: 'En attendant Godot' and 'Fin de partie'* (London: Grant & Cutler, 1981).

McDonald, Rónán, *The Cambridge Introduction to Samuel Beckett* (Cambridge University Press, 2006).

Mooney, Sinéad, *Samuel Beckett* (Tavistock: Northcote House, 2006).

Pattie, David, *The Complete Guide to Samuel Beckett* (London and New York: Routledge, 2000).

Pilling, John (ed.), *The Cambridge Companion to Beckett* (Cambridge University Press, 1994).

Sheringham, Michael, *Beckett: 'Molloy'* (London: Grant & Cutler, 1985).

Translations/editions

Beckett produced his fiction and drama in English and French, translating himself, occasionally with collaborators, out of the language in which he first wrote each text. Paul Auster has commented in his 'Editor's Note' to the *Grove Centenary Edition*: 'Beckett's renderings of his own work are never literal, word-by-word transcriptions. They are free, highly inventive adaptations of the original text – or, perhaps more accurately, "repatriations" from one language to the other, from one culture to the other. In effect, he wrote every work twice.'

A four-volume Grove Centenary Edition of Beckett's principal works, containing *Novels I* and *Novels II*, *The Dramatic Works*, and *The Poems, Short Fiction and Criticism*, was published by Grove Press, New York, in 2006. The novel trilogy (*Molloy, Malone Dies, The Unnamable*) has been published in the Everyman's Library (New York and Toronto, 1997), with an introduction by Gabriel Josipovici. Individual texts have been published in the main by Faber and Faber in the UK and Grove Press in the United States.

DVDs

Beckett on Film (2002). Film versions of all of Beckett's stage plays, with the exception of the early and unperformed *Eleutheria*.

30 French literature into the twenty-first century

New novel, new criticism

Britton, Celia, *The Nouveau Roman: Fiction, Theory and Politics* (London: Macmillan; New York: St Martin's Press, 1992).
Culler, Jonathan, *Barthes* (London: Fontana/Collins, 1983).
Jefferson, Ann, *The Nouveau Roman and the Poetics of Fiction* (Cambridge University Press, 1980).
Sontag, Susan (ed.), *Barthes: Selected Writings* (Oxford: Fontana/Collins, 1983).

A return to tradition

Cloonan, William, *Michel Tournier* (Boston: Twayne, 1985).
Davis, Colin, *Michel Tournier: Philosophy and Fiction* (Oxford: Clarendon Press. 1988).
Gascoigne, David, *Michel Tournier* (Oxford and Washington, DC: Berg, 1996).
Platten, David, *Michel Tournier and the Metaphor of Fiction* (Liverpool University Press, 1999).
Tournier, Michel, *The Erl-King* (also known as *The Ogre*), trans. Barbara Bray (London: Collins; New York: Doubleday, 1972; Baltimore: Johns Hopkins University Press, 1997; London: Penguin, 2000).
  Friday or The Other Island, trans. Norman Denny (Harmondsworth: Penguin Books, 1974; Baltimore: Johns Hopkins University Press, 1997; originally published London: Collins; New York: Doubleday, 1969).
Watt, Ian, 'Michel Tournier's Friday', in *Myths of Modern Individualism* (Cambridge University Press, 1996), pp. 255–67.
Worton, Michael (ed.), *Michel Tournier* (London: Longman, 1995).

Literature as play

Bellos, David, *Georges Perec: A Life in Words* (London: Harvill; Boston: Godine, 1993).
Bridgeman, Teresa, *Queneau: 'Exercises de style'* (University of Glasgow Introductory Guides to French Literature, 1995).
Elkin, Lauren, and Scott Esposito, *The End of Oulipo?* (Alresford: Zero Books, 2013).
Gascoigne, David, *The Games of Fiction: Georges Perec and Modern French Ludic Narrative* (Bern: Peter Lang, 2006).
Levin Becker, Daniel, *Many Subtle Channels: In Praise of Potential Literature* (Cambridge, Mass.: Harvard University Press, 2012).
Matthews, Harry, and Alastair Brotchie (eds.), *Oulipo Compendium*, 2nd rev. edn (London: Atlas Press, 2005).
Motte, Warren (ed.), *Oulipo: A Primer of Potential Literature*, new edn (Normal, Ill.: Dalkey Archive Press, 1998).

Perec, Georges, *Life: A User's Manual*, trans. David Bellos, rev. edn (Boston: Godine, 2008).

Queneau, Raymond, *Exercises in Style*, trans. Barbara Wright, rev. edn (New York: New Directions, 1981; London: Oneworld Classics, 2009); *Exercises in Style: 65th Anniversary Edition* (New York: New Directions, 2013).

Shorley, Christopher, *Queneau's Fiction: An Introductory Study* (Cambridge University Press, 1985).

Thiher, Allen, *Raymond Queneau* (Boston: Twayne, 1985).

Duras and other women writers

Atack, Margaret, and Phil Powrie (eds.), *Contemporary French Fiction by Women: Feminist Perspectives* (Manchester University Press, 1990).

Crowley, Martin, *Marguerite Duras: A Beginner's Guide* (London: Hodder and Stoughton, 2003).

Damlé, Amaleena, *The Becoming of the Body: Contemporary Women's Writing in French* (Edinburgh University Press, 2014).

Davis, Colin, and Elizabeth Fallaize, 'The Story of her Life: Marguerite Duras's *L'Amant* (1984)', in *French Fiction in the Mitterrand Years: Memory, Narrative, Desire* (Oxford University Press, 2000), pp. 18–37.

Evans, Martha Noel, *Masks of Tradition: Women and the Politics of Writing in Twentieth-Century France* (Ithaca, NY: Cornell University Press, 1987).

Fallaize, Elizabeth, *French Women's Writing: Recent Fiction* (London: Macmillan, 1993).

Günther, Renate, *Duras: 'Le Ravissement de Lol V. Stein' and 'L'Amant'* (London: Grant & Cutler, 1982).

Hill, Leslie, *Marguerite Duras: Apocalyptic Desires* (London and New York: Routledge, 1993).

Holmes, Diana, *French Women's Writing 1848–1994* (London: Athlone Press, 1996).

King, Adèle, *French Women Novelists: Defining a Female Style* (Basingstoke: Macmillan, 1989).

Lydon, Mary, *Skirting the Issue: Essays in Literary Theory* (Madison: University of Wisconsin Press, 1995).

Rye, Gill, and Amaleena Damlé (eds.), *Experiment and Experience: Women's Writing in France 2000–2010* (Bern: Peter Lang, 2013).

(eds.), *Women's Writing in Twenty-First-Century France: Life as Literature* (Cardiff: University of Wales Press, 2013).

Sheringham, Michael, *French Autobiography: Devices and Desires: Rousseau to Perec* (Oxford: Clarendon Press, 1993), pp. 316–20.

Stephens, Sonya (ed.), *A History of Women's Writing in France* (Cambridge University Press, 2000).

Wilson, Emma, 'Women Writers, Artists, and Filmmakers', in William Burgwinkle, Nicholas Hammond and Emma Wilson (eds.), *The*

Cambridge History of French Literature (Cambridge University Press, 2011), pp. 680–88.

Winston, Jane, 'Gender and Sexual Identity', in Timothy Unwin (ed.), *The Cambridge Companion to the French Novel: From 1800 to the present* (Cambridge University Press, 1997), pp. 223–41.

Worton, Michael, and Gill Rye, *Women's Writing in Contemporary France: New Writers, New Literatures in the 1990s* (Manchester University Press, 2002).

Autobiography/autofiction

Boyle, Claire, *Consuming Autobiographies: Reading and Writing the Self in Post-War France* (London: Legenda, 2007).

Jefferson, Ann, *Biography and the Question of Literature in France* (Oxford University Press, 2007).

Keefe, Terry, and Edmund Smyth (eds.), *Autobiography and the Existential Self: Studies in Modern French Writing* (Liverpool University Press, 1995).

Lejeune, Philippe, *On Autobiography*, trans. Katherine Leary (Minneapolis: University of Minnesota Press, 1989).

Sheringham, Michael, 'Changing the Script: Women Writers and the Rise of Autobiography', in Sonya Stephens (ed.), *A History of Women's Writing in France* (Cambridge University Press, 2000), pp. 185–203.

French Autobiography: Devices and Desires – Rousseau to Perec (Oxford: Clarendon Press, 1993).

Francophone writing

Aldrich, Robert, *Greater France: A History of French Overseas Expansion* (London: Palgrave Macmillan, 1996).

Corcoran, Patrick, *The Cambridge Introduction to Francophone Literature* (Cambridge University Press, 2007).

Forsdick, Charles, and David Murphy (eds.), *Francophone Postcolonial Studies: A Critical Introduction* (London: Arnold, 2003).

(eds.), *Postcolonial Thought in the French-Speaking World* (Liverpool University Press, 2009).

Hargreaves, Alec, Charles Forsdick and David Murphy (eds.), *Transnational French Studies: Postcolonialism and 'Littérature-monde'* (Liverpool University Press, 2010).

Harrison, Nicholas, 'Francophone Writing', in William Burgwinkle, Nicholas Hammond and Emma Wilson (eds.), *The Cambridge History of French Literature* (Cambridge University Press, 2011), pp. 621–30.

Jack, Belinda, *Francophone Literatures: An Introductory Survey* (Oxford University Press, 1996).

McDonald, Christie, and Susan Rubin Suleiman (eds.), *French Global: A New Approach to Literary History* (New York: Columbia University Press, 2010).

French fiction today

Asibong, Andrew, *Marie NDiaye: Blankness and Recognition* (Liverpool University Press, 2013).

Cruickshank, Ruth, *Fin de millénaire French Fiction: The Aesthetics of Crisis* (Oxford University Press, 2009).

Duffy, Jean H., *Thresholds of Meaning: Passage, Ritual and Liminality in Contemporary French Narrative* (Liverpool University Press, 2011).

Echenoz, Jean, *Cherokee*, trans. Mark Polizzotti (Boston: David Godine, 1987; London and Boston: Faber & Faber, 1991). French original: *Cherokee* (Paris: Minuit, 1983).

Double Jeopardy, trans. Mark Polizzotti (Lincoln: University of Nebraska Press, 1993). French original: *L'Équippée malaise* (Paris: Minuit, 1986).

I'm Off + One Year, trans. Guido Waldman (London: Harvill Press, 2001). French originals: *Je m'en vais* (Paris: Minuit, 1999) and *Un an* (Paris: Minuit, 1997). US edition of the former published as *I'm Gone*, trans. Mark Polizzotti (New York: New Press, 2001).

Lake, trans. Guido Waldman (London: Harvill, 1998). French original: *Lac* (Paris: Minuit, 1989). US edition published as *Chopin's Move*, trans. Mark Polizzotti (Champaign, Ill.: Dalkey Archive Press, 2004).

Lightning, trans. Linda Coverdale (New York: New Press, 2011). French original: *Des éclairs* (Paris: Minuit, 2010).

1914, trans. Linda Coverdale (New York: New Press, 2014). French original: *14* (Paris: Minuit, 2012).

Plan of Occupancy, trans. Mark Polizzotti (Paris: Alyscamps Press, 1995). French original: *L'Occupation des sols* (Paris: Minuit, 1988).

Ravel, trans. Linda Coverdale (New York: New Press, 2007). French original: *Ravel* (Paris: Minuit, 2005).

Three by Echenoz: Big Blondes, Piano, and Running. Gathers together three novels, translated respectively by Linda Coverdale, Mark Polizzotti and Liesl Schillinger (New York: New Press, 2014). French originals: *Les Grandes Blondes* (Paris: Minuit, 1995), *Au piano* (Paris: Minuit, 2003), *Courir* (Paris: Minuit, 2008).

Hippolyte, Jean-Louis, *Fuzzy Fiction* (Lincoln: University of Nebraska Press, 2007).

Houellebecq, Michel, *Atomised*, trans. Frank Wynne (London: Vintage, 2001). US edition published as *The Elementary Particles*. French original: *Les Particules élémentaires* (Paris: Flammarion, 1999).

H. P. Lovecraft: Against the World, Against Life, trans. Dorna Khazeni (London: Gollancz, 2005). French original: *H. P. Lovecraft: Contre le monde, contre la vie* (Paris: J'ai lu, 1991).

Lanzarote, trans. Frank Wynne (London: Vintage, 2004). French original: *Lanzarote* (Paris: Flammarion, 2000).

The Possibility of an Island, trans. Gavin Bowd (London: Weidenfeld & Nicolson, 2005; Vintage, 2007; New York: Knopf, 2006). French original: *La Possibilité d'une île* (Paris: Fayard, 2005).

Platform, trans. Frank Wynne (New York: Knopf, 2003). French original: *Plateforme: Au milieu du monde* (Paris: Flammarion, 2001).

The Map and the Territory, trans. Gavin Bowd (London: Heinemann, 2011). French original: *La Carte et le territoire* (Paris: Flammarion, 2011).

Whatever, trans. Paul Hammond (London: Serpent's Tail, 1998). French original: *Extension du domaine de la lutte* (Paris: Éditions Maurice Nadeau, 1994).

Kemp, Simon, *French Fiction into the Twenty-first Century: The Return to the Story* (Cardiff: University of Wales Press, 2010).

Morrey, Douglas, *Michel Houellebecq: Humanity and its Aftermath* (Liverpool University Press, 2013).

Motte, Warren, *Fables of the Novel: French Fiction since 1990* (Normal, Ill.: Dalkey Archive Press, 1999).

Fiction Now: The French Novel in the Twenty-First Century (Normal, Ill.: Dalkey Archive Press, 2008).

NDiaye, Marie, *All My Friends*, trans. Jordan Stump (San Francisco: Two Lines Press, 2013). French original: *Tous mes amis* (Paris: Minuit, 2004).

Rosie Carpe, trans. Tamsin Black (Lincoln: University of Nebraska Press, 2004). French original: *Rosie Carpe* (Paris: Minuit, 2001).

Three Strong Women, trans. John Fletcher (London: Maclehose Press, 2012). French original: *Trois femmes puissantes* (Paris: Gallimard, 2009).

Sheringham, Michael, 'The Contemporary French Novel', in William Burgwinkle, Nicholas Hammond and Emma Wilson (eds.), *The Cambridge History of French Literature* (Cambridge University Press, 2011), pp. 576–84.

Sweeney, Carole, *Michel Houellebecq and the Literature of Despair* (London: Bloomsbury, 2013).

Index of authors and titles

Titles appear under the author's name. Bold type indicates writers and texts that are discussed in (varying degrees of) detail.

Index of genres, movements and concepts

Cambridge Introductions to . . .

AUTHORS

Margaret Atwood Heidi Macpherson

Jane Austen (second edition) Janet Todd

Samuel Beckett Ronan McDonald

Walter Benjamin David Ferris

Lord Byron Richard Lansdown

Chaucer Alastair Minnis

Chekhov James N. Loehlin

J. M. Coetzee Dominic Head

Samuel Taylor Coleridge John Worthen

Joseph Conrad John Peters

Jacques Derrida Leslie Hill

Charles Dickens Jon Mee

Emily Dickinson Wendy Martin

George Eliot Nancy Henry

T. S. Eliot John Xiros Cooper

William Faulkner Theresa M. Towner

F. Scott Fitzgerald Kirk Curnutt

Michel Foucault Lisa Downing

Robert Frost Robert Faggen

Gabriel Garcia Marquez Gerald Martin

Nathaniel Hawthorne Leland S. Person

Zora Neale Hurston Lovalerie King

James Joyce Eric Bulson

Kafka Carolin Duttlinger

Thomas Mann Todd Kontje

Christopher Marlowe Tom Rutter

Herman Melville Kevin J. Hayes

Milton Stephen B. Dobranski

George Orwell John Rodden and John Rossi

Sylvia Plath Jo Gill

Edgar Allan Poe Benjamin F. Fisher

Ezra Pound Ira Nadel

Marcel Proust Adam Watt

Jean Rhys Elaine Savory

Edward Said Conor McCarthy

Shakespeare Emma Smith

Shakespeare's Comedies Penny Gay

Shakespeare's History Plays Warren Chernaik

Shakespeare's Poetry Michael Schoenfeldt

Shakespeare's Tragedies Janette Dillon

Tom Stoppard William W. Demastes

Harriet Beecher Stowe Sarah Robbins

Mark Twain Peter Messent

Edith Wharton Pamela Knights

Walt Whitman M. Jimmie Killingsworth

Virginia Woolf Jane Goldman

William Wordsworth Emma Mason

W. B. Yeats David Holdeman

TOPICS

American Literary Realism Phillip Barrish

The American Short Story Martin Scofield

Anglo-Saxon Literature Hugh Magennis

Comedy Eric Weitz

Creative Writing David Morley

Early English Theatre Janette Dillon

Early Modern Drama, 1576–1642 Julie Sanders

The Eighteenth-Century Novel April London

Eighteenth-Century Poetry John Sitter

English Theatre, 1660–1900 Peter Thomson

French Literature Brian Nelson

Francophone Literature Patrick Corcoran

German Poetry Judith Ryan